Ingo Berensmeyer
A Short Media History of English Literature

Ingo Berensmeyer

A Short Media History of English Literature

—

DE GRUYTER

ISBN 978-3-11-153459-6
e-ISBN (PDF) 978-3-11-078445-9
e-ISBN (EPUB) 978-3-11-078447-3
DOI https://doi.org/10.1515/9783110784459

This work is licensed under the Creative Commons Attribution-NonCommercial-NoDerivatives 4.0 International License. For details go to https://creativecommons.org/licenses/by-nc-nd/4.0/.

Library of Congress Control Number: 2022936617

Bibliographic information published by the Deutsche Nationalbibliothek
The Deutsche Nationalbibliothek lists this publication in the Deutsche Nationalbibliografie; detailed bibliographic data are available on the internet at http://dnb.dnb.de.

© 2024 Ingo Berensmeyer, published by Walter de Gruyter GmbH, Berlin/Boston
This volume is text- and page-identical with the hardback published in 2022.
The book is published open access at www.degruyter.com.

Cover image: thomas-bethge/iStock/Getty Images Plus
Typesetting: Integra Software Services Pvt.

www.degruyter.com

For my students

Contents

1 **Introduction** —— 1
History? Media? Literature? —— 1
Key Terms —— 5
Instructions for Use —— 16

I The Age of Performance (since c. 70,000 BCE)

2 **Voice and Hand** —— 21
Origins —— 21
Writing on Parchment —— 24
Old English Literature —— 29
Cædmon —— 33
Beowulf —— 37

3 **The Medieval and Early Modern Book** —— 43
Middle English Literature —— 43
Sir Gawain and the Green Knight —— 46
Truth Seekers: Kempe, Langland, and Gower —— 49
Chaucer —— 50
Manuscript and Print —— 56

4 **Theatre and Drama: Liveness on the Stage** —— 63
Early English Drama —— 63
The Play's the Thing —— 68
Metatheatre and Metadrama —— 76
Later Developments —— 78
Theatre and New Media —— 80

II The Age of Representation (since c. 1500 CE)

5 **Print Culture in the Long Eighteenth Century** —— 85
The Rise of the Book Market —— 85
The Subscription Model —— 86
Samuel Johnson and the Age of Authors —— 88
The Battle of the Books —— 89
Newspapers and Coffeehouses —— 93

Grub Street —— 95
Gray's Elegy —— 98

6 **Paper Worlds: The Novel as Object and Form** —— 103
Novel Habits —— 104
Samuel Richardson —— 107
Laurence Sterne —— 111
The Novel in Nineteenth-Century Print Culture —— 112
Serial Fiction —— 116
New Grub Street —— 120
The Battle of the Brows —— 123
The Rise of the Paperback —— 124

7 **Voice and Breath in Romantic and Victorian Poetry** —— 127
Voice in Literature —— 127
Voice as Interior Speech —— 129
Apostrophe —— 131
Ode to the West Wind —— 133
Radical Subjectivity —— 135
Victorian 'Mediums': Tennyson and Browning —— 138

III The Age of Connection (since c. 1850 CE)

8 **Touch: Literature as Telecommunication** —— 147
Literature and the Telegraph —— 147
Deep-Sea Cables —— 153
Wireless Horrors —— 156

9 **Sound: Phonography, Telephony, Radio, Noise** —— 161
Recorded Voices —— 161
Literature and the Telephone —— 165
Radio Plays —— 166
Sound and Noise —— 170
Ultrasound —— 175

10 **Vision: Text and Image** —— 179
Ways of Seeing —— 179
William Blake —— 181
Illustrations —— 181

      Modernist Typography and Visual Thinking —— 186
      The Waste Land —— 191
      Blindness —— 194
      The Graphic Novel and Other Forms of Sequential Art —— 195

11 Screen: Literature and the Moving Image —— 197
      Seeing Mrs. Bathurst —— 197
      Early Cinema and Literary Modernism —— 198
      I am a Camera —— 204
      The Rise of Television —— 207

12 Web: Literature in the Digital Age —— 213
      Publishing and the Digital Revolution —— 214
      Electronic Literature —— 217
      Convergence —— 219
      Literature in the Age of Platform Capitalism —— 223

Acknowledgements —— 227

Timeline —— 229

List of Illustrations and Table —— 233

References —— 235

Index —— 257

1 Introduction

History? Media? Literature?

Scholars and critics have long been arguing about how to write a history of literature, and why. Such histories are still being written, despite vocal opposition from a long line of theorists, from René Wellek to Hans Ulrich Gumbrecht, who claim that these endeavours are conceptually and practically impossible or worthless (Wellek and Warren 1956, 252–271; Gumbrecht 2008). If I add my own contribution to the heap, it is in the hope of doing something slightly different. *A Short Media History of English Literature* intends to show how literature develops in tandem, in concert or competition with different materials, means, and modes of communication. Instead of tracing historical developments through a long line of texts, regardless of their material forms and formats, this book asks questions about the (inevitable?) connections between texts and media. What, for example (if there is such a thing), is the ideal material carrier for literature? Is it the book or, more precisely, the codex (a particular book format)? Is it the printed page? What about drama, which is usually performed on stage in front of live audiences, involving real people in real spaces? Wouldn't we have to say that drama also belongs to literature, but perhaps less to "the book as an expressive form" (McKenzie 1999)? And what about other kinds of literature and other formats, such as the radio play, the audiobook, or the literary podcast, intended not to be read but to be listened to? To what extent are the media in which literary objects are embodied, embedded, and encoded relevant to our enjoyment, appreciation, and understanding of these objects?

Looking at literary history from a media perspective inevitably changes the way such a history can be written. It entails several shifts in emphasis, both in terms of content and presentation. The manuscript, the printed book, the audiobook – these will be some of the key objects or infrastructures that have shaped the media history of literature. If the principal agents of literary history are no longer genres, authors, and texts but configurations of media and technologies, this will affect our sense of periodisation and challenge the customary but unsatisfactory combination of period terms derived from dynasties or monarchs ('Tudor', 'Elizabethan'), art history ('Renaissance'), or wider cultural and philosophical trends ('Postmodernism').

The most basic assumption for a history of this kind is that literature is more than just texts or just words on a page, more than printed books or manuscripts. It comes in many different material – and sometimes apparently immaterial – forms, different sensory environments, and transient media configurations. But we cannot access them without these material forms or without relying on our senses. Some of these forms are very old and apparently simple, they are intuitively there – for example, the voice of someone reciting a poem. Some are more recent and involve complex technologies, such as the e-book or the podcast. Historians of media speak of 'old' as opposed to 'new media', a distinction that is ultimately not very helpful when it comes to understanding how literature exists within a multiplicity of media and 'text technologies' (Treharne and Willan 2020) and has been doing so for a very long time indeed (Marvin 1988; Gitelman 2006).

A related question is whether these changing forms are merely carriers or vehicles for literary content, 'forms' in a merely superficial sense. In this view, it does not matter whether we read *The Hobbit* in book form or listen to an audiobook version of the same text. If we assume that the medium in which we encounter literature in fact matters, we realise that literature is not merely 'content', not merely text or information or data but a complex sensory arrangement that depends crucially on the medium or media in which it is presented. In an extreme version of this view, literature cannot be treated separately from its media. In Marshall McLuhan's famous phrase, "the medium is the message" (1994 [1964], 7). In other words, there is no content without form; the information or message a medium can provide depends on the nature of that medium, not on its content.

For a very long time, literary histories have been neglecting or even avoiding these aspects. One of the reasons for this is the disciplinary divide between literary studies and media studies. Historically, media studies as a discipline has been associated with the social sciences and journalism, while literary studies came to belong to the humanities and liberal arts. Literary studies methods are still markedly historical, aesthetic, and text-oriented, despite branching out into cultural, gender, and postcolonial studies. Media studies are more likely to focus on the technologies, economics, and politics of modern mass communications. The blind spots that arise from this division of labour are many: media specialists are not likely to be interested in the history of print media, for example, while literary scholars tend to read texts without paying attention to their physical, material carriers – which they are more likely to regard as mere packaging. Book historians, on the other hand, are more likely to work in history departments; they are certainly interested in print mediation but have no reason to grant special status to a particular type of text over others as 'literature' in an aesthetic sense. Although crucial differences prevail, there has been an increasing convergence between these separate disciplines, partly because of digitalisation, new research methods involving access to data on a massive scale, and increased awareness of the materiality of texts across different media. In support of such a convergence, Meredith McGill has argued that there could be "common ground between literary studies and media studies" in the media history of literature, which she regards as "a privileged site for thinking about media shifts" (2016, 35).

Shifts and changes between media have long been an object of media history, but it is far from clear how they interact with literary change, for example the rise or fall of genres, literary forms, or movements. McLuhan's strong claims about media are not very helpful when it comes to applying them to more fine-grained developments or complex relationships between texts and media. Yet such sweeping claims have a long tradition, including Walter Benjamin's famous essay "The Work of Art in the Age of its Technological Reproducibility" (1936). Here, Benjamin writes: "Just as the entire mode of existence of human collectives changes over long historical periods, so does their mode of perception. The way in which human perception is organized – the medium in which it occurs – is conditioned not only by nature but by history" (2008, 23). Media, in this view, shape human perception and knowledge; they also, in their symbolic character, serve to enable exchange and conversion. In this sense, the American sociologist Talcott Parsons (1977) identified money as a key medium for modern societies, because money converts a wide variety of different objects into commodities and regulates their exchange. Niklas Luhmann, building on Parsons, identified money, power, even love as media of communication. If all these can be media, is there still a way of using this term in a more concrete, narrowly defined sense that remains useful for literary studies?

Beginning with these basic questions, this book will proceed through the most important stages of a history of literature as a history of media, exploring changing media configurations that have an impact on what literature is or can be, and how its aesthetics develop over time in response to media changes. Obviously, this history is very long in scope, ranging across one and a half millennia from the early Middle Ages to the present. It is short in its presentation, which focuses on key developments and moments of transition rather than aiming for any sense of completeness (which would indeed be impossible). This, then, is not quite a conventional history of English literature, providing a (by now) frequently imitated narrative account of historical periods in which major works and authors are discussed in their literary and social contexts (see, for example, Sanders 2004). Nor is it another history of the book, focusing on the material and institutional conditions of written and printed texts (see, for example, Lesser 2019). Historians of the book would most likely object to my privileging the category of the literary, which I understand in the unoriginal and unexciting sense of imaginative writing, distinct from other kinds of writing by such qualities as its "organization, personal expression, realization and exploitation of the medium, lack of practical purpose, and [. . .] fictionality" (Wellek and Warren 1956, 27). Yet one of the points to make is precisely that literature, because of its "realization and exploitation of the medium", deserves its own media history. This book, then, combines elements of book history, media history, and literary history to present how literature is associated, connected, or entangled with media.

Such a history involves many changes of formats and institutional or performative contexts. It involves continuities as well as discontinuities, survivals and revivals as well as ruptures and revolutions. This is not a history of linear progress; in fact, some of the most archaic forms of enjoying poetry – listening to the voice of a poet – have been revived, in live settings (poetry readings, festivals, or poetry slams) and recorded formats. Printed books, first introduced to Western Europe in the fifteenth century, are now being produced every year in greater quantities than ever before – despite competition by downloadable digital text files or e-books. In fact, the digital revolution has furthered print because most texts, whether printed or downloaded, are now 'born digital' as text files on a computer. On the other hand, new media have always generated anxieties and fears of obsolescence or cultural decline. As the old song has it, "video killed the radio star".[1] In the twentieth century, some writers feared that cinema and television would make novels obsolete because the stories told in novels, with their detailed verbal descriptions, could be much more easily and quickly consumed as films. More recently, there have been concerns that watching TV or playing video games would replace reading as entertainment, or that literary authorship and publishing would be destroyed by the Internet and the combined forces of the corporate giants driving the digital revolution. Yet, so far, literature still lives on, and despite many changes and uncertainties there seems to be no reason to expect its imminent demise.

In fact, as Umberto Eco once said, "the Internet has returned us to the alphabet":

> If we thought we had become a purely visual civilisation, the computer returns us to Gutenberg's galaxy; from now on, everyone has to read. In order to read, you need a medium. This medium cannot simply be a computer screen. Spend two hours reading a novel on your computer and your eyes turn into tennis balls. [. . .] And in any case, the computer depends on electricity and cannot be read in a bath, or even lying on your side in bed. (Carrière and Eco 2012, 4)

Eco was optimistic that the book as an object would not be much affected by these technological changes: "The book is like the spoon, scissors, the hammer,

---

[1] Written by Trevor Horn, Geoff Downes, and Bruce Woolley in 1978 and first recorded by Woolley in 1979 (Wikipedia).

the wheel. Once invented, it cannot be improved. [. . .] Perhaps it will evolve in terms of components; perhaps the pages will no longer be made of paper. But it will still be the same thing" (4–5). Whether a book not made of paper would indeed "still be the same thing" is a moot point; what matters is that such a view of media history runs counter to the cultural pessimism and nostalgia of critics like Allan Bloom, Neil Postman, or Sven Birkerts (2006, 2015), who did not or cannot envisage any positive outcomes from cultural and media change. Personally, I am confident that the codex format will survive for a long time yet as a material carrier of text, and that it is not about to be superseded by 'the Internet', social media, streaming television, or anything else. This is borne out by empirical evidence: the worldwide market share of e-books in relation to physical books has remained constant at less than ten percent since 2017 and is not expected to rise considerably until 2025.[2] As I argue in this book, the media history of literature is not a history of 'one damn thing after another' but of co-evolution and co-adaptation. It begins with our voices and our hands, but these do not get replaced by paper or print, nor later by electronic media. The media history of literature is not a "slaughterhouse", to quote Franco Moretti's gruesome image of literary evolution (2013, 63), but – to stick to a commercial metaphor – a clearing house that facilitates exchanges and transactions between changing forms, formats, and texts.

Key Terms

Before I can begin to trace the continuities and transformations in the long history of literature, I need to set out a few definitions of key terms, beginning with the word 'medium' itself. A useful starting point for this is Raymond Williams's 1976 publication *Keywords: A Vocabulary of Culture and Society*. 'Medium', Williams informs us, means 'middle' in Latin. In English, it was used from the sixteenth century onwards, and since the early seventeenth century it "has had the sense of an intervening or intermediate agency or substance" (1983, 203). Early modern writers like Francis Bacon and Robert Burton use it in this sense, for instance "expressed by the Medium of Wordes". In the eighteenth century, the word can be applied to newspapers: "through the medium of your curious publication" (ibid.). In the early twentieth century, Williams tells us, "the description of a newspaper as a medium for advertising became

---

[2] "Bücher – Weltweit", *Statista*, Statista GmbH, https://de-statista.com.emedien.ub.uni-muenchen.de/outlook/amo/medien/buecher/weltweit. Date of access: 3 Dec. 2021.

common" (ibid.). The plural form 'media' only came into use "when broadcasting as well as the press had become important in communications [. . .]; it was then the necessary general word." Terms like 'mass media' and later 'media studies' and many others evolved from this. Williams already notes (204) that 'media' is often used – incorrectly, one might add – as a singular noun.

Williams's discussion of the terms 'medium / media' leads directly to the problem of defining a medium. He notes that *language* was long considered a medium in the old sense of "an intervening or intermediate agency or substance" but would now (i.e., in the 1970s) be considered a "primary practice" (203). He is probably thinking here of pragmatics as a part of modern linguistics, or speech act theory (the view that language has performative rather than merely constative dimensions) as developed by J. L. Austin in his 1955 lectures *How to Do Things with Words* (Austin 1975). Williams goes on to tell us that "writing (for print) and speaking or acting (for broadcasting) would also be practices. It is then controversial whether print and broadcasting, as in the technical sense [of 'media'] [. . .], are media or, more strictly, material *forms* and sign systems" (Williams 1983, 203, emphasis original). There is, then, a strong sense of the word 'medium' "as something with its own specific and *determining* properties (in one version taking absolute priority over anything actually said or written or shown)" (204, emphasis original). In this technical sense of 'medium', the medium is indeed the message. Williams here probably alludes to Marshall McLuhan's influential books from the early 1960s, *The Gutenberg Galaxy* and *Understanding Media* (McLuhan 1962, 1994). Williams distinguishes this sense of media, which might be called a techno-deterministic one, from "a social sense of media in which the practices and institutions are seen as agencies for quite other than their primary purposes" (Williams 1983, 204). This rather cryptic expression signals his Marxist convictions; he makes the important point that practices and institutions may have multiple, even contradictory purposes, as well as many different functions for and impacts on society. Newspapers, for instance, are important media of information and, as such, have an important role to play in modern democracies, but they are also, as Williams points out, "a medium for something else, such as advertising" (203) – they are complicit in the economic nexus of capitalism that pays for and profits from disseminating the news. Literature in modernity, despite its frequently vaunted autonomy or purity as a form of art, is equally implicated in media and institutions that condition its production, distribution, and reception – whether this is the patronage system in early modernity or the world of commercial publishing in the present.

For the purposes of this history, there are three important lessons to take away from Raymond Williams:

1) There is no single or simple definition of 'media'. The term is a broad umbrella for many different kinds of practices, material forms, sign systems, and institutions.
2) There is a distinction to be made between physical media as related to the human senses: sight, sound, touch (and, less importantly in our case, smell and taste), and technical media such as print or broadcasting.
3) There is a debate about the question to what extent (physical and technical) media determine the content of what is being communicated, "said or written or shown" (Williams 1983, 203).

In another famous expression from McLuhan, media are "the extensions of man" (1994 [1964], 4). In this view, the technical systems we have created for the purposes of communication are supplements to our natural senses, extending the reach of our voices, eyes, and ears. These extensions, or in fact "any new technology", McLuhan argues, introduce a "new scale [. . .] into our affairs" (7); indeed, "the change of scale or pace or pattern" *is,* for McLuhan, "the 'message' of any medium or technology" (8). The railway, for example, takes "movement or transportation or wheel or road" (8) to new levels of acceleration and spatial expansion; the aeroplane, in turn, "tends to dissolve the railway form of city, politics, and association" (ibid.); another of his examples is electric light, which similarly changes "time and space factors in human association exactly as do radio, telegraph, telephone, and TV" (9).

McLuhan has been rightly criticised for his rhapsodic style and his hyperbolic statements. But his view of media is both instructive and suggestive, even for readers who do not agree with his technocratic and techno-deterministic view of history. Even if one does not buy into his sweeping generalisations, one would do well to pay attention to changes in "scale or pace or pattern" (8) when studying media history. Another notable point to take home from McLuhan is "that the 'content' of any medium is always another medium" (ibid.): "The content of writing is speech, just as the written word is the content of print, and print is the content of the telegraph" (ibid.). In this view, a new medium that emerges picks up an older medium (or several older media) and turns them into its 'content'. McLuhan is rarely very precise or analytic, so it is hard to pin down what he means by 'content', unless it is simply the other side of 'form', the raw material that is used for a new form of communication.

'Communication' is another of Williams's keywords. Its meaning has been extended from "lines of communication" such as actual "roads, canals and railways" (1983, 72) to "other means of passing information and maintaining social contact". Here, the interesting point Williams makes is that communication still has two possible meanings, to "transmit" or to "share" (ibid.) – the direction of communication can be a one-way street or a participatory activity. If we apply this to the history of literature, both aspects will be prominent at different times and in different configurations. To speak of 'media configurations' is a way of signalling that media form complex networks that involve various objects and practices. There cannot be a neat separation between literature on the one hand and media on the other – literature and media always belong together, they interact with each other, and the forms and affordances of different media (practices) affect what literature can (be thought to) be in different historical situations.[3] For this reason, this history views literature in relation to media, and often in relation to rivalling media.

The double sense of communication as transferral and connection can be made fruitful for a distinction between "representational" and "connective" media (Trotter 2017, 391). These are not mutually exclusive, but historically different emphases, as David Trotter asserts: "No medium has remained wholly representational or wholly connective in definition and use" (ibid.). Representational media, he explains, "attract the '-graphy' suffix. They involve the storage and deferred release of information: that is, a *writing* in light, in sound, in movement." By contrast, connective "(or 'tele'-) media" place the emphasis "on instantaneous, real-time, and if at all possible interactive one-to-one communication at a distance". Representational media involve "two places at two times", connective media "two places at one time" (ibid.).

Because literature is not a medium in its own right but, in Trotter's words, "a relation to the relation between media" (2017, 394) or the uses of media, literary studies cannot simply be replaced by or merged with media studies. Media studies as a discipline almost exclusively deals with modern mass media, often using empirical, quantitative, and qualitative methods derived from the social sciences, communication studies, and psychology. The media history of literature has to take some of these into account, but its historical reach must be wider, extending back beyond modernity, and its scope is necessarily narrower – trained on the uses and definitions of literature in relation to representational and connective media.

The distinction between media and mass media can be clarified with a little help from Niklas Luhmann (1927–1998). As a sociologist, Luhmann thought about communication as the key to understanding society, and he regarded the

---

[3] The term 'affordance' was coined by the psychologist James J. Gibson in the 1960s to describe useful properties of objects (Gibson 1973); it is now more generally defined as "a quality or utility which is readily apparent or available" (OED). It has been introduced into literary criticism in the work of N. Katherine Hayles (2002) and applied to the study of literary form by Caroline Levine (2015), among others.

operations of communication within media as crucial to how we see the world, or in fact how reality is being constructed for us. To quote a famous saying of his: "Whatever we know about our society, or indeed about the world in which we live, we know through the mass media" (2000b, 1). Newspapers, broadcasting, TV, and now the Internet and social media transmit information. But they are not only representational but also connective and even constitutive of society in the sense of "imagined communities" (Anderson 2006), establishing a fictional connection between large numbers of people who do not actually know each other. By distributing information among large numbers of people, mass media constitute communities, a 'we'. Since we cannot know very much "about the world in which we live" directly, from our own experience or from what our families or neighbours tell us, only mass media allow us to bridge huge physical and geographical distances. We obviously know, or think we know, more about the universe than we could ever observe with our own eyes; in fact, often knowledge contradicts the impression received by our senses – as in the famous case of the 'setting' or 'rising' sun, which we see as such but know to be an effect of the earth's movement in relation to the sun. The increase of knowledge may not be the only purpose of mass media, but it is an intriguing thought that our views of the world, our observations of reality, are crucially shaped – if not entirely determined – by what media allow us to see or to hear.

When Luhmann wrote this, in the 1990s, he was thinking of television and the early Internet rather than of social media, where the priority has shifted from dispensing information about the world to more active and interactive forms of intervention in it, emphasising (in Trotter's terms) connectivity over representation. But his thinking remains useful for exploring the relationship between media and literature. Literature, one might say, also allows us to have knowledge about the world, but knowledge of a somewhat different kind or quality. For Luhmann, imaginative activities open up a "second reality" (2000b, 51). The simplest kind of such second realities are games. He defines games as "a kind of doubling of reality, where the reality perceived as the game is separated off from normal reality without having to negate the latter. A second reality is created which conforms to certain conditions and from which perspective the usual ways of life appear as real reality" (2000b, 51). In this view, entertainment, including a novel, "functions like a game because it inserts a second reality into the 'usual' reality for a certain time period that is identified by a more or less clear beginning and end. The common reality is not denied through entertainment or a game but is temporally kept in the background" (Moeller 2006, 132). Unlike games, Luhmann explains, novels do not require readers to play by rules; they require and work with information. In entertainment, in contrast to games,

> the excerpt from reality in which the second world is constituted is marked visually or acoustically – as a book, as a screen, as a striking sequence of specially prepared noises which are perceived as "sounds" in this condition. This external frame then releases a world in which a fictional reality of its own applies. A world! – and not merely, as in social games, a socially agreed sequence of behaviour. (Luhmann 2000b, 52)

Entertainment, for Luhmann, creates a second reality that enables the distanced, reflective observation of actual (first) reality. Literature, in this view, is a form of *second-order observation*, an observation that observes other observers. In Luhmann's systems theory, 'observation' means any act of perception or even imagination that is directed at a real, mental, or fictional object with the aim to distinguish that object from others and thus to structure reality. Second-order observation can even occur in the same person who is the first-order observer, though not normally at the same time: I can reflect on my own observations of the world but only after I have made those observations. In his history of English poetry, Peter Hühn has made this distinction fruitful for the analysis of lyric poetry, understanding the constellation of an observer observing him- or herself as an analogue of the dual aspect of lyric speech: the lyric speaker speaks his or her mind, but is also subjected to the superior awareness of the poem's textual composition, which structures the text and can point out blind spots in the speaker's observation of the world. The poem's "aesthetic materiality" (Hühn 1995, 15)[4] establishes a higher-order level of observation, making visible hidden implications in the speaker's words on the lower level.

This perspective might be a key to the distinction between literature and other forms of communication. Poetry, imaginative writing, or storytelling more generally, is never *merely* communication; it is never just about imparting information or providing us with knowledge about the world. Rather, it provides us with knowledge about ourselves, revealing the hidden depths and blind spots in the way we – and our societies – carve up reality into more or less neat, well-ordered chunks (or 'systems', or 'fields'). It is *performative* and potentially transformative but – at least in modernity – always *reflective* and *reflexive*. It allows us to see or hear or feel things that we would otherwise be unable to see, hear, or feel. In its reference to an external world, it is imitation or *mimesis*, as Aristotle calls this in his *Poetics* (1448b, usually translated as 'imitation' or 'representation', as in Aristotle 2013, 20). In its evocation of subjective experience (or models of subjective experience), it allows us to reflect on the possibilities and limits of experience, and perhaps on the deficits as well as the joys and

---

[4] Translations from works not originally published in English, as in this case, are my own unless otherwise stated.

pains of our limited points of view, our identities, and their social and cultural foundations. This, too, is *mimesis* – at least if we follow Paul Ricoeur's notion of mimesis as comprising the three stages of prefiguration, configuration, and refiguration (1984, 46, 53–54). While Aristotle speaks of *catharsis* (1449b, 'purification'; 2013, 23) as the purgative effect on our emotions of a fictional narrative, Ricoeur broadens the concept of mimesis to describe readers making sense of a text for their own world, their own lives.

Readers certainly enjoy literature for many reasons, but perhaps one of these is its potential usefulness for reflecting on real-life situations (e.g., moments of crisis, change, transition but also – increasingly in modernity – conditions of stasis or boredom) and thereby receiving a kind of indirect training or coaching: what Kenneth Burke (1961) referred to as "literature as equipment for living". In short, "literary works make you think differently" (Cave 2016, 5). They "alter the cognitive environment of the reader in ways that are powerful, potentially disturbing, and not at all self-evident" (ibid.). But their usefulness may not always be immediately clear. Since literature is both a "*product* and *symptom* of human cognition", according to Terence Cave (14), its relation to thinking is complex and ambivalent. Like the mind itself, it is a blend of cognitive modes (cf. Cave 2016, 31, quoting Mark Turner). Next to many possible functions, its cognitive value may stem from a deep-seated evolutionary place in forms of mental playing with language and concepts – particularly with metaphors.

The reference to Aristotle also shows that the idea of fiction as a second world is not as new as it might seem; for the early modern period, Harry Berger proposed that writers and thinkers used fictional worldmaking "to accomplish intellectual tasks in a second world separate from the confusing everyday world" (Keen 2015, 124, with reference to Berger 1965).

Like other works of art, literary texts establish their own imaginary or fictional reality. According to Luhmann, this creation of a second (fictional) reality by means of art is not merely an addition of more objects to the world; it gives us "a position from which *something else* can be determined *as reality*" (2000a, 142). It confronts reality with alternative possibilities, "on the basis of an increasing freedom and a growing distance vis-à-vis an established reality" (144) until, in modernity, works of art can respond to the contradictory ordering principles of religious belief, financial crises, and scientific rationalism, and, later, even create objects that can no longer be distinguished from real objects (144–145). Fictionality, then, in systems-theoretical terms, is the home of second-order observation.

Literature, to repeat, is not a form of direct observation but of *second-order observation*. Its content is not 'content' – not the story as such – but form: *how* the story is told. And this form, over the centuries, has been shaped by media and in relation to media (and relations between media) – from voice to pen to print to digital media and beyond. Literature as possibility and as reality is formed by changing clusters of practices, institutions, sign systems, and material forms: by what Hans Ulrich Gumbrecht and Ludwig Pfeiffer (1994) have called "materialities of communication". These materialities form the basis of this history.

The last term to be defined, at least in a working definition, is the term 'literature' itself, which Williams with some understatement introduces as "a difficult word" (1983, 183). The question what is or is not literature is deeply involved with the question of media, and I use this word as an even broader umbrella for a wide variety of different historical practices and institutions. It is somewhat anachronistic, but otherwise no history of literature could be written. 'Literature' is not a static object but unceasingly changing, and its development is closely implicated with evolving media relations. When the word was first used in English, in the late Middle Ages, it meant 'literacy' or 'learning'; only much later, in the eighteenth century, was it used to refer to books and to "the practice and profession of writing" (ibid., 185), and much later again it was narrowed down to 'imaginative literature' or 'works of literature' as a form of verbal art. The notion of *English literature* is even younger, associated as it is with the rise of nationalism and the construction of national literatures from the late eighteenth century onwards. In this book, English literature is treated as a case study that allows for a manageable scope, with occasional glances at other (albeit mostly European) literatures, and my history begins long before 'English' was even a word. In modernity, the English language and literature in English spread across the globe like no other, turning Shakespeare and Jane Austen into global cultural icons but also leading to literatures in English written outside of Britain, mostly but by far not exclusively in countries belonging to the former British Empire. This makes 'literature in English' an even more fascinating topic. These migrations and the global, transnational reach of literature in English are only occasionally touched upon in this book because such a reach, though desirable, would have expanded this history beyond a manageable scope. Yet they are in fact built into the literature we call 'English' from the beginnings, as for example the Old English epic poem *Beowulf* attests in its Scandinavian setting, its Latin and biblical influences, and its blend of several cultures (see ch. 2).

Literature is not a medium, but it has throughout history been associated with various media. It may well be, as Salman Rushdie has stated, "the most low-technology of art forms" (2010, 424), requiring little else than pen and paper to produce and only a reader or listener to take it in. In oral cultures or contexts, it requires no more than a voice and an ear. Its medium in this sense (as it is also used by Wellek and Warren in their classic *Theory of Literature*) is simply language. It is open to many different forms and formats of production, distribution, and reception. If literature is sometimes described as a medium, this is in a metaphorical sense, for example as a medium for fame, for cultural creativity, or cultural capital – and it is in this sense that literature has certainly been the most important medium in and of modernity, producing and reflecting forms of subjective experience and representations of the world (Reinfandt 2009). Not tied to the limitations of other audio-visual practices, literature massively raises the meaning potential of communication due to its ability to negate existing realities and to imagine alternative (possible) worlds.[5] But this sense of 'medium', detached from any actual physical or material media, is so abstract as to be almost worthless for the purposes of media history.

An even more abstract but potentially useful concept of medium is again one proposed by Luhmann. According to this definition, a medium can be described as "a malleable set of possibilities into which forms are temporarily fixed" (Luhmann 1987, 81).[6] This extremely general formulation concerns much more than the mass media that Luhmann addresses elsewhere in his theory; arguably, it bridges the representational and connective emphases of Trotter's definition. Also described as a "loose coupling" of elements, this means "an open-ended multiplicity of possible connections that are still compatible with the unity of an element" (Luhmann 2000a, 104). For instance, in language one can use the same word with the same meaning (an element) to form many different meaningful sentences (an open-ended number of possibilities). A form, on the other hand, is a temporarily fixed coupling of these elements. Once the medium of the physical book has been established, it can be filled with an unlimited amount of literary forms.

In this brief introduction, I have tried to show that what is required for a media history of literature is a flexible and pragmatic working definition of these three terms: media, history, and literature. Historically, distinct media often relate to each other or are combined in various ways. In the latter cases, we often speak of 'multimedia' – for instance when images, sounds and music are combined. In the same vein, the study of 'intermediality' has become a rich field of research focusing on the relations between, and combinations of, media (Rippl 2015). Such research involves forms of *ekphrasis* (simply put, the verbal imitation or description of visual images in literature) as well as forms of

---

5 See the foundational work of Ong 2002. For an ambitious systematic (and systems-theoretical) attempt at conceptualising literature as a medium for modern subjectivity, see Jahraus 2003 and cf. Reinfandt 2009.
6 Luhmann's distinction between medium and form follows his reading of Heider 1926.

visuality within literary texts. It can focus on literature and photography, on forms of adaptation of literary texts into other media such as cinema or TV,[7] on graphic novels, multimodal forms of narrative, literature and music, video games, dance, and other forms of performance. There are many areas of enquiry that pertain to the manifold connections between media and literature, many more than can be discussed here.

Among other aspects, I will be neglecting literature and music, dance, video games, and graphic novels – but what is lost in these areas can be gained in others, and there are special studies for all of these that readers can turn to.[8] The principal idea to keep in mind is that literature – just like its writers and readers – usually does not exist on its own, or purely in the medium of language, but that it exists in *ecologies of media,* variable historical configurations in which different media support and compete with each other.[9] Language itself is a medium, and its affordances for literature have been explored not only in the kind of 'close reading' advocated by the New Criticism but also by theories of metaphor, especially cognitive metaphor theory and conceptual blending (Lakoff and Johnson 1980, Turner 1998). In addition to thinking about literature as existing in or supported by different physical media, another perspective on the topic is framed by thinking about cognition. Thus, in a kind of virtual or latent intermediality, we visualise characters or objects while reading (Mendelsund 2014); we may have the impression in our minds of watching a film when reading a novel; or, if a certain feature is not afforded by a medium, we may supplement it in our minds by using what Shakespeare calls our "imaginary forces" (*Henry V* Pro.18) – in his own example, 'seeing' an army where in fact there are only a handful of actors on stage. "Think, when we talk of horses, that you see them" (Pro.26).[10] These mental processes, enabled or constrained by different physical media, are obviously much more difficult to historicise than the physical media themselves. Another obstacle to their historicisation is that they are, though not timeless, possibly quite independent of particular media – and the human mind (and body) will take from these media what they

---

[7] The German language even has a word for this: *Literaturverfilmung,* turning literature into film, the opposite of a novelisation that transforms a film into a novel.
[8] To give only a few examples: for music, see Hollander 1961, Wolf 1999; for dance, Jones 2013, Brandstetter 2015, Marczek-Fuchs 2015; for video games, Aarseth 1997, Domsch 2013, Ensslin 2014; for graphic novels, Baetens and Frey 2015, Williams 2020.
[9] The term 'media ecology' goes back to Postman 1974; see also Fuller 2005, Berensmeyer 2012.
[10] All quotations from Shakespeare in this book are from *The Norton Shakespeare* (Shakespeare 1997).

can get by way of aesthetic experience, just as they can 'see' six or seven actors as an army of thousands. Limitations can be productive, and an empty stage (cf. Brook 1996) can be more effective than the most screen-filling of special effects. Literature has never been, and probably never will be, tied down to any single medium.[11]

Historical media configurations are now also in the purview of a research field called *book history, histoire du livre,* or *history of the book,* or sometimes *history of the material text.* According to one expansive definition, book history is the "social, cultural, and economic history of authorship, publishing, printing, the book arts, copyright, censorship, bookselling and distribution, libraries, literacy, literary criticism, reading habits, and reader response" (Greenspan and Rose 1998, ix). While not too clearly defined, book history deals with aspects of the history of publishing, of how texts exist in different documents, different material forms, including anything from clay tablets to digital texts. This field of studies has raised awareness for the multiplicity of aspects and agencies involved in communication, beyond merely a sender, a message, a medium, and a receiver. In the case of books, these may include publishers, printers, bookbinders, booksellers, perhaps literary agents, reviewers, and journalists, etc. Robert Darnton has called this "the communications circuit" (1982). Beyond these individuals, there are structural factors and processes to consider (Adams and Barker 2006). Within book history, there are now many specialised areas, such as the history of particular types of documents or technologies such as the PDF (Gitelman 2014) or word processing (Kirschenbaum 2016). Obviously, a media history of literature will be narrower in focus than a history of the book, and much narrower than a global history of text technologies (Treharne and Willan 2020). As I have sketched out in this introduction, the aim of this book is to trace the connections between the material history of the production and transmission of texts with the history of (English) literature as an aesthetic phenomenon. I assume a basic continuity throughout history of a type of text (in the widest sense)[12] that can be described as having certain structural or aesthetic features (an open set of features that might include, for example, fictionality, experientiality, formal patterning, self-reflexiveness, etc.) which make it 'literary', or which invite readers, listeners, or viewers to identify it as such. My key interest then is to see the extent to which media and technologies affect the poetics and aesthetics of this type of text: to understand literary history as shaped by the impact of different

---

11 For an anthropological approach to the cultural history of media and literature, see Pfeiffer 2002.
12 Cf. the definition given by Treharne and Willan: "signs, symbols, or sounds of any kind that intentionally convey meaning" (2020, 1).

physical substrates, new technologies, and new configurations of media. As we are experiencing a massive media shift from print to digital technologies in the twenty-first century, such an understanding of literary history seems to me more relevant than ever – if only to take a stand against gloomy scenarios of cultural decline. Though the material forms of production, distribution, and reception may be changing, the history of literature will continue – in some form, some medium or other.

Instructions for Use

A final note on how this book is structured, and the reasoning behind this. Without making a strong claim about periodisation, I propose that the media history of literature can be divided into roughly three ages according to three dominant types of media usage: performance, representation, and connection. These are to be understood not as descriptions of reality but as ideal types (in the sense of Max Weber). *Performance-based media* have the human body, or a community of bodies that interact with each other in the present, as both their origin and their target. Their effects are transient, local, and often experienced as immediate, instantaneous, and present. Oral poetry and storytelling, live theatrical performance, and at least some aspects of written texts fall under this category. *Media of representation* "involve the storage and deferred release of information" (Trotter 2017, 391). They re-present something that is no longer present (i.e., that is removed spatially or temporally, or both) but which can be made to reappear by means of media. They encourage or require acts of interpretation orientated towards discovering the meaning of what they represent. In this part of the book, I focus on early modern and modern print culture, but also on the ways in which literature in print attempts to regain sensual and physical immediacy by appealing to sensory activities like breathing. Thus, the modes of representation and performance are connected, they do not simply replace one another. In the third part, which mainly covers the twentieth and twenty-first centuries, the dominant orientation of ('new') media gradually changes towards the mode of *connectivity* and experiences of *connection* and *disconnection*. With David Trotter, we can define this as a mode that privileges "interactive one-to-one communication at a distance" (ibid.). In other words, these electronic and digital media attempt to return to a (however attenuated) sense of immediacy and directness that seemed impossible in the age of representation. Yet the earlier dominant modes do not disappear; they only cease to be dominant.

Individual chapters within the three parts are each concerned with a particular kind of medium or media configuration. Some of these relate to the senses, others refer to certain objects or technological innovations. They are not intended to convey a sense of teleology or exclusivity; quite the opposite. Although my narrative proceeds roughly chronologically, it does not follow a deterministic or teleological model of history, but it tells a story of expansion, adaptation, and co-evolution across sometimes longer, sometimes shorter periods of historical time. As Umberto Eco reminds us, the book is a very old tool and still in use even though we also now have many different types of screens at our disposal (Carrière and Eco 2012, 4–5). The media history of literature is at least as much a story of continuities as of discontinuities. After all, even though everything else has changed, we still respond to literature with the same senses our ancestors did thousands of years ago. What they did with them (as far as we can know) will be the topic of the next chapter.

I The Age of Performance (since c. 70,000 BCE)

2 Voice and Hand

In 1964, the French anthropologist André Leroi-Gourhan published *Gesture and Speech* (*Le geste et la parole*). He presented a synthesis of then current knowledge about human evolution, giving a systematic account of, among other things, brain development, tool use, society, the birth of language and symbols, the growth and expansion of memory, even questions of style and aesthetics. Following an evolutionary perspective, Leroi-Gourhan was interested in the neuro-physiological coordination between the hand and the face. Ever since human beings learned to walk on two legs rather than four, they enjoyed the freedom to use both their faces and their hands simultaneously – a significant step in human evolution that enabled a wide array of technological and social developments. In its totalising ambition of writing a global account of how human evolution and technological progress were connected, *Gesture and Speech* resembles Stanley Kubrick's (1928–1999) similarly ambitious 1968 film *2001: A Space Odyssey*. The film has an equally sweeping historical scope from the 'dawn of man' to space travel, symbolised in the famous match-cut of a flying bone turning into a spaceship. Although this very sweep may now seem somewhat suspect, given the ever-increasing specialisation in biology, anthropology, and history, similar accounts of 'big history' have recently come back into fashion – consider, for example, the global bestseller *Sapiens: A Brief History of Humankind* (Harari 2015).

Origins

According to Leroi-Gourhan's evolutionary perspective, the free use of their hands releases cognitive capacities and enables humans to speak and communicate better with each other. This important step is now known as the 'Cognitive Revolution', which is thought to have occurred "between 70,000 and 30,000 years ago" (Harari 2015, 23). Also, the first graphic symbols or images, "tight curves or series of lines engraved in bone or stone", date from 35,000 BCE (Leroi-Gourhan 1993, 188). Leroi-Gourhan points out that what he calls "graphism did not begin with naive representations of reality but with abstraction" (ibid.) These first signs represent "rhythms rather than forms" (189). In other words, they are not mimetic depictions of animals or objects in the real world; for this anthropologist, they represent a form of writing:

> It was symbolic transposition, not copying of reality; in other words, the distance that lies between a drawing in which a group agrees to recognize a bison and the bison itself is the

> same as the distance between a word and a tool. In both signs and words, abstraction reflects a gradual adaptation of the motor system of expression to more and more subtly differentiated promptings of the brain. The earliest known paintings do not represent a hunt, a dying animal, or a touching family scene, they are graphic building blocks without any descriptive binder, the support medium of an irretrievably lost oral content. (1993, 189)

The symbolic world that is created here, in other words, depends on *imagination*; its symbols are abstractions from reality, constituting a "second world" (Berger 1965) or a "second reality" (Luhmann 2000b, 51) in parallel to the first one. They are an early form of collective fiction-making. Indeed, Leroi-Gourhan concurs: "These symbols constitute the world of language which parallels the real world and provides us with our means of coming to grips with reality" (195). The development of the brain, of symbolic forms, of fiction, language, and writing is coordinated, in his account, with technological and social developments from agriculture to urbanisation. The visual, image-oriented aspect of graphic notation is not fully lost in the invention of linear, phonetic writing systems; towards the end of his account of language and writing, Leroi-Gourhan agrees with McLuhan's hypothesis of media as the "extensions of man" (1994 [1964], 4) when he notes:

> Tools detached themselves from the human hand, eventually to bring forth the machine. In this latest stage speech and sight are undergoing the same process, thanks to the development of technics [sic]. Language, which had separated itself from the human through art and writing, is consummating the final divorce by entrusting the intimate functions of phonation and sight to wax, film, and magnetic tape.
> (Leroi-Gourhan 1993, 216)

We will never know what the first poetic use of language was like, and what purpose exactly it was meant to serve. It probably begins, again, with forms of abstraction within the second reality that is language: acts of naming, which assign certain sounds to objects or persons in the world (paradigmatic distinctions); acts of verbal association that link persons to objects and actions (in other words, the invention of *grammar* or syntagmatic connections); and most likely simile and metaphor (when something is compared to something else, is identified with something else): *Hercules is like a lion; Hercules is a lion.* Metonymy (something begins to stand for something else that is associated with the object or is a part of the object): *hungry mouths*, where 'mouths' actually means people who are hungry; *lend me your ears*, where 'ears' means 'attention', or *tongues* as a metonym for 'language' because tongues are crucial for speaking. Then, irony, the use of words in opposition to their actual meaning. Such language use against the grain of semantics has its place in jokes and many other social situations of public speaking; it may well be the origin of 'verbal art'. In this sense, there probably was *literature* long before there was writing. The term 'orature' is sometimes used to describe phenomena of oral literature (Ashcroft et al. 2007). The first poems, for all we know, were composed and recited orally and passed on, to use a metonymic expression, 'by word of mouth'. Perhaps they were associated with wisdom, with important cultural knowledge, and they may have had the structure and purpose of proverbs. The voice that speaks those words is not individualised but inhabits a communal function; it does not tell just any story but performs a ritual that is meaningful for the community, establishing and maintaining a bond that is essential for its survival. To such gnomic utterances we can also add jokes and riddles as significant short forms of literature.[13] Singing songs and telling stories are obviously much older human activities than writing. Having a singer or a storyteller naturally involves an audience who enjoy listening to songs or stories. Setting their hands free for manual work not only gave early humans the possibility to speak and watch each other while speaking or listening; it also enabled them to tell each other stories. When this was connected with writing at a much later date, the potential for telling stories to audiences that were remote in space and time – sometimes across millennia – increased vastly.

The first stories to survive in writing are about the kings of Uruk, a city in Mesopotamia (today's Iraq), dating from c. 2150 BCE. (For comparison, the oldest sources of the Hebrew Bible date from c. 1000 BCE.) Uruk is one of the oldest cities in the world, and it had a long tradition of literacy in a pre-alphabetic writing style known as cuneiform because of its wedge-shaped letters, which have been preserved on clay tablets. This form of writing was invented in Mesopotamia around 3000 BCE, but its earliest surviving texts were economic and administrative rather than literary. We do not know the reason why a scribe (or group of scribes) sat down to record the story of Gilgamesh – an epic story of friendship between a king of Uruk and a 'wild man' named Enkidu. Their friendship bridges the gap between the civilisation of the city dwellers and the untamed wildness of the world beyond the city walls. Together, they kill the monster Humbaba and secure trees as building material for the city. For this, Enkidu is punished by a god and dies. Gilgamesh searches for him everywhere, even in the underworld. There he meets a very old couple who tell him about the flood which they alone survived (an account that is similar to the Great Flood in Genesis); but even they cannot give him back his friend or grant him immortality. Even the king must make his peace with death and recognise the limits of his power.

---

13 See ch. 3 for examples of the Old English riddle; for more on poetic voice, ch. 7.

Beyond the story itself, this epic narrative is interesting for the way it incorporates writing and the very material on which it was written: unbaked clay, the very building material of cities like Uruk and thus the very basis of Mesopotamian civilisation. Gilgamesh is "a writer-king", perhaps even "the author of his own tale" (Puchner 2017, 33):

> He who experienced the whole gained complete wisdom.
> He found out what was secret and uncovered what was hidden,
> He brought back a tale of times before the Flood.
> He had journeyed far and wide, weary and at last resigned.
> He engraved all toils on a memorial monument of stone.
> (Dalley 2008, 50)

A few centuries later, the Homeric tales, written in the Greek alphabet, similarly tell of distant journeys and homecoming (*The Odyssey*), of warriors and "toils", human beings and gods, death, and mortality (*The Iliad*). Written down around 800 BCE and given a definitive textual shape around 300 BCE, the two epic poems associated with the name of Homer, but especially the *Iliad*, were the foundational texts of ancient Greek culture – frequently copied and commented on, memorised in large parts, and used as a kind of school textbook and universal reference work. Alexander the Great is said to have carried a copy of the *Iliad* wherever he went and even put it under his pillow every night, in a box also containing a dagger – wisdom and protection side by side (Puchner 2017, 3). The Homeric texts were used to teach reading and writing. They would be written on scrolls made of papyrus, pressed leaves of a plant which were pasted together to create a smooth writing surface which could absorb and preserve traces of ink. Our term 'scrolling' (up or down when reading text on a screen) is a reminder of the physical necessity of unrolling a scroll when reading; the Latin word for scroll, *volumen,* gives us the word 'volume' (as in 'the second volume of *The Lord of the Rings*'). An unrolled scroll could have a length of six metres. Easier to use were "concertina-folded papyrus notebooks" that were first made before the year 100 CE (Raven 2018, 23).

Writing on Parchment

In late antiquity, a different writing material came into use, which was later associated with the rise of Christianity: parchment. The name derives from the library of Pergamum (now Bergama in Turkey). There, librarians began to use prepared sheepskins as a writing surface. The membranes were "dehaired by being soaked in lime and then scraped, stretched and dried, rubbed smooth with pumice and cut into sheets" (Raven 2018, 24). When one handles a manuscript written on membrane, one can still see that one side is rough (the 'hair' side) and the other smooth (the 'flesh' side). While ink and papyrus, and later paper (which arrived through Islamic Spain in the twelfth century and became common in Europe at the end of the fourteenth century; see Kurlansky 2016) are plant-based materials, many early books were written on animal skin. In German, there still survives the expression *Das geht auf keine Kuhhaut* – that won't fit on a cow's skin – to denote something indescribable or unbearable.

In Rome and throughout the Mediterranean world, parchment was increasingly used in combination with a new format, from which the modern book derives: stacked sheets bound on one side and placed between covers. In Latin, this was called a *codex*, and over the years this came to replace the scroll as the preferred format of preserving texts, as membrane and later paper replaced papyrus as the basic substrate for writing. *Caudex* means 'tree trunk' in Latin; *codex*, attested by the first century CE, was first used for notebooks made of wax tablets and wood. Due to its ease of use and its affordances as a text technology (cf. Treharne and Willan 2020, 168–172), the codex became *the* format of the physical book as we know it today. *Liber*, Latin for 'book', from which we get 'library', originally denoted the bark of a tree. The Greek word *biblos*, said to derive from the Phoenician city of Byblos, first denoted a papyrus roll, later a codex book, and still later a very particular book: the Bible. A *charta* referred to "a papyrus roll of no more than twenty sheets or about 4.5 metres" (Raven 2018, 32). Some of the features of books that we take for granted were introduced fairly late: punctuation in Rome c. 200 BCE, and word separation in Ireland in the seventh century CE.

In 537 CE, the Roman statesman and scholar Cassiodorus celebrated writing on papyrus and its possibilities of preserving information so that it stays the same over time:

> For previously, the sayings of the wise and the ideas of our ancestors were in danger. For how could you quickly record words which the resistant hardness of bark made it almost impossible to set down? . . . The tempting beauty of paper . . . opens a field for the elegant with its white surface; its help is always plentiful; and it is so pliant that it can be rolled together, although it is unfolded to a great length. Its joints are seamless, its parts united; it is the snowy pith of a green plant, a writing surface which takes black ink for its ornament; on it, with letters exalted . . . there discourse is stored in safety, to be heard for ever with consistency [*aequaliter*].[14]

---

[14] Cassiodorus, *Variae*, bk. 11, letter 38, as qtd. in Raven 2018, 33. Inserted Latin word from the text at https://www.thelatinlibrary.com/cassiodorus/varia11.shtml.

Yet a text can only remain to be heard in the same way (*aequaliter*) unless the material on which it is located is destroyed. Libraries are flammable. There is a touching letter by the Roman physician Galen from 192 CE describing the impact of such a fire: "When Philides the grammarian's books were destroyed in the fire, he wasted away and died as a result of discouragement and distress. What is more, for quite some time, people went around in black garments – thin and pale like mourners" (qtd. in Raven 2018, 34).

Printing, invented first in China (as woodblock printing) at some point between the seventh and ninth centuries CE (cf. Raven 2018, 34), and much later with different technologies (as printing with movable type) in fifteenth-century Europe, was to mitigate this immediate risk of loss. Printing makes it easier to have multiple copies of the same text (which could of course also be achieved, though more laboriously, through copying manuscripts). Once a text had been set in type, the cost of printing more copies of a book was considerably lower than the cost of making those copies in a scriptorium – which means that there was an added economic incentive to printing and selling more copies of the same text (Treharne and Willan 2020, 160–161). But before Johannes Gutenberg (c. 1400–1468) invented the technologies of modern printing in the mid-fifteenth century, there was no other option than copying texts by hand; the word *manuscript* derives from the Latin for 'written by hand'.

Manuscripts were expensive to produce, both in terms of resources and labour costs. They were written on parchment or vellum, i.e., sheep- or calfskins. While 'parchment', as noted earlier, derives from the ancient city of Pergamum, 'vellum' comes from the Latin *vitulinum*, 'made from calves', or from Old French *velin* (veal). Vellum is of a higher quality and thinner than parchment. It took a community to make a book, and – depending on the book's size – quite a few sheep or calves to obtain the amount of parchment or vellum required. Roughly twenty-five animal skins were needed to make an average book, while an exceptionally large volume like the Codex Amiatinus, one of the few complete manuscripts of the Latin Bible, consisting of 1030 folios, would require more than five hundred (Gameson 1992). One or more scribes would write out a text, and usually several texts would be collected in a unified codex, or composite manuscript. There is little evidence that scribes in monasteries particularly enjoyed their work, "wasting away the daylight hours" in cramped conditions and in silence (Borsuk 2018, 48). One monk's gloss reads like a call for help: "St. Patrick of Armagh, deliver me from writing" (qtd. in Borsuk 2018, 48). But for many, if not most monks and nuns assigned to writing (Gameson 2012, 98), copying Christian texts was a devotional practice that was thought to deliver "spiritual blessings" (119) for the scribe and the entire community.

A later medieval writer, Thomas Hoccleve (1368–1426), complains bitterly about the low pay and the physical strain of working as a professional scribe. They were not allowed to chat or sing while working but had to "laboure in travayllous stilnesse" while 'stooping and staring at the sheepskin' (ll. 1013–14) and doing damage to their stomachs, backs, and eyes.

> What man that thre and twenti yere and more
> In wrytyng hath continuid, as have I,
> I dar wel seyn it smertyth hym ful sore
> In every veyn and place of hys body;
> And yen most it greveth, trewely,
> Of any craft that man can ymagyne[.][15]
> (Hoccleve, *The Regement of Princes* [1411–12],
>   ll. 1023–28, in Pearsall 1999, 331)

Though this complaint may be somewhat exaggerated, there can be no doubt that copying texts by hand was (and still is) laborious and time-consuming. The surviving record of Old English manuscripts (some four hundred are still extant) is probably only a small sample of the original production. Some were destroyed during Viking raids, some went up in flames in Canterbury Cathedral in the late eleventh century, and some perished in the dissolution of the monasteries during the English Reformation. Another disaster occurred in 1731, when a fire broke out in the London library of Sir Robert Cotton, containing the most important collection of medieval manuscripts in England, now part of the British Library. From surviving catalogues, we have evidence of the substantial collections of religious houses in England in the late Middle Ages: St Augustine's, Canterbury, for example, had more than 1,800 books (Bell 2006, 140).

Many texts survive in only one copy, like the *Beowulf* manuscript that was singed in the fire in Cotton's library. Only very few were written by their authors themselves (two later Middle English texts, the *Orrmulum* and *Ayenbite of Inwit*, are notable exceptions). Scribes probably often also edited texts, so that what we read may not always be the original author's words. Medieval texts are usually at least one step removed from their original creators. When there are several manuscripts of one text, there are often variant readings, differences in spelling and

---

15 "Anyone who has persevered in writing / for 23 years and more, as I have, / I daresay it hurts him terribly / In every vein and place of his body; / And most of all it is harmful to the eyes, truly / Of any craft that you can imagine." (My translation) – Hoccleve's *Regiment of Princes* is a book of advice for rulers, but it includes a lengthy prologue containing much information about Hoccleve's life and his disgruntled personality. It was a popular text surviving in over forty manuscripts (Pearsall 1999, 322).

vocabulary. Paul Zumthor (1972) coined the term *mouvance* to describe the rather loose and mobile nature of medieval texts, while Bernard Cerquiglini (1989) speaks of *variance* in connection with scribal practices. Yet, as we shall see below, even printed texts are less fixed or stable than one might assume. This is not to say that poets, at least in the high Middle Ages, did not care for accuracy in textual transmission; one very interesting short lyric by Geoffrey Chaucer (early 1340s–1400) addresses a scribe named Adam; Chaucer complains bitterly about Adam's carelessness and haste (or impatience) in copying his works:

> Adam scriveyn, if ever it thee bifalle
> Boece or Troylus for to wryten newe,
> Under thy long lokkes thou most have the scalle,
> But after my makyng thow wryte more trewe;
> So ofte adaye I most thy werk renewe,
> It to correcte and eke to rubbe and scrape,
> And al is thorugh thy negligence and rape.[16]
> (Chaucer 1987, 650)

Old English texts, by contrast, tend to focus less on the weaknesses of writing but emphasise its near-magical powers. The awe in which writing was held can be clearly felt, for example, in one of the riddles (number 26) from the Exeter Book, which talks about the act of writing with a quill on parchment:

> Mec feonda sum   feore besnyþede,
> woruldstrenga binom;   wætte siþþan
> dyfde on wætre;   dyde eft þonan,
> sette on sunnan   þær Ic swiþe beleas
> herum þam þe Ic hæfde.   Heard mec siþþan
> snað seaxses ecg,   sindrum begrunden;
> fingras feoldan,   ond mec fugles wyn
> geondsprengde speddropum,   spyrede geneahhe.
> Ofer brunne brerd   beamtelge swealg
> streames dæle,   stop eft on mec,
> siþade sweartlast. [. . .]

---

[16] "Scribe Adam, if ever it should fall to you / To write *Boethius* or *Troilus* again, / May you get a disease of the scalp under your long locks, / Unless you write more faithfully according to my creation;/ So many times a day I have to fix your work, / To correct it and also to rub and scrape it off, / And all because of your negligence and haste." (My translation) Chaucer refers to his narrative poem *Troilus and Criseyde* and his translation of Boethius. The poem survives in two manuscripts; in one, its title is "Chaucer's wordes unto Adam, his owne scriveyn", in the other "Chaucers woordes vnto his owne Scriuener" (Chaucer 1987, 1188). These are unlikely to be authorial. The identity of this Adam (who has been traced to a London scribe named Adam Pinkhurst) is disputed (see Lesser 2019, 62).

> An enemy took my life, deprived me
> of my physical strength; then he moistened me,
> he dipped me in water; took me out again,
> and set me in the sun where I rapidly lost
> all of the hairs that I had. Then the knife's hard edge
> cut into me, ground away with cinders;
> fingers folded me, and the bird's joy [i.e. feathers]
> went over me with useful drops, made tracks repeatedly.
> Over the brown rim it swallowed more tree-dye,
> a measure of the liquid, again it stepped on me,
> leaving its black tracks. [. . .]
>   (Treharne 2010, 80–83, ll. 1–11)

As is customary in Old English riddles, the object is speaking in the first person. Giving inanimate objects or animals the power of speech is probably among the oldest poetic strategies – an act of metaphor that transfers human qualities to the non-human environment. Here the emphasis is on the violence that is done to the skin in preparation of writing, which is described as making "tracks" (*spyrede*). As the riddle continues, the speaker describes how "a man covered me, / with boards, stretched skin over me, / adorned me with gold [. . .]" (ll. 11–13). In this weird blend of sexual imagery, violence, and decoration, the riddle describes the finished book (most likely a gospel-book), which it then continues to celebrate as a useful source of wisdom, piety, and virtue.

Old English Literature

Old English literature in the narrow sense (excluding homiletic, historical, and legal texts) consists mostly of poetry. In an edition, this is usually printed like modern poetry, as in the example just quoted: with short lines and a pause (caesura) marked by a gap in the middle of line. However, in the original manuscripts, they are written in continuous form, like prose; mainly because parchment was expensive but also because such conventions for representing poetry on the page had not yet developed. Some 30,000 lines of poetry have survived. Most Old English poems are anonymous and cannot be dated with any precision. Only two poets are known by name: Cædmon and Cynewulf. Most poems have no title. The *Beowulf* manuscript, for instance, starts with the first line of the poem, and its title is a modern addition to the text – introduced, apparently, by J. R. R. Tolkien (1892–1973) in the early twentieth century when he dropped the definite article from what was previously known as *The Beowulf,* in accordance with classical epics like *The Iliad* or *The Aeneid*. His intervention substantially changed the perception of *Beowulf* as a work of literature (Tolkien 1936).

The poems that have come down to us were all mostly written down in a half-century around the year 1000. But the documented history of what is now known as 'English' literature begins in the early fifth century CE. When Northern tribes threatened to invade Rome, the Empire ordered its legions back from the far-flung regions where they had been posted, including Britain. The 'native' inhabitants were left to their own devices. Political struggles erupted into acts of aggression between the different populations of the Isles. In the late 440s, the king of the Britons is said to have invited mercenaries from the continent to help him fight against the Picts and the Irish. According to the Venerable Bede, the first English historian, writing almost three hundred years later, the king's name was Vortigern, and the incoming tribes were led by two brothers, Hengist and Horsa (Bede 2008, 26–27). In a relatively short time, these tribes from areas of what is now Denmark and northern Germany – Bede mentions the Saxons, Angles and Jutes (27), but modern scholars also add the Frisians (Treharne 2010, xxi) – took over and drove the Celtic Britons out to the fringes, to Brittany, Wales, Northern England, and Cornwall. But whether these new settlers replaced or gradually mingled with the native population is an open question (Solopova and Lee 2007, 2). Their language, now known as Old English, emerged out of the West Germanic dialects that the settlers brought with them.

Their religion was pagan, whereas their new country had adopted Christianity under Roman rule, though Bede records a religious decline preceding the arrival of the settlers. Later, in 597, a missionary from Rome began to convert the new inhabitants of the British Isles to Christianity: St. Augustine of Canterbury (not to be confused with the much more famous philosopher-theologian St. Augustine of Hippo). At the same time, missionaries from Ireland and Scotland began to convert people further North. What exactly the so-called Anglo-Saxons[17] believed *before* they became Christian is a matter of much speculation. The mixture of pre-Christian and Christian elements is a fascinating feature of Old English literature. Within a medieval Christian culture, some earlier beliefs and concepts like *wyrd* (fate, destiny) and *middangeard* ('middle-earth', middle enclosure) keep cropping up, lightly retouched to fit a Christian worldview. Christianity itself was far from univocal in the Middle Ages; it was not simply 'Catholic' (a term used in the modern sense only after the Reformation), and there were many groups that did not conform to Roman orthodoxy. Bede, for example, complains about the "Arian

---

[17] The name 'Anglo-Saxon' has come under attack in recent years, mainly because of its abuse by white supremacists. I do not use it in a racial sense but, for the lack of a better alternative, as an inadequate label for the inhabitants of early medieval England, wherever 'English' or 'early English' will not do.

madness" (2008, 20), which denied the equality and co-eternity of the Trinity, and the "treacherous poison" (21) of the Pelagian heresy, which denied that divine grace was a precondition for salvation. In all its multiplicity, Christianity was of crucial importance to medieval literature. Its reliance on the written word (the Scriptures) as the basis of its teaching and its liturgy required an active practice of preserving and producing material texts. Until the ninth century, these texts were predominantly written in Latin. As Elaine Treharne explains, "English was spoken by the ordinary population, and used for the oral recitation of poetry, but it was not yet considered a language suitable for writing" (2010, xxi). It took from the fifth to the eighth century for the first (extant) piece of writing in Old English to emerge. In the ninth century, King Alfred of Wessex, also called Alfred the Great, was the first king to promote English as a written language. He also encouraged teaching in English and initiated a revival of classical learning by having important books translated from Latin into the vernacular (Treharne 2010, xxi–xxii).

Written Old English was used in a more or less standardised form from the ninth century onwards. The incoming Germanic tribes had brought a runic script with them that was mainly used for short epigraphic inscriptions (Hines 1990, Waxenberger 2017; see also https://www.runesdb.eu/en/). The word *writing* (Old English *writan*) originally meant "to cut a figure in something" and "to incise runic letters in stone" (Howe 2002, 5). Runic script was gradually replaced by the Latin alphabet but two of its letter forms were used in combination with Latin letters to write in English: þ (*thorn*) and ƿ (*wynn*, meaning 'joy', used for a 'w' sound). Some other letter forms, æ (*ash*) and ð (*eth*), were adapted from Latin. Thorn and eth could be used for both voiced and unvoiced 'th' sounds. Written English lost the ash, eth, and wynn letters by the thirteenth century, but the thorn was still in use in the early modern period. From the twelfth century, another letter form, *yogh* (ȝ) came into use, derived from the insular form of *g*, used for the initial sound in words like 'yet' and the *gh* in 'night' (which was still pronounced in Middle English like the German word *nicht* [niçt]).

The tribes that migrated to Britain were probably organised in smaller groups, based on kinship ties. Archaeological evidence shows that their settlements consisted of huts built around a large hall for gatherings and celebrations (fig. 1). In many poems, the hall symbolises "a well-ordered society" (Solopova and Lee 2007, 5). This is the place where the *scop* ('poet') would recite poetry, probably accompanied by a harp. Society was based on networks of mutual dependencies, and what people feared most – as can be gleaned from many literary texts – was to be banished from their community, to become an outcast or an exile. Only a minority would have been able to read or write – probably those engaged in administrative tasks and those who chose a religious life as monks or priests, for whom reading and writing were essential.

Fig. 1: Reconstruction of an Anglo-Saxon village hall. West Stow, Suffolk, 2018. Source: Ingo Berensmeyer.

In the surviving record, there is ten times more prose than poetry. English prose (from Latin *proversa oratio*, 'straightforward discourse') was developed into a true literary form from the ninth century onwards, ranging from legal, medical, and historical texts to saints' lives and other religious writings, letters, wills, glosses to Latin texts and translations of classical texts as well as of the Old and New Testament. Latin as the *lingua franca* continued to dominate. Many medieval Latin manuscripts were written in England, such as the Codex Amiatinus, mentioned above, produced in the monastery of Monkwearmouth-Jarrow around the year 800. The influence of Latin on English is already present in early (continental) borrowings, in words like *stræt* (street) from *strata*, *weall* (wall) from *vallum*, *win* (wine) from *vinum*, which may well have been picked up from Roman soldiers. Later influences are in a more literary and religious register, with words like 'altar', 'bishop', 'school' and 'grammar'. Latin would be studied in the monasteries because it was necessary for monks and nuns to engage with the texts used by the Church (Solopova and Lee 2007, 42–44). The use and quality of Latin writing decreased during the time of the Viking raids in the late eighth and ninth centuries, while writers following King Alfred's educational programme continued to model their English writing style on Latin grammar.

Cædmon

Reading in early medieval England must be imagined as a performative event, a shared cultural practice; people did not read texts in private or in silence. There was no clear historical division between an oral and a literate community, but there were "textual communities" (Stock 1983, 88) in which "the way to the truth was through the written word as performed or interpreted within a community" (Howe 2002, 3). The story of Cædmon, the first English poet known by name, is a good illustration of this. Nicholas Howe gives this concise summary of the story as recorded by Bede in his *History* sometime before 731: Cædmon was a cowherd who served a monastery; thus he lived in an oral community of peasants on the margins of a literate community of monks.

> Bede relates that Cædmon would, from a sense of his own lack of talent, quietly withdraw from the banqueting hall when his turn to sing a song and play the harp approached. [. . .] One night, after leaving the hall, he retires to his cowbarn and falls asleep to a dream in which someone calls to him by name and orders him to sing a song. Cædmon replies that he cannot sing, the authority figure repeats his command, and Cædmon asks what he should sing about. After being told to sing of God's Creation, Cædmon recites a vernacular poem that he had never heard before and that now goes by the name of 'Cædmon's Hymn.' The nine-line poem that we have seems to be only a fragment of Cædmon's first creation, but it clearly observes the strict metrical, alliterative, and stylistic conventions of vernacular Old English poetry and is also orthodox in its Christian theology.
> (Howe 2002, 11–12)

Bede reports that, on the following morning, Cædmon notifies the reeve and then the abbess of the monastery about the dream. Everyone agrees that "the Lord had granted him heavenly grace" (Bede 2008, 216), that he had received "the gift of poetic composition" (Howe 2002, 12) from God himself. This narrative account of a cultural encounter between the vernacular oral culture of a Germanic people and the Latin culture of the Church can be interpreted in different ways. Is Cædmon a Christian hero because he applies traditional poetics to the new purpose of propagating Christianity, or does his story demonstrate the survival of a traditional poetics in the face of the cultural invasion of Christianity? According to Howe, the story "marks the end of pure orality in Anglo-Saxon England and initiates a complex interchange between oral poetics and written texts" (2002, 12), with many written texts striving to achieve the (imagined) effect of oral communication in a form of "vocality" (Zumthor 1990, 18) or "fictional orality" (Suerbaum and Gragnolati 2010, 1). It also describes a community flexible enough to include very different languages and social functions.

As Bede's story of Cædmon continues, the monks want to find out if he is more than a 'one-hit wonder', so they put him to the test, reading and explaining a passage from the Bible to him and asking him to put it into verse. Bede emphasises that the monks are fluent in Latin and English; Cædmon himself is illiterate and speaks only English. By explicating the biblical text to him, "the monks incorporate him within their community and also determine that his role will be to expound the text in a different manner to a different audience" (Howe 2002, 13). Cædmon joins the monastic community and continues to compose poetry about Christian topics, none of which have survived. But many other Old English poets wrote about these topics, which shows how close the connections between religious communities and other areas of society must have been when it came to literacy and the reading and writing of texts. Reading and writing were thought of as communal acts. Nobody would read alone and in silence in this period. Silent readers were an exception, an oddity even, as reported by St Augustine of Hippo in his *Confessions* (6.3), where he records how strange it was to see Ambrose, the bishop of Milan, read in silence without speaking the words: "but when he read, his eyes followed the pages and his heart pondered the meaning, though his voice and tongue were still" (qtd. in Howe 2002, 3). The etymology of the English word *reading* (Old English *rædan*) includes the meanings of 'giving advice or counsel' or 'explaining something obscure', which then came to mean 'the interpretation of ordinary writing' (4–5). Reading was thus closely aligned to speech and communication rather than silence, and there was significant overlap between orality and literacy rather than any sense of a clear distinction between them.

Another remarkable fact about Cædmon's hymn, the earliest extant piece of Old English poetry, is that Bede only paraphrased the poem in Latin, adding that "[t]his is the sense but not the order of the words which he sang [. . .]. For it is not possible to translate verse, however well composed, literally from one language to another without some loss of beauty and dignity" (2008, 216). Later scribes added Old English versions of the text in the margins of manuscripts. The poem – or their versions of it – use the pattern that is typical of Old English verse "to praise the Christian God" (Treharne 2010, 2), filling an older form with new content in a first instance of the fusion of Christian and pagan elements in English literature. Bede's *Ecclesiastical History* was translated into English in the reign of Alfred, and there are five extant manuscripts of the work in varying states of completeness at Oxford, Cambridge, and in the British Library. The following is the Oxford Bodleian Library's version of Cædmon's hymn (with a modern English translation):

Nu sculon herigean   heofonrices Weard,
Meotodes meahte   ond his modgeþanc,
weorc Wuldorfæder,   swa he wundra gehwæs,
ece Drihten,   or onstealde.
He ærest sceop   eorðan bearnum
heofon to hrofe,   halig Scyppend;
þa middangeard   moncynnes Weard,
ece Drihten,   æfter teode
firum foldan,   Frea ælmihtig.

Now praise the Guardian of the heavenly kingdom,
the might of the Creator and his conception,
the work of the glorious Father, as he established the beginning,
eternal Lord, of each of the wonders.
He first created for the children of the earth
heaven as a roof, holy Creator;
then the middle-earth the Guardian of mankind,
eternal Lord, afterwards adorned
the world for people, the Lord almighty.
(Treharne 2010, 8–9)

Cædmon's hymn is highly characteristic of the form and structure of Old English verse with its "strict metrical patterns" (Solopova and Lee 2007, 75) and rules for alliteration. Each half-line has "a minimum of four syllables" and usually "two stresses", which "fall on 'meaningful' elements in the verse" (76). A key technique employed frequently in Old English poetry is variation: for example, in this hymn, God is invoked in several different ways, as guardian, creator, father, and almighty lord. Poets would use synonyms to refer to the same object in order to avoid monotony: the same ship at the beginning of *Beowulf* is referred to as *scip* (ship), *cēol* (keel), *fær* (vessel), and *hringed-stefna* (ring-prowed ship). Another typical device is parallelism, the repetition of "a grammatical structure or idea [. . .] elsewhere in the poem" (Solopova and Lee 2007, 77). Often the same expressions are repeated in various poems; these are called 'formulas'. About seventy percent of the text in the first twenty-five lines of *Beowulf* appears elsewhere in Old English verse. This does not mean that poets simply copied from each other. One theory (the 'oral-formulaic theory') claims that this repeated use of stable expressions has its origin in oral composition: in performance, poets would have drawn from a general repertoire of formulas and adapted their words to the requirements of a live audience. However, some poets who were literate also used formulas; thus the oral-formulaic theory "explains the origin of formulaic style in oral pre-literate culture, but not its persistence in later learned and written poetry" (ibid., 79).

Most importantly, there was a special poetic diction, words that poets would use but that would not be common in everyday language or in other forms of literature. Some words only appear in poetry; some compounds only appear in a single work, such as the expression *gūðcyning* ('battle-king') in *Beowulf*. 'Kennings' are a special type of compound, where two separate words are combined to mean something else, e.g., 'whale' + 'road' = 'whale-road' (*hron-rād*) = 'the sea'; *sǣ-wudu* 'sea-wood' = 'ship', *bān-hūs* 'bone-house' = body. These metaphors and metonymies can be difficult to unravel, and they resemble the Old English riddles in miniature.

No other works by Cædmon have survived. But there is a long list of Old English Christian poems about biblical and other topics (many of them in the Junius manuscript): *Andreas, Azarias, Christ I–III, Christ and Satan, Daniel, The Descent into Hell, The Dream of the Rood, Elene, Exodus, The Fates of the Apostles, Genesis A, Genesis B, Guthlac A and B, Judith, Juliana, Menologium, Psalms.* The concern with Christian texts shows the 'English' trying to make sense of their place in the world, situating their lives in the Christian tradition and reminding themselves of this on a regular basis. In many poems, stories from the Old Testament are interpreted as prefigurations of the New Testament. What these poems have in common is, among other things, "an identification [. . .] with the oppression of the Israelites in the Old Testament, and the early Christians" and "a willingness to modify stories" for the benefit of a contemporary audience (Solopova and Lee 2007, 99). For example, in *Judith* (a poem included in the Nowell codex, written by the second of the two scribes who wrote the *Beowulf* manuscript), the biblical story of Judith and Holofernes is augmented with a battle scene (ibid.). *Judith* celebrates a female warrior heroine, a 'woman of elf-like brightness' (*ides ælfscinu*, l. 14) who kills the Assyrian warlord. She is described with adjectives like "prudent" (*snoteran*, l. 55), "holy" (*halige*, 56), "bright" (*beorhtan*, 58) and "courageous" (*eornoste*, 108), and as "the Saviour's / glorious handmaiden" (*Nergendes / þeowen þrymful*, 73–74). The description of how she kills Holofernes is particularly vivid:

> Then, this woman with braided locks struck
> the enemy, that hostile one,
> with the shining sword, so that she cut through half
> of his neck, such that he lay unconscious,
> drunk and wounded. He was not dead yet,
> not entirely lifeless. The courageous woman
> struck the heathen hound energetically
> another time so that his head rolled
> forwards on the floor. The foul body lay
> behind, dead; the spirit departed elsewhere
> under the deep earth and was oppressed there
> and fettered in torment forever after[.]
> (Treharne 2010, 231, ll. 103–114)

The poem goes on to visualise Holofernes's torments in hell. Christian theology and a warrior ethic are also combined in *The Dream of the Rood*, one of the poems in the Vercelli book; part of this poem also survives in runic script on the Ruthwell Cross, dating from the seventh or eighth century (Lesser 2019, 30–31). Narrated by the Cross on which Christ was crucified, this visionary poem presents Christ as a heroic warrior getting ready for battle. After death, he is treated like a Germanic hero. The emphasis is not on Christ's suffering but on his strength and courage. Apparently, Christ had to match or even outdo the adventures of Germanic heroes and Norse gods to fit the norms of this culture. There is some struggle in these poems to balance Christian beliefs with pagan Germanic concepts like *wyrd* (fate), and an ongoing concern with matching and blending these two worldviews. Even in a thoroughly Christian, monastic setting, the old tales obviously retained their appeal.

Beowulf

One of these old tales (and now the most famous) is the epic poem *Beowulf*. It survives in a single manuscript (British Library MS Cotton Vitellius A. xv) that has been dated to the late tenth or early eleventh century, in a more precise dating to the first decade of the eleventh century (fig. 2; see Kiernan 2015 for an online edition). This volume is a composite of at least two different manuscripts; the second (older) one, known as the Nowell Codex, is a compilation of several texts in prose and verse that share an interest in monsters and the marvellous, but the connection may also have been intended "to provide readers with material for moral contemplation" (Scragg 2012, 556), which suggests an ecclesiastical context for its creation. The book was written by two scribes, the second one taking over at line 1939b in mid-sentence. The codex was damaged by a fire at Ashburnham House in 1731, and the text deteriorated further in the nineteenth century, but some of the lost text can be reconstructed on the basis of two transcriptions made in the late eighteenth century.

Beowulf may go back as far as the sixth century, and in part back to even older oral traditions. *Beowulf* is a heroic epic that tells the story of a warrior, an exemplary hero, and his adventures in Scandinavia, but it is steeped in Christianity, the writings of the Church Fathers, and the Bible, especially the Old Testament (Jack 1994; Fulk et al. 2008). It also has some parallels to Virgil's *Aeneid*, the *Odyssey*, the *Iliad*, and Statius's *Thebaid* about the sons of Oedipus fighting over Thebes. Although *Beowulf* is now considered an essential part of English literature, its first printed edition in the early nineteenth century was supported by the Danish government (Lesser 2019, 15) – showing just how inadequate modern national boundaries are for the understanding of medieval texts.

Beowulf sails from what is now Sweden to Denmark, in the hope of defeating a monster or ogre named Grendel, who has been terrorising the court of the Danish king Hrothgar for twelve years. In single combat, Beowulf fights Grendel and tears off his arm, but Grendel escapes to the swamp and there dies of his wound. Now Beowulf has to fight Grendel's mother, a hideous swamp creature, who had killed one of Hrothgar's advisers in revenge. He slays her and cuts off the head of Grendel's dead body, taking it back to Hrothgar as a prize. Beowulf returns as a celebrated hero. Later on, he becomes king and rules wisely and peacefully for some fifty years. But then he is called back to action because the country is threatened by a dragon who brings fire and destruction. Beowulf manages to kill the dragon but is wounded in the fight, and finally killed by the poison from the dragon's bite. His people build a funeral pyre and ceremonially burn his corpse by the seaside, mourning the passing of a great and wise ruler. This fairly simple life-story of a hero fighting three successive enemies, however, is not told in a linear fashion but in a sinuous pattern of interwoven narrative threads running backwards and sideways as well as forwards. Of its total of 3,182 lines, some 700 are narrative digressions. While this nonlinearity used to be regarded as the accidental result of spontaneous (oral) composition or the combination of older textual sources, more recent critics have come to appreciate it as "the work of a highly literate and meditative poet" who knew exactly what he was doing (Lapidge 2019, 268).

The poem is highly original rather than imitative; nevertheless, its alliterative verse and metre are typical of Old English poetry:

Hwæt, wē Gār-Dena   in ġeārdagum,
þēodcyninga   þrym ġefrūnon,
hū ðā æþelingas   ellen fremedon.
        (Fulk et al. 2008, ll. 1–3)

In the Irish poet Seamus Heaney's masterful verse translation, these opening lines are rendered as follows: "So. The Spear-Danes in days gone by / and the kings who ruled them had courage and greatness. / We have heard of those princes' heroic campaigns" (Heaney 2019, 3). *Hwæt,* the first word of the poem, often rendered in modern English as 'lo', 'hark', or 'listen', also occurs at the beginning of other Old English poems, calling the poem's audience to attention in what is a clear reminiscence of the oral/aural context of poetry. Heaney translates it as "so", using an emphatic discourse marker in Hiberno-English, "an expression that obliterates all previous discourse and narrative, and at the same time functions as an exclamation calling for immediate attention" (2019, xxxvii).

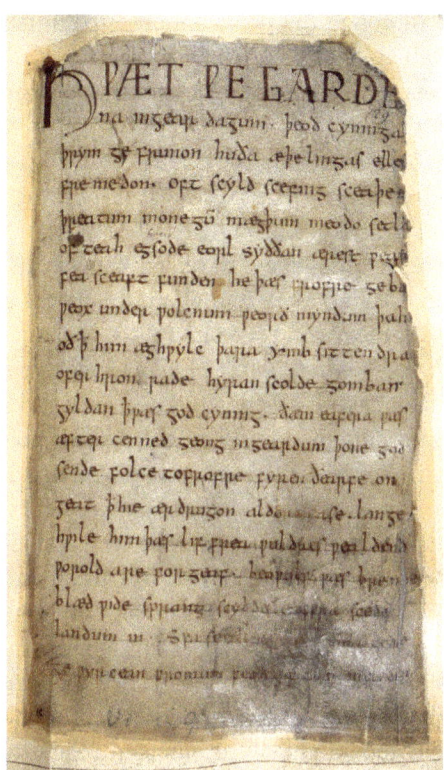

Fig. 2: First page of *Beowulf* manuscript (Cotton Vitellius A. XV, f. 132).
Source: British Library, Wikimedia Commons.

The call for attention probably directed first audiences less to the content of the story, which they would most likely be familiar with, but to the way it was being told or sung, its artful composition. The poem's main interest is not the action as such but how characters respond to events and moral dilemmas. Its tone and mood are on the whole sombre and serious: there is little humour in *Beowulf*. Life is presented as harsh and difficult. The hero constantly has to face dangers that threaten not only his own life and that of his companions but the existence of the entire community. The poet is given to moralising, and he provides his audience with role models. Its ending with the death and burial of the hero is imbued with a sense of pessimism or fatalism. This highlights values of a tribal warrior society like honour, fame, physical courage (though understatement is the rule), and the relationship between chieftain and followers. The warriors were to avenge and defend the chief or king with their lives; the king in turn had to show generosity in dispensing the spoils of raids. Beowulf praises

Hrothgar's generosity (ll. 1473 et seq.). Although the poem is interested in the hero's inwardness, it is not concerned with individuality in any modern sense.

Yet there is a second layer to the poem in which these actions and values are observed and reflected from a Christian point of view. While its characters may be pagans, the poet is not. In what has been described as "double vision" (Osborn 2019, 146), the poem establishes a distinction between "two levels of knowledge", one that belongs to the pagan world of the poem and its "natural wisdom" and one that exists for a Christian audience who enjoy "revealed knowledge" through the Scriptures (150). In Marijane Osborn's interpretation, this is not a problem or a conflict but a crucial feature of the poem. For example, the construction of Heorot, Hrothgar's hall, alludes to the book of Genesis; fabulous monsters (*eotenas, ylfe, orcneas* – giants, elves, demons) are described as descendants of Cain. Also, the Christian God is sometimes presented in terms of Norse mythology, as when he is described as 'weaving' success in war (*wīgspēda ġewiofu*, l. 697a) like the Norns, who were thought to weave the thread of human fate. Finally, at Beowulf's funeral, the hero is praised not only as a courageous man, but also as the mildest of kings. Beowulf's death, which unites heroic struggle and submission to *wyrd* (fate) with self-sacrifice, is important in this respect since the notion of Christ's sacrificial death was incompatible with pagan ideas of heroism. But the design of the epic's conflicts is also significant. Conflicts arise between Beowulf (and his followers) and supernatural evil enemies. Consequently, the poem can heighten the contrast between good and evil, recommend solidarity among people, and channel violence towards a safe non-human dimension. Since killings were frequent in Germanic society and retaliation was a matter of honour, *Beowulf* works towards a compromise here as well (cf. ll. 1383–1398). Hrothgar, for example, does not take vengeance on Grendel himself after the ogre has killed thirty of his men but delegates this task to Beowulf, whose primary motivation is not revenge but to keep people safe from further harm.

Nothing is known about the author, or authors, of *Beowulf* and how the text came to be written down in the version that has survived. There is only one source that allows us to gauge the popularity of such poems with an eighth-century audience of monks – a harsh critique by Alcuin (c. 735–804), who complains in a letter of 797 about worldly entertainment in monasteries and refers to "Hinieldus" (Ingeld), a character who is mentioned in *Beowulf* (l. 1791) but who probably had similar songs sung about his own heroic deeds, asking the rhetorical question *quid Hinieldus cum Christo* – what did Ingeld have to do with Christ?

> Let God's words be read at the episcopal dinner-table. There it is fitting for a reader to be heard, not a harpist: sermons of the Fathers, not the songs of heathens. What has Ingeld to do with Christ? The house is narrow and has no room for both. The Heavenly King does

not wish to have communion with so-called kings who are pagan and damned: for the eternal King reigns in Heaven, while the other, a pagan, is damned and wails in hell.[18]

Alcuin's condemnation of blending Christian and pagan elements does not mean that nobody at the time could have appreciated the *Beowulf*-poet's typological approach to his material. The fact that the text was considered valuable enough to be copied and preserved by monks should be evidence enough that an Anglo-Christian audience thought of *Beowulf* not merely as a 'safe' but as a useful text.

Beowulf also shows clearly how early Scandinavian society dealt with outsiders. Grendel and the other demons in the poem are monstrous exiles. Grendel is a *mearcstapa* ('mark-stepper', l. 103, i.e., one who walks on the boundary of human society). Their plight is associated with the descendants of Cain, condemned by God after having slain his brother Abel (l. 107, 1261). They are called *wræcca* ('wretch', l. 2613). Grendel's exclusion from society is justified by the fact that he refuses to pay compensation and has thus offended against the fundamental law of the blood-feud. When Grendel and Beowulf fight, Beowulf tears off one of Grendel's arms and carries this back to the hall as a token (*tācen*, l. 833) of his victory to prove his valour. But the monsters in *Beowulf* are also depicted as strange, uncanny doppelgangers or doubles of the hero: the poem shows how closely the hero and the monster are connected. Thus, Grendel is called a 'hall-thane', while Beowulf is 'Hygelac's thane' (*þeġn* = fighter, loyal follower; l. 142, 194). Grendel's approach to Heorot parallels Beowulf's subsequent approach of the lair of Grendel's mother. Grendel's "sudden grip" (*fǣrgripe*, l. 738) during the combat is paralleled with Beowulf's "hand-grip" (*mund-gripe*, l. 753); Heorot's construction mirrors its destruction. "Given Grendel's central role as a man-eating monster", Andy Orchard notes, "it seems extraordinary that the *Beowulf*-poet should choose to depict him as a character with a point of view, one that is capable of evoking sympathy [. . .] when the predator becomes prey" (2003, 192).

There has been (and still is) much debate about *Beowulf*, not least about its many unanswered questions and indeterminacies. Recent critics have tried to find some answers by relating the poem to its original audiences (that is, listeners) or

---

18 In the Latin original: "Verba Dei legantur in sacerdotali convivio. Ibi decet lectorem audiri, non citharistam: sermones patrum, non carmina gentilium. Quid Hinieldus cum Christo? Angusta est domus: utrosque tenere non poterit. Non vult rex celestis cum paganis et perditis nominetenus regibus communionem habere; quia rex ille aeternus regnat in caelis, ille paganus perditus plangit in inferno." Latin text in Alcuin 1895, 183; trans. adapted from Bullough 1993, 124 and North 2006, 133.

its earliest readers (for an overview, see Niles 2016, 149–172). In the context of the early history of media in England, *Beowulf* and other surviving manuscripts attest perhaps above all to the power of the written word, the power of literacy (Lerer 1991) and the "self-reflexivity of writers" (Niles 2016, 81). Thus, in one riddle similar to the one about parchment discussed above (Exeter Book, number 60), the speaker has the magical ability to "speak without mouth" (*muðleas sprecan*, l. 9b) and "exchange words" (*wordum wrixlan*, l. 10a). The answer to this riddle is 'reed' or reed pen, with the effect that the poem's "shape-changing speaker turns out to be the very pen that has written the verse riddle that the reader is trying to solve" (Niles 2016, 81). But what is so intriguing about this riddle is that this pen addresses a *reader* but does so in the mode of (mouthless) speech: "*þæt ic wiþ þe sceolde / for unc anum twam ærendspræce / abeodan bealdlice*" (ll. 14b–16a) – "that I should boldly proclaim a message with you, for us two alone" (Klinck 1992, 99). The riddle that the pen silently proclaims "only for the two of us" establishes a social community – communication – between writer and writing tool, in silence and in private, or alternatively between the written word and the reader who voices the words of the poem, whether silently or aloud.[19] It shows a profound (and humorous) grasp of the intricacies of writing and reading as performative media practices.

---

[19] On the origins and functions of silent reading in the Middle Ages, see Saenger 1997.

3 The Medieval and Early Modern Book

The medieval book comes in many different forms and formats: from beautifully illuminated manuscripts, such as the *Book of Kells* (now in Trinity College Dublin), to the earliest printed books, which often still look to the naked eye as if they were handwritten – especially the so-called *incunabula* or 'cradle pieces' dating from before 1501. In the previous chapter, we have seen monks copying and translating religious texts as well as collecting and copying secular poetry, and we have seen monks and scholars writing legal and historical texts, often collected in the format of manuscript books written on membrane. Each copy of a manuscript is unique, and if several copies have survived, they usually include many substantial textual variants. After the scribes had finished writing and/or rubricating and illuminating, the individual sheets would be folded and collected into so-called gatherings or quires, which would then be stitched together to form a codex. Books were bound "with boards", as the Exeter Book riddle 26 explains (l. 12), usually wooden boards covered in leather. Perhaps in contrast to modern times, one can assume that every text preserved in this way was considered useful – space in a manuscript would have been too precious to waste.

Page numbers in medieval manuscripts and early printed books, if they exist at all, can come in two forms: pagination or foliation. In pagination, each side of each leaf gets its own number (as in modern books); in foliation, only one side is numbered, and the two sides of the leaf are then referred to as 'recto' (the right-hand side) and 'verso' (the left). The notation for this is 'f. 5r' or 'f. 5v' (folio 5 recto or verso). Early books usually consist of gatherings of three or more leaves; in early printed books, each gathering would normally be marked by a letter (A, B, C, etc.). The 'signature' consists of this letter and a number to identify the page: e.g., "sig. B6v" refers to the verso of leaf 6 in quire B. Very long books may have quires marked by several letters, e.g. "BB". In this chapter, we will have a look at the uses of handwritten and printed books in the later Middle Ages and the early modern period.

Middle English Literature

The end of the Old English period is conveniently marked by the Norman invasion of 1066. Norman influences on England were already present in the years leading up to this event. By 1100, Normans had occupied important positions of power, and "English ceased to be the language of the monarchy and its related administrative bodies" (Treharne 2010, xxiii), which now communicated in French until the fourteenth and early fifteenth centuries. English manuscripts were still copied, some were newly composed; but they were no longer copied as extensively as before. The English language at this time (known as Middle English) absorbed many loan words from French and from Scandinavian languages. Compared to Old English, Middle English was simplified: it lost most of its inflections; the old system of gender and cases disappeared, and adjectives no longer changed their form according to the case of a noun. There was much regional variation and, unlike Old English, no standard norm of any kind; a new standard only emerged in the fifteenth century.

Works of theology or history, such as Geoffrey of Monmouth's (c. 1100–1155) *Historia regum Britanniae,* which tells the 'history of the kings of Britain' until the arrival of the Angles and Saxons, were now yet again written in Latin rather than English. This was one of the most frequently copied books in the high Middle Ages, with more than 200 surviving manuscripts (Lesser 2019, 52). A favourite among fictional genres was the romance, including Anglo-Norman works on Tristan and Yseut (Thomas of Britain's *Tristan,* c. 1170) or other Arthurian material, but there were also some with an English setting: *Boeve de Haumtone* ('Bevis of Hampton'), set in Southampton, *Waldef* (East Anglia) and *Gui de Warewic* ('Guy of Warwick', c. 1210). These texts focus on local families and powerful barons; they tend to avoid Arthurian material, which is geared towards the idea of "centralised kingship" (Solopova and Lee 2007, 123). Much Anglo-Norman literature is associated with women as authors, readers, and patrons; an important example is Marie de France (fl. 1160–1215), who wrote *lais* (short verse romances) for the royal court.[20] Once Parisian French gained dominance at the French court early in the fourteenth century, and there was a growing political rivalry between England and France, English again became a preferred language for the élite. Anglo-French survived, however, in legal writings even in the sixteenth century. It is important to realise that the Middle English literary tradition was multilingual: "boundaries between languages and cultures were transparent and texts were written by multilingual authors for multilingual audiences" (Solopova and Lee 2007, 124).

Latin and French influences are obvious in *The Owl and the Nightingale,* a poem in octosyllabic couplets. French court poets had made this form popular. *The Owl and the Nightingale* is a debate between these two birds, overheard by a human speaker. Their argument, extending over 1,800 lines of verse and by

---

20 See Ashe 2015 for a selection of twelfth-century Anglo-Norman and English fiction in translation, including *Gui of Warwick,* Marie de France, and Thomas of Britain.

turns entertaining and learned, touches on many different topics of life from marriage to "toilet manners" (Treharne 2010, 468). The outcome remains open: we are not told who wins. Perhaps the point was to make readers think about the issues presented and judge for themselves (ibid.).

Shorter poems from this period include the Worcester Fragments (religious poems about the transience of earthly life), transcribed by the so-called "Tremulous Hand" of Worcester. These poems, which are generally in a poor condition of preservation, show the influence of French and Latin literature in the choice of subject matter and form; they also demonstrate some continuity with Old English poetic traditions. They often use Old English and continental metres, sometimes in combination, and they display a concern with English cultural legacy and poetic technique. The Tremulous Hand, for example, praises earlier monks and scholars like Ælfric and Alcuin, who are mentioned by name. "Through these were our people taught in English", he writes (l. 9), but complains that "now that teaching is neglected" (l. 16). He laments the loss of the binding force of education in English (Treharne 2010, 363–365).

Another remarkable Middle English lyric is "Sumer is icumen in" ('summer has arrived'), a song that appears in a thirteenth-century manuscript (BL Harley 978, f. 11v) in a multilingual and multimedia environment. In contrast to the Tremulous Hand, it is very joyful. The text is set to music, and its English words appear right underneath the musical setting (which is a canon), above a religious lyric in Latin (*Perspice Christicola*) that can be sung to the same melody. The text and its setting thus invite at least two musical performances, one in Latin and one in English, one religious and the other secular.

Sumer is icumen in,	Summer has come in,
Lhude sing cuccu,	Sing loudly, cuckoo,
Groweþ sed, and bloweþ med,	Seed grows and meadow blooms
and springþ þe wde nu.	and the wood springs now.
Sing cuccu!	Sing cuckoo!
[. . .]	[. . .]
	(Treharne 2010, 410)[21]

At this time, lyric poems and music were closely connected. Manuscript poems in the medieval and early modern period were not primarily intended for silent reading but for oral performance and sometimes for musical accompaniment. One of the most important collections of Middle English lyric poems is BL

---

[21] See also Treharne 2010, 409 for speculation about the manuscript's provenance and purpose; also note Ezra Pound's 1915 parody, "Ancient Music", which begins "Winter is icummen in, / Lhude sing Goddamm" (Pound 2010, 50).

Harley 2253, a manuscript from the mid-fourteenth century that contains poems in French, English, and Latin, covering a wide range of religious and secular topics (see Treharne 2010, 567–614).

Longer narrative poems from this period include Laȝamon's *Brut* (BL Cotton Caligula A.ix), a 16,000-line alliterative verse chronicle on Arthurian material that combines French and (Old) English traditions. Dating from c. 1200, the *Brut* uses some archaic expressions to make the story appear more 'literary', dignified, or heroic. In some ways, it harks back to *Beowulf*, especially in its presentation of a heroic ideal of glory or posthumous fame. "Never [. . .] before" had there been "such a king", the speaker asserts, "so courageous in all things" (l. 11467), and we know this because his story has been preserved in writing: "For þat soðe stod a þan writen hu hit is iwurðen" (l. 11468) – "for that truth has remained in writing always, about how it happened" (Treharne 2010, 465). In his prologue, Laȝamon introduces himself as a priest and a careful chronicler, beginning his tale as a writer facing the empty page, with a pious prayer:

> Laȝamon opened this book and turned the leaves:
> He looked at them joyfully: God be merciful to him!
> He took feathers with his fingers and wrote on book-skins,
> And the true words put together,
> And the three books were joined into one.
> (ll. 24–28, Treharne 2010, 459)

He presents himself not as an author in the modern sense but a recorder and an arranger of "true words" – 'truth' understood not necessarily in a modern sense of factual accuracy but in a moral sense of rightness. The purpose of this text was to teach other knights about the values of chivalry. No knight would be "respected", he writes (*wel itald*, l. 11477) "unless he knew of Arthur and of his noble court"; but if he did possess this knowledge, he would be "welcome" wherever he went, "even if he were in Rome" (ll. 11487–11488).

Sir Gawain and the Green Knight

Another story associated with the Arthurian chivalric 'matter of Britain' is *Sir Gawain and the Green Knight*. All we know about its author is that he came from the Northwest, perhaps from Cheshire or Shropshire (because that is where his dialect can be placed), and that the poems were copied into the manuscript (Cotton Nero A.x) around 1400. *Sir Gawain and the Green Knight* is "undoubtedly the most skilful of the many English medieval Romance texts concerned with the deeds of King Arthur and the Knights of the Round Table" (Treharne 2010, 776).

It may have been written for "a provincial aristocratic audience, who were themselves concerned with chivalry and aspects of the knightly code" (ibid.), or a group of Cheshire courtiers at the court of Richard II. Since its rediscovery in the nineteenth century, it has been translated into modern English several times, for instance by Tolkien (1975) and more recently (2007) by the poet Simon Armitage (1963–). It has also been adapted for several films, most recently *The Green Knight* (2021). The story of Sir Gawain follows the basic paradigm of the medieval romance: "The knight rides out alone to seek adventure" (Finlayson 1980/81, 55). He finds himself in an unknown landscape, where he encounters dangerous and often supernatural events. In most romances, the hero solves the problem with his skill in arms and then rides on to yet another adventure; usually there is very little connection with social, political, or religious contexts of actual life.

Sir Gawain and the Green Knight is in alliterative verse, structured into four 'fitts' or sections. The stanzas are of varying length, ranging from twelve to thirty-seven lines, but they all end in a 'bob and wheel': a monometer line (the bob) followed by four trimeter lines (the wheel), rhyming *ababa*. There is a high degree of formal awareness: the last line, for example, is the same as the first, creating an effect of circularity and closure. The main symbol in the text is one of infinity: the "endeles knot" (l. 630) of the image on Gawain's shield, the pentangle or five-pointed star, stands for limitless perfection. Like the poem *Pearl* (by the same poet), *Gawain* has exactly 101 stanzas, "a number symbolizing completeness" (Solopova and Lee 2007, 187), and its additional number symbolism is based on the number five: five principal virtues make up Gawain's pentangle, and the total number of lines in the poem amounts to 2525, a multiple of five plus a final bob and wheel of five lines. This would not have been evident for medieval readers, unless they counted the line numbers in the manuscript, but it can hardly be accidental.

Remarkably, this is not the story of a knight's martial prowess but the story of a knight who embarrasses himself by getting involved with the wrong woman and losing the central single combat with the Green Knight; from then on, he will wear the girdle the woman has given him as a mark of his weakness and shame: "þe token of vntrawþe" (l. 2509, 'untruth' = infidelity) (Treharne 2010, 800). Interpretations of the poem have focused on its being centrally about the virtue of *trouthe* (comprising loyalty, integrity, honour, and consistency). Gawain's plight indicates the fragility of the chivalric code of honour. Derek Pearsall identified this theme as "the invention of embarrassment" (1997, 351). Even though the other knights praise him for having succeeded, Gawain knows only too well about his having failed – he has let himself down. The story sets up a contrast between public honour and private shame. Unlike other heroes of medieval romance, like Yvain or Lancelot, Gawain does not go mad over this or retreat to the wilderness, but he learns to live with his embarrassment. In this theme of what it means to not quite succeed despite the outward appearance of success, *Sir Gawain* is a strikingly modern poem.

The two contracts in the story (the beheading game and the exchange of winnings) are linked in that they serve to test Gawain's *trouthe*; in hindsight, they turn out to have been connected. But the outcome of the story does not result in a clear moral message but leaves Gawain (and the reader) with a conundrum that depends not only on the elements of the plot but also on genre and narration. Any moral message of a 'realistic' heroic story is undercut by the comic elements and exaggerations of romance, which disrupt its moral seriousness, especially in the bedroom scenes. Gawain, an imported character from French chivalric romance, had a reputation for being a ladies' man and a tendency to risk comic humiliation while being tested; the English author of this poem, even though he probably lived far from London, must have been familiar with the French romances about Gawain. But he was not exactly "borrowing" but "drawing on a wider knowledge of his stock character, and he alludes to his audience's memory of that character's literary life" (Butterfield 2009, 207). The story of *Sir Gawain and the Green Knight*, in other words, depended on a subtle and sophisticated knowledge of its source material and literary tradition (cf. Butterfield 2009).

It is remarkable also for its technique of depicting characters and landscapes. To give only one example: the castle of Sir Bertilak is described in an elaborate technique derived from French romance writing, from the changing perspective of Gawain as he approaches it. First it appears when Gawain prays to the Virgin as he is riding alone through the wilderness of the Wirral on Christmas Eve, hoping to find some place to attend Mass. It appears as if "pared out of papure" (l. 802, 'like a paper cut-out'), in sharp contrast to the threatening wilderness that surrounds the young knight.[22] The castle is demarcated from the tangled forest by an encircling palisade that surrounds the park; its name, as Gawain learns later, is "Hautdesert" ('high lonely place'): a courtly French name that is an expression of cultural hegemony, not built for military purpose but for display and to keep out the forces of wild nature. (As we have seen with *Gilgamesh*, the contrast between city and wilderness is one of the oldest topics in storytelling.)

The approach to such a castle is a staple of romance involving a knight errant, and one expects adventure and risk. The safety promised by such a glorious

---

22 The reference to paper – still a very rare and precious material in fourteenth-century England – is most likely to a table ornament or food decoration; see Ackerman 1957, who notes that the phrase "pared out of paper" also occurs in *Cleanness* (attributed to the same poet) l. 1408; he also refers to a paper castle mentioned as a table ornament in Chaucer's *The Parson's Tale*.

castle is deceptive, and danger within may be more difficult to detect than the dangers of nature without. It is important that we get this from Gawain's perspective. This is yet another strikingly modern feature: for the protagonist, the view of the scene changes as he moves through it. There is no overall vision, but the scene is seen bit by bit as each new aspect appears to the hero, in fragments. Gawain cannot anticipate what will await him inside the castle, as he is later unable to foresee the consequences of accepting the Lady's girdle.

Truth Seekers: Kempe, Langland, and Gower

While Gawain's emotional turmoil is contained in an elaborate fictional setting, other writers discovered autobiography as a more direct form of expressing inner experiences. Among these, Margery Kempe (c. 1373–1439) was perhaps the most remarkable. Possibly illiterate but obviously familiar with saints' legends and the Bible, she dictated the text that became known as *The Book of Margery Kempe* to two scribes, recording her spiritual journey and mystical experiences alongside her real-world travels and travails in a form that combined the genre of the saints' lives with a new form of personal life-writing. The text tells its readers that some "worthy and worshepful clerkys" encouraged her to "makyn a booke of hyr felynges and hir revelacyons" (Treharne 2010, 811–812) and to get them in writing ("þat sche schuld don hem wryten", 811). Next to Julian of Norwich (c. 1342–1416), Kempe is one of the earliest women writers in the history of English literature.

The search for religious truth is also a driving force in the work of the Ricardian poet William Langland (c. 1325–1388), the author of *Piers Plowman*, a long poem that is associated with radical reform movements in the Church (Wycliffites and Lollards) and a strong concern for social justice and poor relief. The poem is shaped as a series of dreams in which the dreamer, Will, first sees the rottenness of a society ruled by money and then witnesses the attempt to reform it through the work of Piers, the good honest Christian ploughman. When this attempt fails, Will returns to a more personal search for spiritual truth. "Treuþe is þe beste" of all treasures, as Holy Church has taught him (passus I, l. 210) – but the Church's teachings, even though absolutely true, may be too remote from everyday life; redemption can only come from God according to the believer's conduct in life. The spiritual restlessness that we see in Margery Kempe also haunts Langland, who "refuses to approach a problem from one point of view without putting that perspective to the test against the most cogent alternatives known to him" (Kirk and Anderson 1990, xii, qtd. in Langland 2006, xiv).

Another common form of medieval storytelling was the narrative poem that offered an entire collection of stories. John Gower's (c. 1330–1408) *Confessio Amantis* is one such (written in English, despite the Latin title), first completed in 1390 and revised two years later. Much of the *Confessio Amantis* is in the form of a 'mirror for princes', a popular medieval genre of political instruction. Here, King Richard II is mirrored in the historical figure of Alexander the Great, an ambiguous figure who is a mighty conqueror and an honest ruler but at the same time a rash tyrant. The storytelling voice of Genius often slides into that of the poet-narrator, Gower himself. The *Confessio* was popular in its time; it survives in 49 manuscripts, which show considerable revision perhaps to adapt the poem "to changes in the political situation" (Solopova and Lee 2007, 189). Gower understood the role of the poet to be that of a political advisor and learned moralist, giving advice to members of the ruling élite. The learned character of his work is also attested by the fact that he added "summaries, glosses, and notes in Latin" to the English text of the *Confessio Amantis,* which "were set in the margins of the manuscripts" (190). Presentation copies were made for Henry IV and for Thomas Arundel, the bishop of Canterbury. The genre of the 'mirror for princes' or 'mirror for magistrates' remained popular until the sixteenth century (Hoccleve, *The Regiment of Princes*, 1410–1412; Lydgate, *The Fall of Princes,* 1431–1439; Baldwin, *The Mirror for Magistrates*, 1555), but later writers did not openly acknowledge Gower's influence (Watt 2009). The *Confessio* was printed by William Caxton (c. 1415/20–1491) in the fifteenth century and still read in Shakespeare's time (1564–1616); one of its stories became the source for Shakespeare's and George Wilkins's (d. 1618) play *Pericles* (1607?), which also features Gower as a narrator figure.

Chaucer

Gower probably knew his fellow poet Geoffrey Chaucer (1340s–1400), as he was one of the dedicatees of Chaucer's poem *Troilus and Criseyde* (1382–1386). Chaucer is by far the best-known and still most widely read Middle English author. He is also the one whose life is most amply documented (Turner 2019). He came from a family of wine merchants in Ipswich, and he held many different official positions: among other things, he was a soldier, a diplomat, a customs officer, and a member of Parliament. He also travelled widely on official business to France, Spain, and Italy. The circumstances of his death following the overthrow of Richard II and the accession of Henry IV in 1399 are less clear. Chaucer's death date is given as 25 October 1400 (on a tomb erected some 150 years later), and he was buried in Westminster Abbey; he had a house nearby and was a member of that parish – his burial there had nothing to do with his being a poet, yet his tomb was to be the beginning of what is now Poets' Corner.

The frontispiece of an early fifteenth-century manuscript of *Troilus and Criseyde* depicts Chaucer reciting his work from a pulpit to a courtly audience (Coleman 2010). If Chaucer had not written *The Canterbury Tales*, he would now be famous for this courtly romance in five books, based on an episode from the stories about the Trojan War that focuses largely on earthly and spiritual love, inspired by Boccaccio's *Il Filostrato*. It follows Troilus's change from someone who arrogantly looks down upon love to someone who turns into a devoted lover and is then cast into utter despair. Chaucer's handling of characters is psychologically complex: Criseyde is both calculating and generous, pragmatic in her infidelity but also driven by fear. The figure of Pandarus, who acts as a go-between, is a manipulator but also a kind of spiritual advisor to Troilus. The narrator keeps his own counsel and hides behind a (probably fictional) authority figure called Lollius ('the stutterer'). The activity of storytelling is frequently reflected in the poem itself, which abounds in scenes of reading and listening.

Chaucer throughout his work cultivates an ironic persona, presenting himself as an inept poet and hiding his skills behind a façade of self-deprecation. He usually presents a variety of perspectives on human life without pronouncing a final judgement upon them. Multiple views on life are contained in *The Canterbury Tales*, an unfinished collection of twenty-four tales, presented as a storytelling contest among pilgrims on their way from London to Canterbury (inspired by Boccaccio's story collection *Il Decamerone*, 1353). The first lines of the general prologue are still very well known and have frequently been parodied, for example in T. S. Eliot's (1888–1965) *The Waste Land* (1922) or Patience Agbabi's (1965–) *Telling Tales* (2014) (more on this below):

> Whan that Aprill with his shoures soote
> The droghte of March hath perced to the roote,
> And bathed every veyne in swich licour
> Of which vertu engendred is the flour;
> Whan Zephirus eek with his sweete breeth
> Inspired hath in every holt and heeth
> The tendre croppes, and the yonge sonne
> Hath in the Ram his half cours yronne,
> And smale foweles maken melodye,
> That slepen al the nyght with open ye
> (So priketh hem nature in hir corages),
> Thanne longen folk to goon on pilgrimages,
> ....
> (Chaucer 1987, 23, ll. 1–12)

As in *Troilus and Criseyde*, the narrator of the *Canterbury Tales* suspends judgement on the narrated events instead of providing, like Gower, a moral of the story. The pilgrims are most of them strangers to one another before they embark on their journey. They stop at the Tabard Inn in Southwark, where the host proposes a contest: he will ride to Canterbury with them, and they will take turns telling stories. The pilgrim who comes up with the best story will be rewarded with a free dinner at the Tabard at the end of the trip. The pilgrims are a representative mix of medieval English men and women from all social spheres: each of them is vividly individualised, and they all get to tell a story: the Knight, the Miller, the Reeve, the Cook, the Man of Law, the Wife of Bath, the Friar, the Summoner, the Clerk, the Merchant, the Squire, the Franklin, the Physician, the Pardoner, the Shipman, the Prioress, the Monk, the Nun's Priest, the Yeoman, the Parson, etc. In a moment of self-parody, Chaucer himself makes an appearance and tells the tale of Sir Thopas, an old-fashioned verse romance; the tale is quickly interrupted by the host, who tells him how inept he is as a poet, so that Chaucer has to go on with another story, this time in prose. All the tales are bursting with life; they belong to different genres (the romance, the sermon, the saint's life, the fabliau or bawdy tale, the beast fable, etc.), and they rely on vivid contrasts between different social strata and between contrasting models and attitudes about how to live. The characters present a range of vices and virtues, but we get a sense of them not only as emblematic representations but also as individuals.

Since the fictional pilgrims are responsible for their own stories, Chaucer's narrator can use this as an excuse for telling morally dubious or downright obscene tales. For example, after the Knight has told a highly stylised tale of two friends, Palamon and Arcite, who fall in love with the same woman and have to fight it out in a tournament (a "noble storie" [l. 3111] based on the conventions of courtly romance which pleases "the gentils everichon" [l. 3113]), it is the Miller's turn to tell a story replete with dirty practical jokes. Chaucer (or the narrator) comments:

> For Goddes love, demeth nat that I seye
> Of yvel entente, but for I moot rehurce
> Hir tales alle, be they bettre or werse,
> Or elles falsen som of my mateere.
> And therfore, whoso list it nat yheere,
> Turne over the leef and chese another tale;
> ....
> Blameth nat me if that ye chese amys.
> ....

Avyseth yow, and put me out of blame;
And eek men shal nat maken ernest of game.
(ll. 3172–3186)

This passage is interesting in several ways: as an excuse for fiction and for low comedy in fiction (a "game" that should not be taken seriously), but also as a direct address to a community of readers, even an individual reader, who is imagined no longer as a listener but as a reader of texts who is turning the pages: "whoso list it nat yheere, / Turne over the leef". If the reader has a choice over what to read, the author cannot be blamed for that choice. Notably, the distinction between author and narrator – a staple of modern criticism – is "neither here nor there" in Chaucer and other examples of medieval literature (von Contzen 2018, 64, see also Spearing 2015).

"The Miller's Tale" is a good example of the complexity and humour in medieval fiction. It is the story of a carpenter who is married to, and very jealous of, a beautiful young woman named Alison. Alison, however, is tempted by the overtures of a young clerk named Nicholas. Nicholas cooks up a plot to trick the carpenter, persuading him that the end of the world is near and that a flood is coming, so that like Noah the carpenter should build himself an ark. Believing this, the carpenter hangs three large troughs underneath the roof of his house; while he sleeps in one of them, waiting for the flood, Nicholas and Alison make their escape. But there is a third man in love with Alison, a parish clerk named Absolon, who in the darkness of night is cruelly punished for his desire. The noise wakes up the carpenter; thinking that the flood has come, he cuts the cords and breaks an arm in his fall. The whole town thinks he has gone mad, and no one believes his reasoning. The tale resonates with medieval theatricality; there is a great 'staginess' about the window scenes, and Noah's Flood was a staple of medieval drama, usually a scene staged by the carpenters' guild (see ch. 4 below). Furthermore, it resonates with thematic and verbal echoes of the Knight's Tale, so it can be read as a low parody of romance conventions: in the Knight's Tale, also, two men compete for the same woman.

The contrast between the Miller's and the Knight's Tale illustrates the different levels of 'high' and 'low' style that Chaucer combines in *The Canterbury Tales* and that expresses a range of possible experiences of the world, within an overarching Christian worldview. He invents a variety of 'realistic' characters who tell different types of stories in different ways, thus showing different kinds of subject position in relation to medieval beliefs and ideologies (M. Miller 2009): the Knight's Tale appeals to the chivalric ethos of 'aristocratic formalism', a strong belief in cosmic order and socially encoded forms of stylised or ritualised behaviour; the Miller's Tale invites its readers or listeners to laugh at bawdy humour and physical comedy in a fallen world. The Wife of Bath, whose name – like the woman's in the Miller's Tale – is Alison, is the only secular female pilgrim and one of Chaucer's liveliest and most memorable creations. In the prologue to her tale, she presents the tensions between systems of order and common ways of living as a conflict between "auctoritee" and "experience" ("The Wife of Bath's Prologue", l. 1). Alison's reasoning is based on life as it is lived, not on learned authorities or written texts. Authorities may teach, she says, that the genitals ("membres [. . .] of generacioun", l. 116) were only made for excretion and in order to distinguish males from females: "The experience woot wel it is noght so", she argues (l. 124), insisting that they were also made for pleasure. But her outlook on life is also an expression of a modern commercialism in which everything is for sale ("al is for to selle", l. 414), including the body, and in which sexual relationships are expressed in terms of debts and payments. "Different views of reality" are thus "brought into contact" (Solopova and Lee 2007, 201), especially through the use of different genres.

Some of the tales open up a world that is invested in ideals of ethical perfection and moral purity, with concomitant anxieties about moral failure and moral pollution. In the figure of the pardoner, a self-described conman who sells bogus relics and indulgences, *The Canterbury Tales* criticise corruption within the Church while at the same time emphasising the concern with sin and genuine repentance, which becomes visible despite the obvious inauthenticity of the pardoner's theatrical self-presentation. For modern readers, it is easy to forget that the *Tales* end with a lengthy sermon by the parson, in a move away from fictional storytelling to a didactic manual for confession and penance. In the contrast between the pardoner and the parson, Chaucer compares false religious sentiments with genuine beliefs, criticism of institutional corruption with religious devotion. The setting of the stories is, after all, a pilgrimage, which has a religious purpose. In the "Retraction", a final authorial comment, Chaucer as "the makere of this book" takes "his leve" and revokes all his "translacions and enditynges of worldly vanitees", supplying us with a catalogue of his works and asking Christ for forgiveness for sinful texts (Chaucer 1987, 328).

Chaucer left the *Canterbury Tales* incomplete; according to the general prologue, every pilgrim was supposed to tell two stories on the way to Canterbury and two on the way back, but this plan was probably aborted. In the surviving manuscripts, there are only twenty-four tales, and their order varies. The stories were transmitted as part of ten longer fragments, many of which contain groups of tales linked by dialogue and interaction between the pilgrims. We can only speculate why Chaucer did not produce a final version, whether he gave it up or even intended the text to be complete in its fragmentary form. No manuscripts have survived from Chaucer's own lifetime; even the earliest copies of his works vary in textual detail and contain evidence of scribal errors – perhaps some from the pen of Adam, berated by Chaucer in his poem "Adam scriveyn" (see ch. 2) – and editing.

There are many reasons why Chaucer has remained attractive to later generations of poets. For writers of today, what may be most appealing about the *Canterbury Tales* is the energy and diversity of its cast of characters. One proof of their longevity are the many retellings, plays, and poetic remixes of this text. The most complete new version is Patience Agbabi's *Telling Tales* (2014). In this sequence of poems, Agbabi captures the orality of Chaucer's narrators, who now travel on a Routemaster bus, giving them distinctly modern identities, such as the Nigerian-born 'Mrs Alice Ebi Bafa' as the Wife of Bath, and including new linguistic and media phenomena such as texting language (e.g., Agbabi 2014, 81, 88–90). Agbabi grafts the urban and culturally diverse inflections of today's English onto the structure of Chaucer's *Tales* and thereby injects them with a renewed authenticity: "Chaucer Tales, track by track, here's the remix / [. . .] / [. . .] they're authentic / cos we're keeping it real [. . .]" ("Prologue (Grime Mix)", ll. 32–37; Agbabi 2014, 1–2). The rhythms of Chaucer's already multilingual Middle English are reworked and translated into a modern "cosmopolitan vernacular" (Coppola 2016, 310). This is just one of several recent adaptations of *The Canterbury Tales* and the Wife of Bath character; others include Jean 'Binta' Breeze's (1956–2021) poem "The Wife of Bath in Brixton Market" (2000), the monologue *Alisoun Sings* (2019) by Caroline Bergvall (1962–), and Zadie Smith's (1975–) play *The Wife of Willesden* (2021), which places the Wife's prologue and tale in a pub in North West London, reinvesting it with very contemporary cultural and social energy.

Chaucer's lasting fame was made in print. One of the first books printed by Caxton in his Westminster shop was an edition of Chaucer (fig. 3). Caxton's activity as a printer-publisher was vital in securing a canon of Middle English poetry by making the works of earlier authors more widely available (Gillespie 2006). Next to religious and didactic books, he also printed some entertaining prose works such as Thomas Malory's (d. 1471) Arthurian narrative *Le Morte Darthur* in 1485, which would have appealed to a wider audience beyond the gentry. Many medieval texts that were only available in a few manuscript copies could now be read for the first time in print by a wider readership. Chaucer in particular was hailed by sixteenth-century writers as the "English Homer" (Gillespie 2006, 70). Without printing, this renaissance of Middle English poetry would probably not have happened, and their influence on Edmund Spenser (1552–1599), Shakespeare, and others would be much less considerable (Cooper 2014, Coldiron 2015). The impact of Caxton's printing of Chaucer is also attested, for example, in William Morris's

(1834–1896) endeavour of painstakingly recreating early printing techniques in his Kelmscott Press edition of *The Works of Geoffrey Chaucer* at the end of the nineteenth century (1896). With this book, "Morris reverse-engineered an incunabulum" (Treharne and Willan 2020, 157) in a beautiful – if utterly nostalgic – protest against the mechanisation and industrial production of cheap books in modernity (fig. 4). Following in Caxton's footsteps, Morris's choice of Chaucer is also highly eloquent of Chaucer's Victorian status as an English national poet.

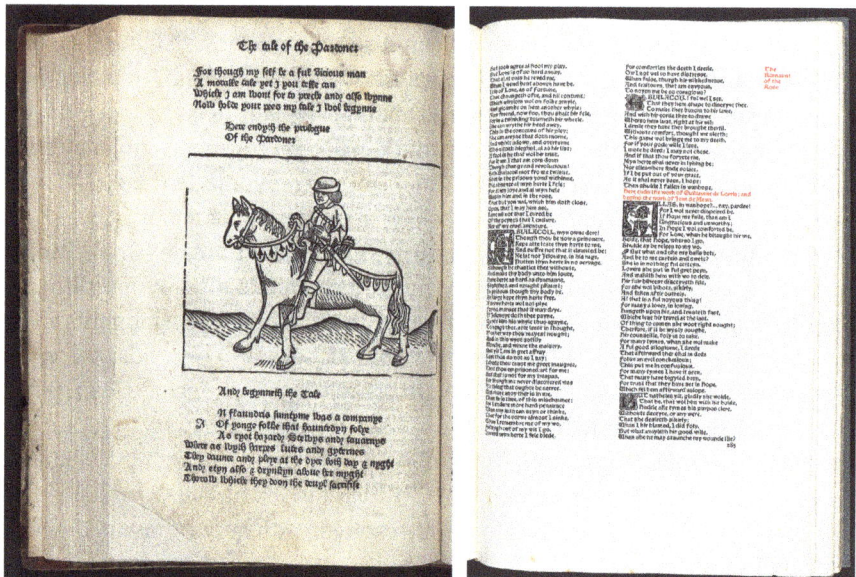

Figs. 3 and 4: A page from Caxton's edition of *The Canterbury Tales* (1483), woodcut and letterpress, and a page from the Kelmscott Chaucer (1896), letterpress.
Source: Paul Mellon Collection, Yale Center for British Art.

Manuscript and Print

William Caxton started out as a mercer (a textile merchant), moving between England and Flanders in the 1460s and becoming governor of the English merchants in Bruges in 1463. In the early 1470s he travelled to Cologne, apparently to learn the art of printing and to acquire a printing press. Having recognised the economic possibilities, his idea was to establish a monopoly on printing texts in English. He became Britain's first printer, publisher, and bookseller. He set up his own press in Bruges in 1473 and three years later at Westminster. Caxton published some hundred titles, and the work was continued by his successor, the aptly named Wynkyn de Worde (d. 1534/5). Though the transition from manuscript to print was gradual rather than revolutionary, print had a major impact on various aspects of literary culture, including the standardisation of English, the dissemination of national norms, transmission and availability of texts, and ideas of literary ownership and copyright.

Writers at this time may have had a sense of authorship, in the sense of a feeling of responsibility for their work, which might involve showing remorse (as shown by Chaucer) or the desire to be remembered (as shown by Malory, for example), but they did not own their work and could not hope to profit from selling copies of it. The notion of copyright was introduced in the early modern period in order to secure the rights of printers, not writers. In England, these rights were administered by the Worshipful Company of Stationers (founded in 1403, incorporated in 1557). No book could be officially printed without the permission of this guild, although in practice offenses against this rule were rarely sanctioned. The cost of a license was standardised at sixpence in the 1580s, and it was optional at first for publishers to enter their right in the Stationers' Register for an additional fee of four pence as a kind of "insurance policy" against piracy (Blayney 1997, 404); this became mandatory in 1637.

The idea that such 'copy' could be valuable property emerged only gradually from the sixteenth to the eighteenth century, until 'literary property' (ownership of an immaterial text as opposed to ownership of printed books) came to be protected by English law (Feather 2006, 55–56, 64–68). The requirement to register copyright with the Stationers was only abolished in 1911. Stationer's Hall, the centre of London's book trade for centuries, was hit by an incendiary bomb during the Blitz in 1940 but the Company records were saved.[23]

For a long time, there was continuity between print and manuscript, with "considerable movement across [this] divide" in both directions (Lesser 2019, 77). Copies made by professional scribes remained an alternative mode of publication into the seventeenth and even the eighteenth century. Sometimes, especially with printed books that were suppressed, but also other forms such as letters or speeches, the direction was from print back into manuscript, allowing individual readers to preserve their own copies of texts (Woudhuysen 1996, 25). Readers frequently wrote in their books. Some printed books even had blank pages, to be filled by their users with notes, aphorisms, and commonplaces under printed

---

[23] On the history of the Stationers' Company, see Blagden 1960; Blayney 2013; Myers 2001. It is now "The City of London Livery Company for the Communications and Content Industries".

headwords. In some instances, reading communities like the extended family of Nicholas Ferrar at Little Gidding cut and pasted printed materials into new combinations (Lesser 2019, 100–101).

Writers often shared their texts with others in social networks, which later scholars called 'coteries' (circles of friends); frequently, but not always, poems circulated in such coteries were written for specific occasions or for specific people; they could have special meanings and distinct social functions (Marotti 1995). Some poetry collections were written in collaboration by many hands, for example the Findern Manuscript (CUL MS Ff. 1.6) dating from the fifteenth century, compiled by "as many as 30 or 40 scribes" (Lesser 2019, 65), and the Devonshire Manuscript (BL MS Add. 17492) dating from the 1530s and early 1540s. For this anthology, a group of men and women at the Tudor court contributed almost two hundred items, most of them love lyrics attributed to Thomas Wyatt (c. 1503–1542). The Devonshire Manuscript offers a glimpse of early modern literature as a form of social interaction and a complex negotiation of public and private interests, since the persons who contributed to this miscellany were male and female members of the early modern aristocracy who communicated about their amorous relationships by the indirect means of transcribing lyric poems (Siemens et al. 2014).

When the printer Richard Tottel imitated the form of the verse miscellany in print in 1557, in a book titled *Songes and Sonettes*, he opened this courtly pursuit for a wider readership, probably sensing the commercial possibilities of publishing poetry in English. This paved the way for an increasing popularity of poetry on the print market, including work by women poets such as Isabella Whitney (fl. 1566–1573) and Aemilia Lanyer (1569–1645) (Clarke 2000), and early bestsellers such as Shakespeare's *Venus and Adonis* (1593). At the same time, already in the Elizabethan era, popular prose fiction like George Gascoigne's *The Adventures of Master F. J.* (1573), Robert Greene's *Pandosto* (1588), Thomas Deloney's *Jack of Newbury* (1597), and Thomas Nashe's *The Unfortunate Traveller* (1594) was being created for a large and diverse audience, best targeted and reached through the medium of print.[24] This audience included women, who were also active as writers, literary patrons (Ezell 2019) and, occasionally, publishers like Joan Broome and Margaret and Elizabeth Allde. Women readers were increasingly addressed as potential customers in the book trade, and the reading habits of some of these women can be reconstructed from inscriptions in books they owned and other documents (Lesser 2019, 92–93).

---

24 See Salzman 1998. For a more extensive survey of English Renaissance literature, including its media contexts, see Berensmeyer 2019. For a history of a single Renaissance lyric traversing the worlds of manuscript and print, see Murphy 2019.

If money was no incentive for having one's works printed, why did writers choose to appear in print at all? Compared to manuscript publication, print certainly offered a much wider potential audience and could make a writer famous. Shakespeare, for example, while he was still an emerging playwright in the early 1590s, wrote two narrative poems on classical topics, adding a bit of spice by focusing on fashionable erotic topics. He dedicated these to the young earl of Southampton – hoping, one can safely assume, to win the earl's patronage and thus gain not only a financial reward but also the more lasting and more valuable currency of prestige by being acknowledged as one of the earl's servants. One of these poems, *Venus and Adonis,* turned out to be a bestseller in the book market (Kesson and Smith 2013) – but here, as usual, the only ones to make money were printers and booksellers (the word was still largely synonymous with 'publisher' in the seventeenth and eighteenth century). Other early modern poets equally discovered the possibilities of gaining more widespread public attention through print – most notably Edmund Spenser, who has been described as a "print-fixated poet" (Love 1993, 145).

The increasing attractiveness of print could also consist in "the thrill of disclosing to a wider public materials formerly confined to a privileged readership" (McCabe 2010, 467), moving poems out of the closed circles of a coterie into the wider world of curious readers, as Richard Tottel did with his printed miscellany of *Songes and Sonettes* in 1557. While the "stigma of print" (the claim that having one's work printed was generally frowned upon in the early modern period) has been debunked as a scholarly myth (Saunders 1951, May 1980), there was a wide range of contemporaneous opinions about the value of print and its affordances of publicity as opposed to the more traditional and exclusive system of manuscript circulation (Love 1993). The lasting esteem of manuscripts as opposed to print can be seen, for example, in these lines by John Donne (1572–1631): "What presses give birth to with sodden pangs is acceptable, but manuscripts are more venerated. A book dyed with the blood of the press departs to an open shelf where it is exposed to moths and ashes; but one written by the pen is held in reverence, and flies to the privileged shelf reserved for the ancient fathers" (orig. in Latin, qtd. in van der Weel 326).[25]

The boom in English-language publications in the early modern period cannot be explained by the advent of print or by commercial interests alone. Another

---

[25] From a Latin manuscript poem by Donne, "De libro cum mutuaretur", first printed in 1635. See *Digital Donne: The Online Variorum,* F14400B, http://donnevariorum.dh.tamu.edu/volume-5-de-libro-cum-mutuaretur-parturiunt-madido-quae-nixu-praela-recepta/. Date of access: 18 Aug. 2021.

(indirect) cause was the Reformation. Isolated from other European countries through its break with Rome in 1532–1534, England had to prove that it was also a culturally independent country, a worthy successor to the ancient civilisations of Greece and Rome. "Literary and political nationalism worked hand in hand" (Alexander 2004, xxii). For example, in translating French and Italian sonnets and then writing their own, Tudor poets engaged in a project of cultural as well as literary translation. The sonnet had first been adapted by Chaucer (though not in the fourteen-line form) in *Troilus and Criseyde,* where an embedded poem was introduced as *Canticus Troili* (the song of Troilus) (book 1, before l. 400; Chaucer 1987, 478). This was based on one of the Italian poet Petrarch's (1304–1374) sonnets (no. 132), *S'amor non è.* In the sixteenth century, the sonnet became the privileged medium for expressing tensions within and around the self – not (yet) primarily as the self-expression of the poet but as a rhetorical way of communicating common ideas and feelings. The affective economy of the early modern sonnet has recently been likened to the economic form of double-entry bookkeeping, another early modern invention, which provides a balance sheet of its subject's inventory, debit, and credit (Bethke 2021). After the early experiments of Thomas Wyatt and Henry Howard, earl of Surrey (1517–1547), later poets like Philip Sidney (1554–1586) wrote sonnet sequences (*Astrophil and Stella,* 1591). In the 1580s and 1590s, a 'sonnet craze' developed – even playwrights like Shakespeare started writing and circulating sonnets, which often ended up in print with or without their approval.

In early modernity, the book became a commodity. A large-format folio book would still have been a luxury item, but the smaller quartos attracted buyers of the 'middling sort' (what would today be called the middle class). Even smaller, inexpensive chapbooks were affordable to many who could read; though literacy was still not very widespread, and many people would still have had no difficulties getting on with their daily lives without knowing how to read and write. Printing and binding books were still often separate activities; one could buy the unbound sheets of a book from a bookseller (usually identical with the publisher and sometimes the printer) at his – and very occasionally her – shop, and then choose from a range of bindings, which could add considerable cost to the purchase. Most books, however, would be sold bound (Lesser 2019, 210). There was as yet no centrally organised book trade; one would need to know which shop to go to for a particular book. Title pages of early printed books usually contained information on who the printer was and where they were being sold. These title pages could be displayed away from the shop as advertisements.

Printers, working from manuscript exemplars, also began to care about the textual quality and correctness of their copies and used this to advertise their books. Caxton, for example, did so in the preface to his second edition of *The Canterbury Tales* (1483), claiming access to a "trewe and correcte" manuscript of the text and justifying his decision "to enprynte it agayn, for to satysfye thauctour, where as to fore by ygnouraunce I erryd in hurtyng and dyffamyng his book in dyuerce places" (sig. A2^v). The editors of the First Folio likewise asserted that they had edited Shakespeare's plays "according to the True Originall Copies" (Taylor et al 2017, xxv), indeed that "as where (before) you were abus'd with diuerse stolne, and surreptitious copies, maimed, and deformed by the frauds and stealthes of iniurious impostors", they had now "publish'd them [. . .] cur'd, and perfect of their limbes" (lxxvii). Such claims, whatever their truth value, were a common marketing strategy in print publishing (Lesser 2019, 78–80).

During the sixteenth and seventeenth centuries, print developed its own media language, codes, and conventions for presenting texts. These ranged from title pages and tables of contents (which manuscripts usually did not have) and other paratexts such as printers' marks and devices to woodcut illustrations and the use of different typefaces such as Roman, *italic*, DISPLAY TYPE (such as capitals), and 𝔅𝔩𝔞𝔠𝔨 𝔩𝔢𝔱𝔱𝔢𝔯 (or Gothic). Black letter dominated printed texts in English, but Roman – first used in England by Richard Pynson in 1509 (Lesser 2019, 70) – became the norm by the end of the sixteenth century. Some early printers used different typefaces indiscriminately (because type was expensive and scarce) but some used them strategically, e.g. drawing on national or religious associations. For instance, Roman type became associated with Calvinism, so English bibles and the Book of Common Prayer were frequently printed in black letter to signal their Englishness and their opposition to Puritan dissent (Lesser 2019, 72); Edmund Spenser's epic romance *The Faerie Queene* (1590/1596) was printed in Roman, possibly to give this long poem a fashionable 'classical' look by imitating the Aldine editions of Virgil and other ancient authors, and at the same time to give it a more 'modern' look by setting it apart from other poems in English for which black letter would still have been the norm at this time (Bland 1998, 107). Such design choices, whether the authors' or the printers', could be complex forms of communication.

Literature in the sixteenth and seventeenth centuries was still far from being a mass medium. There were some forms that already reached potentially large popular audiences – ballads, for example, which were printed on single sheets (called 'broadsides') and accompanied by woodcut illustrations and suggestions for tunes to sing them to. These would be sold by street vendors ('balladmongers') and performed in public so that they reached many, even among the illiterate. A conservative estimate suggests that "3,000 distinct ballads" were printed in the Elizabethan period in multiple copies (Watt 1994, 11). Some books went through several editions very quickly and constitute the category of early 'bestsellers' – a term usually reserved for a later, more commercialised era in publishing (Kesson and Smith 2013). And there was one form of literature with wide popular appeal, drawing large audiences, that we have to turn to now: plays.

4 Theatre and Drama: Liveness on the Stage

In the early modern period, a wide range of literary forms and genres catered to a diverse range of audiences from the barely literate to the highly educated. Books could come in many forms: from the cheap printed chapbook to the elaborate presentation copy of a manuscript made by a professional scribe. Poems could be sent in letters, transcribed into commonplace books, or printed in miscellanies. Plays were performed on the public stage but also printed and sold in the quarto book format. If all of these were 'literature', this was not the name for a single institution but a manifold of textual practices in a continuum of media (manuscript, print, performance, and any combination of these). Two configurations stand out as 'new media' in this period, both in the sense of their novelty and because they propagated and reflected social and cultural change: printed books and commercial theatre. The public playhouse was the most exposed and vulnerable of these, being both marginal and central to early modern English culture. It was frequently attacked for allegedly undermining public morality and inciting 'licentious' behaviour (Mullaney 1988), but it also served to promulgate norms and values that were important to this society.

Early English Drama

Drama is among the oldest forms of literature. In the fourth century BCE, Aristotle uses drama as his main reference point for a theory of mimetic art in his *Poetics*. In the classical world, theatre was a central element of civic life, and the amphitheatre was a key architectural feature of many cities throughout the Roman empire. In the Middle Ages, drama moved away from the theatre and turned to churches and public spaces as locations for performance. What is known about drama in medieval England largely depends on surviving texts from the end of the fourteenth century onwards. The earliest reference to the York Cycle dates from 1376 (Walker 2000, xii), but it is probably older that that; it reached its final form in 1415 (5). These plays were religious in their basic orientation, but they also addressed matters of politics, social order and disorder, and "anxieties about male sexuality" (ix), among other topics. It is debatable whether certain ritual elements of the Christian liturgy can be considered a form of proto-drama. If so, dramatic performances as part of the ecclesiastical year could be regarded as a form of early medieval theatre. Æthelwold's *Regularis Concordia* of c. 970, a Benedictine rule book, describes a ritual performed in churches on Easter morning focused on the visit to the Sepulchre (Christ's burial chamber), involving a short dialogue between the angel at the empty tomb and the three women coming to anoint Christ's body. This ritual playlet would have been performed by monks.

Little is known about secular drama before the late Middle Ages, although it is likely that street performers would have entertained their audiences with improvised or sometimes scripted plays, which have not survived. Outside of the guild system, which provided social control and a religious reason for the performance of plays, drama would have been difficult to justify. If they did not take place in a church or a hall, medieval performances were open-air productions. Plays were a mobile form, performed in the streets or on specially constructed pageant wagons, usually on or around religious holidays. In York, these wagons would follow a prescribed route through the city and stop "at between twelve and sixteen different stations" along the way (Walker 2000, 5). Performances would last from very early in the morning to late at night on Corpus Christi day. The stage floor would have been at audience head height, about 1.5 metres above street level, but some people would have been able to watch from the windows of their houses.

'Mystery plays' are so called because they dealt with mysteries of faith but also because they were organised by different trades (*ministerium* in Latin, from which we get the word 'métier'). These were enormously popular and held sway for three centuries. Other notable genres were the 'morality plays' or 'moral plays' (discussed below) and plays about saints' lives, which depicted crucial episodes like conversions or miracles in the lives of holy men and women. They often featured sensational effects such as torture and execution scenes. The mystery plays aimed to depict "the whole history of the universe from the creation of Heaven and Earth to Doomsday (the Last Judgement)" (Walker 2000, 3), and they did so in English rather than Latin, making biblical stories accessible to everyone.

Especially in Northern England, religious drama flourished in urban centres and was supported by local guilds (i.e., unions of craftsmen), which had a great influence in the rising cities. Whole play cycles survive from Northern England: from York, Chester, and Wakefield. The York Cycle had over fifty plays, each delegated to a particular guild (e.g., the Fishers and Mariners presented the story of Noah and the Flood, the Bakers presented the Last Supper, the Pinners – makers of pegs and nails – were responsible for the Crucifixion). Every guild member paid a contribution to fund these performances. Women's roles were performed by men, and the style of performance would not be realistic; stage spaces were small, texts were in verse, and characters could directly communicate with the audience.

These plays were all based on the Old and New Testament. Performed by laypersons, they would cover episodes such as the Fall of Angels, Abraham and

Isaac, the story of Moses and the Pharaoh, the birth of Christ, the Resurrection, etc., illustrating the pattern of salvation in human and cosmic history. They engaged with medieval cosmology and the modes of making the divine present in the world, and they did so in the vernacular. This was "a form of theater that explore[d] theology through the very logic of performance" (Beckwith 2009, 85) and reflected the shared values and concerns of both the local community and a wider Christian world. As may be imagined, the focus was less on the finer points of theology than on the dramatic potential inherent in these stories. For example, when the four soldiers nail Jesus to the Cross in the York *Crucifixion*, they discuss the "practical difficulties" of their job "in graphic detail" (Walker 2000, 134), and when they raise the Cross, it is with shouts of "Owe, lifte!", "Holde þanne!" and "Heve uppe!" (139, ll. 211–212, 223). On a particularly elaborate wagon, the Mercers' Guild performed *The Last Judgement* to great effect, with thrones for Jesus and the Apostles, a mouth of Hell below, and a Heaven above with mechanical "Aungels payntid red to renne about" (159). The Chester *Pentecost* calls for God to send forth the Holy Spirit "*in spetie ignis*" ('in the form of fire'), and two angels "cast fire upon the apostles": the actors may well have been showered with real sparks (Twycross 2008, 38).

Four cycles have survived: York (c. 1467), Towneley (c. 1500, associated with Wakefield but named after the Towneley family who owned the manuscript), Chester (1591–1607) and N-town (c. 1468–1500), where the N stands for *nomen* (Latin for 'name'): hence any town where any play from the cycle could have been performed. The best-known play, from the Towneley cycle, is the *Wakefield Second Shepherds' Play*, whose author is referred to as the Wakefield Master. Five plays from the Towneley cycle are attributed to him. The *Secunda Pastorum*, as this play is also known, combines a pious presentation of the Birth of Christ with elements of comedy. It is based on the account of the Nativity in Luke, chapter two: the birth of Christ as seen by the shepherds keeping their flock near Bethlehem. This extract is from the beginning (ll. 1–9):

1 PASTOR
Lord, what these weders ar cold! And I am yll happyd.[26]
I am nere hande dold,[27] so long have I nappyd;
My legys thay fold, my fyngers ar chappyd.
It is not as I wold, for I am al lappyd
In sorow.
In stormes and tempest,
Now in the eest, now in the west,

---

26 Not dressed properly for the cold weather.
27 'Dulled' = numb.

> Wo is hym has never rest
> Myd day nor morow.
>
> (Walker 2000, 42)

The play combines this Christian story with realistic detail, putting on stage shepherds and soldiers who complain about the cold, the taxes, and the treatment they receive from the gentry. The Wakefield Master links the Christian story to a comic subplot in which a sheep is stolen and disguised as a baby boy lying in the cradle. The play's bleak beginning – which suits the Yorkshire moors better than Bethlehem – is counterbalanced by the optimistic ending, whose focus is on charity and harmony.

The second major type of English medieval drama is the 'morality' or 'moral play'. These plays were allegorical: their protagonists stood for the whole of humankind and were often called 'Everyman' or 'Mankind'. They engaged with what it meant to be human, with the complexities of human life, which they presented as a journey through temptation, fall, and redemption: a struggle between good and evil that is ultimately resolved by the grace of God. The forces of good and evil were personified, most notably in the 'vice' figure, as opposed by virtues. The moral purpose of these plays is difficult to miss as audiences were encouraged to identify with the protagonist, to reflect on their own lives, and to repent before it would be too late.

The earliest surviving morality is *The Castle of Perseverance* (c. 1405). In a later example, *Mankind* (c. 1465–1470), the eponymous protagonist is first educated by Mercy and then tempted by three riotous vice characters: Nowadays, New Guise, and Nought, who make fun of Mercy's Latinate expressions. In a parody of key words of the Mass, New Guise (= 'the latest fashion') answers Mischief's question "Mankynde, *ubi es*?" ('where are you?') with the words "*Hic, hyc, hic, hic, hic hic, hic hic!*" (Walker 2000, 276, ll. 775–776) – at the same time saying 'here' in Latin and emitting a violent hiccup, thus undermining the very ability of language to communicate meaningfully. The power of words was a key theme of these plays, and words and performance were closely intertwined. Elements of the morality plays, like the personification of vice, survived into the Renaissance in plays like Christopher Marlowe's *Doctor Faustus* (c. 1588–1592) or Ben Jonson's *The Devil is an Ass* (1616). They established a vigorous comedy of crime with powerful ingredients, notably "ignorance and folly, a disposition to mock the virtuous, a callous lack of sympathy for victims, obscenity, and indulgence in lechery, drunkenness and petty theft" (Happé 1972, 18).

A subgenre of the moralities were the interludes; like the moral plays, these would be performed in the halls of manor houses or of London livery companies, or indeed in the hall of a royal palace. They would address a socially diverse public, both speaking to higher and lower-status members of their audience in these settings (Walker 1998). The interludes were more political and secular in their outlook, discussing topics such as good government (in John Skelton's *Magnyfycence,* c. 1519–1520) or the aristocracy's function in society (in Henry Medwall's *Fulgens and Lucres* – written before 1501 and one of the first English plays to appear in print, between 1510 and 1516). After the English Reformation in the 1530s, Protestant writers like John Bale and David Lindsay tried to give their plays a decidedly anti-Catholic spin, also to counter the general anti-theatrical prejudices of their time and to create a genuinely Protestant drama. John Bale (1495–1563) wrote a series of plays in the 1530s under the patronage of the Lord Chancellor Thomas Cromwell (c. 1485–1540), intended to move King Henry VIII further on the path of religious reform. These included plays – now lost – titled *The King's Two Marriages* and *The Impostures of Thomas à Beckett* (Walker 2000, 480). In Scotland, Sir David Lindsay of the Mount (c. 1486–1555) provided similar court entertainments for James V (1512–1542), one of which was later reworked after James V's death into *Ane Satyre of the Thrie Estaitis,* a long and spectacular play addressing the religious and political concerns of its time (Walker 1998). Some of these polemical plays would not only be performed at court but also printed for a wider readership, beginning the media transition of early modern drama from 'pure' performance and preservation in manuscript towards a wider distribution in printed texts.

The authors of plays before the sixteenth century remained anonymous. Most plays were probably co-authored by various writers and frequently revised throughout their existence. One manuscript of the York cycle that has survived probably was the 'master copy' used to check the actors' text against the official version. Plays were written down for performance purposes only, or to be inspected by authorities, but not to be read by readers in a different context; only much later did the idea arise to preserve plays as works of literature. Generally, there are fewer surviving medieval plays from the British Isles than from continental Europe.

Mystery plays continued to be performed into the sixteenth century, when they were suppressed by Protestant authorities as tainted remnants of Catholicism. Anti-theatrical prejudice had a long tradition in the Church since Tertullian's *De spectaculis* (c. 200 CE), and the Reformers shared this hostility of the Church Fathers. The anonymous author of the early fifteenth-century *Tretise of Miraclis Pleyinge* condemns the performances as "scornyng of God" (Walker 2000, 198). In this hostile atmosphere, the plays were ultimately discontinued mainly "because they be Disagreinge from the senceritie of the Gospell", as the dean of York, Matthew Hutton, advised the mayor and Council of York in 1567 (ibid., 205).

Although a number of early play texts have survived, medieval drama was an ephemeral form, not made to last but conceived and performed for special purposes, occasions, or audiences. It depended on a collaborative effort of many people since the text of a play needed to be complemented and completed in performance. This did not change much in the next centuries, well into the seventeenth. Many early plays have come down to us only in the form of titles (about 2,000 are known by title between 1533 and 1623), some seven hundred were printed between 1580 and 1660, and about five hundred of these have survived. There was a market for printed plays in the quarto format, although scholars are divided over the question whether printing plays was a profitable or a risky business for printers (Farmer and Lesser 2005). Only a tiny fraction of early modern playwrights had their work collected in the large and expensive folio format, as in the case of Ben Jonson's *Workes* (1616) and the posthumous First Folio of *M[aste]r William Shakespeare's Comedies, Histories and Tragedies* (1623). As William Prynne's (1600–1669) antitheatrical polemic *Histrio-mastix* (1633) documents, this privileged treatment of plays in print was not to everyone's liking: "Some Play-books [. . .] are growne from *Quarto* into *Folio*, which yet beare so good a price and sale, that I cannot but with griefe relate it, they are now [. . .] new-printed in farre better paper than most Octavo or Quarto *Bibles*" (sig. **6v, italics reversed). Not only the Puritans (radical Protestant zealots who pushed for more drastic religious reforms) may have envied the luxury treatment that some of these secular entertainments were given by the book trade.

The Play's the Thing

To be performed on stage, plays depended on handwritten documents more than on printed texts. The word 'role' for the part played by an actor derives from the physical roll of paper on which their lines and cue-lines were written out for them. Only few handwritten documents pertaining to the early modern stage have survived (Stern 2009). There were almost no established conventions for what a play could or should look like or what it might or might not contain. Playwrights employed a huge range of variation and experimentation to find out what would or would not work with audiences. Depending on the performance situation, these could include all social ranks. Even plays performed at court in the early sixteenth century addressed not only courtiers but also the servants attending (Walker 1998). Consequently, styles of theatrical performance ranged from elaborate stylisation to popular entertainment, from high tragedy to low comedy and farce, often embodying a mixture of many different tones and registers to find a middle ground on which to unite a segmented audience.

Plurality and multiplicity were also the order of the day when it came to different performance venues. Early on, before there were playhouses, secular plays used to be acted by 'strolling players', troupes of actors who travelled the country and performed in public spaces or manor houses. Their social status was insecure. Actors were often treated with suspicion or even contempt because, for one, they tended to move around and did not stay in one place, at a time when vagrancy was a punishable offence. Because of their mobility, actors came close to – and often mixed with – beggars, criminals, and low-life delinquents. Secondly, they raised suspicion because they dressed up in the clothes of their social superiors and pretended to be something they were not, at a time when sumptuary laws regulated which colours or fabrics could be worn by which part of the population. Because rank and status were clearly marked by dress, the theatrical disguise of one's social identity could be considered offensive, possibly because it revealed that the authority of those in power depended less on their inherent qualities than on external appearances – a social fiction that worked only as long as their audience could be persuaded to believe in it.

Itinerant actors performed in public places or private households, often in London inn-yards. In the sixteenth century, these included the Bull, the Cross Keys, the Bell, and the Bel Savage. Other theatrical venues were the universities, where students performed plays in Latin, either derived from classical sources or newly written, and London's Inns of Court, where courtiers and lawyers enjoyed the performance of plays. Large halls or tennis courts could also be used for this purpose. Specific buildings for performing plays were an innovation of the late sixteenth century. In 1567, John Brayne converted an inn, the Red Lion in Whitechapel, into what was probably the first purpose-built playhouse in Europe since classical antiquity. Its remains were discovered by archaeologists in 2020. In 1576, James Burbage built what was simply called "The Theatre" just outside the city walls to the North, in Shoreditch – to avoid the repressive city administration and to make it easily accessible to Londoners. This must have been a profitable venture because it was quickly followed by another theatre, the Curtain, built almost next to it. The Curtain was not named after a proscenium curtain – this was not a feature of early modern playhouses – but apparently "after the walled-in (or 'curtained') field in which it stood" (Scott-Warren 2005, 103). The number of professional theatres built in London from the mid-sixteenth to mid-seventeenth century amounts to "at least twenty-three" (ibid.). They were built in areas – the so-called 'liberties' – which were free from city jurisdiction, a territory "over which the city had authority but, paradoxically, almost no control" (Mullaney 2005, par. 4; see also

Mullaney 1988), permitting a greater artistic license than the (Puritan) city officials would otherwise allow.

There are a few historical drawings that show what these playhouses looked like from the outside. They were circular or polygonal, built of wood, about thirty metres wide and ten metres high. The only extant picture of the interior of an Elizabethan playhouse is a sketch and a description by Johannes De Witt of Utrecht (which survives in a copy by Aernout van Buchel, c. 1596) of the interior of the Swan, which also depicts a performance in progress (fig. 5). The Latin names given to parts of the building in this sketch display an awareness of classical stage traditions. This is, unfortunately, the only contemporary illustration that has survived. Anything else that one can find in pictures,

Fig. 5: Interior of the Swan playhouse. Copy by Aernout van Buchel of a sketch by Johannes de Witt (1596); from Arnoldus Buchelius, *Adversaria*, fol. 132r.
Source: Utrecht University Library Special Collections Ms. 842, Wikimedia Commons.

models, films, and reconstructions is based on a blend of reliable information and fanciful speculation.

The stage, surrounded by the audience on three sides, was an elevated rectangular platform as much as twelve metres wide. There was no artificial lighting, so performances took place in the afternoon, probably between two and five o'clock. The audience would stand around the stage in the yard (admission: one penny), and there were seats (at double price) in the three tiers of galleries that lined the inside walls. Here one could sit on a bench protected from the elements. Above the stage was a canopy supported by two massive wooden pillars, painted to look like marble, which could also serve as trees onstage if needed. At the back, there was a gallery used – depending on the play being performed – as an upper stage (e.g., Juliet's balcony in *Romeo and Juliet*), a lords' room, or a music room for a band of musicians. Underneath this gallery were two or three doors leading to the 'tiring house' (dressing room and prop store); here there was a curtained area where actors could be 'discovered' by pulling the curtains aside. Due to the lack of elaborate scenery, the plays' effect depended on the audience's willingness to enter scenic conventions of illusion, to suspend their disbelief for the duration of the performance. Willingness to entertain such illusions was the foundation of the early modern playhouse. This also extended to the gender identities of boys or men playing women, and sometimes playing women who disguised themselves as boys. "to the point where in [Shakespeare's] *As You Like It* Rosalind was played by a boy playing a girl pretending to be a boy playing a girl" (Gurr 1997, 3282).

Playhouses had to make a profit, so their managers had to find plays – and ever new plays – that would fill their houses. They were performance spaces in more than one sense. The theatre was not only a place to watch plays being performed, but also a space where people of all social spheres could watch each other performing their social identities. Those sitting in the more expensive seats paid for watching the play but also (probably) enjoyed being on display for their fellow audience members, their peers and those socially above or beneath them. Around the theatre, an entire culture industry emerged that attracted writers (often university graduates) who tried for a career as professional playwrights.

Actors' companies sought the patronage of a nobleman to escape punishment for vagrancy. This is why Elizabethan and Jacobean companies have names like Lord Strange's Men, the Admiral's Men, the Chamberlain's Men, the Earl of Leicester's Men, Oxford's Men, Worcester's Men, etc.; 'men' on this context means 'servants', but in fact also men only – no women were allowed as actors until after the Restoration in 1660. Next to these all-male troupes, there were the boys' companies (the Children of Paul's, the Children of the Chapel, the Children of the Queen's Revels), who performed in smaller venues with a reduced repertoire (mostly comedy). These became increasingly popular with city audiences until they were suppressed by James I – possibly because of lobbying from the adult companies, who wanted to oust their competition. Companies might perform at various playhouses, but some of them became regulars. The actors of the Lord Chamberlain's men, for instance, financed, and profited from, the Globe Theatre by owning a share of their playhouse. Shakespeare paid about 12.5 percent of the building costs and purchased his share of the Globe, the first playhouse to be owned by its players. It was built in 1599 using the timber of the old Theatre, whose lease of land had expired. It became the Lord Chamberlain's men's permanent playhouse. Profits were shared between members of the company as such and the owners of the theatre (called 'housekeepers'), who included the two Burbages (James and Richard) and five others, one of them Shakespeare.

From 1594 onwards, only two companies were licensed to perform within London's city limits: these were the Lord Chamberlain's Men (the company Shakespeare joined in 1594), later (from 1603) known as the King's Men, and their only serious rivals, the Admiral's Men (later known as Prince Henry's Men). The records of performances given at court show that the Lord Chamberlain's Men were by far the most favoured of the theatrical companies. From the summer of 1594 to March 1603, they seem to have been playing almost continuously in London. They did a provincial tour during the autumn of 1597 and travelled again in 1603 when the plague was in town; after this, they toured during part of the summer or autumn most years.

Performances were sometimes introduced by a musical overture and closed with a dance or a jig, often involving a clown's antics. Even tragedies were rounded off in this way, closing on a light-hearted note. There is a fascinating eyewitness account of a performance of Shakespeare's *Julius Caesar* at the Globe (September 21, 1599) by a Swiss traveller, Thomas Platter:

> On the 21st of September after lunch, about two o'clock, I crossed the water [the Thames] with my party, and we saw the tragedy of the first emperor Julius Caesar acted very prettily in the house with the thatched roof, with about fifteen characters; at the end of the comedy, according to their custom, they danced with exceeding elegance, two each in men's and two in women's clothes, wonderfully together.
> (Trans. Noah Heringman in Greenblatt 1997, 3329)

Because plays appealed to a diverse audience, they could become a forum for addressing widespread social concerns and debating, directly or indirectly, conflicts that arose between competing and conflicting values, such as the economic concerns of early capitalism in contrast to traditional social and familial bonds.

Such conflicts, for instance, drive the action of plays like Shakespeare's *The Merchant of Venice* (c. 1596). Early modern theatre presented problematic aspects of life and heightened conflicts in a manner that oscillated between ritual and entertainment, involving the audience to a great degree. Playwrights and companies sought out material that would hold, fascinate, or puzzle their audiences and make them come back for more. Audiences would respond to plays about characters caught up in tragic or comic situations in which traditional beliefs and codes of chivalry, charity, or honour would clash with new economic or political realities, or simply with the exigencies of a dramatic situation. Hamlet's famous soliloquy on suicide, "To be or not to be", is an example of this, pitting the abstractions of canon law against a moment of extreme mental anguish, as is Falstaff's speech about honour in *1 Henry IV* (1596–1598). Beyond speeches as such, there is in many plays a tension or discrepancy between what characters say and what they do (or fail to do), illustrating on yet another level the conflict between verbal arguments and human action or inaction, the fact that words can be used or abused for all kinds of purposes or intentions.

The first English tragedy, *Gorboduc* by Thomas Norton (1532–1584) and Thomas Sackville (1536–1608), was performed at the Inner Temple and at Whitehall for Queen Elizabeth in 1561 and first printed in 1565. It constitutes an important link between the moralities and interludes of the previous decades and the neo-Senecan tragedies by Marlowe, Shakespeare, and others. It was also the first English play to be written in blank verse (unrhymed iambic pentameter), a form that was built to last and proved to be immensely influential on later playwrights. Tragedy, or serious drama, depends on generating powerful affective responses in the audience –similar to medieval drama, but usually without an explicit religious framework. This demanded a heightened language, for which blank verse was the perfect template in English, combined with literary models of Roman plays by Seneca, which were translated and adapted for English audiences.

Theoretical considerations about drama – as laid down, for example, in Aristotle's *Poetics*, with its emphasis on the unities of place, time, and action – would not have played a significant role in this development. The *Poetics* would only have been available in Greek or Latin. Ben Jonson is known to have owned a Latin translation printed in 1623 (McPherson 1974, 26). There was an Italian translation from 1570, but none in French or English until the late seventeenth and early eighteenth century. Aristotelian ideas did enter the wider culture, however, for instance in Sir Philip Sidney's *Defence of Poesie* (c. 1579). Other classical precepts about drama – such as the five-act structure – came from different sources such as Horace's *Ars poetica*. Early modern English playwrights were, for the most part, more interested in experiments than classical precedents.

Anyone who has seen the film *Shakespeare in Love* (1998) – a very useful introduction to the social and economic world of early modern English drama – will remember that the real star playwright in the early 1590s was not Shakespeare but Christopher Marlowe (1564–1593). Marlowe was one of the so-called "university wits", a fashionable group of young writers who came to fame in London in the 1580s and who all had a university education, most of them at Cambridge. Their classical training did not keep them from having a violent and at times criminal temperament; Marlowe was stabbed and killed in a Deptford tavern, apparently after quarrelling over the bill. He was highly admired for his poems and plays, which broke new ground in dramatic poetry. Marlowe's plays – *Tamburlaine* (1 and 2), *The Jew of Malta, Edward II, Dido Queen of Carthage, The Massacre at Paris,* and *Doctor Faustus* – all deal with megalomaniac protagonists who are ultimately destroyed. *Tamburlaine* tells the story of a self-willed tyrant, an outsider and usurper who became a type for the dramatic figure of the "overreacher" (Levin 1952). In the process, Marlowe proclaimed a new dramaturgy exalting individual achievement and power, pinpointing the audience's response on terror rather than pity. The protagonist faces a series of military enemies and defeats them one after the other; the only serious enemy left at the end of part two is Death, to whom even Tamburlaine must finally succumb. Tamburlaine delivers thundering speeches to his followers and opponents, juxtaposing horror and beauty, "pairing blood and guts with poetic contemplation" (Hunter 1997, 46) in Marlowe's signature blank verse:

> I will, with engines never exercised,
> Conquer, sack, and utterly consume
> Your cities and your golden palaces,
> And with the flames that beat against the clouds
> Incense the heavens and make the stars to melt,
> As if they were the tears of Mahomet
> For hot consumption of his country's pride;
> And till by vision or by speech I hear
> Immortal Jove say 'Cease, my Tamburlaine',
> I will persist a terror to the world,
> Making the meteors that, like armèd men,
> Are seen to march upon the towers of heaven,
> Run tilting round about the firmament
> And break their burning lances in the air
> For honour of my wondrous victories.
> (*2 Tamburlaine* 4.1.194–208;
> Marlowe 1999, 121)

Marlowe wrote his *Tamburlaine* not only in blank verse but in a kind of blank verse designed for a particular kind of acting. "[T]he verse-speaking of Tamburlaine requires an extraordinary combination of force and control, more in the mode of opera than of the modern stage, if the combination of line and paragraph rhythms is to be mastered" (Hunter 1997, 47). The play was a model of how humanist learning could be repurposed for popular stage entertainment. Like all of Marlowe's plays, it works with a basic tension between strong individual personalities and their surrounding social and historical frameworks, which they attempt to control but which are ultimately uncontrollable and stronger than any individual. Marlowe's innovations in dramatic technique had a powerful impact on his fellow playwrights, including Shakespeare.

Many early modern plays combined elements of tragedy and comedy. A good example are the comic relief scenes in Shakespeare, like the Porter in *Macbeth* (1606). As a mixed genre, tragicomedies were also very popular with audiences. Playwrights probably did not spend too much time thinking about genre as a fixed set of rules that had to be followed (unlike in France, for example, where such precepts were adhered to much more faithfully). They had to supply a demand for entertainment, so they turned genre into "a technique of multi-layering" (Hunter 1997, 94), trying to offer something for everybody. Shakespeare wrote plays that were announced on playbills as comedies, tragedies, or histories; but these labels were extremely flexible. Comedies could include more serious elements, tragedies could include persons of lower rank and comic scenes, and history plays included bits of everything. Genres were not fixed, but highly dynamic, and 'comedy' could be a general term for all kinds of plays.

Through print, early modern drama reached a wider literate and literary audience. But – like any drama – it was principally written to be performed by actors, live on a stage, in front of an audience. There are numerous elements (or codes: visual, acoustic, spatial) that cannot be scripted into the text but that emerge from the performance situation. These effects of immediacy connect theatre back to some of the oldest forms of entertainment that are predominantly visual, oral, and aural: physical movement, spoken words, song and dance, religious ritual. As Jonathan Bate explains (2008, 101), the effects of drama are "achieved not by rhetoric alone, but by the combination of eloquent speech and 'lively' (lifelike) acting. [. . .] The two dimensions of the poetic words on the page are transformed into life by the third dimension of performance on stage." This third dimension, however, could reflect back on itself, addressing and highlighting the medium of theatrical performance in a turn towards metatheatre and metadrama – familiar features of early modern plays that will be the topic of the next section.

Metatheatre and Metadrama

Performance on stage has essentially two dimensions, distinguished by Robert Weimann (2000) as *locus* and *platea*. *Locus* is the place where the dramatic fiction is located; *platea* is a kind of contact zone between this and the audience, a space that a character can enter in order, temporarily, to leave the fiction. This boundary zone between the fictional world of the play and the reality of the performance can be breached, often in a playful manner to remind the audience that they are watching a play. In modern drama, this is also known as 'breaking the fourth wall'. A character might, for example, refer to characters in a different play (as when Polonius in *Hamlet* 3.2.104–112 mentions a play about Julius Caesar); or might point out that they have acted in such a play, breaching the distinction between character and actor (as Polonius also does, linking *Hamlet* to Shakespeare's *Julius Caesar*). In the first case, we have metadrama; in the second, metatheatre. An audience remembering a performance of *Julius Caesar* at the Globe would have associated the actor playing Polonius with Julius Caesar and possibly the actor playing Hamlet – Richard Burbage – with Brutus, and they might realise how meaningful this association is when Hamlet later stabs Polonius in act 3, scene 4.

The stage may add to the impression that what we witness when we watch a play is separated from the everyday world and is thus fictional – a "second reality" in Luhmann's term (2000b, 51) – but this distinction is brittle. Especially in the early modern playhouse, the audience was visible to the actors and there was less of a physical or psychological barrier between actors and audience. Sometimes audience members would sit very close to the stage or even on the stage. In such a setting, the "aesthetic screen"[28] of theatrical fiction may break down. Alternatively, the play itself may stage a breakdown of the barrier between fiction and reality in forms of metadrama and metatheatre. This happens, for example, in Francis Beaumont's (1584–1616) *The Knight of the Burning Pestle* (c. 1607), where a grocer, his wife, and their two apprentices interrupt the performance and demand changes to the play. The grocer's wife even gets to speak the epilogue. These characters who interrupt the action are scripted into the play, but first audiences may well have wondered about the boundaries between playing and reality.

Metadrama and metatheatre can be connected to what Thomas Corns has called "multilayered mimesis" in Shakespeare: the actors, Corns writes, play

---

[28] I adapt this term from Morton 2007, 35, who uses it to denote the separation between "the perceiving subject" and "the object". See also Berensmeyer 2013.

"characters who then both play roles and comment on the distinction between those roles and a depicted interiority that conflicts with them" (2007, 47). By allowing different frames of reference and different roles to comment on each other, Shakespeare and other early modern dramatists made use of theatrical mimesis and metatheatrical references to explore the performative conditions and the possibilities for transformation that are (not only according to Aristotle) deeply imprinted in human nature. Through many productions across the ages, *Hamlet* in particular has become a paradigmatic instance of theatrical meta-reflection, gaining an ever-growing layer not only of prestige but of cultural inquiry which new productions cannot simply ignore. In effect, *Hamlet* has thus over the centuries become a kind of theatrical palimpsest, a many-layered "meta-commentary" on theatre in general (Mosse 2014, 114).

Many plays, but perhaps particularly Shakespeare's, oscillate between *representation* and *performance*, between showing something that may already be known in other ways or based on history (e.g., the history of the Wars of the Roses, or the life of King Richard III) and expanding the known by creating genuinely new, startling, or surprising experiences for the audience (e.g., feeling 'sympathy for the devil' that is Richard III as performed by a good actor), bringing a play to life. Those performance effects that arise from a theatrical production and go beyond mimetic representation are probably what draws an audience into the theatre in the first place, but they are also the most difficult to analyse. At the Globe, but also in early modern halls or the smaller indoor playhouses, audiences were close to the stage. In these settings, especially in an indoor playhouse, candles would highlight the actors' faces, making these their "chief visual medium of communication" (Astington 2001, 109). What happens on stage, and in the connecting space between actors and audience, is not merely the mimetic representation of an external reality, nor a merely verbal circulation of various competing discourses, but the creation of a genuinely new social space of communication and aesthetic experience. It is "a simulation of social communication" (Schwanitz 1990, 100), but it is also a *stimulation* of cognitive and emotional responses that is experienced as pleasurable. Theatre and theatricality may *also* be about representing something given or criticising dominant ideas of their time, but they tend to go beyond these dimensions, beyond symbolism and reference, towards forms of pure play. They remain tethered to reality, if only in the most tenuous of ways – a play like *A Midsummer Night's Dream* has few things to connect it to the reality of Elizabethan England, but it does have some – so that they do not descend to mere fantasy. There are usually some serious matters at stake, even in the most abstruse comedy. If this were not the case, audiences would stop caring for the characters and their stories, and boredom would set in. An empty spectacle might be entertaining for a while but not for an entire afternoon or evening.

Later Developments

From the early modern period onwards, drama retained a dual character of performance and literariness. Some plays were apparently not written for public performance but for private theatricals or for reading – notably, plays by women, like Mary Wroth's (1587–1653) *Love's Victory* (c. 1620) or Elizabeth Cary's (1585–1639) *The Tragedy of Mariam* (printed in 1613), which was rediscovered by twentieth-century feminist critics as engaging with questions of patriarchal authority and female disobedience (Ezell 2019, 196). The later term 'closet drama', applied to plays not intended for the stage but solely for the page, is rightly associated with Romanticism, with dramatic poems like Byron's (1788–1824) *Manfred* (1817) or Percy Shelley's (1792–1822) *Prometheus Unbound* (1820). In modernity, there is again a greater overlap between these formats, as some twentieth-century plays demonstrate: T. S. Eliot's (1888–1965) verse dramas *Murder in the Cathedral* (1935) and *The Cocktail Party* (1949), for example, as well as Christopher Fry's (1907–2005) *The Lady's Not for Burning* (1948) were commercially successful in London's West End and on New York's Broadway despite their literariness, their use of poetry. Closer to the contemporary world of theatre, plays in verse are still going strong, for example with Mike Bartlett's (1980–) 'future history play' *King Charles III* (2014), written in Shakespearean blank verse, or Zadie Smith's *The Wife of Willesden* (2021) in Chaucerian decasyllabic metre. With Shakespeare, the literary aspects (or the 'poetry') of his plays has dominated critical discussion from the eighteenth century onwards; performative aspects then had a comeback among scholars in the second half of the twentieth century, enshrined in the *Oxford Shakespeare* edition of 1986, which chose to print the plays in versions as close as possible to the plays' first performances. More recently, the pendulum has swung back again to a more literary and book-historical emphasis in the *New Oxford Shakespeare* of 2016. Most likely it will keep swinging between the media poles of representation and performance.

One might argue that the media conditions for theatre, and for Shakespeare's theatre in particular, have always been fragile. Early modern audiences appreciated the "strong, effective, above all self-contained, emotional statement" of actors' speeches within a conventional system of signs. "A play", Richard Sennett explains, "did not 'symbolize' reality; it created reality through its conventions" (2002, 79). Audiences responded immediately and spontaneously, loudly, and sometimes violently, so that "many [eighteenth-century popular] theaters had to be periodically gutted and redecorated" (76). Performances in the eighteenth century were no longer directed mainly towards the principal patron but to the audience at large (77); stage seats, allowing audience members to sit right next to the actors, were removed at the Comédie Française in 1759 and in David Garrick's (1717–1779) Drury Lane in 1762 (80). Yet later architectural developments in stage design cut off the direct contact between actors and audience, putting the audience into a darkened auditorium and screening the actors off by means of artificial lighting. This changed the very foundations of theatrical expression and experience, from a system of repeatable signs that encouraged spontaneous emotional expression to a form of symbolic representation that was to be enjoyed in silence. In the nineteenth century, silence had become the norm as theatres were larger and middle-class audiences demonstrated their respectability by keeping their emotions in check (Sennett 2002, 206–207). Watching a play in a darkened auditorium became a proto-cinematic experience long before cinema was invented (see ch. 11).

Productions of Shakespeare, especially in the Victorian period, became increasingly realistic and spectacular, following historical research on costumes and props – *Macbeth* and *King Lear*, for example, were performed in medievalist settings and *Julius Caesar* in elaborate reconstructions of ancient Rome. Once cinema could compete with this kind of 'photorealism', productions tried to bring Shakespeare into the present by using modern dress, though, strictly speaking, modern dress had been the norm for costumes before the rise of historicism in the nineteenth century. The first performance of this kind took place at the Birmingham Repertory Theatre in 1923. More recent concerns have been with casting: directors and audiences have become more aware of diversity, and since 2000 there have been more productions featuring all-female, all-Black, or multi-ethnic casts. Colour-blind or colour-conscious casting has become a matter of much debate. These questions lead back to issues of representational realism or authenticity in theatre: should non-Black actors be cast to play Black characters, and vice versa? Or should actors be able to play anything and anybody, regardless of their colour, size, gender, or able-bodiedness? The line between the individual actor as a performer of a (fictional) role and as the representative of a particular (real-life) group has become more difficult to draw, and it is now almost impossible to imagine a 'white' actor donning blackface to play Shakespeare's Othello, as was common practice in former times.

Theatre and New Media

The coming of radio, cinema, and television (see ch. 9–11 below) added new technological possibilities to mediate performed drama to an expanded audience – either reducing drama to voices, music, and sound effects in the case of radio, or filming and broadcasting a live performance using camera movements, recorded sound, and differently framed shots to guide the viewer's experience. The close-up may appear an unusual distortion of ordinary theatrical experience, but less so when we remember that audiences in early modern indoor playhouses would also have been very close to the stage and paid close attention to the actors' faces. The impressive description of Garrick's performance of *Hamlet* in Georg Christoph Lichtenberg's letters from England (1775; see fig. 6) even anticipated the cinematic effects of slow motion or the freeze-frame in its meticulous attention

Fig. 6: Mr Garrick in Hamlet. Mezzotint by James MacArdell after a painting by Benjamin Wilson, 1754.
Source: Metropolitan Museum of Art, Wikimedia Commons.

to detail, as if Lichtenberg had been able to stop time while watching the play.²⁹ After early experiments with Shakespeare in silent cinema, full-fledged film productions, instead of filmed theatrical performances, became feasible, with established actor-directors like Laurence Olivier (1907–1989) or Orson Welles (1915–1985) at the helm. Olivier's *Hamlet* (1948) – the first sound film of that play in English – even won the Best Picture Oscar. After a period of decline, a late bloom and boom in Shakespeare films was associated with Kenneth Branagh (1960–) in the 1990s, following the success of his *Henry V* (1989) and *Much Ado About Nothing* (1993). Later notable big-screen adaptations of Shakespeare plays include Michael Almereyda's *Hamlet* (2000) and Julie Taymor's *The Tempest* (2010). More recently, some theatres have started to expand their global cultural presence through live broadcasts shown in cinemas around the world; the National Theatre, for example, launched its first broadcast in 2009. Its 2015 production of *Hamlet* with Benedict Cumberbatch (1976–) in the title role was reportedly seen by more than a million viewers by 2020.³⁰ This "virtualization of liveness" (Worthen 2008, 311) was first attempted in the 1960s, but it only reached an acceptable technological level in the early 2000s.

Conversely, film was integrated into stage performances in the twentieth century, first in the form of projections or filmed scenery – apparently as early as 1898 in a Chicago production of Lincoln J. Carter's play *Chattanooga* (Waltz 2006, 547) – and gaining traction with Erwin Piscator's productions in the 1920s. Such scenographic projections became increasingly sophisticated and effective, leading towards forms of hybrid theatre and the use of live video recording and projection on stage in combination with performance. In the Wooster Group's *Hamlet* (2006–2007), for example, directed by Elizabeth LeCompte, the filmed recording of Richard Burton's and John Gielgud's 1964 Broadway production – called a 'theatrofilm' at the time – was remediated within a live theatre performance. The Wooster Group referred to their production as a 'reverse theatrofilm'.³¹ A digitally manipulated version of the Burton/Gielgud film was rear-projected onto a screen at the back of the stage, with the actors in front of the screen following every movement of their video avatars (which are sometimes wholly or partially erased from the video) and adding their own live video feed

---

29 Lichtenberg 1994, 3: 334–336. An English translation of this letter can be found online at https://theatregoing.wordpress.com/tag/georg-christoph-lichtenberg/, date of access: 30 June 2020.
30 National Theatre website, http://ntlive.nationaltheatre.org.uk/about-us, date of access: 30 June 2020.
31 A performance of this production has been published on DVD, and some extracts are available on YouTube.

on a smaller TV screen mounted in front of the larger screen. On the large screen, when not fast-forwarding through the Burton film, the word 'play', as on an old videotape, supplied a generic metareference to what was going on. In addition to the manipulated segments from Burton's film, the production also in some scenes included extracts from Michael Almereyda's *Hamlet* film (2000) and Kenneth Branagh's 1996 film of the same play. This, then, was a form of metatheatre with a vengeance, a play with the ghostly presences and absences of *Hamlet* and an entire dramatic tradition. The Wooster Group's shrewd take on the multiply premediated history of Shakespeare's most familiar play turns the play into a spectral act of reproduction, re-enactment, and remembrance: a *Hamlet* as "the collection of all Hamlets" (Scott Shepherd, qtd. in Callens 2009, 544; see also Worthen 2008) or a *Hamlet* as embodying the ghostly presence of theatre history.

Whereas this "postdramatic" production (Lehmann 2006) was an example of "nonidentificatory acting" (Callens 2009, 545) in a Brechtian tradition that did not want the audience to become immersed in the representation, a couple of recent Shakespeare productions tried just the opposite approach: to make the experience of watching a play live on stage more immersive again by means of 'promenade staging'. This involved no video technology but a new kind of shared theatrical space, in effect abolishing the conventional architectural separation between the stage and the stalls. The Bridge Theatre in London, founded in 2017, produced two Shakespeare plays in its first seasons: *Julius Caesar* (2018) and *A Midsummer Night's Dream* (2019), both directed by Nicholas Hytner (1956–). In these productions, part of the audience shared the central stage space with the actors, who performed on platforms that could be raised or lowered and combined or removed at will. The audience in this standing room were very close to the actors and performed as extras, guided by a large group of crew members so that the actors' movements and scene changes remained undisturbed. For the audience (including myself), this was a very special and very physical, even visceral experience. At the end of *A Midsummer Night's Dream*, the moon rose in the form of a couple of big lighted balloons thrown into the audience; club music was playing, and after a few seconds everybody in the house was dancing. This was a nod to early modern stage practices, certainly, but it was also the most immediate and direct involvement of the audience in a play that one could – so far – imagine theatre to achieve, a physical and communal experience that no other technology will ever be quite able to replicate.

II **The Age of Representation (since c. 1500 CE)**

5 Print Culture in the Long Eighteenth Century

Live theatre shows no sign of disappearing; on the contrary, in an age where many people spend a lot of time in front of various screens, it continues to be a highly attractive alternative to other forms of entertainment. As we have seen in the previous chapter, this is precisely because of its promise of immediacy. But drama has always (at least from the sixteenth century onwards) also been a *literary* genre, geared towards representation, towards reading as well as performance. In the sixteenth and seventeenth centuries, there was a market for plays beyond the theatre, in print. Many play-texts were published as quartos, and some even made it into collected works of their authors in the prestigious folio format. Books like *M[aste]r William Shakespeare's Comedies, Histories and Tragedies* (1623) gave a cultural authority and canonical status to drama that had previously been conferred on a few poets only, most notably Chaucer. (After Caxton had published *The Canterbury Tales* – see ch. 3 – William Thynne's edition of *The Workes of Geffray Chaucer* first appeared in print in 1532.) These were expensive books, intended to preserve the plays as 'works' to be read, but also – in Shakespeare's case – probably to secure ownership of these profitable plays for the King's Men (Marino 2013). Heminges and Condell, the editors of the First Folio, addressed their commercial interests head-on in the preface "To the great Variety of Readers" with the words: "Well! It is now publique, & you wil stand for your priuiledges wee know: to read, and censure. Do so, but buy it first" (Taylor et al. 2017, lxxvi). We have already heard their contemporary William Prynne complain about the luxury treatment of such scurrilous literature, perceived as irreligious and sinful, in the book trade, where plays now competed with Bibles (see ch. 4).

The Rise of the Book Market

In the seventeenth and eighteenth centuries, literature increasingly became a marketable commodity from which printers and authors could make – at least in theory – a handsome profit. Initially, the economics of literature were still dominated by the concept of patronage. By dedicating their work to a patron – male or female, usually from the nobility or gentry – authors could hope to gain not only a financial reward, but also the more lasting and valuable currency of protection and prestige. It could also mean access to an elite audience, to a well-stocked library, and possibly other kinds of jobs such as secretarial work or some official post somewhere. The literary world of Elizabethan England was still firmly based on this model rather than a modern commercial understanding of literature as a business. It was grounded in personal relationships of exchange between writers and patrons as part of an early modern gift economy (Fumerton 1991, Scott 2006, Heal 2014). A writer's choice of subject matter or genre usually reflected the taste of the patron, rather than aiming for commercial success and/or the writer's self-expression. The exception to this is drama (see ch. 4), where plays needed to be commercially viable, otherwise theatre companies would not pay dramatists to write them. In this case, the audience in the playhouse takes the place of the patron and is often addressed directly in prologues and epilogues asking for a show of support, for applause, as in the epilogues to Shakespeare's *A Midsummer Night's Dream* and *The Tempest*.

As the modern system of royalties did not yet exist, any profits from print publication would accrue to the printer rather than the authors, who sold their work for a flat fee. In April 1667, John Milton (1608–1674) sold the copyright to his epic poem *Paradise Lost* to the printer Samuel Simmons for a mere £ 10 – five down and another five after 1,300 copies had been sold. Based on purchasing power, this would roughly mean £ 1,500 in today's money.[32] This contract, preserved in the British Library, is said to be "the earliest known example of a contract between an English author and their publisher" (Tuppen 2017).

The Subscription Model

In the seventeenth century, yet another way of financing literary authorship was invented: the subscription model. In one of the first well-known cases, the publisher Jacob Tonson (1655–1736) got together with the poet John Dryden (1631–1700) for a project of translating the works of the Roman poet Virgil (published 1694–1697). Translators had been paid by publishers before, especially in the profitable field of popular romances from France and Spain, containing heroic or vagabond adventures. Now, Tonson secured a number of signatories and financial backers for the translation of a classical author's works, enabling Dryden to complete this project. Subsequently, the poet Alexander Pope (1688–1744) came to a similar agreement with Bernard Lintot (1675–1736) to publish a translation of the *Iliad* by subscription. Subscribers agreed in advance to buy one or more copies of the book, sometimes in a more prestigious format, and they usually paid half the book's retail price in

---

[32] The historical worth of money is notoriously difficult to calculate; I have used the purchasing power calculator on measuringworth.com.

advance. Their names would then be printed in a list of subscribers included in the book, displaying their patronage. With the move away from single patrons, something like 'crowdfunding' is born.

Even though Dryden and Tonson fell out at some point, Dryden made a lot of money out of this transaction; estimates range around £ 1,000 from Tonson and the subscribers and another £ 400 or £ 500 for his three dedications to individual patrons. Altogether, that is more than £ 220,000 in today's money. For Pope and the six-volume *Iliad* project started in 1713, expectations were even higher – at least four times higher – than for Dryden, but there were difficulties in securing a large enough number of patrons, so that Pope's profits were not as generous as he expected.

The Anglo-Irish essayist and satirist Jonathan Swift (1667–1745) made fun of this "*modern* way of *subscription*" (2008, 66) in his *Tale of a Tub* (written 1697, published 1704): books, "the children of the brain", could now have "a multiplicity of *godfathers*" (2008, 33). In a later addition to this text, Swift satirically announces "A Project, for the universal benefit of Mankind" which should "produce a handsom Revenue to the Author", namely "to print by Subscription in 96. large volumes in *folio*, an exact Description of *Terra Australis incognita*" (2008, 146), to be "bought at the publick Charge [. . .] for every Parish Church in the three Kingdoms" (147). In the eighteenth century, subscriptions not only helped to fund authors and publishers but could also serve to signal one's political allegiance, as some literary projects and persons attracted strong Whig or Tory support (Lesser 2019, 198–199).

In the early eighteenth century, the publisher began to replace the patron as the author's commissioner. This was a gradual transition; the market did not immediately supersede earlier economies of writing and publishing. The eighteenth century is often depicted as the age of the professionalisation of authorship; but this is not a simple story (from dependence on patronage to being free agents in a market). There were always authors who did not get paid for having their works printed, and there was also a continuing practice of authors paying for their works to be printed. For many poets, this was still the case in the early nineteenth century (Byron, Keats, Shelley). Only very few writers like Dryden and Pope made a lot of money from having their work published (Downie 2014). Towards the end of the eighteenth century, there was "a range of authorial models or identities on offer, whether professional or amateur, individual or sociable, original or imitative, proprietary or anonymous" (Schellenberg 2019, 143). Authorship had become a complicated business.

Samuel Johnson and the Age of Authors

Probably the most famous anecdote about the change from patronage to professionalism concerns Samuel Johnson (1709–1784), also known as 'Dr Johnson', the most famous man of letters in eighteenth-century Britain. Johnson was a prolific writer and critic who had an interest, among other things, in literary biography. His *Lives of the Poets* (1779–1781) is a fine example of this. It is also an illustration of the changes brought to the book market through profitable reprints of earlier works that had gone out of copyright, because Johnson wrote these biographies as prefaces for a series of such reprints, beginning in 1779. Many of Johnson's sayings were made famous in the biography that his Scottish follower and friend James Boswell (1740–1795) wrote about him, the massive *Life of Johnson* (1791). Johnson's most lasting claim to fame, however, is that he compiled the first *Dictionary of the English Language* (1755). Naturally, he needed patrons for a project of this magnitude, so he asked the Earl of Chesterfield for some financial support. Chesterfield, however, made Johnson wait so long that he finally gave up; but then, when the work was a success, the earl apparently claimed he had supported it. Johnson's response is recorded in an angry letter to his would-be patron (7 February 1755):

> Seven years, My lord have now past since I waited in your outward Rooms or was repulsed from your Door, during which time I have been pushing on my work through difficulties of which it is useless to complain, and have brought it at last to the verge of Publication without one Act of assistance, one word of encouragement, or one smile of favour. Such treatment I did not expect, for I never had a Patron before.
>
> (Johnson 2020, 509)

Johnson's letter to Chesterfield continues with a *Dictionary*-style definition: "Is not a Patron, My Lord, one who looks with unconcern on a Man struggling for Life in the water and when he has reached ground encumbers him with help" (509–510). In his *Dictionary*, Johnson defines a "patron" as "commonly a wretch who supports with insolence, and is paid with flattery" (1755). The *Dictionary*, comprising more than 2,300 folio pages and defining some 40,000 words, made Johnson famous, and he went on to become the most celebrated author in Britain; but he started out poor. "I was miserably poor", he later told Boswell, "and I thought to fight my way by my literature and my wit" (Boswell 1992, 39). Johnson wrote many essays and numerous poems, a classical tragedy (*Irene*, 1749), a philosophical novel (*Rasselas*, 1759), an account of his journey through Scotland (1775), more than forty sermons acting as a ghost-writer for several priests, and 52 critical biographies of British authors.

But few writers had or could afford to have the chutzpah of Samuel Johnson or the gentlemanly detachment of Alexander Pope. For any single one of these successful individuals, there were hundreds of struggling writers competing for attention and reputation, or merely trying to survive. The eighteenth century was "the age of authors" (Johnson 2014 [1753], 210) not just because authors were becoming more independent from patrons and publishers, but also because there were now so many authors that it was a cliché to complain about this overcrowding of the public sphere with printed matter, and to apologise for adding yet another text to the multitude that was already out there:

> The present age, if we consider chiefly the state of our own country, may be stiled with great propriety THE AGE OF AUTHORS; for, perhaps, there never was a time, in which men of all degrees of ability, of every kind of education, of every profession and employment, were posting with ardour so general to the press. The province of writing was formerly left to those, who by study, or appearance of study, were supposed to have gained knowledge unattainable by the busy part of mankind; but in these enlightened days, every man is qualified to instruct every other man, and he that beats the anvil, or guides the plough, not contented with supplying corporal necessities, amuses himself in the hours of leisure with providing intellectual pleasures for his countrymen.
>
> (Johnson 2014, 210)

In the same essay in *The Adventurer* of 1753, Johnson goes on to lambast "this universal eagerness of writing" (210) as an "epidemical conspiracy for the destruction of paper" (211), of which his own essay is of course a part. The "cure" he suggests is that authors should be properly qualified and refrain from writing unless they have "the power of imparting to mankind something necessary to be known" (211).

The Battle of the Books

To this multitude, one needs to add another conflict: a controversy about the relative merits of 'ancient and modern learning', which was imported to England from Paris by Sir William Temple in the late seventeenth century. This led Jonathan Swift to write *The Battle of the Books (A Full and True Account of the BATTEL Fought last FRIDAY, Between the* Antient *and the* Modern *BOOKS in St JAMES's LIBRARY)*, written by 1697 and published in 1704. In this satire, the 'battle of the books', ancient against modern authors, is imagined as an actual battle taking place in the royal library, which at that time was housed in St James's Palace and directed by Temple's nemesis, the classical scholar Richard Bentley. Swift literalises the metaphor of the book as a vessel that preserves its writer's spirit, as this was (for example) memorably phrased by Milton in *Areopagitica* (1644): "Books are not absolutely dead things, but doe contain a potencie of life in them to be as active as that soule was whose progeny they are; nay they do preserve as in a violl the purest efficacie and extraction of that living intellect that bred them" (1953, 492). Swift concurs: "In these books", he writes, "is wonderfully instilled and preserved the spirit of each warrior, while he is alive; and after his death his soul transmigrates there to inform them. [. . .] So, we may say, a restless spirit haunts over every book till dust or worms have seized upon it" (2008, 107). Now the 'armies' of the ancients and the moderns are starting to fight each other, triggered by a comment made by Aesop, the ancient fabulist, that the ancients are like honeybees and the moderns like spiders, the ancients producing "sweetness and light" as opposed to the "dirt and poison" of the moderns. In the ensuing battle, described in mock-heroic fashion modelled on Homer's *Iliad*, one encounter is between Virgil and his modern translator, "the renowned Dryden". Virgil is "in shining armour, completely fitted to his body", whereas Dryden's "helmet was nine times too large for the head [. . .] and the voice [. . .] sound[ed] weak, and remote" (118–119). Clearly Swift was not a fan of Dryden. The text imitates a manuscript from which several passages are missing, indicated by typical Latin phrases that philologists used: *hic pauca desunt, ingens hiatus hic in manuscripto*, etc., and the end of the battle is also missing, leaving the question of superiority of the ancients or the moderns undecided. By treating this (alleged) manuscript like an ancient text that he pretends to edit, Swift enacts the quarrel between the ancients and moderns in a media setting of print.

In this satire, Swift defended his patron, William Temple, who held that ancient learning was superior to modern innovations, against Bentley, the philologist who had demonstrated that some of the ancient writings admired by Temple were in fact later forgeries. But he also ridiculed the entire debate about priority and superiority in the field of literature by personifying authors as epic heroes and warriors on a battlefield. His *Battle of the Books* also shows that writing and publishing at the turn of the eighteenth century could be regarded as a sort of battlefield in which all kinds of writers and critics were fighting for supremacy.

Publication had become easier because, in 1695, the Licensing Act expired so that there was no effective censorship anymore (for plays, licensing was reintroduced in 1737). Printing presses, which had been limited to London, Oxford, Cambridge, and York, could now be installed anywhere in the country. All this led not only to an increase in book production but also in newspapers and magazines that offered new outlets for aspiring writers. In practice, censorship had never been very effective. For the Jacobean period, Cyndia Clegg has calculated that fewer than one percent of all books published in England were affected by restrictive measures (2001, 19) – though press regulation grew stricter in the run-up to the English Civil War in the mid-seventeenth century. The

Presbyterian William Prynne was harshly punished as a 'seditious libeller' in the 1630s, having his ears cut off and his cheek branded 'S. L.' (Lesser 2019, 166) – though not because he had railed against the fact that some plays were better printed than Bibles (see ch. 4), but because he was thought to have maligned Queen Henrietta in his critique of women actors.

In the eighteenth century, attempts to control publications shifted from pre-publication censorship to the libel laws – laws against blasphemy, insults, and sedition. Obscenity became another punishable offence. The first person to be punished for this, in 1727, was the publisher Edmund Curll (c. 1675–1747), convicted of "disturbing the King's peace" and "corrupting the morals of the king's subjects" because he had printed a book called *Venus in the Cloister or the Nun in her Smock*, the translation of a French work of erotic fiction (Feather 1988, 89; see also Travis 2000).[33] Thus, even though books no longer needed to be licensed before publication, authors still had to be careful or risk the consequences. When Daniel Defoe (1660–1731), the author of *Robinson Crusoe* (1719), was fined, imprisoned, and pilloried in 1703, suffering public abuse, this was on account of a satirical pamphlet (*The Shortest Way with the Dissenters*) and a sentence under the new libel legislation. However, for most of the eighteenth century, the press enjoyed greater freedom in Britain than in any other major European country (Feather 1988, 90).

From the early eighteenth century onwards, publishers were also better protected by the law. In 1710, the Copyright Act was passed, also known as the Statute of Anne.[34] This Act followed a successful petition by the publishers, and it cemented their rights in their copies, which were now protected for a period of twenty-one years (for existing copies) and fourteen years for new ones, with the possibility of extending them for another fourteen years after that. Lobbying for legal protection, the same Daniel Defoe compared piracy with adultery and burglary, arguing that "the printing of other Mens Copies" was "every jot as unjust as lying with their Wives, and breaking-up their Houses" (Defoe 1704, 21, qtd. in Lesser 2019, 200). Yet the law's actual name was "An Act for

---

33 The Obscene Publications Act of 1857, intended to suppress pornography, also led to prosecutions against English translations of Zola in 1888 and Radclyffe Hall's (1880–1943) lesbian novel *The Well of Loneliness* in 1928 (Feather 2006, 129). The law was changed in 1959 to allow "a defence on the grounds of literary merit" (205). Its first test came when Penguin published D. H. Lawrence's (1885–1930) *Lady Chatterley's Lover* in 1960, which ended in their acquittal (see also Lesser 2019, 401–403).

34 If its date is sometimes given as 1709, this is because the new year in the Julian calendar began on 25 March. According to the new style (introduced in Britain in 1752), the Act was passed in the spring of 1710.

the Encouragement of Learning", and it effectively implied the concept of a public domain, by limiting a right that had previously been considered permanent, although it did not change publishing and bookselling practices immediately. In many cases, publishers bypassed the law by adhering to an idea of 'honorary' copyright and using their connections within the trade to defend what they considered their property against cheaper editions (Lesser 2019, 232). In crucial parts, the law was rather vague, and subsequent trials against book piracy within the British Isles sometimes favoured the copyright holders and sometimes the alleged pirates. This ended in 1774, when the House of Lords decided in favour of a Scottish printer, Alexander Donaldson, who had made a successful business of cheap reprints of English texts that were legally out of copyright. The London printers harassed him with lawsuits, especially when he sold these reprints in his London shop for almost half the usual price, advertising his business as "*The Only Shop for* CHEAP BOOKS" (qtd. in Lesser 2019, 220). When he reprinted James Thomson's (1700–1748) quartet of poems *The Seasons* (1730) in Edinburgh in 1772 – one of the steadiest sellers in eighteenth-century poetry – Donaldson was sued by the poem's English copyright owner, Thomas Becket. In this case, *Donaldson v. Becket,* the Lords finally ruled that copyright did not exist in perpetuity beyond the limits stated in the law.

Subsequently, the length of copyright was extended in 1814 to twenty-eight years or the life of the author if that was longer, and extended yet again in 1842 to the author's life plus seven years, and again in 1911 to life plus fifty years, and again in 1988 to life plus seventy years. But effectively, the law acknowledged the existence of a public domain in which texts would ultimately be unrestricted by copyright. This was "a significant turning point in the history of the book in Britain" (Lesser 2019, 221). Even though book prices did not immediately fall, this meant that older texts could be made much more widely available, and it allowed publishers to collect literature into anthologies and reprint series, making it "possible to comprehend, say, 'British Theatre' or 'the English poets' as a whole" unlike ever before (ibid.).

Even though the idea of copyright as arising not from publication but from the author's act of creation was only recognised by the law in 1911, authors also profited from the increasing recognition of 'literary property' in earlier centuries. They could negotiate profitable terms with their publishers, who operated at no small financial risk. Henry Fielding (1707–1754), for example, sold the copyright to his novel *Tom Jones* (1749) for the proud sum of £ 600 (about six times the annual income of an average lower-middle-class family) – nearly £ 100,000 in today's money – and went on to earn £ 800 for *Amelia* two years later (Hammond and Regan 2006, 229). Authors and texts, novelists and poets began to compete for the attention of their readers in a more and more volatile literary marketplace.

Newspapers and Coffeehouses

This emerging marketplace also witnesses the invention of newspapers. The first "coranto" or newsbook in English was a single-sheet publication printed in Amsterdam in 1620; the first English weekly of home news appeared in November 1641, shortly followed by various other publications, mostly eight pages, sometimes illustrated with woodcuts. Newspapers boomed during the English Civil War: fourteen different papers were on sale in England in 1645, mostly pamphlets from both sides of the political divide (Frank 1961). The first regular newspaper was the *Parliamentary Intelligencer,* founded in 1659, which prudently changed its name in 1660 to the *Kingdom's Intelligencer* and came to be the official government newspaper, followed in 1665 by the *Oxford Gazette,* which later continued as the *London Gazette* (Feather 1988, 53–54). The "first successful daily newspaper" (Feather 2006, 58) was the *Daily Courant*, from 1702 onwards, which was soon "selling 800 copies a day" (58) and reaching as many as twenty readers with a single copy (Lesser 2019, 179). The mail coaches would carry periodicals to the countryside three days a week, connecting the provinces with the metropolis and providing a welcome diversion. Sometimes dangerously so – at least one East Anglian farmer is said to have fallen off his horse while reading "the Northampton news paper" (qtd. in Lesser 2019, 180).

Beginning in the mid-seventeenth century, coffeehouses came into fashion in London as well as Paris. These were places where people from different ranks and backgrounds could come together as strangers, discuss freely, and exchange information. They developed an art of civilised conversation and served as "prime information centers" (Sennett 2002, 81). Newspapers picked up or initiated coffeehouse debates and distributed new ideas. Coffeehouses and periodicals entered a constellation from which a mediated public sphere emerged. Periodicals and books could be borrowed and read in coffeehouses, which would usually charge a membership fee that was much lower than that of a circulating library (but one would be obliged to pay extra for coffee and other beverages). Periodicals and coffeehouses broke down traditional barriers to communication (such as rank and status) and, for a while, had an integrating social function. Notions of civility, cultivation, education, and taste provided a common ground for (almost) everybody, most of all the rising bourgeoisie. Such notions were promoted, for instance, in the periodicals edited by Joseph

Addison (1672–1719) and Richard Steele (1672–1729) at the beginning of the eighteenth century: *The Tatler* and *The Spectator*.

Essay periodicals share many features of the early English novel: fictional editor personae, invented situations, multiple perspectives, and a plurality of voices. The most important of these are Daniel Defoe's *The Review* (1704–1713), Richard Steele's *The Tatler* (1709–1711), Richard Steele's and Joseph Addison's *The Spectator* (1711–1712); *The Guardian* (from 1713); and later those journals mainly authored by Samuel Johnson: *The Rambler* (1750–1752) and *The Idler* (1758–1760), the latter "published as a series of essays in a newspaper, *The Universal Chronicle*" (Feather 2006, 58). The *Tatler* was published three times a week, the *Spectator* even more frequently, each lasting for about two years and selling as many as 4,000 copies a day, a success rate that was not replicated by its later imitators. Johnson's *Rambler* was published twice a week and sold about 500 copies (Feather 2006, 58). Steele's and Addison's *Spectator* was "one of the most spectacular bestsellers of the early eighteenth century" (Feather 2006, 58); it was re-issued in book form (in four volumes) between 1711 and 1713 and frequently reprinted.

Periodicals also developed into an outlet for literary criticism (*Monthly Review*, from 1749; *Critical Review*, from 1756) as well as for shorter fictional texts, thus turning into an aid to the formation of a recognisably modern system of literature. Within a growing overabundance of print, these journals allowed readers access to even more literature that they could at least know about if not read in its entirety, and they saw themselves as a kind of "literary *police*" (*Critical Review*, January 1766, 61, qtd. in Lesser 2019, 209) with a gatekeeping function – inviting readers to spend their time and money wisely and not waste them on unworthy products of the print market. Periodicals and 'part books', which were delivered to provincial areas by post, allowed early forms of serial publication already in the 1730s.

The coffeehouse/newspaper constellation linked direct, face-to-face interaction with distant print communication. The thirst for information made many new readers familiar with the printed word. By the end of the eighteenth century, the public sphere was almost exclusively based on print media, and print was widely available for a largely literate population. An ever-increasing number of readers had access to books and periodicals. For the first time in European history, reading and writing attained the status of the central cultural medium: the medium in which a large part and the most important part of social communication was being conducted. For the novel, one of the most fascinating cultural objects to emerge from this constellation, the ubiquity of print was an ideal incubator (see ch. 6 below).

Grub Street

If the eighteenth century was the first age of the professional author, it was also the age of the literary hack: a writer who did it for the money, offering his services "for bread"; a writer whose talents were for sale. "Hackney for bread" became a phrase (Hammond 1997). The literary market, grown along with an increase in literacy and disposable income, created demand for writers to produce copy for the printing presses. Along with original content, booksellers supplied reprints of older texts, classical or religious material, but there was also demand for writers who could translate, compile, or abridge texts that already existed. These content providers or 'hacks' were derided by authors like Pope or Fielding, but not all of these "drudges of the pen, the manufacturers of literature, who have set up for authors" (Johnson 2020 [1751], 351; *The Rambler* no. 145) were 'slaves' to the booksellers; some of them enjoyed a good reputation, were respectably middle-class, and worked with leading publishers; these include Thomas Birch (1705–1766), Oliver Goldsmith (1728–1774), Charlotte Lennox (c. 1730–1804), Tobias Smollett (1721–1771), and others, some of whom are still remembered as original authors of new works but who also dabbled in many literary projects, editions, and compilations on the side. They usually worked on commission and were paid by the sheet (the printed output of their writing) by a publisher who then owned the copyright (Feather 1988, 104).

In 1758, the Grub Street hack James Ralph (1705–1762) published his pamphlet *The Case of Authors by Profession or Trade, Stated*, in which he demanded fair payment for writers within the structures of the book trade. Writers were to be treated just like other professionals; he contrasted these against the "Voluntier, or Gentleman-Writer" who did not need to earn money from writing. The 'gentlemen-writers' created false expectations with the public that authors were not like other tradespeople and did not need remuneration for their labour. With this pamphlet, Ralph began a debate about literature as a profession which would be picked up again in the early nineteenth century in the "dignity of literature" controversy (Salmon 2013). Literature became a form of work, of labour: "the work of writing" (Siskin 1998). This was offensive to the amateurs, to gentlemen like Alexander Pope, who looked down upon 'jobbing' writers. In his mock-epic poem *The Dunciad* (1728), Pope vividly and viciously lampooned the reign of 'Dulness', and in the *Epistle to Dr Arbuthnot* (1735) he railed against the inept hacks of "Grub Street" (2006, 340, ll. 109–114):

> One dedicates in high heroic prose,
> And ridicules beyond a hundred foes:
> One from all Grub Street will my fame defend,

And more abusive, calls himself my friend.
This prints my *Letters*, that expects a bribe,
And others roar aloud, 'Subscribe, subscribe.'

Grub Street was an actual London street that quickly became the name for a new condition of text production: hard graft, and often precarious living, in the literary equivalent of a sweatshop. Johnson himself, in his *Dictionary*, defines Grub Street as "Originally the name of a street in Moorfields in London, much inhabited by writers of small histories, dictionaries, and temporary poems; whence any mean production is called *grubstreet*" (1755).

'Grub Street' writers and printers were busy experimenting with new forms under new conditions of production and reception. In his satire *A Tale of a Tub*, Swift's author persona refers to himself as an "adopted [. . .] member of that illustrious fraternity", "the Grub Street brotherhood" (2008, 29), writers of low repute whose "productions" were "designed for the pleasure and delight of mortal man" – not, in other words, destined for immortality and eternal fame – and whose "post in the commonwealth of wit and learning" was assured (29). In a letter to his publisher, Benjamin Tooke, Swift referred to the *Tale of a Tub* as "so perfect a Grubstreet piece, it will be forgotten in a week" (29 June 1710; 2008, 200).

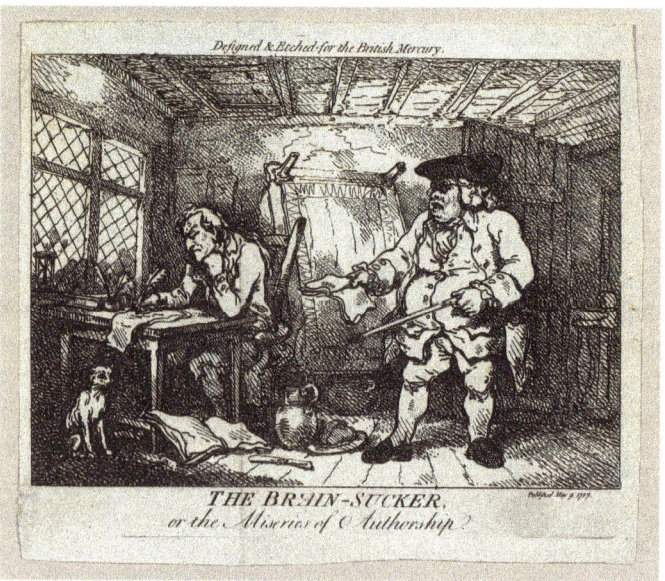

Fig. 7: The Brain-sucker, or the Miseries of Authorship (1787), etching attrib. to Thomas Rowlandson.
Source: Royal Collection, London.

Towards the end of the eighteenth century, the image of the hack as an impoverished writer exploited by evil booksellers had become a firmly established literary trope (see Böker 1987, Berensmeyer 2014, Berensmeyer et al. 2015). In one satire from 1787, "The Brain-Sucker: Or, the Distress of Authorship", starvation and madness await the young genius who leaves his rural home for London and ends up trapped in a garret where he must do literary slave work for a ruthless publisher (fig. 7) – until the young writer's father comes to the rescue. This satire may be directed at the bookseller as a capitalist exploiter of talent, but also at the idea of uneducated country boys lighting out for the literary territory. It refers to poetry as a "disorder", an infection (Oswald 1787, 22), a "dreadful distemper" (47); the poet is described as displaying "the strongest symptoms of insanity" (15). As an authorship satire, "The Brain-Sucker" takes part in the polemic about writing as a profession. In an implicit contrast to the cultural ideal of the autonomous gentleman author, it presents the world of literary labour as dangerous, contaminated, and contaminating, and it shows poetic inspiration as a disease. Because "The Brain-Sucker" is narrated from a socially inferior position, in a letter by the young writer's father, Farmer Homely, it could be taken as arguing for a more moderate view on authorial professionalism, as claiming, in other words, that it is better to be a freelance professional than a poor enslaved genius and a puppet of cruel market forces. Most notably, "The Brain-Sucker" is a satire in prose rather than verse; this seems fitting for its unpretentious narrator, but it also places this text outside of the much-discussed genre of English verse satire from Dryden to Pope and Swift. Its manner is more directly urban and realistic in an almost (proto-)Dickensian way, fusing the material reality of the "distress of authorship" with imaginary and conceptual resources such as the inflated idea of the Romantic genius.

In this chapter, we have mostly been looking at the material conditions of literary life in the eighteenth century. The idea that the biography of an author could make for interesting reading, or yield a coherent story worth telling, is itself symptomatic of this new-found interest in the literary life. Early in his career, Samuel Johnson set a trend by publishing, anonymously, *An Account of the Life of Mr Richard Savage, Son of the Earl Rivers* (1744), possibly the first full-length literary biography in English. Savage (c. 1697–1743) had died the previous year in a debtors' prison in Bristol after a scandalous and eventful life on the edge of destitution, even though he claimed to be the illegitimate son of an earl. Johnson, himself an ambitious young hack at the time, saw the commercial and artistic potential of writing down the story of Savage, whom he had known personally and whose friend he had been. In writing this biography of a writer, Johnson was interested in the conditions of literary production and how they affected a work's final form. He shaped Savage's rather chaotic life into a tragic story that combines sensationalism with moral instruction. His narrative is often defensive about Savage, but also critical of his folly and his moral failings. This was the crucial departure: Johnson did not produce a one-sided account but a nuanced portrait of his subject, a truly modern biography. It may also have contributed to the formation of the realist novel (Johnson 2016).

Gray's Elegy

In the eighteenth century, the 'lives of the poets' became amenable to being turned into literature; but there was also a clear awareness that fame would not be available to everyone – most authors, like most people, would be forgotten. A focus on transience and mortality is notable in eighteenth-century poetry of the so-called 'graveyard' school (Thomas Parnell, Edward Young, Robert Blair, and others). One poem stands out: Thomas Gray's (1716–1771) *Elegy Written in a Country Church-Yard,* perhaps begun 1746–1747, completed in 1750, printed as a seven-page pamphlet in 1751. Gray's "Elegy" achieved immediate fame and ran through eight editions in only two years – showing how poetry, in eighteenth-century print culture, could be a popular literary genre, rivalling the novel. The poem marks a shift from neoclassical lucidity towards the obscure and the sublime around mid-century. Like Ann Finch's (1661–1720) "Nocturnal Rêverie" from 1713 (Fairer and Gerrard 2015, 33–35), its speaker describes the 'solemnity' of a night scene: "Now fades the glimmering Landscape on the Sight / And all the Air a solemn Stillness holds" (ll. 5–6). But here the speaker's solitude and his individuality are emphasised much more strongly. The speaker is not in unison with nature but separate from it.

The speaker, visiting a village graveyard, reflects on the obscure destinies of the villagers who lie buried there, "to dumb Forgetfulness a Prey" (l. 85), and begins to imagine what their lives may have been like. He then, in an ironic turn of self-scrutiny and self-reflection, addresses himself (ll. 93–100):

> For thee, who mindful of th' unhonour'd Dead,
> Dost in these Lines their artless Tale relate;
> If chance, by lonely Contemplation led,
> Some hidden [later ed.: kindred] Spirit shall inquire thy Fate,
>
> Haply [= perhaps] some hoary-headed Swain may say,
> 'Oft have we seen him at the Peep of Dawn
> 'Brushing with hasty Steps the Dews away
> 'To meet the Sun upon the upland Lawn.

The poet has changed roles: he imagines himself dead and imagines an old villager remembering him. It is the villager, an illiterate rustic, who is given direct speech here. The way in which he remembers the poet as a somewhat quirky stranger and outsider figure is perhaps intended as a form of self-reflecting irony by the poet himself. It is uncertain how seriously Gray took his own writing: he engaged in many other activities apart from poetry, from antiquarian studies to botany; although people saw him as a potential new Milton, he turned his back on a poetic career when he was forty years old and declined the offer of the poet laureateship in 1756. But this poem certainly prefigures the idea we have of the typical 'romantic' poet:

> 'Hard by yon Wood, now frowning [later ed.: smiling] as in Scorn,
> 'Mutt'ring his wayward Fancies he wou'd rove,
> 'Now drooping, woeful wan, like one forlorn,
> 'Or craz'd with Care, or cross'd in hopeless Love.
> (ll. 105–108)

The villager then goes on to recall how one day the poet was gone, and how he witnessed the poet's funeral. He then directly turns to address the speaker: "'Approach and read (for thou canst read) the Lay, / 'Grav'd on the Stone beneath yon aged Thorn.'" In the next three stanzas, which bring the poem to a close, we are given "The EPITAPH" – the speaker, and we as readers, are reading the inscription on the poet's headstone. It is detached from the rest of the text by a heading and is printed in italics. It describes the poet as "*A Youth to Fortune and to Fame unknown*", prone to melancholy but blessed with a heightened sensibility. The headstone also directly addresses its reader:

> *No farther seek his Merits to disclose,*
> *Or draw his Frailties from their dread Abode,*
> *(There they alike in trembling Hope repose)*
> *The Bosom of his Father and his God.*[35]
> (ll. 125–128)

Apart from serving as a trigger for melancholy reflection and self-reflection, the graveyard in the poem opens a space for a cascade of situations of reading and writing, from reading the inscriptions on other peoples' headstones to composing one's own imaginary epitaph. On one level, its theme is the poet's achievement of "moral choice and resolution" in the face of likely future obscurity (Weinbrot

---

[35] Qtd. from the William Andrews Clark Memorial Library copy of the first edition (1751), available online at http://www.gutenberg.org/files/15409/15409-h/15409-h.htm, where one can also consult a facsimile of the Eton College manuscript. Fairer and Gerrard (2015, 419–423) print a 1753 version of the text with a few minor authorial corrections and revisions.

1978). But the poem also reflects the more complex media situation of literary writing in the eighteenth century by evoking its multiple dimensions: public writing, primary orality (the illiterate villager speaking), secondary orality (the poet's interior speech and poetic composition which follows oral patterns of memory), poetic literacy/intertextuality (levels of intertextual allusions to older poetry, which turn the text into "an ample page / Rich with the spoils of time" [ll. 49–50]), and finally print, the medium in which Gray's poem was published.

Fig. 8: A Country Churchyard. Verse from Gray's Elegy, 1790. Aquatint on paper by Marie C. Prestel after Thomas Gainsborough.
Source: Paul Mellon Collection, Yale Center for British Art.

One could read this poem as a reflection not only on fashionable melancholy subjects and as a prefiguration of Romanticism, but also as a reflection on cultural memory and on different media of tradition and remembrance, including poetry itself and its communicative function in eighteenth-century print culture. Poetry as a literate and literary form of memory can record the speech patterns of the illiterate villager, whose memory is based on oral tradition; it is equally capable of including an inscription sculpted on a gravestone. The poem stages itself as a meeting-place of several media of memory. It demonstrates that eighteenth-century poetry had become 'multi-medial' in a context of a generalised print culture (see also fig. 8; Berensmeyer 2009).

Gray's "Elegy" displays and reflects upon its condition of having been *written* rather than composed, and having been written in an unusual location: a rural graveyard. In its printed form, it embodies a series of cultural discontinuities: between an older form of poetry that was usually distributed in manuscript or in limited print-runs for a select audience, a form that was still to a great extent oral and aural (as well as tactile), and a modern form of textuality printed and distributed widely for an unknown and diverse readership. In this media-historical shift, these two distinct forms of communication (intimate, close, and familiar on the one hand; uncertain, cast adrift, and distant on the other) place a new kind of tension and stress on the elegy, one of the most highly charged traditional lyric forms (Mulholland 2008). To produce an elegy in this media-historical context is risky, but Gray's may be one of the most successful attempts to bring together, in a cohesive if not fully coherent form, the tensions and discontinuities of eighteenth-century culture and media.

As Michele Sharp argues, Gray's "Elegy" replaces the elegiac trope of "transmission of voice" with "a transmission of texts" (2002, 6). It translates specific acts of mourning into a more general dynamics of cultural remembrance from a distance, thereby confirming the potential of poetry as a form of literary expression in the age of the novel. Unlike Milton's "Lycidas" (1637), Gray's "Elegy" has no immediate occasion such as mourning the death of a friend. Its act of commemoration is directed towards the numerous unremembered villagers, "rude Forefathers of the Hamlet" (l. 16), who are buried in the churchyard. By removing the poet from the centre of urban modernity (London) to a rural graveyard, the poem invokes and projects its own alternative vision of community. Paradoxically, this creation of an alternative audience is only possible by means of print: the handwritten text must leave the graveyard and, by means of the printing press, return from the country to the city to achieve its goal of becoming culturally performative. If eighteenth-century poetry wished to compete with the novel, it needed to adapt to the new conditions of literary production and consumption.

6 Paper Worlds: The Novel as Object and Form

Of "Golden Age" do poets tell,
The "Age of Brass" they laud as well;
While ev'ry age hath serv'd by times
A peg on which to hang their rhymes.
But as the world goes rolling on,
Strange times indeed we've chanced upon,
For Fashions progress never lags –
And now we're in the "Age of Rags".
– For paper now is all the rage
And nothing else will suit the age.[36]
  "The Age of Paper", popular song, 1862

In the eighteenth century, printed texts came to dominate public forms of communication. Professional practices of authorship and publication were consolidated. The growing print industry created an ever-increasing demand for paper. Paper at this time was made from linen rags, but the supply of recycled textiles (sold by ragpickers) was not sufficient, so prices for paper rose and inferior materials began to be used. Production sped up with the invention of the Fourdrinier machine, which allowed paper to be produced in a continuous roll instead of single sheets, from 1807 onwards. Machine-made paper became common in the 1830s (Lesser 2019, 230). Paper made from wood pulp was introduced in 1843. The figures are quite staggering: "production of paper in the United Kingdom increased from about 11,000 tons [. . .] in 1800 to 100,000 tons in 1861 [. . .] and to 652,000 tons [. . .] in 1900" (Innis 2007, 184). Such a high demand for paper cannot be attributed to a single type of book or literary genre, of course, and books were not the only product of print culture – handbills, posters, greeting cards, newspapers, and magazines all needed a steady supply of paper. But the novel, and the continuing demand for new novels all the time, depended on paper more than any other literary form. The novel was, after all, "the only [or at least the first] literary genre to have been invented since the invention of printing" (Feather 1988, 57), and its history cannot be properly understood without looking more closely at the connection between novels, print, and paper.

---

36 Music and lyrics by Henry Walker, performed by Howard Paul in a suit made entirely of paper. For the complete lyrics, see https://rhollick.wordpress.com/2018/09/17/the-age-of-paper/. Date of access: 21 Aug. 2021.

Open Access. © 2022 Ingo Berensmeyer, published by De Gruyter. This work is licensed under the Creative Commons Attribution-NonCommercial-NoDerivatives 4.0 International License.
https://doi.org/10.1515/9783110784459-006

Novel Habits

What aided the wide-ranging circulation of novels among potential readers was Francis Kirkman's (1632– c. 1680) idea to open the first commercial circulating library in 1661. This created new possibilities for distributing books to readers who could not afford to, or did not want to, buy them but were willing and able to borrow books for a fee. Provincial bookshops soon caught on, and by the end of the eighteenth century there were circulating libraries all over the country, creating a much larger market for novels (Feather 2006, 49, 62–63). In 1862, *Chambers's Encyclopaedia* defined "circulating library" as "a collection of books lent out on hire – circulated from hand to hand".[37] Novels – fictional stories with a built-in obsolescence that would be read once and then discarded for new novels – were an ideal literary form for this new system of distribution, and they usually made up the biggest part of a circulating library's stock.

Due to economic, legal, and social changes, the market for books grew steadily in the eighteenth century. Popular books could now exceed the traditional size of a print-run of about 1,000 copies. Publishers began to advertise their books to retail booksellers in quarterly lists of recent publications, the so-called 'term catalogues', from 1668 to 1711 (Feather 1988, 61). The term catalogues are an interesting source of evidence, giving us a better sense of the role of literature in the book market. According to one study, most books announced in 1700 belonged to the category of 'divinity' (theology), 52 %. Only six percent were poetry, and fictional texts made up only about three percent of the total (Simons 2010). But these catalogues were highly selective, and the number of titles actually published was much higher.

Most publishers and printers resided in London, but they became increasingly interested in provincial customers. After 1732, lists of new books regularly appeared in *The Gentleman's Magazine*, a monthly with a wide circulation that was succeeded by similar book trade journals such as *Bent's Monthly Literary Advertiser* (1805–1858), *The Publishers' Circular* (1837–1939) and *The Bookseller* (from 1858) (Feather 1988, 78, 99; Lesser 2019, 296). *The Gentleman's Magazine* established the word 'magazine', which had previously meant 'storehouse' (from Arabic *makzin*) as a term for a periodical publication. Its business model consisted to a large extent of reprinting a selection of that month's essays from weekly journals.

---

37 *Chambers's Encyclopaedia: A Dictionary of Universal Knowledge for the People* (London: W. and R. Chambers, 1862), Internet Archive, https://archive.org/details/cu31924087904631/page/n8/mode/2up. Date of access: 3 March 2020.

Journals included more advertising for books, and reviews began to appear in newspapers and magazines in the mid-eighteenth century, such as the *Monthly Review* (from 1749), edited by Ralph Griffiths (c. 1720–1803), and the *Critical Review* (from 1756), edited by Tobias Smollett. Smollett was also the first writer to pen a novel specifically for periodical publication: his *Launcelot Greaves* was "published in twenty-five parts in *The British Magazine* between January 1760 and December 1761" (Feather 2006, 61). Over the century, there was a marked rise in the production of titles that we would categorise as fiction. While these remained a tiny minority until 1700, they increased up to more than 140 titles per year in the 1790s (Simons 2009). Titles that were explicitly labelled as 'novels' took off from the 1760s onwards. The 'rise of the novel' is a very real phenomenon, whatever its cause or causes may have been; there has been some disagreement on this question ever since Ian Watt published his classic study, *The Rise of the Novel*, in 1957 (Skinner 2001, 3–28; Hammond and Regan 2006).

One such 'novel' kind of story, published in the *London Magazine* in 1779, purports to be narrated by the very paper it is printed on. The pretence that the narrative voice emanates from the printed text of a sermon highlights the proximity of fiction and religious literature on the eighteenth-century book market (Stein 2020, 139, 153). Told in the first person, "Adventures of a Quire of Paper" recounts the entire production process of paper from flaxseed to linen rags as a cruel experience, similar to the trials and tribulations of writing materials in the Old English riddle (see ch. 2). It then proceeds to the various uses to which cloth and paper can be put, not all of which are as innocent and clean as a printed sermon. For example:

> In the form of a pastoral I was rubbing the grease off a gridiron in an eating house; and as A kind Warning to Christians, clapped under a pot of porter just taken from the fire, over which a chairman and a drayman were quarrelling, and damning each other with all their might. Here, as A Picture of Delicate Tenderness, I was pinned round the fat of a haunch of venison, in an alderman's kitchen; and there, as An Essay on the Powers of Harmony, strained over half an old comb, out of which a chimney sweeper's imp twanged something like the Black Joke. ("Adventures" 1779, 451)

Readers of this 'it-narrative' (i.e., a story told by an object, a popular eighteenth-century genre) were pointed to the history of the very stuff they were holding in their hands while reading, turning the material text into a self-conscious medium (Lupton 2012).

Most novels, like the "Adventures of a Quire of Paper", were ephemeral products, written because there was popular demand for some light reading. Novels were soon forgotten and replaced by new ones. That is also why they were called 'novels', the alternative name 'romance' being soon pushed to the margins: they catered to a new desire for permanent novelty. As John Feather remarks, the novel's value for the book trade was precisely "not in its literary merit but in its essential triviality"; there was a demand for a "continuous supply of new novels" which publishers were only too happy to satisfy (2006, 60–61). The market gradually changed its focus from reprinting profitable old texts to printing ever new ones, and this created a permanent demand for authors to write new works, the majority of which were never reprinted. The "slaughterhouse of literature" (Moretti 2013, 63–89) was born together with the consumer society (Plumb 1982). Novels were the first literary genre created not to be read, exactly, but *consumed*, enjoyed, devoured, gobbled up, then discarded and replaced. One customer of a circulating library in Warwick, a butcher named John Latimer, is on record to have borrowed, and likely consumed, a volume a day for one winter month in 1771 (Fergus 2006, 113).

Together with the novel, new reading habits emerged. Reading became extensive rather than intensive, a pursuit of leisure rather than learning, and a mode of distraction instead of focused attention (Engelsing 1974; Moretti 2013, 174). However, this reading for entertainment did not mean that people were less interested in facts and information; history and travel literature were also in great demand. The novel profited from this, too, because it grew increasingly what we now call 'realistic': it catered less for readers' appetites for the exotic and fantastic (though it did that, too) but it supplied stories about real life – stories about social climbing, moral pressures, funny incidents, families and individuals, aunts and uncles, crime and criminals, wealth and poverty, love and desire, in short: the stuff of life. Next to plausible characters, settings, and events, and a marked interest in particularity – "particular individuals having particular experiences at particular times and at particular places" (Watt 1957, 31), Ian Watt identifies "formal realism" (32) as a key feature of the novel: techniques of writing that evoked an atmosphere of credibility, authenticity, and verisimilitude. Examples of this are the eye-witness or survivor narrative; these formed the basis of travel writing, but they were also prominent in early novels like Aphra Behn's (1640–1689) *Oroonoko* (1688) and Daniel Defoe's *Robinson Crusoe* (1719).

What eighteenth-century readers looked for in a novel was neatly summed up by William Congreve (1670–1729), writing in 1692: novels, he says, "Come near us, and represent to us Intrigues in practice, delight us with Accidents and odd *Events*, but not such as are wholly unusual or unpresidented, such which not being so distant from our Belief bring also the pleasure nearer us" (qtd. in Hammond and Regan 2006, 29). According to this early definition, novels were presented as more familiar, more credible, and more down-to-earth than other literary forms; but the keyword here is, above all, "pleasure".

Most early eighteenth-century novels, from Aphra Behn onwards, belonged to the genre of 'amatory fiction' – steamy potboilers filled with intrigue, seductions, and duels (Ballaster 1992). These went out of fashion in the 1730s. Given its ephemeral nature, the novel was under pressure, early on, to reinvent new genres that had a novelty appeal for readers. When readers tired of amatory fiction, they took to Samuel Richardson's (1689–1761) moralising or Henry Fielding's social comedy, and later they moved on to sentimental novels, Gothic novels, historical novels, Newgate novels, silver-fork novels, *bildungsromane*, sensation novels, detective novels, science fiction novels, and so on. The novel is the 'dirtiest' of literary forms in that contamination is its basic principle. There is nothing a novel cannot include: letters, memoirs, journalism, philosophy, satire, travel, poetry, etc. A corresponding sense is that the novel is the only literary form to do justice to the full complexity of an increasingly complex and quickly changing modern world. Fielding, in the preface to his novel *Joseph Andrews* (1742), was only half joking (and echoing Polonius on dramatic genres in *Hamlet*) when he ennobled the novel by calling it "a comic epic-poem in prose" (1985, 25). Theorists of the novel would later follow him in referring to the novel as "the epic of an age in which the extensive totality of life is no longer directly given, in which the immanence of meaning in life has become a problem" (Lukács 2000, 186). Whatever else they did, early novels also often provided guidance for life in a world that had become more complex, by presenting models of possible experience. Conversely, readers would use literature – essay periodicals as well as novels – as media for self-fashioning, either as a means of self-education or as a way of enhancing their social reputation, for example by demonstrating their sensitivity through crying in public over a copy of a fashionable sentimental novel like Henry Mackenzie's (1745–1831) *The Man of Feeling* (1771) (Lesser 2019, 226).

Samuel Richardson

Such guidance could take the form of moral orientation; nowhere more so than in the novels of Samuel Richardson. One of the most highly respected novelists of the eighteenth century, Richardson was also a printer, and not a minor one at that: starting out as a joiner's son, he owned three printing-houses and employed more than forty people in the 1750s (Sale 1950, Dussinger 2012). He produced not only books but also journals, posters, and other jobbing work, but he apparently also began writing early on. It is said that he composed letters for young lovers at the tender age of thirteen. After his first wife and all their six children had died young, he married the daughter of a fellow printer in 1733, and four daughters of this marriage survived. In the same year he wrote and published a conduct book intended for readers from the lower ranks of society: *The Apprentice's Vade Mecum; or, Young Man's Pocket-Companion*. A series of 'familiar letters' that he composed on the problems and concerns of everyday life was published in 1741 as *Letters Written to and for Particular Friends, on the most Important Occasions. Directing Not Only the Requisite Style and Forms to Be Observed in Writing Familiar Letters; but How to Think and Act Justly and Prudently, in the Common Concerns of Human Life*. This inspired Richardson to write a novel in letters. *Pamela, or Virtue Rewarded* (1741) became a massive hit. It combines the form of fictional letters with the titillating story of a fifteen-year-old servant girl who must defend her virtue and virginity against her employer and molester, Mr B—. Written in a mere two months between November 1739 and January 1740, *Pamela* is told in letters and extracts from Pamela's journal. By focusing on her experiences, her mental anguish, and her inner conflict between obedience and self-protection, *Pamela* can be considered a forerunner of the psychological novel. The letters among six correspondents aim for a sense of urgency, realism, and immediacy, as if events were being described as they happen. Richardson called this "writing to the moment" in a letter to his friend, Lady Bradshaigh (14 Feb. 1754; Richardson 1964, 289). While he did not invent the epistolary novel as a form, Richardson gave it a new sense of purpose and perfected its use. In an age when letters were being written and delivered promptly all the time, this was not only the normal way of communicating with people who did not live in the same place. Letters as a medium also afforded new ways of exploring the inner lives of literary characters in a novel.

The trials and tribulations of Pamela, who in the end manages to transform Mr B—'s desire into love and to steer him towards marriage, made the novel into a huge success, even internationally. It became a "media event" (Warner 1998, 176–230; Keymer and Sabor 2005). *Pamela* went through six editions in the first year and was serialised in the newspaper *All Alive and Merry*. There were *Pamela* plays, translations, continuations, and parodies, waxworks, even *Pamela* merchandise, such as fans. Richardson quickly wrote a sequel, *Pamela in her Exalted Condition* (1741), showing Pamela as the perfect wife and mother, to protect his literary property from other continuations that were less morally inclined. The moral debate about *Pamela*, however, has never really ended. Is Pamela's virtue sincere or sham? Is she an ingénue or a gold-digger? The early readers of *Pamela* were divided into "pro-Pamelists" and "anti-Pamelists". Other authors made fun of Richardson's earnestness and of the lowly station of his heroine. Among the immediate literary responses to *Pamela* are Eliza Haywood's (1693–1756) *Anti-Pamela* and Henry Fielding's *Shamela* (both 1741).[38] Fielding's spoof not only replaces Pamela's morality with expediency, he also has her write at ludicrously inappropriate moments, making fun of Richardson's signature technique of "writing to the moment":

> *Thursday Night, Twelve o'Clock.*
> Mrs. *Jervis* and I are just in Bed, and the Door unlocked; if my Master should come — Odsbobs! I hear him just coming in at the Door. You see I write in the present Tense, as Parson *Williams* says. Well, he is in Bed between us, we both shamming a Sleep, he steals his Hand into my Bosom, which I, as if in my Sleep, press close to me with mine, and then pretend to awake. (Fielding 2004, 247)

The parodies of *Pamela* show the novel struggling for its place in culture (high or low, or somewhere in the middle?) and argue about its literary respectability. What were novels for? Was their success to be celebrated or deplored? Richardson sought to resolve this dilemma by combining sensational stories with a consistent moral vision. In *Pamela,* this is declared in the subtitle, *Virtue Rewarded*; but perhaps the title implies that, normally in life, it is not, or other attitudes are rewarded instead. Richardson continued to use the epistolary form in his subsequent novels, *Clarissa* and *Sir Charles Grandison*, which grew longer and more complex, sacrificing plot for intricate social and psychological nuance. As Samuel Johnson remarked, "if you were to read Richardson for the story, your impatience would be so much fretted that you would hang yourself. But you must read him for the sentiment, and consider the story as only giving occasion to the sentiment" (Boswell 1992, 427). The sentiment is a key to a growing interest in authentic depictions of emotion in the novel, depictions that could be enjoyed alone or in public. Richardson regularly read aloud from his manuscripts to a growing circle of male and (mostly) female friends who met in his weekend house in Fulham. He apparently worked hard to keep his texts short, but his interest in minute psychological analysis inevitably made them expand more and more.

Clarissa (1747–1748) tells "the history of a young lady" (thus the subtitle) in letters among over twenty correspondents, running to a million words, making this one of the longest novels in English. This time, the heroine is a young woman from a rich and ambitious family, and her antagonist, the aptly named Lovelace (= loveless), is an aristocratic rake. But this time, unlike in *Pamela*, there is no happy ending. After being drugged and raped by Lovelace, Clarissa almost loses her sanity; she begins to prepare for death and finally dies. Lovelace is killed by her cousin in a duel.

---

[38] For a collection of *all* contemporary responses, see Keymer and Sabor 2001.

Richardson set out to correct what he perceived as the early novel's devious ways of appealing to lower instincts rather than the intellect and nobler sentiments. But he also built on earlier romance fiction, most notably the amatory fiction of Aphra Behn, Eliza Haywood, and Delarivier Manley (1663 or c. 1670–1724; e.g., *The Adventures of Rivella*, 1714). He adapted these stories, in which women were regularly seduced and abandoned by men, for the moral benefit of his readers – or so he claimed. Richardson explained his agenda in a letter to Aaron Hill, saying that certain stories, "if written in an easy and natural manner [. . .] might possibly introduce a new species of writing, that might possibly turn young people into a course of reading different from the pomp and parade of romance-writing, and dismissing the improbable and marvellous, with which novels generally abound, might tend to promote the cause of religion and virtue" (1964, 41). Yet, as a printer and a businessman, he also knew what kind of book would sell, and *Pamela* in particular attests to his shrewd sense of commerce in its combination of virtue-mongering and sensationalism.

The conflict that came to a head with *Pamela* was built into the novel from its beginnings. Was reading novels meant more for the mind or for the body? Were its pleasures cognitive or emotional, even physical? In other words, was novel-reading good or bad? This question was to pursue the novel for quite a long time and has never disappeared entirely – although, in the twentieth century, moral panics about reading the wrong kinds of texts were gradually replaced by anxieties about not reading at all. In the mid-eighteenth century, above all, the success of *Pamela* "made clear the novel's cultural possibilities and financial rewards, and established the respectability of the form" (Ingrassia 2004, 7).

Novels were closely associated with the medium of the printed book and its new modes of nationwide and even international distribution, reaching a potentially large audience of men as well as women from all social classes, even children. The first publisher to introduce a uniform 'edition binding', one John Newbery (1713–1767), is also considered the father of children's literature because he published the first books specifically for children, beginning with *A Little Pretty Pocket-Book* (1744) and *Goody Two-Shoes* (1765). He must be one of the first publishers to think of product placement. He also sold a patent medicine, Dr. James's Fever Powder, and in the children's book *Goody Two-Shoes* (1765) the heroine's father is "seized by a violent Fever in a Place where Dr *James's* Powder was not to be had, and where he died miserably" (Grenby 2013, 93, italics original).

Laurence Sterne

Already in the mid-eighteenth century, some novelists were aware of the strangeness and newness of this form of communication, addressing a large number of readers, even creating a new form of social community through novels. Richardson saw himself as "introduc[ing] a new species of writing" (1964, 41); Fielding likewise declared himself to be "the Founder of a new Province of Writing" (2005, 77), asserting a new, more intimate relationship between authors and readers made possible through print. The novel thus became a forum for competing discourses, and its formal flexibility made it ideal for presenting epistemological, moral, and political issues from different viewpoints (Nünning 1992, 64). The Anglo-Irish writer Laurence Sterne (1713–1768), like Richardson and Fielding, used the novel as a testing ground for ideas of human nature, perception, individuality, and virtue that were currently being debated in society. In *The Life and Opinions of Tristram Shandy, Gentleman* (1759–1767), Sterne also reflected in a parodic and playful manner on the novel's forms of mediation, its dependence on the printed page. "Tristram Shandy" is a telling name, "shandy" meaning "wild" or "somewhat crazy" (*OED*), and the novel has a lot of fun with conventions of narration but also with typography, including different typefaces, diagrams, dashes, asterisks, blank pages, and other devices. At the end of chapter twelve in volume one, there are two black pages, to mourn the death of Parson Yorick (named after the dead jester from Shakespeare's *Hamlet*). In volume four, there is a chapter missing between chapters 23 and 25, and Tristram tells us that he has torn out ten pages, claiming that "the book is more perfect and complete by wanting the chapter, than having it" (1985, 311). In the original edition, the pages following the missing chapter were wrongly numbered, jumping from 146 to 156, with the even numbers now on the right-hand pages, something that is never done in printing. Something had seriously gone wrong here – and the book as artefact signalled this flaw deliberately as part of its communicative purpose. Another famous visual moment in the book is the blank page in volume six, where the reader is introduced to the lovely, desirable widow Wadman. Here is the text of chapter 38:

> To conceive this right, – call for pen and ink – here's paper ready to your hand. – Sit down, Sir, paint her to your own mind – as like your mistress as you can – as unlike your wife as your conscience will let you – 'tis all one to me – please but your own fancy in it.
>
> [blank page]
>
> — Was ever any thing in Nature so sweet! – so exquisite!
> – Then, dear Sir, how could my uncle Toby resist it?

> Thrice happy book! thou wilt have one page, at least, within thy covers, which MALICE will not blacken and which IGNORANCE cannot misrepresent. (450–452)

Sterne and his printers went to great lengths to insert some marbled pages into every copy of the book, each a unique, hand-stamped specimen (de Voogd 2006, 110). His narrator refers to this as the "motley emblem" (Sterne 1985, 232) of his work – each buyer of the book gets their own. No modern edition has yet replicated this, rendering them instead in black and white. Sterne's novel, in its original form, thrived on the conflict between text and typography, their "ever surprising layout" and "constant flux" (de Voogd 2006, 117) turning every page into "a living unit" (116). In this novel as a print artefact, words and nonverbal features of the book combine to create an entirely new visual experience that points forward to the experimental procedures of some modernist and postmodernist fiction and the design features of art books that blur the line between text and image, as in Tom Phillips's (1937–) *A Humument* (1970, 2016).

The Novel in Nineteenth-Century Print Culture

In the nineteenth century, all processes of book production were gradually mechanised. Using water and later steam presses, a large number of sheets could be printed more quickly. These new technologies were first used for newspapers; the *Times* had the first steam press in 1814. The technique of lithography, invented by the German Alois Senefelder in 1798, made it possible to print high-quality illustrations, in addition to existing technologies of woodcuts and engravings, which were also made easier and cheaper by using steel plates instead of copper. The photomechanical reproduction of photographs in print became possible towards the end of the nineteenth century. In France, Honoré de Balzac (1799–1850) opens his novel *Lost Illusions* (*Illusions perdues*, 1837–1843) with a reflection on the technological progress in the print industry, where wooden presses are being replaced by "ravenous machines" like the British "Stanhope press" (Balzac 2004, 3). Their hunger, increased by the rise of periodicals, demands an ever-growing supply of paper, and the search for a cheaper method of papermaking dominates the third part of the novel, "An Inventor's Tribulations". It describes how the struggling young printer David Séchard is robbed of the fruits of his innovation by several scheming antagonists. More poignantly, *Lost Illusions* describes the world of publishing as brutally materialistic and only interested in short-term gain, a world in which books will be cheaper not only in their price, but also in their material and literary quality. Thanks to cheaper ways of making paper pulp out of "vegetable substances" (515), books can become ephemeral, disposable commodities. "What a shame it is", exclaims David, "that our era cannot make books which will last!" (112). He is talking about the quality of paper, but the novel extends this lament to the quality of literature. The fate of David's best friend, the aspiring writer Lucien de Rubempré, illustrates the debasement of literature in his stellar rise and fall as author and journalist. Ironically, Lucien's real name is Chardon ("thistle"), referring to the very same material that David uses as his raw material for pulp ("nettles and thistles", 515). Lucien's weed-like opportunism and short-termism turns him briefly into a "fashionable commodity" (Moretti 2000, 134) but prevents him from achieving any lasting literary fame. The age of disposable reading matter has begun.

Next to new technologies of printing and papermaking, the most important infrastructure that ensured faster distribution of books and newspapers was the railway. By 1850, Britain had a complete railway system. This created a new readership for novels yet again, because there was now a demand for books to be sold at train stations to be read during the journey. Cheap book series were the answer. The newsagent W. H. Smith (1825–1891) had an exclusive contract with the London and North Western Railway. Beginning at Euston station, he built a small empire of railway bookstalls, counting more than five hundred by the end of the 1860s (Wilson 1985). In 1848, when Smith opened his first shop, George Routledge began publishing a profitable book series called the *Railway Library*, cheap one-volume novels and other books aimed at the rail travellers' market. Other publishers followed: John Murray launched *Reading for the Rail* in 1851, and Longman came up with a *Traveller's Library* series in the same year (Lesser 2019, 280). William Henry Smith went on to be an eminent Victorian politician, given the nickname "Old Morality" by *Punch* (Davenport-Hines 2009). He would not have enjoyed his name being associated with the phenomenon of the "railway novel", which became a byword for popular entertainment, the nineteenth-century equivalent of the airport thriller. These so-called sensation novels, including Wilkie Collins's (1824–1889) *The Woman in White* (1859–1860) and Mary Braddon's (1835–1915) *Lady Audley's Secret* (1862), were bestsellers notorious for their allegedly unhealthy physical effects on readers' nerves. If read on a train, it was feared that the strain on the nervous system might be downright dangerous; readers, however, did not seem to mind (Daly 1999). 'Railway literature' became a byword for these cheap books from 1849 onwards. Their printed paper bindings inaugurated an "explosion of color" (Lesser 2019, 283) made possible by the new technique of chromolithography (see fig. 9 for a lurid example that literally shows an explosion on the cover).

Enormous amounts of paper were consumed in the nineteenth century to satisfy an ever-growing mass market in literature, first and foremost the novel. Taxes on paper were abolished in 1861, and the technology of stereotyping gave

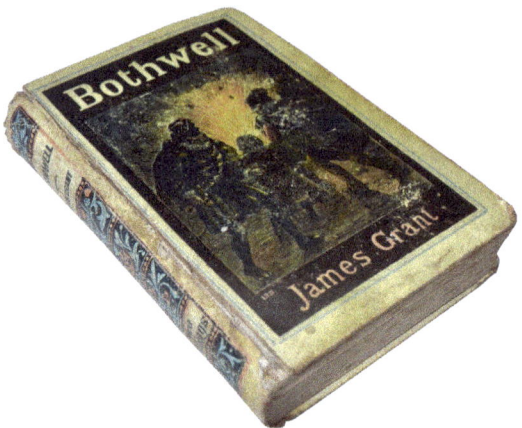

Fig. 9: James Grant, *Bothwell* (London: Routledge, n.d. [c. 1884]), priced at 2s and part of Routledge's Railway Library.
Source: Ingo Berensmeyer.

publishers a cheap and simple way of keeping text in type and producing reprints or new editions of older texts at very low cost. The literary world became ever more professionalised and industrialised, diversifying and creating new jobs such as the publisher's reader, someone who evaluated incoming manuscripts for a publishing house, and the literary agent, who represented authors in business negotiations with publishers. The market became increasingly competitive. There was a price war among publishers in the 1880s, when the price for a reprint volume fell to a shilling or less – about the cost of a dozen eggs at the time (Borsuk 2018, 97, 103). In 1899, the Net Book Agreement was introduced, determining a fixed price for every book published. This remained in place until 1994. At the end of the nineteenth century, there were "at least 1,000 bookshops in England and Wales" (Feather 2006, 93). The number of (independent) bookshops in the UK is currently well below that figure at 883 (in 2019).[39] In London's West End, many nineteenth-century bookshops, including Hatchard's in Piccadilly, attracted leisured and moneyed customers by designing their shops to look "like retailers of luxury goods" (Lesser 2019, 299). Trade in second-hand books also picked up, with 72 antiquarian bookshops being listed in *Leigh's New Picture of London* in 1830 (ibid.). Less reputable retailers

---

39 https://www.thebookseller.com/news/growth-bookshops-record-number-shops-disappear-high-street-985381. Date of access: 25 February 2020. Feather 2006, 93 refers to the eighteenth century but it is clear from the context that he must mean the nineteenth; the first edition (1988, 135) reads "century".

resided in Holywell Street near the Strand, and casual buyers – including working-class and lower-middle class customers who would feel unwelcome in a West End bookshop – could find reading material at street bookstalls and barrows (300).

Most new novels in the nineteenth century were published in three volumes, based on the precedent of Walter Scott's (1771–1832) immensely successful historical novel *Waverley* (1814). In 1850, buying such a 'triple decker' – named, it seems, after "the three decks of guns that large warships would have" (Lesser 2019, 256) – would have set potential readers back one and a half guineas (31s 6d), about £ 165 in today's money. The market for these books was mainly in the circulating libraries, which had existed since the seventeenth century but grew along with the desire for novels. They made the triple-decker format commercially viable (Bassett 2010, 74–76). At the turn of the nineteenth century, there were already between 1,000 and 1,500 circulating libraries in Britain (Lesser 2019, 236), many operating as a side-line of bookshops. These would offer books on loan for a subscription fee. The libraries could loan a novel's separate volumes to three readers at the same time (Shillingsburg 2010), and they certainly help to explain the novel's popularity in the long nineteenth century. But they also included substantial holdings of non-fiction books and other reading matter besides.

One of the most famous circulating libraries of the Victorian era was Mudie's Select Library, founded by Charles Edward Mudie (1818–1890) in 1842. By 1875 he owned 125 branch libraries in the UK (fig. 10). His company regularly ordered as many as 2,500 copies of a new book and made a profit from renting them to eager readers for a fee – about the same amount for a year that it would cost to buy a three-volume novel. In the 1850s and 60s, he "was adding anything up to 100,000 volumes a year" (Feather 2006, 137). Mudie's was a 'select' library, which means that it chose which books to include or not. Standard attitudes and even the plots of novels were thus directly or indirectly influenced, promoting middle-class morality (Griest 1970, 78). "Novels of objectionable character or inferior ability" were excluded.[40] But this should not be taken to mean that Mudie's exercised anything like systematic literary censorship. In fact, book historians have pointed out that "Mudie's was more often attacked for its *inclusion* of popular sensation novels in the 1860s than for its *exclusion* of immoral works" (Lesser 2019, 314), and it did not shy away from stocking controversial titles such as Charles Darwin's (1809–1882) *Origin of Species* (1859). Mudie was such an important customer

---

40 Quote from a Mudie's catalogue of 1860; http://britishcirculatinglibraries.weebly.com/mudies-select-library.html. Date of access: 25 February 2020.

of the publishers that they even discreetly bailed him out when the company got into financial difficulties in 1863 (Finkelstein 1993; see also Roberts 2006). It was Smith's, not Mudie's, who banned George Moore's (1852–1933) novel *Esther Waters* (1894) from its premises – a novel about a servant girl who becomes a single mother –, leading to a debate about the libraries' obstruction of literary realism.

Fig. 10: Mudie's Select Library sticker, n. d.
Source: Ingo Berensmeyer.

Serial Fiction

The increasingly professional production of literature in the nineteenth century meant that authors who had to earn a living by writing depended to a large extent on success in the circulating libraries. In tandem with their publishers, they were likely to self-censor their product to make it fit these implicit or explicit expectations. But censorship was not systematic, and a ban by the commercial libraries "could actually lead to increased sales" (Lesser 2019, 230) because it provided free advertising for the book or the author in question. Another factor in the professionalisation of authorship was the expansion of the periodical press, which allowed easy entry to the literary marketplace for a wide variety of writers from different backgrounds, including many women.

Alongside the commercial libraries, public libraries were established in many places from 1850 onwards. Increased access to literature was also provided by reprint editions and cheaper popular fiction. There was a growing market for single-volume reprints of older novels, like Bentley's *Standard Novels* series (1831–1856; 126 titles), which were priced at six shillings each (about £ 30 in today's money), and Routledge's *Railway Library* (1849–1898, 1,277 titles), which cost two shillings or only one. Bentley's series included the first reissue of the novels of Jane Austen (1775–1817) in 1833. Now among the most widely read classics of English literature, they were much less appreciated in the early nineteenth century, and Bentley's Standard edition helped keep Austen's witty and profound novels in circulation. Routledge's later series and similar competitors were known as 'yellowbacks' because of their coloured paper bindings. These appealed to a less genteel readership. Even cheaper were the 'penny dreadfuls' or 'penny bloods', popular fiction and periodicals aimed at a working-class audience, which were sold for a penny a part (less than 50p in today's money). Titles like *Reynold's Miscellany* and *Lloyd's Penny Weekly Miscellany, The Family Herald*, and *The London Journal* targeted a mass audience with cheap print, often combining text and illustration. Clearly, there was much demand in this market for older titles as well as for new fiction for various segments of the population. Wilkie Collins, in 1858, estimated that these penny journals "had one million purchasers and three million readers" (Lesser 2019, 273).

Nobody knows exactly how many novelists there were in Victorian Britain or how many novels were published, but the quantity is staggering. John Sutherland estimates that there were about 3,500 authors of novels between 1837 and 1901, and "a probable total output of around 50,000 novels" over these 64 years (2006, 159), which means that each novelist produced about fourteen titles. Charles Dickens's (1812–1870) output of fifteen novels was about average, then; some prolific authors, like Anthony Trollope (1815–1882), managed forty-seven, others even twice as many (Sutherland 2006, 169). At the end of the century, two thousand novels were published every year – more than five per day. By that time, even new novels were sometimes published in paperback, in what is known as the 'shilling shocker' format – including Robert Louis Stevenson's (1850–1894) *The Strange Case of Dr. Jekyll and Mr. Hyde* in 1886. After 1900, the 'yellowbacks' were displaced by even cheaper pocket-sized books called 'sevenpennies' (Lesser 2019, 319).

Elements of popular fiction and middle-class respectability joined in the novels of Charles Dickens, by far the most successful of all Victorian novelists. As a young man, Dickens started writing for Chapman & Hall, an enterprising duo of young publishers who were looking for a text to accompany a series of comic engravings they wanted to publish in parts. This became *The Pickwick Papers* (1836–1837), a huge popular success. Dickens's celebrity allowed him to dictate his own terms to publishers, and he became the editor of a sequence of magazines in which his own novels appeared in serial form, alongside the work of other writers he curated, before they were printed in book editions. Dickens's journal *Household Words* became a household name, later changed to *All the Year Round*. He made a lot of money – just one of his novels, *Dombey and Son* (1846–1848) earned him a profit of nearly £ 10,000 (which would be more than a million today). As an editor, Dickens adopted the serial format of the working-class penny journals and took it to a more middle-class market, though his journals were still cheap enough to reach some working-class readers as potential buyers. Instead of weekly parts at a penny, he published new fiction in monthly episodes, each part exactly thirty-two pages long at the price of one shilling.

The novelist William Thackeray (1811–1863) edited the *Cornhill Magazine* for Smith Elder, and George Eliot (Mary Ann Evans, 1819–1880) was associated with *Blackwood's Magazine* and the publishing house of Blackwood. Nineteenth-century changes to copyright law strengthened the position of authors in relation to their publishers. Many authors took an active role in this, including Thomas Carlyle (1795–1881) and Dickens, who also fought tooth and nail for protection against book piracy, especially in the US. New laws forbade the import of foreign reprints of British books. In Germany, the Leipzig publisher Christian Bernhard Tauchnitz (1816–1895) made an enormous fortune by reprinting English-language books for a European and later global market, mainly for English-speaking tourists travelling outside of the British Empire or the US, starting his *Collection of British Authors* in 1841 (later expanded to include American authors as well). These cheap paperbacks could not be sold in Britain or the US, and British buyers were not allowed to take the books home. There are reports of Tauchnitz books being thrown overboard on the ferry, as well as of customs officers tearing out those pages that had already been read so that the book could not be resold in Britain (Feather 1988, 255). Similar continental reprint series of books in English, undercutting British book prices, were established in Paris by Galignani in 1805 and Baudry in 1831. In these early years of the nineteenth century, before international copyright agreements were in place, reprint book piracy was rampant. Tauchnitz was unusual in offering 'his' authors generous sums for being allowed to include their titles in his series, and he made friends with many British writers, including Dickens (see Mienert et al. 2017).

The publishing of novels in serial form, in periodicals or parts, also had consequences on plot construction. If authors wanted to get their readers hooked, they needed to create suspense: "Make 'em laugh, make 'em cry, make 'em wait", was Wilkie Collins's maxim.[41] The end of a monthly instalment and the end of a volume were ideal places to keep the reader waiting – the "cliffhanger" was born (Lodge 1992, 13–16). For instance, in Charlotte Brontë's (1816–1855) *Jane Eyre* (1848), the female protagonist begins to establish trust and respect for her employer, Mr. Rochester; she falls in love with him in the

---

[41] Frequently quoted, though Bachman (2006, 2) refers to it as "apocryphal".

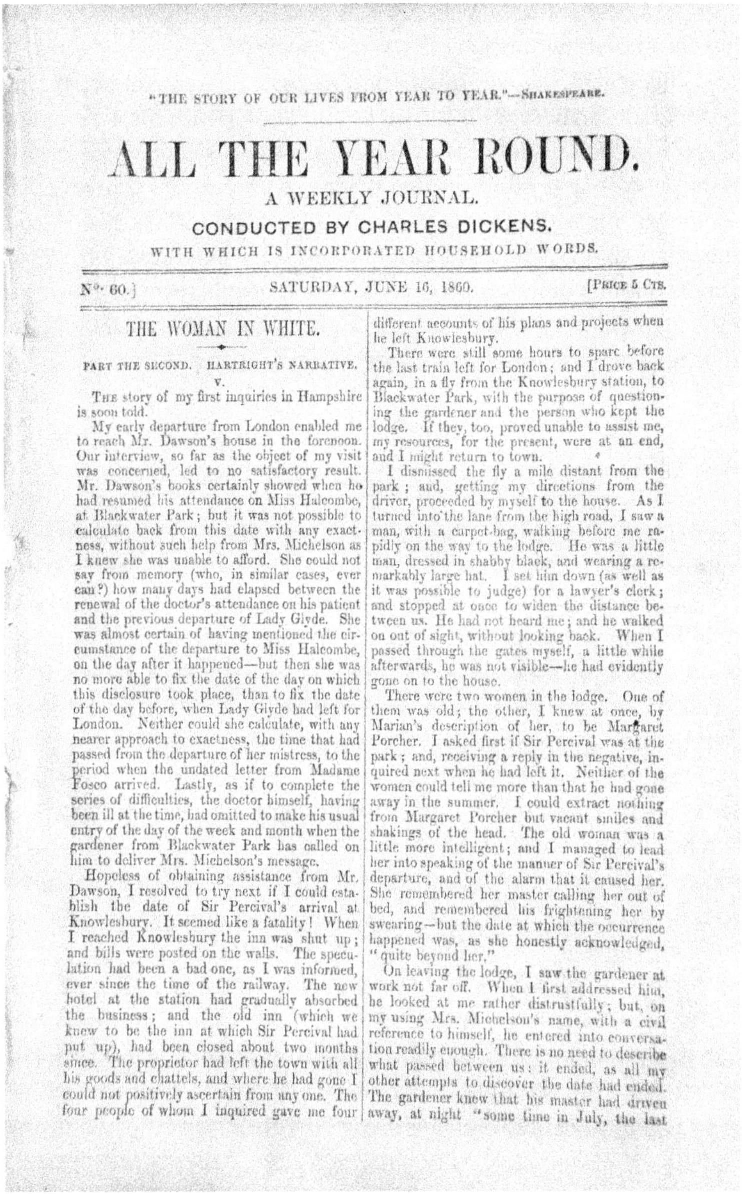

"THE STORY OF OUR LIVES FROM YEAR TO YEAR."—SHAKESPEARE.

ALL THE YEAR ROUND.
A WEEKLY JOURNAL.
CONDUCTED BY CHARLES DICKENS.
WITH WHICH IS INCORPORATED HOUSEHOLD WORDS.

N°. 60.]　　　　SATURDAY, JUNE 16, 1860.　　　　[PRICE 5 CTS.

THE WOMAN IN WHITE.

PART THE SECOND.　HARTRIGHT'S NARRATIVE.
V.

THE story of my first inquiries in Hampshire is soon told.

My early departure from London enabled me to reach Mr. Dawson's house in the forenoon. Our interview, so far as the object of my visit was concerned, led to no satisfactory result. Mr. Dawson's books certainly showed when he had resumed his attendance on Miss Halcombe, at Blackwater Park; but it was not possible to calculate back from this date with any exactness, without such help from Mrs. Michelson as I knew she was unable to afford. She could not say from memory (who, in similar cases, ever can?) how many days had elapsed between the renewal of the doctor's attendance on his patient and the previous departure of Lady Glyde. She was almost certain of having mentioned the circumstance of the departure to Miss Halcombe, on the day after it happened—but then she was no more able to fix the date of the day on which this disclosure took place, than to fix the date of the day before, when Lady Glyde had left for London. Neither could she calculate, with any nearer approach to exactness, the time that had passed from the departure of her mistress, to the period when the undated letter from Madame Fosco arrived. Lastly, as if to complete the series of difficulties, the doctor himself, having been ill at the time, had omitted to make his usual entry of the day of the week and month when the gardener from Blackwater Park has called on him to deliver Mrs. Michelson's message.

Hopeless of obtaining assistance from Mr. Dawson, I resolved to try next if I could establish the date of Sir Percival's arrival at Knowlesbury. It seemed like a fatality! When I reached Knowlesbury the inn was shut up; and bills were posted on the walls. The speculation had been a bad one, as I was informed, ever since the time of the railway. The new hotel at the station had gradually absorbed the business; and the old inn (which we knew to be the inn at which Sir Percival had put up), had been closed about two months since. The proprietor had left the town with all his goods and chattels, and where he had gone I could not positively ascertain from any one. The four people of whom I inquired gave me four different accounts of his plans and projects when he left Knowlesbury.

There were still some hours to spare before the last train left for London; and I drove back again, in a fly from the Knowlesbury station, to Blackwater Park, with the purpose of questioning the gardener and the person who kept the lodge. If they, too, proved unable to assist me, my resources, for the present, were at an end, and I might return to town.

I dismissed the fly a mile distant from the park; and, getting my directions from the driver, proceeded by myself to the house. As I turned into the lane from the high road, I saw a man, with a carpet-bag, walking before me rapidly on the way to the lodge. He was a little man, dressed in shabby black, and wearing a remarkably large hat. I set him down (as well as it was possible to judge) for a lawyer's clerk; and stopped at once to widen the distance between us. He had not heard me; and he walked on out of sight, without looking back. When I passed through the gates myself, a little while afterwards, he was not visible—he had evidently gone on to the house.

There were two women in the lodge. One of them was old; the other, I knew at once, by Marian's description of her, to be Margaret Porcher. I asked first if Sir Percival was at the park; and, receiving a reply in the negative, inquired next when he had left it. Neither of the women could tell me more than that he had gone away in the summer. I could extract nothing from Margaret Porcher but vacant smiles and shakings of the head. The old woman was a little more intelligent; and I managed to lead her into speaking of the manner of Sir Percival's departure, and of the alarm that it caused her. She remembered her master calling her out of bed, and remembered his frightening her by swearing—but the date at which the occurrence happened was, as she honestly acknowledged, "quite beyond her."

On leaving the lodge, I saw the gardener at work not far off. When I first addressed him, he looked at me rather distrustfully; but, on my using Mrs. Michelson's name, with a civil reference to himself, he entered into conversation readily enough. There is no need to describe what passed between us: it ended, as all my other attempts to discover the date had ended. The gardener knew that his master had driven away, at night "some time in July, the last

Fig. 11: First page of *All the Year Round*, June 16, 1860, with an instalment of Wilkie Collins's *The Woman in White*.
Source: Ingo Berensmeyer.

final chapter of the first volume. At the end of volume two, they must call off their wedding because of the shocking news that Rochester is already married to someone else. This leaves the continuation of the story completely open and makes the reader extremely curious for what will happen next. The sensation novel of the 1860s, which usually focuses on one or more secrets to be uncovered, is the most obvious product of this media configuration. Collins's *The Woman in White* was first published as a serial in Dickens's *All the Year Round* (fig. 11). The mystery or detective novel (with Collins's *The Moonstone* of 1868 an early example) is another child of this era. Serialised novels remained a strong presence in the market until the late nineteenth century, when magazines began to prefer publishing self-contained short stories instead (Lesser 2019, 326).

New Grub Street

Most professional writers could only dream of a success like Dickens's or George Eliot's, the sale of whose novels alone kept their publishers afloat. George Gissing (1857–1903) is an interesting late Victorian example of a professional writer who, like many, had to survive on the income of his writing, combining novels with short fiction and work for magazines. He published twenty-three novels in as many years. Starting out as a kind of English Zola with novels about poor people, prostitutes, and young educated men without means who must support themselves by teaching and other low-paid jobs (*The Unclassed,* 1884), Gissing later turned to more middle-class topics. One of his best-known novels is *New Grub Street* (1891), a realistic portrayal of the exigencies of writers who must survive in the print market and thus of the typical situation of professional writers in late nineteenth-century London. Like the old term 'Grub Street' for hack writing (see ch. 5), writing for money is the key theme of the novel *New Grub Street,* too, as emerging writers like Jasper Milvain and Edwin Reardon must learn to curb their idealism as artists and cater to the audience and to the powerful institutions of publishers, journal editors, and circulating libraries in order to sell books, stories, and articles. From the very start of the novel, literature is explained by Jasper, who wants to persuade his sisters to also support themselves by writing, as "a trade", "a business" (Gissing 2016, 8, 12), as a matter of supply and demand. Jasper is quite sure of his place in this world; he is no genius, and he lacks the skill and talent to produce outright "trash" for the "multitude". Hence, as he says, "I shall write for the upper middle-class of intellect, the people who like to feel that what they are reading has some special cleverness, but who can't distinguish between stones and paste" (13). In effect, Jasper/Gissing here diagnoses the literary phenomenon that will later be called 'middlebrow' writing, aiming neither too high nor too low for its readers and leaving them "with the agreeable sensation of having improved themselves without incurring fatigue" (Leavis 1979, 44).

A key moment in the novel comes when Marian Yule, Jasper's female love interest and the daughter of another writer, one foggy day reflects on the sheer overproduction of literature that makes survival in this market almost impossible. The scene of this is the Reading Room of the British Museum, the professional and social centre of literary activity in London since its opening in 1857, thus a highly symbolic location for a novel about writers and writing.

> She kept asking herself what was the use and purpose of such a life as she was condemned to lead. When already there was more good literature in the world than any mortal could cope with in his lifetime, here was she exhausting herself in the manufacture of printed stuff which no one even pretended to be more than a commodity for the day's market. What unspeakable folly! To write – was not that the joy and the privilege of one who had an urgent message for the world? Her father, she knew well, had no such message; he had abandoned all thought of original production, and only wrote about writing. She herself would throw away her pen with joy but for the need of earning money. And all these people about her, what aim had they save to make new books out of those already existing, that yet newer books might in turn be made out of theirs? This huge library, growing into unwieldiness, threatening to become a trackless desert of print – how intolerably it weighed upon her spirit! (Gissing 2016, 95)

Writing as a commodity, as "the manufacture of printed stuff"; writing about nothing else but writing (as Gissing himself does in this novel), leads to a vision of endless recycling of books that have already been written, accumulating in a "trackless desert of print". Marian in the next paragraph even imagines an inventor like Thomas Edison (1847–1931) inventing a "Literary Machine" that would do this automatically: "Only to throw in a given number of old books, and have them reduced, blended, modernised into a single one for today's consumption" (96). In the fog and the growing darkness, she even has a vision of the library turning into one great prison – the prison-house of literature: "the book-lined circumference of the room would be but a featureless prison-limit" (96). Gissing's characters are prisoners of the literary market; their creativity is turned into forced labour as they must support themselves and their families, having learned no other trade. The novel offers a harsh portrayal of literature and of the possibilities of survival for professional writers in late Victorian print culture.

The end of the three-decker came in 1894, when all major publishers, Mudie's, and W. H. Smith agreed to let it die (Menke 2019, ch. 4). Rudyard Kipling (1865–1936), whose own novels up to that point (*The Light that Failed*, 1891, and *The Naulahka*, 1892) had not been published in this format, nonetheless paid nostalgic tribute to it in a poem, invoking the nautical metaphor of the novel as a ship and novel-reading as a journey:

> Fair held the breeze behind us – 'twas warm with lovers' prayers.
> We'd stolen wills for ballast and a crew of missing heirs.
> They shipped as Able Bastards till the Wicked Nurse confessed,
> And they worked the old three-decker to the Islands of the Blest.
> (Kipling, "The Three-Decker" [1894], ll. 5–8; 2015, 472)

In contrast to the old-fashioned Victorian triple-decker, Kipling compared modern novels to steamships, which would never reach this pleasant destination. His poem mocks the two main trends of literature in the 1890s: naturalism (influenced by the French novelist Émile Zola and aiming for a scientific outlook on life) and aestheticism (preaching the doctrine of 'art for art's sake'): "You're manned by Truth and Science, and you steam for steaming's sake?" (l. 46; Kipling 2015, 473). In England at the time, the first alternative was represented mainly by Gissing and George Moore, the second by Walter Pater (1839–1894; *Marius the Epicurean*, 1885) and Oscar Wilde (1854–1900; *The Picture of Dorian Gray*, 1890; *The Importance of Being Earnest*, 1895).

Despite the new one-volume format being priced at six shillings and thus more affordable, circulating libraries continued to be key distributors of books well into the twentieth century: Mudie's ran until 1937, W. H. Smith until 1961, and Boots Booklovers' Library until 1966. Boots was a middle-class institution to the extent that John Betjeman (1906–1984) included it in a list of things "our Nation stands for" in a poem of 1940 (qtd. in Lesser 2019, 346). More popular in the 1930s and 1940s were the "twopenny libraries" or "mushroom libraries", so called because they sprang up everywhere, like the Argosy & Sundial Libraries and Foyle's Libraries. These served a lower-middle-class and working-class clientele and were often run "by small shopkeepers such as newsagents and tobacconists" (Lesser 2019, 347). Their type is memorably described in George Orwell's (1903–1950) essay "Bookshop Memories" (1936) and his novel *Keep the Aspidistra Flying* (1936), which in many ways resembles Gissing's *New Grub Street* in its dire view of the opportunities offered by a literary career for a down-at-heel young man. In 1932, the critic Q. D. Leavis (1906–1981) decried the decline of cultural standards when she described how the discount retail chain Woolworths sold "paper-covered novels [. . .,] American magazines [. . .,] and sixpenny books" (1979, 30). Customers and readers did not seem to mind.

The Battle of the Brows

In the modernist period, the field of fiction became increasingly stratified into three segments: 'highbrow', 'middlebrow', and 'popular'. In the last category would be what is now called 'genre fiction', including mostly crime and romance but also science fiction and fantasy. The field of what is now called 'literary fiction', however, would be subdivided further into high- and middlebrow, with highbrow modernists cultivating "a distinctive economy" (Lesser 2019, 351) that was culturally and socially exclusive, centred on a handful of small magazines, small metropolitan bookshops (Chambers 2020), and small publishing firms producing limited editions (such as Virginia and Leonard Woolf's Hogarth Press). This close-knit community, geographically concentrated in the London boroughs of Holborn and Bloomsbury, was firmly opposed to the wider world of commercial literary publishing ('middlebrow'). Such a contrast between "purists" and "profiteers" (McDonald 1997, 14) had been in place since the 1880s. At that time, the aesthetes, who believed in 'art for art's sake', flocked to new publishers like Methuen, Grant Richards, and the Bodley Head, who were considered "purists" in the publishing business (ibid.). The only commercial publisher to establish a foothold among the purists in the 1930s was the firm of Faber and Faber, whose prestige as a publisher of avantgarde poetry rested on T. S. Eliot as their poetry editor and board member.

George Orwell was visibly uncomfortable with these categories, being neither a Bloomsbury elitist nor wanting to be seen as a lightweight or a provider of 'middlebrow' fiction. He deplored the popularity of authors like Ethel M. Dell (1881–1939), a prolific writer of romance novels (Orwell 2012, 52), and what he regarded as the "cultureless life" of the modern masses (314). But he also wanted his books to sell, which may explain the moderate aesthetic and commercial success of his realist novels in the 1930s. Class prejudice and concerns about cultural decline were a major factor in this division of the fiction market in the interwar period. They were vividly expressed in Q. D. Leavis's study *Fiction and the Reading Public* (1932), in which she railed against what she described as "commonplace sentiments" (1979, 43), "a taste for the second-rate" (34), and the "*faux-bon*" (45), anticipating by a decade Theodor Adorno's and Max Horkheimer's invectives against the 'culture industry' and its brainwashing of gullible populations. Queenie Leavis's husband, the critic Frank Raymond Leavis, similarly polemicised against "mass civilisation", which he saw as in contrast to the "heritage" of a "culture" that he thought had always been the prerogative of a "minority" (Leavis 1930, 25, 30). This polemic later fed into the 'two cultures' debate, when Leavis complained about the dominance of science in education and its alleged threat to literature and the arts (Leavis 1962; Abravanel 2012; Ortolano 2009).

Where the Leavises saw the danger of a "standardization of taste" (Leavis 1979, 33) being propagated by such popular institutions as the commercial lending libraries, the book-tables at Woolworth, and the Book of the Month Club, recent critics have identified these institutions as offering spaces for alternative forms of cultural expression below the highbrow waterline. The 'feminine middlebrow' (Humble 2001) but also its masculine counterpart (Macdonald 2011) have been reinterpreted as cultural spaces with more to offer than mere "standardization", affirmation, or paltry collections of stereotypes and clichés. The "supposedly antagonistic relationship between modernism and the middlebrow" (Sterry 2017, 3) aided the consecration of a modernist aesthetic as predominantly public, urban, experimental, and masculine. The middlebrow and lowbrow segments of literature and culture significantly widen this range, expanding our ideas of modernism to include contested, different, and dissenting aesthetics (see also Ehland and Wächter 2016).

Most readers at the time would not have cared much about the "battle of the brows" (Brown and Grover 2012) one way or the other. The runaway bestseller of the 1930s was *The Citadel* (1937) by A. J. Cronin (1896–1981), a novel that perhaps best embodies what 'middlebrow' stood for: a conventional work of narrative fiction, not presuming to be high art or challenging in a literary way, but of great topical interest – in this case, addressing the state of public health in Britain. It is said to have had a major impact on the creation of the National Health Service after World War Two (Lesser 2019, 359). Sometimes literature does make things happen.

The Rise of the Paperback

For the wider public, there were even more outlets for books in the first half of the twentieth century. The libraries received competition from book clubs, which sold books to members at discount prices, such as the Times Book Club (1904), the Book Society (1929), and – with a decidedly political angle – the Left Book Club (1935) (Norrick-Rühl 2019). What really killed them, however, was the invention of the mass-market paperback. Paper-covered editions had been around for a while. These had been dominated, outside Britain, by Tauchnitz (see above). Towards the end of the nineteenth century, cheap reprint series of classics satisfied a lucrative education and self-improvement market. For example, the Everyman's Library series, published by J. M. Dent (from 1906 onwards), combined Arts and Crafts design and low prices with "a size convenient for the pocket, one that could be taken for a country ramble, or for a railway journey or on shipboard" (Rhys 1932, xiv). This and similar series, like the "World's Classics" started by Grant Richards in 1901 and continued by Oxford University Press in 1905, or Collins Illustrated Pocket Classics (1903), strove to bestow respectability and "a new sense of cultural authority" to the reprint business (Lesser 2019, 320). Dent also introduced the idea of different-coloured covers for different thematic sections in the series. This was picked up by paperback publishers such as Albatross Books, which were based in Hamburg. In Britain, Allen Lane also published a cheap paperback reprint series in a new format with colourful covers, with the innovative idea of selling them in unconventional places: in large department store chains and later supermarkets. This was the birth of Penguin books in 1935 (fig. 12). Priced at sixpence, "the cost of a pint of milk" (Borsuk 2018, 105), they sold three million copies within the first year. The modern design of their typographic covers was inspired by other publishers (Gollancz, Albatross Books); what was new was their long print-run and the business model of buying copyrights from hardback publishers (rather than reprinting out-of-copyright titles).

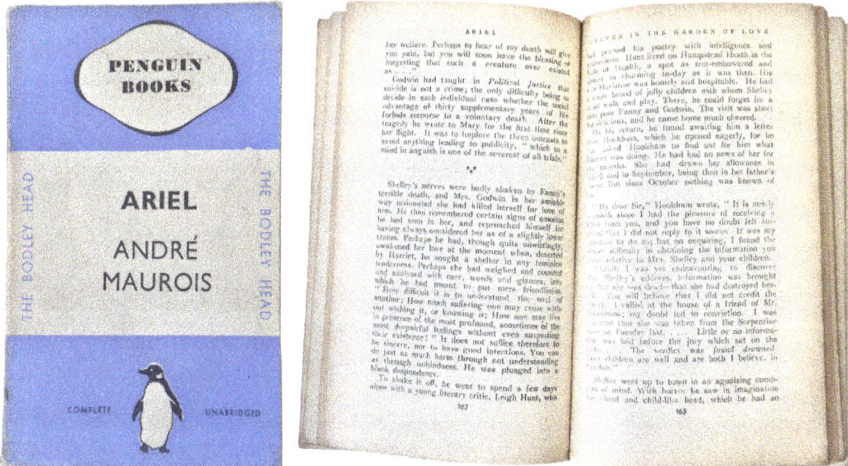

Fig. 12: The first Penguin paperback, 1935. Cover and page spread.
Source: Ingo Berensmeyer.

The success of Penguin books was consolidated during the War, when other publishers suffered from paper rationing. But because Penguin had printed so many books in the last year of peace, it was allotted a much bigger share of paper than anyone else (Lesser 2019, 373). After the War, Penguin launched its Classics series, at first focused on translations from Greek and Latin, beginning with E. V. Rieu's (1887–1972) translation of the *Odyssey* – whose commercial success was a surprise – and later expanding into classics of English literature. Publishing classics in cheap editions became a commercially viable enterprise. Their house style, typography, and layout received a facelift after the War by the German designer Jan Tschichold (1902–1974), who formulated the Penguin Composition Rules in 1947. Tschichold's main guideline was: "We do not need pretentious books for the wealthy, we need more really well-made ordinary books" (qtd. in Borsuk 2018, 106). Finally, in the mid-twentieth century, books really became a mass-market commodity, affordable for everyone and sold in huge quantities almost everywhere. The era of commercial libraries came to an end.

In this chapter, we have followed the history of the modern novel in tandem with the history of popular reading matter and its chief medium: paper and the modern mass-produced book. Even the arrival of e-books and e-readers in the early twenty-first century has so far not been able to kill the paperback. For novels, and much else, paper is still the preferred medium, and the paperback book the preferred format in which novels (and many other kinds of texts) are bought and read.[42] In the following chapters, we will pause before this threshold and reflect on other physical and sensory modalities and their impact on literature in modernity. For this, we will first turn back to Romanticism and ask about the role that breath, the human voice, and bodily rhythms play in the mediation of poetry.

---

[42] "Bücher – Weltweit", *Statista*, Statista GmbH, https://de-statista.com.emedien.ub.uni-muenchen.de/outlook/amo/medien/buecher/weltweit. Date of access: 3 Dec. 2021. On more recent developments in the digital era, see ch. 12 below.

7 Voice and Breath in Romantic and Victorian Poetry

It was a long journey from the first inscriptions in clay to the mass-produced paperback. But this is not a linear history of progress in technologies of writing and disseminating texts, but a history of changing cultural practices. In this history, forms of mediation in the mode of performance have never completely disappeared. One of these forms is the human voice. Listening to the voice of a poet, a bardic singer, or a storyteller is among the oldest experiences of literature. Moreover, we experience listening as more immediate than silent reading. It is no accident, then, that a novelist like Charles Dickens, whose success was built on print and its built-in distance between author and audience, should seek to form a more direct bond with his readers by embarking on extended reading tours around the globe (Dickens 1975, Andrews 2006). People flocked to hear his voice and his impersonations of the characters – up to twenty in each performance – whom they had so far known only from the printed page, or from reading aloud in their own or someone else's voice, or from their own vocal imaginations. Polyvocity or 'heteroglossia' (*raznorečie*) is a key term in the theory of the novel as proposed by Mikhail Bakhtin (1895–1975), who argued that the modern novel was characterised by a tension between many different voices and forms of speech (Bakhtin 1981). But this could also be applied to modernist poetry: "He do the police in different voices" was T. S. Eliot's working title for his poem *The Waste Land* (Eliot 2010, 4; see ch. 10 below). In this chapter, we will look more closely at the concept of voice in literature, and breath and other bodily rhythms in poetry, mainly in the nineteenth century. The world of printed paper did not make these physical forms of mediation as performance disappear; it remediated them in modes of representation.

Voice in Literature

The concept of 'voice' in literature is nowadays used in a metaphorical sense (unless we are in fact dealing with public readings, radio transmissions, or audiobooks): we speak of an individual or a group, a community 'having' or 'not having a voice'; 'making one's voice heard' means achieving attention and recognition; a new writer may be described as a 'new voice'. In poetry, the term 'voice' is also used figuratively for the poem's speaker. In general, it seems there is a mental process that occurs when we read a text, which makes us "infer a voice even though we know that we are reading words on a page" (Parker 1985, 16), i.e., we automatically translate "writing into imaginary speech" (Furniss and Bath 2007, 209). The genres of fiction, drama, and poetry can be easily told apart as different modes of presenting speech: characters without a narrator in drama, characters framed or filtered by a narrator in narrative fiction, and the representation of "personal utterances" in lyric poems (Smith 1978, 8).

For poetry, there is a long tradition of hearing a bard or a poet sing or recite poems aloud. Even well into the eighteenth century and beyond, poetry was a part of eloquence, of rhetoric, and recitation would have been regarded as a performative aspect of its public production and reception. Even later still, in the twentieth century, poetry would sometimes serve as an exercise in elocution. This is demonstrated, with some sarcasm, in Muriel Spark's (1918–2006) novel *The Girls of Slender Means* (1963), in which girls in a London boarding house immediately after World War Two receive elocution lessons based on poems by Donne, Tennyson, Hopkins, and others.

Poets who failed to recite their poems convincingly could be subjected to scathing critique. An early example of this can be found in the seventeenth century. We hear from Roger L'Estrange (1616–1704), a contemporary witness (1686), about a particularly weak performer of his own verses:

> He was One of the *Soundest*, the *Smoothest*, and yet One of the *Sharpest Witts* perhaps, of This *Last Age*. He was a man of *Letters*, an *Excellent Poet*; a *Philosopher*; an *Easy,* and a *Happy Pen*, which way soever he Turn'd it: And yet I have been ready to Snatch the *Paper* out of his *Hand,* to **Hear** him **Read** *his Own Pieces*, sometimes. He *Read* 'em, as if he had not **Understood** 'em, and a man could hardly *make 'em out,* without *Reading* them after him. He did, really, *Spoyle the Best Things in the World,* in his way of Mouthing them: No more *Motion,* then a *Statue,* and All, just in a *Tune,* like the *same Key* on an *Organ,* from One end to the Other. You cannot Imagine, I presume, that he was putting *Tricks* up ⟨-⟩ on *Himself*; and yet if he had *Read* any *Other man's Writings* at the *Same Rate,* it would have been taken for an *Affront* . . .[43]

Harold Love (2001) established convincingly that the target of L'Estrange's scorn was none other than John Dryden; he corroborated this by quoting similar criticism made by Colley Cibber (1671–1757), who described Dryden's reading of his play *Amphitryon* (1690) to the actors as "cold, [. . .] flat, and unaffecting" (qtd. in Love 2001, 400). Apparently, the English liked their poetry to be recited in a more musical manner. Love also quotes a French visitor in the 1690s who vents his astonishment about the English habit of reading poetry aloud in a tuneful tone of voice:

---

[43] *The Observator,* vol. 3, no. 79 (Wed., 2 June 1686), 1, qtd. in Love 2001, 398–399 (emphases original).

> The English have a mighty value for their Poetry. If they believe that their Language is the finest in the whole World, tho' spoken no where but in their own Island; they have proportionatly [sic] a much higher Idea of their Verses. They never read or repeat them without the most singular Tone in the World. When they happen in reading to go out of Prose into Verse you would swear you no longer heard the same Person: His Tone of Voice becomes soft and tender; he is charm'd, he dies away with Rapture.
>
> (Misson 1719, 220–221, qtd. in Love 2003, 49)

Actors in the seventeenth century, especially in serious tragic roles, would also cultivate such a "Tone" towards a more musical manner of delivery, somewhat resembling operatic recitative. This went out of fashion in the mid-eighteenth century (Love 2003, 50), when it was replaced by a more 'natural' style of vocal delivery.

In the antebellum US, the poet and critic Edgar Allan Poe (1809–1849) was referred to, in not exactly complimentary terms, as "the jingle-man", for writing poetry that depended on sound and melody for much of its effect (Guttzeit 2017, 173). A contemporary witness, Thomas Wentworth Higginson, described Poe's voice in a recitation of his poems as "attenuated to the finest golden thread; the audience became hushed, and, as it were, breathless; there seemed no life in the hall but his; and every syllable was accentuated with such delicacy, and sustained with such sweetness, as I never heard equalled by other lips" (qtd. in Guttzeit 2017, 205). In one of Poe's fantastic tales, "Loss of Breath" (first published 1832, revised version 1846), an actor named Lackobreath loses his breath and, in searching for it, loses several parts of his body as well, before finally regaining both breath and voice when he meets his neighbour and rival Mr Windenough in a crypt. This tale has been read as a "a satire of literature and the literary marketplace" (Tally 2014, 15), reading the actor as a stand-in for the author and loss of breath for "lack of inspiration" (Guttzeit 2017, 209) – from the Latin verb *inspirare*, 'to inhale, to breathe in'. Breath, voice, and literary creativity have been closely connected since ancient times – and this connection returns in modernity, with particular intensity around 1800.

Voice as Interior Speech

For poetry, a new tradition emerged in the eighteenth century, which shifted the focus from a rhetorical mode composed for public performance towards a more interiorised form of speech, more in the manner of verbalised thoughts rather than words spoken aloud and addressed to an audience. In poetry, especially in lyric poetry since the Romantics, a conventional view of this lyric 'voice' has been that it is a representation of the poet's own thoughts and feelings; that these thoughts are expressed spontaneously, in solitude, and are meant to be sincere – not made to impress an audience but spoken (or written) as if there were no audience. In 1833, John Stuart Mill (1806–1873) defined poetry as "overheard" speech, in contrast to "eloquence" or rhetoric, which is "heard": "Eloquence", Mill wrote (1859, 71), "supposes an audience; the peculiarity of poetry appears to us to lie in the poet's utter unconsciousness of a listener. Poetry is feeling confessing itself to itself, in moments of solitude." This definition of poetry as "soliloquy" (ibid.) in part echoes statements by William Wordsworth (1770–1850) and Percy Bysshe Shelley (1792–1820), among others, such as Wordsworth's famous assertion that "all good poetry is the spontaneous overflow of powerful feelings" and Shelley's comparison of the poet to "a nightingale who sits in darkness and sings to cheer its own solitude with sweet sounds."[44]

In the historical context of the early nineteenth century, it is remarkable that poetry was (re-)defined as soliloquy and unmediated expression at a time when literature, and the novel in particular, had long adapted itself to a literary market, a media culture, and a public sphere saturated by print. Was this a form of rearguard action or nostalgia, a programme intended to secure a status for poetry that was no longer actually attainable – the futile assertion of a lost cause? Or was it a shrewd (and not entirely unsuccessful) attempt to translate a residual conception of poetic immediacy into the mediated bookscape of the nineteenth century? In any case, many poets from the Romantic period express an idea of poetry as a form of *speech, sound, and song*, emphasising its spontaneity and naturalness (even comparing it to birdsong in the figure of the nightingale), even though – or because – they did so mostly in the medium of print and sometimes at considerable distance from each other and from the general audience. Like Thomas Gray's rural graveyard setting in the *Elegy Written in a Country Church-Yard* (see ch. 6), many of these poets actively pursued a retreat from civilisation and the cities, some of them settling down in the remote Lake District in Cumbria, in the North of England; but their publishing strategies were notably modern and metropolitan. The lyric voice that asks to be (over-)heard by its "auditors" (Shelley 2006a, 1189) most often did so in print, and the "auditors" were actually readers.

From a media-historical perspective, the Romantic celebration of authenticity, sincerity, and immediacy appears as a response to the media configuration of 1800, which predicated indirectness, distance, and silent reading rather than

---

[44] Wordsworth, "Preface to Lyrical Ballads" (1800); Shelley, *A Defence of Poetry* (written 1821, published 1840) (Wu 2006, 498, 1189). Mill could not have known Shelley's *Defence* in 1833 unless he saw the manuscript.

a community of "auditors" or listeners in direct contact with a poet or singer. Consider how Shelley's definition of a poet continues: "A poet is a nightingale who sits in darkness and sings to cheer its own solitude with sweet sounds; his auditors are as men entranced by the melody of an unseen musician, who feel that they are moved and softened, yet know not whence or why" (2006a, 1189). Poets are "unseen" precisely because they, their bodies, their persons, are absent from the text, and the readers are "moved" by this "melody", but they do not know where the music is coming from. They do not even know why they are moved by it. In other words, the modern textual environment does not easily allow for such effects to happen. If they do, against the odds, this miraculous feat is due to the special power of the poets who can 'move and soften' the hearts and minds of their readers despite the limitations of print.

Apostrophe

The voice of the poet had yet another specialty: it could speak to animals as if they understood human language, and it could address inanimate objects as if they were alive and endowed with human faculties. In this mode, the poet did not speak directly to an audience or readers but to another person or object – taking up a long poetic tradition of "apostrophe" or 'turning away' from an audience to addressing a third person or object. Any time a poet says 'O', this constitutes an apostrophe or invocation: "Oh Rose thou art sick" (Blake); "O Contemplation! when to Memory's eyes / The visions of long-past days arise" (Southey); "Oh Sensibility! Thou busy nurse / Of inj'ries once received" (Ann Yearsley); "Oh Solitude, to thy sequestered vale / I come to hide my sorrow and my tears" (Charlotte Smith); "Oh spirit of the days gone bye" (Clare); "Oh Hope thou soother sweet of human woes!" (Smith); "Oh golden-tongued Romance, with serene lute!" (Keats). Occasionally a country is invoked in this manner: "O England, may God punish thee" (Hardy), or the reader – "O reader! hast thou ever stood to see / The Holly Tree?" (Southey) – or indeed a poet: "O poet, come you haunting here" (Hardy again).[45]

This tradition of apostrophe goes back to classical Greek poetry, especially the odes of Pindar (c. 518 – c. 438 BCE), which were frequently translated and imitated in eighteenth-century England. But it also ties in with "one of the

---

[45] These examples of first lines are from poems that can easily be found online or in standard anthologies such as Wu 2006; I have decided not to cite sources in these cases for reasons of space.

characteristic beliefs of Romanticism", namely "that, thanks to literal-minded scientific philosophy, and to commercial worldliness, we humans have lost the ability we once had to communicate with animals and inanimate things" (Ferber 2012, 69; cf. Culler 1977). One of the tasks of poetry and poets, then, was to take us back to a time when "[e]verything had the ability to look at us and to speak" (Ferber 2012, 70), including trees, mountains, rivers, the wind, or a nightingale, which could be anthropomorphised (endowed with a soul or other human qualities) in poetic speech – without seriously turning every poet into an animist or a panpsychist. Like personification, anthropomorphism is one of the oldest techniques of poetic speech and was hence also quite conventional by 1800. Poetry is the one form of speech that allows us to talk to plants, toys, or machines without having to fear ridicule or being taken for a crank.

A different kind of apostrophe occurs when the speaker does not address any concrete person or object, but perhaps him- or herself – "O could I be as I have been" (Clare), "O, I am frightened with most hateful thoughts" (Keats) – or when the speaker uses the 'Oh' as an exclamation, for the sake of emphasis, as an "intensifier" (Culler 1977, 60): "Oh my love's like the red, red rose" (Burns); "O! how I love, on a fair summer's eve" (Keats), "O there is blessing in this gentle breeze" (Wordsworth), "Oh place me where the burning noon" (Smith), "Oh for a lodge in some vast wilderness" (Cowper), "O! were I one of the Olympian twelve" (Keats); "Oh, when I was in love with you, / Then I was clean and brave" (Housman). This 'Oh' is surely related to the equally frequent exclamation 'Ah', which can also be plaintive: "Ah! what a weary race my feet have run" (Thomas Warton), or an exclamation of awe or nostalgia: "Ah, hills beloved! – where once, an happy child" (Smith); "Ah! sunflower! weary of time" (Blake); "Ah! why will Mem'ry with officious care / The long lost visions of my days renew?" (Smith); "Ah, child, thou art but half thy darling mother's" (Hardy).

Jonathan Culler has argued that the 'O' is ultimately an invocation of poetry itself, a sign that what we are reading or hearing is poetic speech: "O Poesy! for thee I hold my pen", as John Keats (1795–1821) writes in "Sleep and Poetry" (1816). The 'O' or 'Oh' does not have a semantic content but is an expression of "poetic presence", "an image of voice" created by "the pure O of undifferentiated voicing" (Culler 1977, 63), asserting the power of poetry. It is, we might add, a figure of the poet's breath: language as natural sound.

Ode to the West Wind

The poet's voicing and the wind are brought together most explicitly in Shelley's "Ode to the West Wind" (written in 1819, published in 1820), in which the wind is addressed as a "thou" and anthropomorphised as a kind of "breath" and "voice":

> Oh wild west wind, thou breath of autumn's being;
> Thou from whose unseen presence the leaves dead
> Are driven, like ghosts from an enchanter fleeing,
> ....
> Wild spirit, which art moving everywhere,
> Destroyer and preserver, hear, oh hear!
> (Shelley 2006b, ll. 1–3, 13–14)

The first three sections of this ode culminate in the entreaty "oh hear!", asking the wind to listen to the poet's voice. The wind itself not only has power over leaves, clouds, and waves, it also has a "voice" (l. 41). In the fourth section, the poet-speaker recognises qualities of himself in the wind: he too is "tameless, and swift, and proud" (l. 56). In the fifth and final section, he asks to become one with the "spirit" of the wind: "Be thou, spirit fierce, / My spirit! Be thou me, impetuous one!" (ll. 61–62). He asks to unite his voice with that of the wind:

> Drive my dead thoughts over the universe
> Like withered leaves to quicken a new birth!
> And, by the incantation of this verse,
>
> Scatter, as from an unextinguished hearth
> Ashes and sparks, my words among mankind!
> Be through my lips to unawakened earth
>
> The trumpet of a prophecy! Oh wind,
> If winter comes, can spring be far behind?
> (ll. 63–70)

Shelley is here asking for the poet's voice, his voice, to become one with a force of nature, to be a force of nature like the west wind. "Spirit" is of course, if we look at its Latin origin, just another way of saying "breath" (*spiritus*; in Greek, *pneuma*). Shelley also associates wind and human utterance in his *Defence of Poetry*: "Man is like an instrument over which a series of external and internal impressions are driven, like the alternations of an ever-changing wind over an Aeolian lyre, which move it, by their motion, to ever-changing melody" (Shelley 2006a, 1185). In a reading of Samuel Taylor Coleridge's (1772–1834) poem "The Eolian Harp" (1796), M. H. Abrams refers to the harp that is played by the wind as "a persistent Romantic analogue of the poetic mind, the figurative mediator between outer motion and inner emotion" (1984, 26).

Shelley wrote the "Ode to the West Wind" only a couple of months after the Peterloo Massacre (16 August 1819), when cavalry forces brutally suppressed a demonstration for political reform in Manchester. In addressing the wind as "breath", he also activates a metaphorical association of breath with freedom, with a sense of being allowed to 'be oneself'.[46] The poem can be read as a response to Shelley's sense of despair in the face of poetry's inability to effect social change, here expressed in the images of "a new birth" and "spring". As W. H. Auden (1907–1983) would write much later, in the 1930s, "poetry makes nothing happen", yet "it survives, / A way of happening, a mouth" (Auden 2005 [1939], ll. 36, 40–41). Even though Auden here diminishes the poetic voice from Shelley's "trumpet of a prophecy" to the more sceptical "a mouth", he still retains the emphasis on the orality, the spoken quality of poetry, its immediate connection to an individual speaker and voice.

It is tempting to read these invocations of the lyric poet's voice as a compensation for the actual shortcomings of print publication. Poetry is meant to be retranslated from the "withered leaves" of paper, the "dead thoughts" on a page into a direct and effective form of speech, scattered "among mankind" so that new "sparks" can fly (Shelley 2006b). A similar form of compensation can be seen in the space given to a printed poem on the page, usually surrounded by a vast amount of white, unmarked, 'negative' space: a poem, this tells us, has value, is special, a luxury item that deserves this waste of paper. This is a crucial part of the visual codes of poetry in print: "The proportion and shapes of text blocks and white margins reflect print conventions of indentation, word spacing and line length that distinguish poetry from prose [. . .] at a presemantic level as the reader's eye skims over a printed page" (Houston 2016, 40). The relationship between the printed text and the white space around it structures the reading experience and assigns value to the poem. It remediates the impression that words in poetry have more 'weight' than in prose and expect to be read more carefully.

---

[46] Cf. Matthew Arnold's (1822–1888) draft notes to "The Buried Life" in the Yale ms. (1849–1852): "hardly for an hour between birth and death have we been on our own one natural line, have we been ourselves, have we breathed freely" (Arnold 1965, 274).

Radical Subjectivity

From a social perspective, Romantic poetry often celebrated the individual as opposed to a group, crowd, or class of people, often emphasising the speaker's loneliness and the act of walking long distances or standing in an elevated place: "I wandered lonely as a cloud", "I travelled among unknown men" (Wordsworth); "I wander thro' each charter'd street", "I travelled through a land of men", "I walked abroad in a snowy day" (Blake); "If I walk in autumn's even", "I dreamed that, as I wandered by the way" (Shelley) "Ive left my own old home of homes" (Clare); "I stood tip-toe upon a little hill" (Keats); "I stood upon a heaven-cleaving turret" (Shelley); "I stood on Brocken's sovran height, and saw" (Coleridge); or withdrawing into the self, as in "My heart aches, and a drowsy numbness pains / My sense [. . .]" (Keats), "I went into the deserts of dim sleep" (Shelley), "I dropped my pen; and listened to the wind", "My heart leaps up when I behold /A rainbow in the sky" (Wordsworth); "My thoughts arise and fade in solitude" (Shelley); "My soul was mantled with dark shadows born / Of lonely fear" (Hemans); "I had a dream, which was not all a dream" (Byron), etc.

A search of texts included in the LION database shows that the verb of motion 'to wander' occurs 421 times in poetry between 1730 and 1780 but 2044 times between 1780 and 1830. This is not merely an increase in absolute numbers; taking into account the total number of poetic texts in the database for these date ranges, this represents an increase from 5.1 to 9.4 percent of all poetry published in this period containing the word 'wander' and its variants.[47] The verb 'to go' remains fairly constant (rising from 25.1 % to 26.6 %); 'to walk' even declines from 9 to 7.8 %, and 'to run' from 15.9 to 11.59 %. Variants of the word 'stand', however, decline from 23.1 % of all texts (1730–1780) to 19.2 % (1780–1830). If these calculations hold up, poetry, in other words, became perhaps less static in Romanticism but not generally more mobile, though definitely more inclined to wandering.[48] Possibly, this indicates an increased cultural focus on solitary (self-) experience in nature, as in one of the earliest master texts of European Romanticism, Jean-Jacques Rousseau's (1712–1778) *Reveries of the Solitary Walker* (*Les rêveries du promeneur solitaire*, 1782).

The Romantic ideas of radical subjectivity and self-expression had their precursors in the mid-eighteenth century, most notably in the idea of the

---

[47] The total number of poetic texts in the database is: for 1730–1780, 8314; for 1780–1830, 21,675.
[48] The total number of texts in LION (poetry, drama, and prose) for 1730–1780 is 9125; for 1780–1830, 23571. 'Wander': 650 / 7.1 % vs. 2839 / 12.0 % = 4.9 % rise in total; for poetry only, the rise is 4.3 %.

"original genius" as proposed by the poet Edward Young (1683–1765) in his essay *Conjectures on Original Composition* (1759). Young argued that unique literary writing sprang from the uniqueness or "mental individuality" (Young 1968, 561) of an original person. For some later poets, including Wordsworth, it followed that authors expressed their individuality in their works. This powerful idea, also known as "expressivism" (Lamarque 2009, 84–85), made it possible for Wordsworth to write an epic poem about himself, about, more precisely, "the growth of a poet's mind", a poem he never quite finished and which he referred to as "the poem to Coleridge", but which we now know as *The Prelude*. It was published posthumously in 1850. This stance of creating poetry, even a sort of heroic poetry, from the innermost self earned him the scorn of John Keats, who referred to this as "the egotistical sublime" (Keats 1988 [1818], 547).

For Keats, the poet's innermost self was unknowable, and its genius consisted in its infinite possibilities. According to a famous letter to his brothers George and Tom, the "quality" that "went to form a Man of Achievement especially in Literature" was not mental individuality but "*Negative Capability*, that is when man is capable of being in uncertainties, Mysteries, doubts, without any irritable reaching after fact & reason" (Keats 1988 [1817], 539). In another letter of 1818, he writes about the "poetical Character" saying that "it is not itself – it has no self – it is every thing and nothing – It has no character" (547). For Keats, what is decisive for literary creativity is not the presence of something in the poet's mind but an absence, a lack of definite characteristics.

Such conflicting theories about the "poet's mind" or the "poetical Character" lay bare the contradictions that characterise Romantic views of literary creation and the connection between authors' lives and their works. They follow on from the eighteenth-century concept of genius, one of the most potent narratives about authorship in modern Western cultures, and they become caught up in what Peter Lamarque has called "the paradoxes of inspiration and expression" (2009, 96): is the poem that derives from inspiration the experience that the poet has *before* writing it down, so that the written text is only a copy of the experience, or is the linguistic expression identical to the poet's inspiration, and thus something given to the poet by a higher power than his "own voice", and hence not an act of self-expression at all? In that case, "genius" would be defined as heteronomous rather than autonomous, characterised by "impersonality" rather than a unique and original personality.[49]

---

[49] On the formative impact of genius discourse in Europe around 1800, see Woodmansee 1984; Haynes 2005.

Towards the end of the eighteenth century, the "myth of lyric voice" was established as "a medium that vibrates forth from the irreplaceable singularity of the speaking body but at the same time merges with conceptuality (thought) such that the utmost in tonal personality coincides with a universality" (Wellbery 1996, 188). But reconciling the singular and the universal in the figure of the poet is rather a challenge. For the Victorians, it was increasingly difficult to stick to this Romantic ideal of harmonising the particular with the universal in the poet's mind and lyric voice. Whereas for Shelley "the mind of the [poetic] creator" was "itself the image of all other minds" (2006a, 1189), such confidence was no longer available in the later nineteenth century without risking solipsism. Consequently, the poet's voice was reimagined as "a drained and reinhabitable voice not tied to an identifiable character or concerned with historical topicality" (Alfano 2017, 5; cf. Christ 1975, 12). In the early twentieth century, this impersonal voice became part of a neo-classicist literary ethos for poets and critics like Paul Valéry (1871–1945), T. S. Eliot, Vernon Lee (1856–1935), F. R. Leavis (1895–1978), T. E. Hulme (1883–1917), and others (Rives 2012), while the dilemma of particularity and universality was relegated to the Freudian unconscious, which in turn "revitalized the Romantic model of the expressive artist" (Wexler 1997, 73–74).

For Keats, the poet's voice and breath had an intensely personal and physical significance. When he died in 1821 at the age of twenty-five, he had been ill for two years, suffering from pulmonary tuberculosis, a disease that had already killed his mother and his brother Tom, whom he had nursed in 1818. At the beginning of his long poem *Endymion* (1818), he writes some of his most famous lines:

> A thing of beauty is a joy for ever:
> Its loveliness increases; it will never
> Pass into nothingness, but still will keep
> A bower quiet for us, and a sleep
> Full of sweet dreams, and health, and quiet breathing.
> (Keats 1988, 107, ll. 1–5)

The emphasis on "quiet breathing" is even stronger because the line in which these words occur is hypermetrical: it has six stresses rather than the usual five. The line is literally 'filled' with goodness; it takes a lot of breath to finish it. Keats knew only too well what he was saying in this line. Here, the voice and breath of poetry, though also linked to a universal 'we' ("a bower quiet for *us*"), are intimately connected to the poet's physical experience and the limitations of his body: his mortality. For a precious moment, the personal and the impersonal were held in a fragile balance.

Victorian 'Mediums': Tennyson and Browning

The idea of poetry as a voice that speaks and as a living breath was continued and extended after Romanticism. Among the Victorian poets, Robert Browning (1812–1889) perfected the poet's ability to speak in the voices of literary characters, like a ventriloquist, in a form known as the 'dramatic monologue' – using a historical or fictional character and giving that character an illusion of dramatic immediacy in the form of direct speech. His contemporary Alfred Lord Tennyson (1809–1892), in his official function as poet laureate, tried to achieve not only public significance and exemplarity for his individual experiences but even a universal significance or wisdom, as when he spoke on behalf of the entire human species in his long poem *In Memoriam* (1850), trying to come to terms with mortality at a time when conventional Christian piety was challenged by scientific discoveries in geology and zoology.

Combining his private and public roles, Tennyson asserted towards the end of his long poem: "I trust I have not wasted breath" (CXX, l. 1; Tennyson 2014, 466). As he explained the purpose of *In Memoriam A. H. H.*, a sequence of 131 lyric poems written to commemorate his friend Arthur Henry Hallam and published, at first anonymously, in 1850, "in the poem altogether private grief swells out into thought of, and hope for, the whole world" (Tennyson 2014, 339). Numerous apostrophes enhance the poet's voice, even to the point of exaggeration:

> O friendship, equal-poised control,
>   O heart, with kindliest motion warm,
>   O sacred essence, other form,
> O solemn ghost, O crownèd soul!
>   (LXXXV, ll. 33–36;
>   Tennyson 2014, 424)

The whole of *In Memoriam* is an apostrophe of Tennyson's dead friend Hallam, whose loss is rhetorically transformed into a gain. He is sent off and at the same time preserved: as something else, as an "other form". Apostrophe, as we have seen, is a poet's vocal training unit. In Tennyson, this is not merely a metaphor, but – as in Keats – can be understood in a concrete physical sense. The rhythmic ebb and flow of verse is intended as equivalent to the poet's breath. Reportedly, Tennyson thought he was the only one who could properly read his own poems aloud because "nobody had lungs like his" (Griffiths 1993, 35; cf. Griffiths 2018). Form and voice are used as a medium whose unity is defined by body rhythms. This "materiality of communication" (Gumbrecht and Pfeiffer 1994) – or, in Tennyson's words, "matter-moulded forms of speech" (XCV, l. 46;

Tennyson 2014, 439) – turns Tennyson's poetry in its more intimate moments into a poetry of the body, a poetry that suggests the possibility of a fusion between the physical and the spiritual (Vernon 1979). Breath here functions as the medium of a communication (if only as a wish that can never be fulfilled) which transcends the boundaries of the communicable: "commerce with the dead" (LXXXV, l. 93; Tennyson 2014, 427) beyond the limit of death.

The Victorians were very interested in 'mediums', that is persons who were thought to be able to make contact with the dead. The poet's breath as the medium of "commerce with the dead" can also be read in the context of contemporary spiritualist techniques such as "insufflation" and "magnetic breathing" intended to strengthen the "life force":[50]

> Ah yet, even yet, if this might be,
>   I, falling on his faithful heart,
>   Would breathing through his lips impart
> The life that almost dies in me [.]
>   (XVIII, ll 13–16; 363)

In elegy 95, this contact is achieved, if only in the form of a fantasy, in a "trance" (XCV, l. 43; 439) which overcomes Tennyson while he is rereading Hallam's letters:

> And strangely on the silence broke
>   The silent-speaking words [...]
> ....
> So word by word, and line by line,
>   The dead man touched me from the past,
>   And all at once it seemed at last
> His living soul was flashed on mine,
> And mine in his was wound [. . .]
>   (ll. 25–26, 33–37; 2014, 438–439)

This is the only instance in the poem where a reunion with dead Hallam is realised, if only in a dream. The wish "O for thy voice to soothe and bless!" (LVI, l. 26; 400) is here fulfilled, the loss absorbed. It is the turning point of the entire

---

[50] See Owen 1989, 129: "Some healers liked to breathe directly on to the patient's body, but Chandos preferred to use the intermediary of a clean handkerchief, breathing deeply through the nose and exhaling through the mouth so that her breath passed through the linen on to the patient's skin. This process was thought to increase the organism's vitality and was recommended as an antidote to the loss of life force, as in the aftermath of a haemorrhage". Following this parallel – Hallam died of a brain haemorrhage –, *In Memoriam* could also be read as just such a transparent texture, like a linen handkerchief through which Tennyson, the healer, applies his breath to the body of dead Hallam, to reinspire him with new vitality.

sequence, the point that finally enables the speaker to construct an optimistic conclusion to the poem. It is at the same time a spiritualist turning point because this mystical experience confronts him with a transcendence that authorises his wishful fantasies. On reading this, professional spiritualists were eager to claim Tennyson as one of their own and expected prophetic wisdom from him – they were quickly disappointed, though (Myers 1967 [1889]). Already in an early talk on "Ghosts", which he gave to the Cambridge Apostles in 1830, Tennyson noted about the poet and the "spiritual world" that it was possible for the poet to access this world but not to illumine the darkness it contained. Paradoxically, the process of discovery would only intensify the obscurity. All the poet could achieve was an occupation of the silence by his voice: "He lifts the veil, but the form behind it is shrouded in deeper obscurity. He raises the cloud, but he darkens the prospect. [. . .] The voice of *him* who speaks alone like a mountain stream on a still night fills up and occupies the silence" (qtd. in Thorn 1992, 61).

Tennyson's poetic voice certainly, for a while, succeeded to occupy this silence as he turned himself into a major public institution, uniting the Romantic ideal of individual experience with the function of public speech as comfort, consolation, and consolidation: here, the poet's voice becomes the central location where universal values of humanity are being desired, contested, and confirmed. For the poet, this could include the consolation of the head of state. Tennyson was summoned to a personal audience with the Queen on 14 April 1862, on which occasion Victoria –an avid reader – compared her widowhood to the situation of Mariana in Tennyson's poem of that name. There were several more visits in the next twenty years, the last one on 7 August 1883. On this occasion, it was Queen Victoria who had to console the aged Tennyson "when he talked despairingly of the irreligion and socialism pervading modern life" (Martin 1980, 539). She did so by quoting, from memory, these lines from *In Memoriam*: "Oh yet we trust that somehow good / Will be the final goal of ill" (LIV, ll. 1–2; Tennyson 2014, 396) and "Eternal form shall still divide / The eternal soul from all beside; / And I shall know him when we meet" (XLVII, ll. 6–8; 390). Tennyson was flattered: "I thought that very pretty, to quote my own words in answer to me" (qtd. in Martin 1980, 539). As the mourning Queen is reported to have said: "Next to the Bible, *In Memoriam* is my comfort" (qtd. in Sinfield 1986, 1).

This function seems intended in the poem itself, which comments on its own effect as an opiate substitute:

> I sometimes hold it half a sin
>   To put in words the grief I feel;
>   For words, like Nature, half reveal
> And half conceal the Soul within.

> But, for the unquiet heart and brain
> A use in measured language lies;
> The sad mechanic exercise,
> Like dull narcotics, numbing pain.
> (V, ll. 1–8; Tennyson 2014, 348–349)

Here poetic speech, the writing and reading of poetry ("measured language"), is presented as a "mechanic exercise" whose rhythmic regularity has a soothing effect. It is part of the stoic attitude that Tennyson calls "self-control" (CXXXI, l. 9; 477), a will to believe "the truths that never can be proved" (ibid., l. 10). Yet, besides the faith, there is a sense of doubt in these poems that melodic palliatives alone cannot satisfy. Tennyson wrote this sequence before Darwin published his theory of evolution; but he responded to then current theories of geology and progressive succession as laid down in Charles Lyell's *Principles of Geology* (1830) and Robert Chambers's *Vestiges of the Natural History of Creation* (1844). Influenced by these theories, he expressed widespread fears of a world without God, a world in which nature was cruel and meaningless, "red in tooth and claw" (LVI, l. 15; 399):

> O life as futile, then, as frail!
>   O for thy voice to soothe and bless!
>   What hope of answer, or redress?
> Behind the veil, behind the veil.
> (LVI, ll. 25–28; 400)

As Christopher Ricks explains in his edition, the veil most likely refers to the veiled statue of truth at Sais in Egypt, which can only be uncovered at the cost of one's life (in Tennyson 2014, 400). The veiled nature of truth calls for a medium to lift this veil but it denies direct access or communication with the sphere that is occluded "behind the veil". The spiritualist medium promises a revelation of this kind but his or her authority is (to say the least) dubious. Such a 'medium' is exposed as a sham in Robert Browning's dramatic monologue "Mr. Sludge, 'the Medium'" (1864). The dramatic nature of this poem, spoken by the medium himself, Mr. Sludge, is immediately evident from the start: his most recent client has discovered that it's all a trick, this speaking with the dead:

> Now, don't, sir! Don't expose me! Just this once!
> This was the first and only time, I'll swear, —
> Look at me, – see, I kneel, – the only time,
> I swear, I ever cheated, – yes, by the soul
> Of Her who hears – (your sainted mother, sir!)
> All, except this last accident, was truth –

> This little kind of slip! – and even this,
> It was your own wine, sir, the good champagne,
> I took it for Catawba, you're so kind)
> Which put the folly in my head!
>
> (ll. 1–10)[51]

This medium's breath is in danger of being extinguished by the angry client: "Aie —aie—aie! / Please, sir! your thumbs are through my windpipe, sir! / Ch—ch!" (ll. 16–18). Browning – or the angry client in the poem – then has Sludge sit down to explain the tricks of his trade, the attraction of the supernatural in a world of "cold philosophy",[52] commerce, and materialism. In a sardonic manner, Sludge extols the powers of "story-telling, brightening up / Each old dull bit of fact that drops its shine" (ll. 192–93), and notes how tables have a manner of tipping of their own accord, "and pens, good Lord, / Who knows if you drive them or they drive you?" (ll. 196–97), referring to the practice of automatic writing (Miller 2018, 122–150). Doubts about the truthfulness of the medium's reports are expelled mainly because there is a *social* desire for trust and belief. The medium is a sham who gives his audience what they want to see and hear, and they will interpret his ravings as spiritual communication ("read wrong things right", l. 308). This culminates in the 'conjuring up' of a dead child, that most Victorian of topics: "a certain child who died, you know, / And whose last breath you thought your lips had felt" (ll. 469–70):

> [. . .] Sludge begins
> At your entreaty with your dearest dead,
> The little voice set lisping once again,
> The tiny hand made feel for yours once more,
> The poor lost image brought back, plain as dreams[.]
>
> (ll. 471–475)

Ultimately, this medium's message is that his host has been complicit in the trickery all along, as he, his family and friends have all the while "fed fat / Their self-conceit which else had starved" (ll. 641–642). Sludge regains his breath to spew reams of verses in contempt and condemnation of his host, ridiculously named "Hiram H. Horsefall" (l. 1032), and his host's gullible friends, but also to argue the closeness between his trickery and Christian beliefs in an

---

[51] Catawba refers to an American grape variety that was used to make Ohio sparkling wines, which, in the mid-nineteenth century, were considered to rival French champagne. The poem's location is Boston (l. 60).
[52] "Do not all charms fly / At the mere touch of cold philosophy?" asks the speaker in Keats's "Lamia", part 2, ll. 229–230 (Wu 2006, 1417).

afterlife, or children's belief in Santa Claus (l. 887). He claims that what he does is to give modern adults back their belief in the miraculous (l. 1221): "Truth questionless though unexplainable" (1220) – indeed, like the poet: "Bless us, I'm turning poet!" Sludge exclaims (l. 1184), and later goes on to compare his lying to the inventions of Homer, "who sings how Greeks / That never were, in Troy which never was, / Did this or the other impossible great thing!" (ll. 1436–-1438). He also compares himself to modern American writers such as Henry Wadsworth Longfellow (1807–1882) and Nathaniel Hawthorne (1804–1864), as well as to historians who play narrative tricks to make the past seem to come alive. At the end of the poem, Sludge has managed to persuade Horsefall not to expose him after all. Alone in his bedroom, he plans to leave Boston behind, to slander his host as a murderer and a bully, and seek new victims elsewhere.

Published in 1864, Browning's poem targets the dishonest practices of spiritualism, but at numerous points it also draws interesting parallels between the spiritualist medium, Mr Sludge, and the very medium of poetry as a form of imaginative writing with a similar bag of tricks at its disposal: fiction as a form of make-believe (J. H. Miller 2009). It marks, as it were, the other side of the medal of Tennyson's earnest attempts to use poetry as a spiritual practice. Browning's "Mr Sludge" documents a disillusionment with the impassioned speech of Romantic poetry and its ability to establish contact with an ideal, numinous world – this, Browning seems to say, is all a sham invented to bamboozle and hoodwink people. But the voice of Sludge has its own fascination as a man who is not evil but who makes the best possible use of his talents for himself, holding up a mirror to the crass materialism of the modern world and its desire for a materialistic version of spirituality. Browning's borrowed voices in the dramatic monologue offer a new pathway for poetic speech, away from close identification with the poet him- or herself (if only in the form of a 'negative capability' or endless potentiality, as we saw in Keats) towards an ideal of modernist neo-classical 'impersonality'. From the borrowed voices of Browning's dramatic monologues, we arrive, on the one hand, at the multiple, discordant, "different voices" of T. S. Eliot's *The Waste Land* (Eliot 2010, 4), while, on the other hand, we approach the emerging stream-of-consciousness technique of the modernist novel, which attempts to represent mental processes in language as if they were unfiltered, as for example in the final chapter of James Joyce's (1882–1941) novel *Ulysses* (1922).

Moreover, like the Victorian realist novel, the world of Browning's poems is filled with stuff – with food, furniture, and other material objects that exceed his speaker's control: "stuffed chairs" and "sideboards" (ll. 78–79). Earlier poets addressed single objects, virtues, or qualities; Browning's poems presents furnished spaces full of objects. Like the novel, they not retreat into a poet's inner world but aim to represent, on paper, the complexity and plenitude of the real world. As they do this, they are critical and self-critical about the performance of media even as they explore their potential. They discount the possibility of direct and instantaneous connection with the "dearest dead" or any other higher power. "Mr Sludge, 'the Medium'" unmasks the performance of the medium as a theatrical sham – a process that begins with the quotation marks in the poem's title. More than Tennyson's, Browning's scepticism encompasses poetry and its possibilities, questioning its meaning and distrusting exaggerated claims about the performative and connective powers of media in general. "Mr. Sludge, 'the Medium'" thus belongs firmly to the age of representation. As we will see, however, 'new media' and new technologies of mediation from the late nineteenth century onwards will come to challenge the Victorian realist paradigm of representation and push towards a new dispensation of media affordances that encourage instantaneous connectivity.

III The Age of Connection (since c. 1850 CE)

8 Touch: Literature as Telecommunication

We have seen in the previous chapter how spiritualist practices – automatic writing, but also to some extent poetry – could be harnessed to establish communication with the beyond, to make contact with the dead:

> So word by word, and line by line,
>   The dead man touched me from the past,
>   And all at once it seemed at last
> His living soul was flashed on mine,

as Tennyson writes in elegy XCV of *In Memoriam* (ll. 33–36; 2014, 439). Overcoming great distances of time and space had been the chief task of writing from very early on (Innis 2007, 26–27), and epic poems from *Gilgamesh* to Dante's (1265–1321) *Divine Comedy* usually contained reports from the world of the dead, in the form of journeys to the underworld. What was new in 1850 was that messages from the beyond were being transmitted sequentially, "word by word, and line by line", and that they should be imagined and experienced as a form of physical contact, mediated through the sense of touch.

At this point, Victorian poetry met modern telecommunications, not merely in the form of spiritualism but also in the technology of the telegraph. Tennyson himself was fascinated by this. In 1897, his son reported an anecdote in which the poet stood by a telegraph pole to listen to "the wail of the wires, the souls of dead messages" (1897, 2: 325). The electric telegraph, from the 1840s onwards, made it possible to send and receive messages across long distances – this was literally 'writing at a distance' (*tele-graphy*), but it was writing in code, using an input device called a 'telegraph key'. The operator would tap this key, and at the other end a 'sounder' would respond with a sequence of clicks.

Literature and the Telegraph

Poets, as we have seen, are naturally interested in communication, also in communication across great distances of space and time – from Keats's reading of Homer ("On First Looking into Chapman's Homer", 1816) to Tennyson's elegiac invocation of his dead friend Hallam in *In Memoriam* and Browning's critique of "Mr Sludge, 'the Medium'" (see ch. 7). Telegraphy, the technical feat of sending and receiving encoded messages through wires, will have seemed to many observers as amazing and mysterious as telepathy (Luckhurst 2002) or telekinesis – the ability to read somebody else's mind or move objects without touching them. It seemed to transgress the laws of nature as they had hitherto been known.

The first electrical telegraphs were introduced in the 1840s, using an electric current through wires to transmit messages. The first commercial model was the Cooke and Wheatstone telegraph, invented in 1837. Samuel Morse invented Morse code in 1838. Telegraph offices in most cities and towns soon made it possible to send and receive messages called telegrams. The first transatlantic cable connecting the British Isles and North America was laid in 1858 between Ireland and Newfoundland. A second, more durable cable was laid in 1866, and several others were put in place in the coming decades. Poems were written in praise of the cable to celebrate the newly won connectivity, including one by the British physicist James Clerk Maxwell (1831–1879) in 1860:

Valentine from a Telegraph Clerk ♂ to a Telegraph Clerk ♀

> "The tendrils of my soul are twined
>   With thine, though many a mile apart,
> And thine in close-coiled circuits wind
>   Around the needle of my heart.
>
> "Constant as Daniell, strong as Grove.
>   Ebullient throughout its depths like Smee,
> My heart puts forth its tide of love,
>   And all its circuits close in thee.
>
> "O tell me, when along the line
>   From my full heart the message flows,
> What currents are induced in thine?
>   One click from thee will end my woes."
>
> Through many an Ohm the Weber flew,
>   And clicked this answer back to me, –
> "I am thy Farad, staunch and true,
>   Charged to a Volt with love for thee."
>   (Campbell and Garnett 1882, 630–631)

Apart from the potential pun on the gender-neutral term 'clerk', which also happens to be one of the author's first names, this poem is remarkable for its daring combination of conventional love imagery with technical words and objects: "coiled circuits", the telegraph's "needle", "the line", "currents" – many of these terms are themselves metaphors, taken from natural language and adapted to scientific phenomena ("currents" originally means and is still used for running or flowing water as well as electron flow; the reference to electricity is first attested, according to the OED, in the mid-eighteenth century). The names in the second stanza refer to inventors and manufacturers of electrochemical batteries (John

Daniell, William Grove, and Alfred Smee), and in the last stanza there are references to units named after scientists Ohm, Weber, Faraday, and Volta – in effect turning the words of physics into poetry. Maxwell's poem established a new form of communication between science and literature, translating poetic language into science and scientific language into poetry. Maxwell wrote poetry for much of his life, including another poem on the failure of the first transatlantic cable (Bruton 2019).

It is significant that Maxwell chose the valentine, a conventional love lyric associated with Valentine's Day, for his telegraphic poem. From John Donne in the early seventeenth century ("Hail Bishop Valentine, whose day this is") to Carol Ann Duffy (1955–) in the late twentieth ("Valentine"), the valentine has been and continues to be a popular genre of the love lyric. It is a truism that many love lyrics imply the physical distance between lover and beloved, a distance that can be merely spatial but is often also social, as in the courtly love tradition of the Middle Ages and its post-medieval continuations and transformations. Physical separation between lover and beloved leads to intense expressions of longing and assertions of powerful emotions ("though many a mile apart", "constant", "strong", "staunch and true", etc.), and the hope that contact with the beloved will result in a release of tension, an end to pain: "One click from thee will end my woes". Though not composed in the sonnet form, Maxwell's valentine touches many bases of the Petrarchan sonnet (see ch. 3).

The point of this poem, then, is to assert a certain continuity of the human "heart" despite technological change (including, though this is far from remarkable in the mid-nineteenth century, normative heterosexuality). The only difference would be that, instead of posting letters or greeting cards, lovers would send each other telegrams. Poetic communication would stay the same in form and content, it would only be mediated in a different way. In this, it resembles the media condition of the early modern sonnet in the age of print, which had to deal with the fact that its apparently private, made-for-manuscript verses were made available for a wider public in the form of print – not always, or not usually, against the poet's wishes. Of course, in many cases one can assume that there was only a tenuous link between the 'stories' told or implied in the sonnets or sonnet sequences and their authors' amorous exploits in real life. But there are bibliographical indications that some sonnets, at least, were originally composed to be included in personal letters, as private communications, and only later gathered into longer sequences (Warkentin 1980; Marotti 1990, 147).

In the early modern dispensation, the distance that needed to be bridged so that intimate lyric communication could take place in writing was that between the heart and the pen or quill (instead of the telegraphic "needle" of Maxwell's valentine). A prime example of this is the opening sonnet of Philip Sidney's sequence *Astrophil and Stella* (1581–1582), which negotiates between emotional authenticity ("[l]oving in truth", l. 1) and the inevitable reference to literary antecedents for inspiration ("[o]ft turning others leaves, to see if thence would flow / Some fresh and fruitful showers upon my sunburnt brain", ll. 7–8). This first of 108 sonnets and eleven 'songs' ends with the Muse's exhortation to "look in thy heart, and write" (l. 14) (Sidney 2002, 153) – the irony being that this was, at the time, already a literary cliché, well-worn through its use in many "others' leaves". This opening salvo sets the scene for many subsequent iterations of the paradoxical associations between feeling and speaking, nature and writing, original and copy throughout the sequence. The paradox of distance and proximity is explored quite strikingly in sonnet nine, which plays on the polysemy of the word 'touch', which can also mean black marble (touchstone) – here designating the colour of Stella's eyes – and touchpaper or touchwood, which is used to light a fire:

> Of touch they are, that without touch doth touch,
> Which Cupid's self from Beauty's mine did draw:
> Of touch they are, and poor I am their straw.
> (2002, 156, ll. 12–14)

Lighting the lover's inward fire, Stella's eyes establish a physical contact even at a distance – triggering, in Shakespeare's words, "the inly touch of love" (*Two Gentlemen of Verona* 2.7.18). Visuality and tactile experience are indeed frequently connected, and the sense of touch is often invoked as a substitute for sight, as when blinded Gloucester in Shakespeare's *King Lear* longs to meet his son Edgar with the words: "Might I but live to see thee in my touch / I'd say I had eyes again" (4.1.23–24).[53] In the context of love poetry, however, both sight and touch are not to be trusted:

> In faith, I do not love thee with mine eyes,
> For they in thee a thousand errors note;
> But 'tis my heart that loves what they despise,
> Who in despite of view is pleased to dote.

Shakespeare's sonnet 141 then goes on to riff on the other senses, including "base touches" (note the plural, here denoting a sexual connotation), which cannot "[d]issuade one foolish heart from serving thee" (l. 10) In the hierarchy of the senses, touch was always 'base', i.e., sordid or ignoble.[54] This changes

---

[53] 'Seeing is touching' is one of the basic conceptual metaphors identified in Lakoff and Johnson 1980.
[54] For an in-depth discussion of the sense of touch in the early modern period, see Moshenska 2014 and Classen 2012; I am also indebted to Gabel 2022.

somewhat in the seventeenth century with Milton's *Paradise Lost*. When he connects "the sense of touch" to human procreation (Milton 1998, 8.579–580) and shows Adam and Eve touching or holding hands (ibid., 5.17, 12.648), he depicts an emerging concept of coupledom: the companionate marriage.

There is a long line of literature, from the metaphysical poetry of John Donne to the eighteenth-century cult of 'sensibility' and beyond, which explores the fusion of the spiritual and the erotic on the basis of the sense of touch. Laurence Sterne, whose *Sentimental Journey through France and Italy* (1768) gave a name to an entire genre of 'sentimental fiction', celebrates this fusion in no uncertain terms:

> Dear sensibility! source inexhausted of all that's precious in our joys, or costly in our sorrows! thou chainest thy martyr down upon his bed of straw – and 'tis thou who lifts him up to HEAVEN – eternal fountain of our feelings! – 'tis here I trace thee – and this is thy divinity which stirs within me – not that, in some sad and sickening moments, *my soul shrinks back upon herself, and startles at destruction* – mere pomp of words! – but that I feel some generous joys and generous cares beyond myself – all comes from thee, great, great SENSORIUM of the world! which vibrates, if a hair of our heads but falls upon the ground, in the remotest desert of thy creation. (Sterne 1986, 141)

Sterne's "sensibility", here expressed by his narrator, Yorick, is a sensory response to the sympathetic 'vibration' of the world, triggered by the mutual (physical) touch of self and environment – a harmony between the individual and the universe that is here also expressed in the form of faith in the divine nature of "creation". This celebration, however, is somewhat undercut by the text, when the narrator's ideals encounter a rather harsh social and physical reality. This applies not only to the famous episode of the caged bird, which leads Yorick to deplore slavery, but also to the very end of the novel, when he is compelled to share a room at an inn with a lady and her maidservant. The room is narrow, so involuntary physical contact is inevitable. The last sentence reads: "So that when I stretched out my hand, I caught hold of the fille de chambre's – " (148). In early editions of the book, Tim Parnell notes, the dash encouraged readers to connect this sentence to the centred and capitalised word 'END' below it, forming a typographical joke and a verbal pun (2003, 246). Touching, indeed.

As David Trotter has argued, the world was ready to be connected long before the new technologies of the nineteenth century arrived; connectivity precedes connection (Trotter 2020). This is also borne out in Anthony Trollope's short story "The Telegraph Girl" (1877). Like Maxwell's valentine, it is a love story about the difficulties of "getting the message through", to quote the motto of the US Army Signal Corps of 1860 (Trotter 2020, 1). It is a story set in the midst of a communications revolution: a widowed printer, Abraham Hall, falls in love with Lucy Graham, a twenty-five-year-old 'telegraph girl', one of 800 women employed in the headquarters of the National Telegraph Department in London. The Telegraph Bill of 1868 had given the Post Office a monopoly on the new technology. The versatile novelist Trollope, who had himself worked for the Post Office, knew this subject well. His story documents important changes in the social landscape of Victorian Britain, after the Universal Education Act of 1870 expanded literacy and numeracy and provided new opportunities of employment and independence for women from lower classes.

One interesting aspect of this story about an unmarried young woman living in London is the former scarcity of jobs outside of domestic service or – the unmentioned, unmentionable – descent into prostitution. Lucy Graham is proud of her freedom and her professionalism as a government employee. But technological changes exert pressure on her skills, as the older technology of needle-punch codes is replaced by a new acoustic system that requires her to listen to rather than "read [. . .] her telegraphic literature" (Trollope 1995, 365). "But now that this system of little tinkling sounds was coming up, – a system which seemed to be very pleasant to those females who were gifted with musical aptitudes, – she found herself to be less quick, less expert, less useful than her neighbours. This was very sad [. . .]" (365–366). This will be part of her motivation to leave the service and marry the printer, Mr. Hall. But before this can happen, before a connection between the two can be achieved, Hall needs to get his message through. This, ironically, is more difficult than one would assume in a "department [. . .] engaged in sending and receiving messages" (378). He cannot ask her by sending a telegram; his is the kind of private message, "of vital importance" (ibid.), that needs to be delivered face to face. But "the staff [. . .] who are engaged in sending and receiving messages, the privacy of which may be of vital importance, should be kept during the hours of work as free as possible from communication with the public. [. . .] Therefore, when Abraham Hall pressed his request the doorkeeper told him that it was quite impossible" (378).

Of course, this being a Trollope story, these difficulties of communication can be overcome, a channel is established, and the message is gotten through. Despite Lucy's lack of musicality, the narrator assures us, "[h]er sense of hearing was at any rate not deficient" (381). "The word had been spoken [. . .] which of course, – of course, – must be a commandment to her" (ibid.). In the context, the stuttering repetition of this "of course" belongs to Lucy's consciousness and refers to her remaining doubts about her being "not fit for him" (ibid.). These doubts are then alleviated by nonverbal signals by her future husband: "he caught her in his arms and kissed her. [. . .] Then in his own masterful manner he put on his hat and stalked out of the room without any more words" (382). The happy ending is secured, no more words are needed, and the story can end.

The short story is itself a piece of "telegraphic literature", to use Trollope's own term (365), a speeded-up version (in five chapters) of a typically much longer Trollope novel. Here, it seems as if the author was self-consciously playing with possibilities of telegraphy, a medium that was not yet exactly threatening older ways of literary communication. This was still the heyday of stories in magazines, read by masses of recently educated people with previously unknown amounts of leisure and money to spend, a part of the 'paper worlds' discussed in ch. 6 above. Still, the pairing of a young telegraph girl and an older printer in 1877 seems oddly apt for a story in which the obstacles to love and marriage reside primarily in communication technologies and the institutional infrastructures around them.[55]

Deep-Sea Cables

In the late nineteenth century, Rudyard Kipling's poem "The Deep-Sea Cables" takes its readers to "the deserts of the deep" (l. 3) and its "great grey level plains of ooze where the shell-burred cables creep" (l. 4). In this poem from 1893, which was included in his 1896 collection *The Seven Seas* (Kipling 2015, 471–472), Kipling revisits Tennyson's deep-sea poem "The Kraken" (1830), whose alien world "far, far beneath" (l. 2) still existed outside of any human time frame and whose "sleep" was as yet "uninvaded" (l. 3) by any form of human presence as it waited for the apocalypse, "the latter fire" to wake it up (l. 13) (Tennyson 2014, 17–18). In Kipling's radical modernisation of this vision, submarine cables have invaded this alien space with frantic if invisible human activity: "Here in the womb of the world [. . .] / Words, and the words of men, flicker and flutter and beat" (ll. 5–6). This radical change, the irruption of (masculine) technology into (feminine) nature and the destruction of the "timeless" order of things (l. 9), is not deplored, however, but greeted at the poem's end with the hope of establishing connection and unity between the parts of the British Empire:

> They have wakened the timeless Things; they have killed their father Time;
> Joining hands in the gloom, a league from the last of the sun.
> Hush! Men talk to-day o'er the waste of the ultimate slime,
> And a new Word runs between: whispering, 'Let us be one!'
>
> (ll. 9–12)

---

[55] Henry James's novella "In the Cage" (1898) is another interesting story about a woman telegraphist; I cannot discuss this here for reasons of space.

Although it is sometimes assumed that this poem refers to the transatlantic cable (e.g., Karlin in Kipling 2015, 663), the plural "cables" in the title and the context of this poem within the sequence *A Song of the English* make it more likely that it refers to the expansion of British cable to other continents, which connected the far-flung reaches of the Empire in the 1870s. Bombay, for instance, was connected to London via cable in 1870, Australia in 1872, and New Zealand in 1876 (fig. 13).[56]

The poem intriguingly combines a vertical axis of depth – the vast distance of the deep sea from the surface, which is understood to be temporal as well as spatial, and is associated with vast amounts of geological and millennial time – with a horizontal axis of travel, connection, and control. The spatial distance between Britain and its colonies has been transformed from a space of separation into a conduit for near-instantaneous communication that makes Kipling hope for a closer union among them. Clearly, the horizontal axis triumphs over the vertical, turning the sea-bed into "waste" (void and/or useless space) which is meaningful only as a distance to be crossed when "men talk [. . .] o'er" it (l. 11) and, at least metaphorically, "join[] hands" (l. 10), establish a connection, even a unity ("Let us be one!"). Technology bridges formerly unimaginable distances, transforming the waste into a channel for telegraphic signals. Steam globalisation has killed the Kraken. Instead of threatening sea-monsters, the deep now only harbours some harmless "blind white sea-snakes" (l. 2).

Whereas Tennyson invoked immeasurable aeons of deep time, Kipling has taken the measure of the seabed ("a league from the last of the sun") and found nothing but emptiness and monotony, "grey level plains of ooze" (l. 4) and "slime" (l. 11). The deep sea has been demystified and disenchanted; it has become boring, a mere medium for transoceanic communication. In establishing high-speed connections between continents, the cables have "killed" not only sea-monsters and mystery but "Time" itself. Sacred time as the father of "the timeless Things" (l. 9), eternal but also unpredictable essences, has been ousted by what Jacques Le Goff has called "merchant's time", a "measurable [. . .] oriented and predictable time" that is "superimposed [. . .] on that of the natural environment, which was a time both eternally renewed and perpetually unpredictable" (1980, 35).

Kipling's later science fiction story "With the Night Mail" (1905) replaces the ocean with the sky as a medium. Distances are abolished not only for the benefit of information but for human beings and commodities as well. For the year 2000, that story imagines a global postal service administered by the "Aerial Board of Control" sending airships around the world. Kipling's vision of

---

56 Wikipedia, "Submarine communications cable", date of access: 22 Feb. 2021.

technological modernity is summed up in the slogan "Transportation is Civilisation" (1994c, 667) – an optimistic Edwardian catchphrase from the heyday of Empire to set beside E. M. Forster's (1879–1970) more famous and also more sceptical motto "Only connect" (from the novel *Howards End*, 1910).

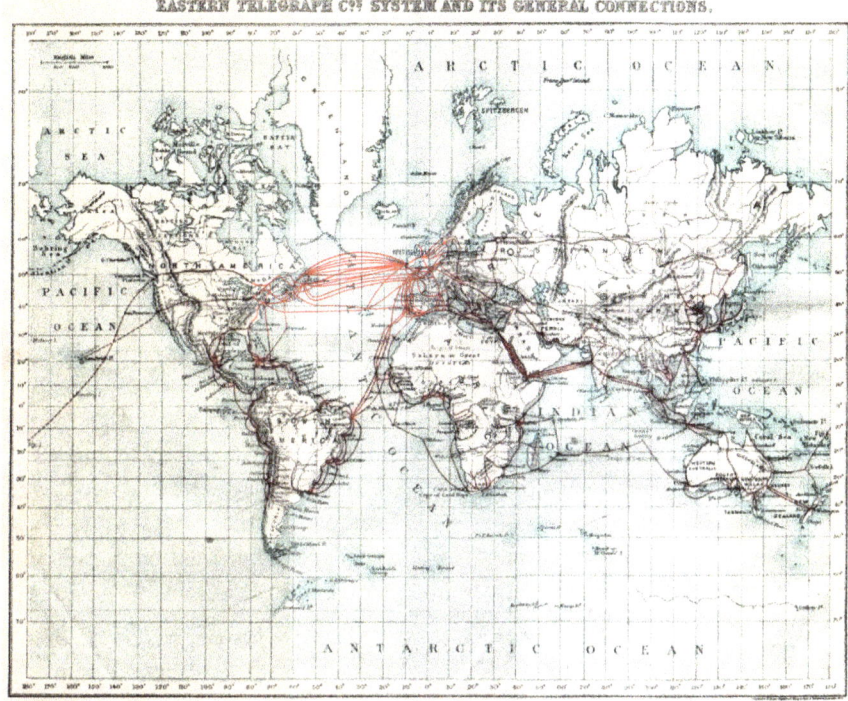

Fig. 13: The Eastern Telegraph Company network in 1901.
Source: Alamy Stock Photo.

There is an additional media comparison to be made between Tennyson's and Kipling's deep-sea poems. "The Kraken" was published in Tennyson's 1830 collection *Poems, Chiefly Lyrical*. In this original publication, the poem is set in a generous amount of negative space, which, besides conforming to typographical convention, enhances this poem's associations of timelessness and isolation. Kipling's poem first appeared in a periodical, the *English Illustrated Magazine* of May 1893. Its context is *A Song of the English*, a sequence of poems that articulate Kipling's imperialist convictions, culminating in the call-and-response of "The Song of the Cities", ranging from Bombay to Auckland, and "England's Answer" to them. The sequence is framed by two drawings: a heraldic design of

Britannia and a picture of three early modern sailing ships reminiscent of Francis Drake (c. 1540–1596) and the *Golden Hind*. In this politically charged textual and visual context, international communications secure what is envisaged as a lasting connection between 'Mother England' and her imperial "sons", scattered across the globe. The contrast between book and periodical is also one of limited audience as opposed to large-scale commercial distribution. Towards the end of the nineteenth century, Kipling's poems and stories easily reached a global audience.

Wireless Horrors

Next to its practical usefulness for communication and contact at a distance, and its naturalisation (as in Maxwell's valentine) into a conventional tradition of love poetry, the telegraph also inspired anxieties, as in Trollope's story "The Telegraph Girl". Further technological development may have contributed to this sense of something uncanny, as long-distance communication soon no longer required physical, visible wires. Electromagnetic waves, called 'radio waves', were first identified by Heinrich Hertz in 1886, and the first transmitters and receivers were built by Guglielmo Marconi in 1895–96. Marconi made the first demonstration for the British government in 1896. Radio technology was widely used around 1900, referred to as 'wireless telegraphy' in Britain. The first transatlantic radio signals were transmitted by Marconi from Nova Scotia in 1902. After the First World War, public broadcasting began in 1919 in the Netherlands and in 1920 in Britain. At first, there were doubts that public broadcasting might interfere with military and other important civil messages; but by 1922 there were many wireless societies in Britain with more than 3,000 members (Briggs 1961).

One literary genre that picked up such anxieties of communication with an invisible world was late Victorian gothic fiction as it slowly developed towards modern horror fiction. A Neoplatonic separation between the real world, or the world that appears real to us, and an invisible but nonetheless real or even more real world of (usually evil) spirits and demons was held up for inspection in the fiction of the Welsh author Arthur Machen (1863–1947). In one of his best-known stories, "The Great God Pan" (1890/1894), the connection between this epistemology of the spirit world and telegraphy was made explicit. Dr Raymond, about to perform a horrible experiment on the brain of a young woman, explains to his friend Clarke:

> this world of ours is pretty well girded now with the telegraph wires and cables; thought, with something less than the speed of thought, flashes from sunrise to sunset, from north

to south, across the floods and the desert places. Suppose that an electrician of to-day were suddenly to perceive that he and his friends have merely been playing with pebbles and mistaking them for the foundations of the world; suppose that such a man saw uttermost space lie open before the current, and words of men flash forth to the sun and beyond the sun into the systems beyond, and the voices of articulate-speaking men echo in the waste void that bounds our thought. (Machen 2019, 11)

What Raymond wants to achieve in his gruesome experiment is to bridge "the unutterable, the unthinkable gulf that yawns profound between two worlds, the world of matter and the world of spirit"; he wants to "set free the current, [. . .] complete the communication" between these two worlds "with a touch" (11). Needless to say, the effect of this "communication" will not be benign. This and similar stories used the available technology of the day as a metaphor for otherwise "unutterable" mysteries of reality, and they operated in the mode of a media fantasy in the boundary zone of literary realism and an imaginary remainder that conventional Victorian realism could not satisfy. They hinted at a hidden dimension of reality or even, as in Machen's extreme case, an utterly other world "behind the veil" (Tennyson 2014, 400) – they "pined for the unseen" (Machen 2019, 15) as did, each in their different way, George Eliot's tale "The Lifted Veil" (1859), Rudyard Kipling's "The Mark of the Beast" (1890), and Richard Marsh's *The Beetle* (1897), to name only three among many Victorian gothic tales.

In Machen's demonic fantasy, the telegraph was merely a metaphor for connection between otherwise distant and strictly separate spheres of reality. In another late Victorian story, it became an agent not of connection but of displacement, temporal as well as spatial. In Kipling's uncanny story "Wireless", first published in 1902 (the quotation marks are part of the title), we see the past invading the present. On a winter evening, the narrator visits his friend, a chemist, as the chemist's nephew, an electrician, is just about to conduct another experiment with radio signals inspired by "this Marconi business" (Kipling 1994a, 553). He explains the physics behind "Hertzian waves" and "induction" (562) to the narrator; his admiration for the technology is clear: "There's nothing we sha'n't be able to do in ten years", he says. The story was written two years before amateur broadcasting without a license was made illegal in 1904. While they are waiting and drinking alcoholic beverages concocted from the chemist's stock, the narrator's attention wanders to the young chemist's assistant, Mr Shaynor, who is suffering from a severe cough and shows signs of tuberculosis. Shaynor is briefly taken for a walk by a beautiful young woman, whose name is Fanny Brand, around the nearby church of St. Agnes. Later, after trying a couple of the narrator's cocktails, Shaynor falls into a kind of trance and begins to write poetry. In fact, he begins to recreate a famous poem; what he writes is largely identical to parts of

Keats's poem *The Eve of St. Agnes*. But he is not rewriting the poem from memory, but literally re-*creating* it. He stops now and then, writes parts of it first in prose and then in verse, and in between seeks inspiration in an advertisement that shows a picture of a woman.

The narrator is astonished, the more so as he later hears from Shaynor that the young man has never read anything by Keats. Shaynor is a druggist by profession, like Keats, suffers from consumption, like Keats, and his girlfriend's name is Fanny Brand, which resembles the name of Keats's girlfriend, Fanny Brawne. The narrator concludes that something must have happened in analogy to the electrical induction of the radio waves, by means of which signals from a great distance have been transmitted. Shaynor, the young assistant, has been turned into a receiver; his head, while writing, is described as" moving machine-like" (565). "Night, my drink, and solitude were evidently turning Mr. Shaynor into a poet", the narrator muses (565). The result of the similarities between Keats and Shaynor appears to him "logical and inevitable. As inevitable as induction", he thinks (566): "If he hasn't [read Keats], it's the identical bacillus, or Hertzian wave of tuberculosis, *plus* Fanny Brand and the professional status which, in conjunction with the mainstream of subconscious thought common to all mankind, has thrown up temporarily and induced Keats" (567). In places, Shaynor has even improved on Keats's poem (568). The spiritualist association with this sort of literary induction is made explicit at the end, when the narrator asks the young poet *manqué* Shaynor whether he has ever "seen a spiritualistic séance" and suggests that radio transmission has a lot in common with spiritualism: "odds and ends of messages coming out of nowhere" (573). But Shaynor only retorts that "mediums are all impostors" and are only in it "for the money they can make" (573). He agrees, in other words, with Browning and his Mr. Sludge (see ch. 7).

In this story, Kipling draws on the new technology of radio waves ('Hertzian waves') and electromagnetism (induction) to write a literary ghost story, combining a crude but fascinating blend of current discourses of technology, materialist determinism, psychoanalysis, and spiritualism. Kipling himself was critical of spiritualism throughout his life, warning against it in his story "The Sending of Dana Da" (1888) and his poem "En-dor" (1919). His sister Trix, who was mentally ill, dabbled in crystal gazing and automatic writing (Lycett 1999, 478; Miller 2018, 122–150).

"Hertzian waves" clearly captured the literary imagination around 1900. For Kipling, they made an interesting metaphor for the sources of literary inspiration: "something coming through from somewhere" (565). Where does poetry, or literature, come from? What is its channel or medium? How does it get its message through? The story does not suggest a single answer to these questions but offers an entire (and rather strange) cocktail of current concerns from "subconscious thought [. . .] common to all mankind" (567) to particular social and personal factors. Its ultimate source remains mysterious. Apparently, Kipling himself shared this fascination, writing in a letter to Rider Haggard in 1918: "We are only telephone wires" (Kipling 1965, 100).

The fascination and anxiety in this story is about the reach of these waves and signals that pass through human bodies and threaten to dissolve the integrity of the self: Shaynor is transformed into a wireless receiver, invaded by poetry or by the ghost of Keats, and the narrator himself begins to feel that his self is being split apart for a while, "my own soul most dispassionately considered my own soul" (1994a, 566) until, reassuringly, "I found myself one person again" (567). In this story, Kipling explored the technological uncanny, the scary aspects of wireless technology: simultaneity, physical dislocation, the possibility "to be in two places at the same time" (Kern 2019, 147). Most importantly, Keats's poem *The Eve of St. Agnes* is about bodily possession and rape; similar to Porphyro's rape of Madeline, a telepathic entity takes possession of Shaynor's body and mind. If this story is "an evocation of the power of writing itself" (Grimes 2011, 32), it is so only with the irony that this power has spun out of control in the era of electromagnetism and radio waves. The story questions how these new technologies will affect an older media dispensation of authorship, writing, and selfhood (see also Luckhurst 2002). Its narrator's limited understanding of events also places this story in the context of modernist impressionism, "situating the wireless at the origin of the impressionist subject" (Fielding 2015, 27) and shattering the narrator's belief in "objectivity, reliability, and authority" (29) as what was thought of as knowledge is transformed into (not more than) consciousness (33). Paradoxically, the new technologies of connection, in these stories, do not lead towards a utopia of universal connectivity, but to horrifying experiences of mental, physical, and social dissociation.

A similarly destructive view of new technologies of communication can be seen in E. M. Forster's science fiction short story "The Machine Stops" (1909). Forster imagines a future humanity living underground, out of touch with the world and each other, residing in isolation each in a cell of their own, while their every need is being provided for by a gigantic machine. They listen to music, lectures, and audiobooks on a sort of radio. The machine can also connect people from opposite ends of the planet by means of a form of instant messaging or video conferencing. In this future world, books have become a thing of the past, indeed "a survival from the ages of litter" (Forster 2001, 95). Forster here seems to be playing with the similar sound of "litter" (rubbish) and "letter": literature has become 'litterature'. Only one book remains, and that is the "Book of the Machine" (95, 97, 115), an instruction manual published by the "Central

Committee" (95). When the machine finally breaks down, its type of civilisation is destroyed; at the end there is hope for renewal with a rediscovery of the earth's surface and its "untainted sky" (the final words of the story) (123). "The Machine Stops" is an early instance of many twentieth and twenty-first-century scenarios of an apocalyptic future dominated by inhuman technology. In their novels about human clones and humanoid robots, for example, authors like David Mitchell (1969–; *Cloud Atlas*, 2004), Kazuo Ishiguro (1954–; *Never Let Me Go*, 2005; *Klara and the Sun*, 2021), Ian McEwan (1948–; *Machines Like Me*, 2019), and Jeanette Winterson (1959–; *Frankisstein*, 2019) have explored looming scenarios of future technologies and possible futures in which humanity might lose touch with nature and its own kind. These novels all hark back, in one way or another, to a key ancestor of modern science fiction, Mary Shelley's (1797–1851) novel *Frankenstein* (1819), in which a scientist fatally succeeds in bringing to life a creature made from dead body parts. Ever since, fascination and fear of the possibilities of science and technology have been hallmarks of science fiction.

The telegraph and the possibility of wireless broadcasting inspired not only optimism but also anxieties about technology and its effects on society. Fascination for the "unseen" (Henry James, Arthur Machen) was joined by horror of its unknown possibilities and consequences. H. G. Wells's (1866–1946) technological romances *The Island of Doctor Moreau* (1896) and *The Invisible Man* (1897) also tapped into these anxieties and transformed them into entertainment. Would these new technologies bring humanity closer together or create new distances and new forms of inequality? And what would be their impact on literary creativity? In the next chapter, we will turn to new technologies of sound recording and transmission around 1900 to explore these questions further.

9 Sound: Phonography, Telephony, Radio, Noise

The Victorians and Edwardians were fascinated by technologies of communication. Tennyson liked to imagine "the souls of dead messages" in the sound emitted by telegraph wires (1897, 2: 325); Kipling compared people to "telephone wires" as recipients of messages from obscure sources (1965, 100; see ch. 8 above). Among these new technologies were the transmission of sound via the telephone (1876) and the recording of sound using the phonograph (1877). The transmission and recording of disembodied human voices stimulated the literary imagination for years to come.

In March 1876, the first successful telephone transmission came about when Alexander Graham Bell spoke into his device the words "Mr. Watson, come here, I want to see you", and Watson could distinctly hear each word. Several inventors claimed to have built the first electric telephone, but the first to be granted a US patent was Bell in 1876. The phonograph was invented only a year later by Thomas Edison, using a waxed cardboard cylinder and a stylus. This was literally a form of writing, as on a wax tablet. Machines using flat disc records were developed a bit later, and the word 'gramophone', originally a brand name first marketed by Emil Berliner in 1895, came into general use in the early twentieth century. The first words Edison recorded, on tinfoil, were apparently from the nursery rhyme "Mary had a little lamb" – the first instance of recorded verse. The new technology of recording voices and sounds is represented in late nineteenth and early twentieth-century literature in many novels and stories such as Villiers de l'Isle-Adam's (1838–1889) *Tomorrow's Eve* (*L'Ève future*, 1886), Jules Verne's (1828–1905) *The Castle of the Carpathians* (*Le château des Carpathes*, 1893), Arthur Conan Doyle's (1859–1930) "The Japanned Box" (1899), Joyce's *Ulysses* (1922), and Thomas Mann's (1875–1955) *The Magic Mountain* (*Der Zauberberg*, 1924). In *The Magic Mountain*, the hero, Hans Castorp, discovers the sanatorium's collection of gramophone records featuring classical music as a source of private aesthetic pleasure; it is one of many modern technologies referenced in this novel (Picker 2001, Symes 2005). Likewise, *Ulysses* is criss-crossed by telephone conversations, telegrams, postcards, gramophone records, and many more kinds of communications media (Derrida 1992).

Recorded Voices

Obviously, writing is already a technology of preserving vocal sounds that can be reactivated in reading. The Roman statesman and scholar Cassiodorus praised writing for exactly this capability in 537 CE: "there discourse is stored in safety, to be heard for ever with consistency" (qtd. in Raven 2018, 33; see ch. 2 above). But the phonograph made it possible to preserve traces of the actual, physical voice of a speaker. Early recordings had authors recite from their works, preferably poems, as if to emphasise the connection between writing and recording, between authorship and the poet's own voice (cf. ch. 7 above). Poetry was among the first items of recorded sound when this technology was still in its infancy. Among the oldest surviving phonograph recordings is a reading of Alfred Lord Tennyson reciting from his poems "Maud" and "The Charge of the Light Brigade", preserved on a wax cylinder in 1890, two years before his death. Robert Browning beat him by one year to become the first recorded poet in 1889, only a few months before he died, reciting a few lines of "How they brought the good news from Ghent to Aix" into an Edison machine at a dinner party; Browning apparently forgets his text after a mere three lines and apologises; then we hear some shouts of "hip hip hooray!" Even though such antics seem more like a parlour game, they accentuate the connection between sound recording, memory and death, a topic of much concern in literature inspired by the phonograph.

The new medium quickly created fantasies and anxieties, as when the magazine *Punch*, in 1878, published a cartoon by George Du Maurier (1834–1896) claiming that soon "the work of 'our best poets' could be publicly disseminated by young women using phonographs, taking the place of the 'hirsute Italian organ-grinders' who walked about the streets of London" (qtd. in Gitelman 2019, 164; for the cartoon, see Roberts 2017, 7). Audiobooks were being imagined long before they became technically possible, as in a drawing from the *Daily Graphic* (New York), April 2, 1878: "The phonograph at home reading out a novel". Thomas Edison had envisaged "[p]honographic books for the blind" as a potential use for his invention (qtd. in Sterne 2019, 170). The first audiobooks, or 'Talking Books', were produced by the American Foundation for the Blind in 1932, using texts that were in the public domain and thus could be reproduced without costs. They were recorded on shellac or vinyl LPs and made available exclusively to the blind. In the 1950s, Caedmon records was the first company (named after the Old English poet, see ch. 2) to publish dramatisations and readings of literary works commercially on long-playing records, beginning with a reading of poems by Dylan Thomas (1914–1953) in 1952 (Rubery 2011 and 2016; see fig. 14).

The human voice has been traditionally thought of as "the paradigmatic sign of presence" (Schaeffer and Gorman 2009, 51). Now the possibility of the recorded, phonographic voice in the age of mechanical reproduction was perceived as lacking emotion, being speech without (physical) presence: "Rather than bearing testimony to individuality and the presence of a consciousness, it

Fig. 14: An early 'audiobook': Caedmon TC 2005, vinyl LP and sleeve, 1956.
Source: Ingo Berensmeyer.

speaks of mechanical reproduction and threatens an absence at the heart of speech" (Enderwitz 2015, 157). As the French philosopher Jean-Marie Guyau wrote in 1880: "[T]he phonograph is incapable of reproducing the human voice in all its strength and warmth. The voice of the apparatus will remain shrill and cold; it has something imperfect and abstract about it that sets it apart" (qtd. in Kittler 1999, 31–32). It is a speech without presence, but also one that is outside the normal experience of temporality: a recorded voice on a phonograph is disconnected from its human and temporal or spatial origin; it can be played back more quickly or more slowly, and it will persist in time, possibly beyond its owner's death. There is, then, a connection between the phonograph and memory, an uncanny effect of lifeless life beyond mortality. The phonograph is a persistent record that counteracts the transience of human life; yet as a representation it can never be more than a semblance of life – an undead presence.

In Arthur Conan Doyle's short story "The Japanned Box" (1899), a widower is held back from relapsing into alcoholism by listening, morning and night, to the phonographic record of his dead wife's voice admonishing him to abstain. Since he keeps this a secret from everyone, his servants think there must be a ghost in the house. Only at the end of the story is the supernatural voice revealed to be an effect of technology, hidden in a lacquer box. While, in this story, the wife's artificially extended presence beyond death is a positive force for the living, anxieties about the undead abound in Bram Stoker's (1847–1912) horror novel *Dracula* (1897). Here, vampire hunters use all the available modern technologies to fight the monstrous Transylvanian count, whose bite confers immortality at the price of losing one's humanity, one's soul. Dr Seward keeps a voice diary on his phonograph, which is later typed up by Mina Harker together with all the other notes and documents that, when assembled, constitute Stoker's novel. This mode of constructing a novel out of a series of documents was inspired by Wilkie Collins's sensation novel *The Woman in White* (1859–1860), but the panoply of media is here expanded to include audio and typescript. In Friedrich Kittler's phrase, *Dracula* is "that perennially misjudged heroic epic of the final victory of technological media over the blood-sucking despots of old Europe" (1999, 86). These media include the phonograph and the typewriter – technologies of Western modernity that help to vanquish an atavistic intruder from the East. There is, however, an unvanquishable fear that the technological superiority of the British Empire may not be strong enough to prevail against the barbaric despotism of Count Dracula and his subterfuge of poisoning the blood of Western men and women and thereby corrupting Western civilisation from within. Such anxieties of 'degeneration' abound in the fiction of the *fin de siècle*, and attitudes to media technology in this context remain at best ambivalent.

In *Dracula*, Mina Harker is the novel's heroic record-keeper, a woman wielding a typewriter. The first commercial model of the typewriter was introduced in 1874, revolutionising office work and, as in Mina Harker's case, creating new jobs for women (Wershler-Henry 2005; Kittler 1997). Typists, like telegraph operators (see ch. 8 above), were for the most part female. The first typewritten work of fiction to be sent to a publisher is said to be Mark Twain's (1835–1910) *Life on the Mississippi* (1883); this fact was even used in advertisements for the Remington typewriter. Other early adopters of typewriters – or typewriting services – included Oscar Wilde (1854–1900), Friedrich Nietzsche (1844–1900), and Henry James (1843–1916). In the early twentieth century, the word "typewriter" could still denote a woman operating the machine as well as the machine itself (Rainey 2009). Whereas many modernist authors feared the mechanisation of culture and the "industrialization of writing" (Latham 2019, 180), some writers relished the possibilities offered by new technologies of communication. In Stevie Smith's (1902–1971) modernist variation on the artist novel genre, *Novel on Yellow Paper* (1936), the "symbiosis of writer and machine" (Berensmeyer 2020, 8) allows a new creative freedom to emerge from the boring, mechanical routines of office work. The typewriter is internalised as a 'Typing Ghost' in Muriel Spark's *The Comforters* (1957), a novel in which the main character, who is also a writer, hallucinates about the author-narrator who is writing her story and controlling her destiny. Like the phonograph, the typewriter could be experienced as a disruptive technology, a machine that acts as a prosthesis, distancing the voice and the hand of the author from the text and rupturing the 'natural' connection between the word and the human person who utters it.

Disruptions in the natural order of things also occur in Joseph Conrad's (1857–1924) and Ford Madox Ford's (1873–1939) collaborative novel *The Inheritors* (1901), which imagines a woman from the future invading the present. If Stoker's Dracula is a relic from Europe's feudal past, Conrad and Ford imagine a no less threatening harbinger from the future. Echoing current anxieties of human degeneration, as evoked for example in H. G. Wells's *The Time Machine* (1895), Conrad and Ford present this 'Fourth Dimensionist' as a future version of humanity with fewer scruples and ethical concerns. Listening to the woman explaining where she comes from, the narrator remarks on her "expressionless voice" and compares it to "a phonograph reciting a technical work" (1999, 9). In the future, apparently, human voices will have assumed the qualities of the machine. As in E. M. Forster's "The Machine Stops" (1909; see ch. 8), there was concern that cybernetic control systems might take over and drastically alter human life and human nature. Technology could help to defeat Dracula, but it could also become a danger to humanity in its own turn.

Literature and the Telephone

The new technologies of the telegraph, phonograph, typewriter, and wireless radio waves were viewed as ambivalent in their potential benefits and the risks they brought along, dissociating communication from human bodies, even further than writing already did, and threatening to dissolve the boundaries of space and time. They were frequently not imagined as establishing connectivity but as metaphors of dissociation, as in Ford Madox Ford's novel *Some Do Not . . .* (1924), the first part of his *Parade's End* trilogy. Here, the shell-shocked protagonist Christopher Tietjens feels disconnected from himself. He hears his own voice as coming through a telephone, from a distance: "his voice – his own voice – came to him as if from the end of a long-distance telephone. A damn long-distance one! Ten years . . ." (2012, 281). The telephone is a medium of connection and expresses the desire for connection, though it threatens to split the subject apart (like the 'wireless' effect in Kipling's story "Wireless") and to disconnect the senses of hearing and seeing. When Mr Bankes in Virginia Woolf's (1882–1941) 1927 novel *To the Lighthouse* speaks to Mrs Ramsay on the telephone, he has a visual impression of her beauty: "He saw her at the end of the line, Greek, blue-eyed, straight-nosed. How incongruous it seemed to be telephoning to a woman like that" (2006, 27). Modernist literature is full of such incongruities between sensory perception and technological mediation.

In literature, the telephone is probably more often depicted as a medium of disconnection and dissociation than one of connectivity (Menke 2019, ch. 2; Trotter 2020). As David Lodge explains, "the 'blindness' of telephonic communication lends itself to deception, and easily generates confusion, misunderstanding and alienation between the participants" (1992, 170). The "narrative potential" (ibid.) of this medium was quickly exploited in the novel, as in Evelyn Waugh's (1903–1966) *Vile Bodies* (1930). In chapter twelve of this society novel about London's *jeunesse dorée* of the interwar years, the 'Bright Young People', the narrator only provides the minimal first sentence "Adam rang up Nina", which is then followed by their voices in dialogue, and then the sentence "Later Nina rang up Adam", followed by the transcript of their second telephone conversation (Waugh 2003, 183–184). Their curt telephonic interactions are about disconnection rather than connection: Adam and Nina are breaking off their engagement over the telephone, and Nina announces she is going to marry someone else. "The effect", Lodge notes, "is both funny and sad" (1992, 170).[57] Some years later, in Muriel Spark's novel *Memento Mori* (1959), the telephone is an "antagonistic medium of surveillance and betrayal" (Tease 2016, 75): a group of elderly ladies repeatedly receive phone calls from a voice telling them "Remember you must die". Of course, the characters who get these calls die soon after. Here the telephone is a medium that invades and threatens the intimacy and security of private spaces, in similar ways to what Avital Ronell proposes in her deconstructionist media analysis in *The Telephone Book*: "the call as death sentence" (Ronell 1989, 6). David Trotter sums up the verdict of a British GPO telephone sales representative from the 1930s that, in literature, "a telephone call is usually bad news" (2013, 56).

Radio Plays

In 1922, the General Post Office decided to establish a national broadcaster. This was the birth of the BBC (British Broadcasting Company Ltd; now the British Broadcasting Corporation), founded in 1922, the oldest national broadcaster in the world. Its first director, Lord Reith, established its mission: "to inform, educate and entertain". During the 1920s and 1930s, the BBC quickly grew into an important national institution. Lovingly if somewhat disparagingly nicknamed 'Auntie' or the 'Beeb', the BBC turned radio into the first acoustic mass medium.

---

[57] See Lodge 1992, 169–173 for an analysis of another telephone scene in Waugh's *A Handful of Dust* (1934) and Nicholson Baker's 1992 novel *Vox*. Another example of a 'telephone novel' would be William Gaddis's *J R* (1975).

In contrast to the US, where there were numerous private stations funded by investors and advertising, programming in Britain was largely funded publicly and controlled by the corporation. Broadcasting was (and is) understood as a public service, paid for (then as now) at least in part by licence fees from listeners and (later) viewers. Only some programmes received financial assistance from newspaper publishing companies. For newspapers, broadcasting also provided new material to review, comment on, criticise, or make fun of (Briggs 1961, 225).

In the early days of wireless broadcasting, a large part of the programming was devoted to news and information, but also literature and classical music, usually ending the day with a live performance of a piano solo. About a quarter "of the total BBC daily transmissions" in the 1920s "took the form of speech", including "women's programmes, news bulletins, weather reports, and the Children's Hour" (Briggs 1961, 235). Big Ben was first heard on the radio to usher in the new year at the end of 1923 (236). At first, only about two to four percent of broadcasting time were dedicated to entertainment (Briggs 1965, 51, 54), also because radio was regarded as competition by the entertainment industry. Quiz shows and contests were viewed with caution (Briggs 1965, 77). There was at first almost no influence from American radio, and no attempt to copy, for example, US radio sitcoms (Briggs 1965, 109, 117). The first British sitcom, *Band Waggon*, was only introduced in 1938–1939, its fictional premise being that two comedians reside in a flat in the top storey of the BBC's broadcasting house (Berensmeyer 2017). Generally, programming until well into the mid-twentieth century and beyond was under moral and political restrictions; for instance, in 1947 there was a rule at the BBC against impersonating politicians. The 'family audience' remained the target group for broadcasting (Briggs 1979, 194–195). Content was reviewed and selected by the Programme Board with the help of "a network of advisory committees [. . .] both local and national" (Briggs 1961, 219). Among its most important concerns early on was religion; Lord Reith was a very strict Protestant believer, and from the outset he regarded the BBC as a promoter of Christian values (Briggs 1961, 219). Next to its religious and social mission, the BBC had an enormous influence on education and on the pronunciation of 'standard English' in the twentieth century.

The BBC began broadcasting plays in the mid-1920s, with the formation of the London Radio Repertory Players in 1924. These were well-received, but early attempts to create realistic sound effects were not too successful. Despite many attempts to make a gunshot sound real, it merely came off as a soft 'plop' as if from a bottle of flat champagne (Briggs 1961, 183). One of the first specially written plays for radio was *A Comedy of Danger* by Richard Hughes (1900–1976), broadcast in January 1924, about a group of people trapped in a Welsh coalmine. Well into the 1930s, dramatic programming tended to be highbrow, including plays by Shakespeare, classical Greek tragedies, and modern plays by writers such as Anton Chekhov (1860–1904) or Henrik Ibsen (1828–1906).

The first attempts at a new form of programming "combining narrative, dialogue, sound effects, and music" (Briggs 1961, 235) date back to 1925, when there was "a series of dramatized episodes in the history of famous British regiments" (235–236). This was the birth of radio drama as a new form combining different acoustic media: human voices, sound effects, and music. Drama got its own department at the BBC in 1927. Henceforth, also adaptations of nondramatic literary works (novels, short stories, etc.) became a staple of radio broadcasting. Lighter forms such as soap operas were introduced in the 1940s, most notably *The Archers* (1950–), the world's longest running show of its kind (it is still running, as of 2022, with six twelve-minute episodes per week on Radio 4). Radio soon became an immensely popular medium; 98 % of the population had access to a set in 1935 (Briggs 1965, 253).

Radio broadcasting, and later television, also created new channels for promoting and reviewing books. The *Listener,* the BBC's own journal (1929–1991), became an important outlet for book reviews and other literary content. Radio also provided new job opportunities for writers as presenters and producers, including the poet Louis MacNeice (1907–1963), who began working for the BBC in the 1940s, and most famously George Orwell, who worked for the BBC as a Talks Producer from 1941 to 1943, and whose dystopian novel *Nineteen Eighty-Four* (1949) was in part inspired by his experiences with the BBC and the wartime Ministry of Information.

More importantly, radio offered the possibility to adapt existing literary material and to create entirely new literary forms and formats, such as the radio play. The most famous radio play ever must be Orson Welles's adaptation of H. G. Wells's science-fiction novel *The War of the Worlds* (1897) for CBS radio in the US in 1938. The realism of this adaptation – with built-in 'news bulletins' seeming to interrupt the programme – caused panic among listeners who believed the Martians had actually landed. Wells and Welles combined proved irresistible. The fact that this was broadcast on October 30 (Halloween) might have given the game away, but "[b]y 8:30, thousands of people were praying, preparing for the end, and fleeing the Martians" (Stirling and Kitross 2019, 214).

Famous postwar radio plays include Samuel Beckett's (1906–1989) productions for radio: *All That Fall* (1957), *From an Abandoned Work* (1957), *Embers* (1959), *The Old Tune* (1960), *Words and Music* (1962), *Cascando* (1964), and *Rough for Radio* (1976). These are minimalist avantgarde plays using voice actors, music, and sound effects. In one of Beckett's plays for the stage, too, recorded sound plays an important role: in *Krapp's Last Tape* (1958), audio technology and the possibility of recording the human voice make a dialogue out of a monologue, as the play's protagonist listens and responds to recordings of his own voice on a tape recorder, reacting to the thoughts and memories of his earlier self. The exchange between the (recorded) past and the present has been a staple of 'phonographic fiction' since Arthur Conan Doyle's "The Japanned Box" of 1899.

The most famous British radio play is Dylan Thomas's *Under Milk Wood* from 1954. A 'comedy of humours' (Kenneth Tynan) set in a fictional Welsh fishing village, Llareggub, the play follows the dreams and thoughts of the inhabitants: Mrs. Ogmore-Pritchard, who has two dead husbands, Captain Cat, Organ Morgan, Polly Garter, a baker who has two living wives, and many others. Thomas had begun working on early drafts of a play set in a Welsh village in the 1930s, originally titled "The Village that was Mad", with a final shape emerging in the 1940s to depict the village from midnight to the following nightfall. Thomas himself gave public readings of the play in the US in 1953, and it was also performed on stage in New York, but he had been ill for a while and died in New York in November 1953. It was first broadcast by the BBC's Third Programme in January 1954.

While the place name 'Llareggub' looks and sounds plausibly Welsh, it is in fact the phrase 'bugger all' in reverse – suggesting a certain stubbornness of the locals. The play introduces its main characters through their dreams and then follows them into their day and accompanies them through it until night falls and they return to their dreams again. During the day, the characters' desires, obsessions, and daydreams take up most of the play. The focus is less on events than on emotions, hopes, memories and love. Because it focuses on an entire community rather than a single individual or family, it can be compared to Thornton Wilder's (1897–1975) play *Our Town* (1938). But Thomas makes full use of the possibilities of radio to present a play for voices that concentrates on his characters' inner lives. The narrator, referred to as "First Voice" in the script (performed by Richard Burton in the original production), repeatedly urges us to "listen" but also, paradoxically, to "look", i.e., to imagine the village and its inhabitants visually; to "come closer now" because "only you can hear" and "only you can see" the details he then evokes verbally: "the [. . .] petticoats over the chairs, the jugs and basins, the glasses of teeth" (Thomas 1988, 2–3). Thomas's poetic language encourages listeners to "hear and see, behind the eyes of the sleepers, the movements and countries and mazes and colours and dismays and rainbows and tunes and wishes and flight and fall and despairs and big seas of their dreams" (3). This is made possible by radio, by the (presumably) attentive posture of the listeners: "From where you are, you can hear their dreams" (ibid.). Called 'a play for voices', *Under Milk Wood* combines different types of texts including lyric poetry and song. The play is filled with wordplay, grotesque fantasies, and surrealism, but overall, it can also be read as a celebration of such a close-knit regional community, with its odd, eccentric characters depicted lovingly and as loving persons despite their flaws and weaknesses. Here, a play for radio creates a sense of community – an "imagined community" (Anderson 2006) – by means of sound that draws listeners in and wraps them in a warm sonic environment. Thomas used radio, a medium with a wide geographical distribution, to achieve an effect of auditory immediacy, as if to compensate for the distance implied by the medium, suggesting to listeners that they formed part of a privileged group of observers or could indeed imagine themselves members of this community that was being established or suggested by the medium. With its idealised, nostalgic depiction of a Welsh village, *Under Milk Wood* may be read as a retreat from the political realities of postwar, postimperial Britain into the vision of an organic community. Yet it also has features that resist such a reading, and the play has also been interpreted as subverting the BBC's agenda of "sanctimonious [. . .] cultural uplift" (Epstein 2019, 249) by means of multiple layers of irony – beginning with the place name 'Llareggub' that is both Welsh and, in reverse, English –, its "aural textures of 'near-madness'" (260), and its focus on "ritual activities of the body" (267). Its combinations of sound, silence, and noise considerably shaped the new art form of radio drama.

Sound and Noise

In wartime and postwar Britain, technologies and literary responses to sound changed considerably, towards thinking more about the relationship between (meaningful) sound and (meaningless or disturbing) noise. This was accompanied by a public discourse about technology that wavered between affirmation and scepticism, the latter frequently tinged with ideas of cultural decline and nostalgia (e.g., Leavis 1962). One example of this is the response to the technological realisation of the 'jet age' and supersonic flight, which was first achieved in the 1940s. Flying faster than the speed of sound became a cultural obsession in the 1950s, manifested for example in David Lean's (1908–1991) film *The Sound Barrier*, which was a box office hit in the UK in 1952. A few years later, Iris Murdoch's (1919–1999) novel *The Bell* (1958) includes a rural idyll that is disturbed by the "shattering" roar of jet planes flying overhead (Murdoch 2004, 130–131). The overwhelming "noise and speed and beauty" makes one of the novel's central male characters touch a boy's arm. Their connection is mediated by witnessing a technological spectacle, a modern miracle even, which evokes a physical sensation like religious or indeed sexual ecstasy – "head back and heart thumping," "almost unconscious" – and that is described in the register of the sublime: "a great tearing roar", "gleaming like angels" (ibid.). This is a Miltonic 'war in heaven', but its description is also interspersed with the discourse of the beautiful: "noise, speed and beauty". The allusion to J. M. W. Turner's painting *Rain, Steam and Speed – The Great Western Railway* (1844) expresses a fascination with technology and the technological sublime that is about to replace, or has already unseated, traditional forms of the numinous or sacred, literally splitting the sky and human ears with supersonic, superhuman possibilities and thus breaking apart the boundaries of the human world as previously known.[58]

The sheer noise of the jets is an emblem of technology transcending the scale of humanity – a key topic in the postwar world, which was dominated by fears of 'the bomb' and nuclear war. It inspires awe and admiration but is also potentially destructive. Jets and other technological innovations not only stimulated Miltonic survivals in the otherwise familiar form of the novel; they also challenged established modes of writing. These new technologies or new uses of older technologies – remembering Friedrich Kittler's quip that electrified music is an "abuse of army equipment" (1999, 96) – challenge traditional definitions of communication, social behaviour, and cultural self-understandings in a changing world.

It is not surprising, given its prominence in the socio-cultural imaginary of the 1950s, that the jet plane features in numerous literary texts from the late Fifties – not as a necessary plot device that propels the narrative forward, but for the most part as an accidental or ornamental element, fulfilling an almost decorative or (paradoxically) retardational function while also serving as a symbol of modernity and a harbinger of the future. In *The Bell*, the jet plane evokes an ecstatic but also potentially destructive experience. It is a curious moment in a novel that otherwise rarely refers to modern technology. Its appearance leaves behind "complete silence", a silence pointing to the possibility that conventional literary language may not be able to represent this phenomenon adequately.

Even a rather staid detective novel like Agatha Christie's (1890–1976) *4:50 from Paddington* (1957), better known for its murder on a train, contains a reference to jet planes. In the novel's penultimate chapter, Christie's characters self-consciously reflect on their being "rather an anachronism" in the modern postwar world (Christie 2011, 340). Miss Marple deplores the omnipresence of noise and complains about jet planes breaking the sound barrier *and* a couple of

---

[58] My discussion of *The Bell* and "The Sound-Sweep" (below) has been adapted from Berensmeyer 2016.

windows in her greenhouse. The reference to jet planes is a signal to contemporary readers that Christie is still up to date despite her long career in the pre-war 'Golden Age' of detective fiction.

The speed of these developments and their accompanying cultural changes challenged the usually more sedate pace of literature, exerting pressure on established habits of reading, notions of cultural value, and related ideas of belonging and social class. This general observation exceeded the discussion of jets, as is evident, for example, in Richard Hoggart's (1918–2014) *The Uses of Literacy* (1957), a book that is often regarded as the birth document of cultural studies in Britain. Hoggart, a student of F. R. Leavis, laments the decline of working-class cultural standards when he describes teenagers gathering around the jukebox in a suburban milk bar, listening to pre-recorded American music rather than engaging in live communal singing. The jukebox was invented in 1927, and the same topic of singing songs as opposed to listening to "music 'on tap'" is broached by Eric Gill as early as 1931 (Gill 2013, 4.) It is open to debate what is worse for Hoggart – the fact that no one sings anymore, or that the music they listen to comes from the US. Mass culture and pop culture had arrived in 1950s Britain, as had cybernetic entertainment machines that interact with – and constitute – audiences. If communal singing constituted and reflected an 'organic' community, listening to pre-recorded "hackneyed songs" (Gunn 1957, 31, l. 10) on a jukebox was taken as a symptom of a newly globalised world of capitalist entertainment.

Technological optimism and cultural pessimism were coupled in many left-leaning arguments from the 1950s. They were united with the right in condemning such modern phenomena as rock'n'roll, which a psychiatrist of the time compared to "the hysterical dancing mania which occurred in Europe in the fourteenth century" and certain US evangelical groups handling poisonous snakes (Sargant 1957, 120). It should be noted that a similar culture war was waged earlier about the deleterious effects of jazz (which is more likely the music Hoggart had in mind when writing *Uses of Literacy*). There are other things afoot here as well. In a marriage advice book from the early 1950s, for example, the writer Leonora Eyles (1889–1960) expresses her disapproval of dancing to jazz music in strongly racialised terms:

> the dancing and its accompany [sic] music that have come to us from the jungle, the bebop and such-like, are not fit for the British temperament. These dances are often accompanied by drugging and in some cities bring people of different races (not nations, that is all to the good) too intimately and too provocatively together: the rhythms of the jungle dances, the throbbing drums, the repetitive tunes or the langorous [sic] swaying may be all very well in the jungles of Africa and the West Indies [. . .] But this is all too strong meat of [sic] the young people of our cold, grey land; their pulse-rate, their blood pressure can't stand it. (Eyles 1952, 35–36)

Eyles's racist discourse resembles earlier cultural panics about new media, such as the mid-nineteenth-century concern that sensational 'railway novels' might be too strong for the nerves of British rail passengers (see ch. 6 above). By contrast, Thom Gunn's (1929–2004) 1957 poem about the voice of Elvis Presley "[u]nreeling from a corner box" (l. 2) is much less depressed about popular culture, despite the phonemic closeness of 'unreel' and 'unreal'. In the last stanza of "Elvis Presley" (1957, 31), the speaker decides that it does not matter whether Elvis's comportment is a "stance" or a "pose" (l. 14):

> Whether he poses or is real, no cat
> Bothers to say: the pose held is a stance,
> Which, generation of the very chance
> It wars on, may be posture for combat.
> (ll. 11–14)

Like W. B. Yeats's (1865–1939) assertion that dancer and dance are impossible to distinguish (in his poem "Among School Children", 1926), Gunn refuses to separate the artificial or staged "pose" from the genuine – and politically meaningful – "stance". Rather than isolating themselves from their own class, as Hoggart observes, Gunn's collective of listeners express their experience in the first person plural: "We keep ourselves in touch with a mere dime" (1957, l. 9) as Elvis "turns revolt into a style" (l. 10). There is a new community to be found in listening to this music. As a literary response to rock music and popular culture, Gunn's poem constitutes a more optimistic vision of connection, of 'keeping in touch'. At times, it can even sound celebratory, especially when compared to the discussions of rock'n'roll in the popular press – at its most controversial when the first regular television show to feature rock'n'roll music and dancing, the *Six-Five Special*, launched in February 1957, once again triggering anxious responses about cultural decline and degeneration.

Even more provocatively, the tables are turned when, in *A Clockwork Orange*, a 1962 novel by Anthony Burgess (1917–1993), the 'ultraviolence' of youth gang member Alex is triggered not by rock music but by listening to classical music on a hifi stereo system. This is first a "new violin concerto" by fictional composer "Geoffrey Plautus", followed by Mozart and Bach. Stanley Kubrick's 1971 film replaces this with parts of the second movement from Beethoven's Ninth Symphony. Alex waxes poetic (in the Russian-inflected lingo the novel uses as the speech of delinquent youth) when he describes this music and its effects on him:

> Oh, it was gorgeousness and gorgeosity made flesh. The trombones crunched redgold under my bed, and behind my gulliver the trumpets three-wise silverflamed, and there by the door the timps rolling through my guts and out again crunched like candy thunder.

> Oh, it was wonder of wonders. And then, a bird of like rarest spun heavenmetal, or like silvery wine flowing in a spaceship, gravity all nonsense now, came the violin solo above all the other strings, and those strings were like a cage of silk around my bed. Then flute and oboe bored, like worms of like platinum, into the thick toffee gold and silver. I was in such bliss, my brothers.
>
> (Burgess 2012, 38–39)

But perhaps the one postwar writer whose work is most symptomatic of the engagement with new technologies of sound, and its concomitant phenomenon of noise, is J. G. Ballard (1930–2009). Ballard's unique way of combining modern technology, social satire, and surrealism in his fiction constitutes one of the most impressive achievements of late twentieth-century British literature when it comes to responding to challenges of technological change. In his novel *Crash* (1973), Ballard turns the car, an emblem of technological progress and mobility, into a site of carnage and mayhem, a symbol of the imminent breakdown of so-called Western civilisation – a breakdown that was widely feared and expected during the Oil Crises of the 1970s. In the media history of literature, these examples are more than merely another turn of the screw of postmodernist self-reflection; they are paradigmatic markers of the way in which literature responds to technology and redraws its own boundaries as a medium.

In his science fiction story "The Sound-Sweep" (1960), Ballard envisages a culture in which classical music has been replaced by "ultrasonic music" that transcends the range of human hearing, making opera singers obsolete. "Ultrasonic music [. . .] provided a direct neural link between the sound stream and the auditory lobes, generating an apparently sourceless sensation of harmony, rhythm, cadence and melody uncontaminated by the noise and vibration of audible music" (Ballard 1963, 48). In contrast to the silence of this new music, the world of the story is filled by the relentless noise of everyday urban life: "a frenzied hypermanic babel of jostling horns, shrilling tyres, plunging brakes and engines" (41) that has to be removed from walls and surfaces with a kind of vacuum cleaner, the sonovac. In a key moment of the story, the mute sonovac operator Mangon and the ex-opera singer Madame Gioconda drive out to the "sonic dumps" (61) where the sound-sweeps' collections are kept. There, they are overwhelmed by the "ceaseless mind-sapping roar" (62) of the stored noises of jet airliners. Ballard's narrator goes on to describe this soundscape in terms that intensify the sublimity associated with the sound of jet turbines in the passage from Murdoch's *The Bell*: it is a physical, visceral experience of ambient noise as pressure, which he identifies with modern civilisation and an avant-garde style of music, "*musique concrète*" (62) – music that makes use of recorded sounds and noises.

Ballard's story may serve as a reminder that the postwar musical avant-garde from Karlheinz Stockhausen onwards embraced electronics, noise, and cacophony in previously – literally – unheard und unheard-of ways, moving beyond traditional concepts of beauty or even humanity in its search for radically new forms of artistic expression (Sellars 2009). In the way it relates the human media of the singing or speaking voice to the super- or post-human sounds and noises of "cars, express trains, fairgrounds and aircraft" (62), Ballard's story is alive to the changing relationship between human beings and modern technology that transcends human capacities of rational understanding and control as well as conventional aesthetics. What Murdoch in *The Bell* and Hoggart in *The Uses of Literacy* hint at – the idea that 'man' in the postwar world may no longer be the measure of all things, that established values and forms of living together have come under immense pressure – is perhaps most fully developed in "The Sound-Sweep". It is only a small step from this to postpunk 'industrial' music, to the German band *Einstürzende Neubauten* (founded in 1980) and their use of drills and jackhammers as musical instruments, and later literary texts that work with ideas of visual and auditory noise – works by Will Self (1961–), for example (*My Idea of Fun*, 1993), Tom McCarthy (1969–; *C*, 2010), Steven Hall (1975–; *The Raw Shark Texts*, 2007), Nicola Barker (1966–; *H(a)ppy*, 2017), and many others.

Ultrasound

Where can we go from here? Perhaps to poetry – to the way in which the soundscapes of poetic language can imagine, imitate, or mimic not only human speech or the sound of human voices in our heads, or imitate natural sounds through onomatopoeia, but even sounds associated with forms of life and ways of experiencing the world that are entirely alien to us. One may wonder what it would be like to be a bat, as the philosopher Thomas Nagel did in his essay of 1974, where he argued that even if one might be able to imagine what it is like to be a bat, one would never be able "to know what it is like for *a bat* to be a bat" (Nagel 1979, 169). One would never know what it would *feel* like to experience the world with completely different sense organs and capabilities, for instance orienting oneself in space by means of ultrasound signals. Yet there is a poem that does just that: "Bats' Ultrasound" by the Australian poet Les Murray (1938–2019), dating from 1987.

The poem starts out in the voice of a naturalist, resembling the presenter of a nature programme on TV, who attempts to make this animal species somewhat less strange by resorting to metaphors and anthropomorphic descriptions of bats and their world, also assuring readers that only "few" bats "are vampires" (Murray 2014, 118, l. 6) and none of them have those qualities that vampires are commonly said to have, like the ability to move through mirrors. Yet the speaker also emphasises the differences between bats, other insects, and humans: while the insects they hunt emit sounds that humans can still just about hear, the bats aim for their prey by means of ultrasound signals, inaudible to the human ear. Then, in the third and last stanza (set off from the rest of the poem by italics), something remarkable happens. The poem appears to translate what the bats are 'saying' into human sounds, into English, speaking in the first person plural and addressing humans in the second person plural:

> *ah, eyrie-ire, aero hour, eh?*
> *O'er our ur-area (our era aye*
> *ere your raw row) we air our array,*
> *err, yaw, row wry – aura our orrery,*
> *our eerie ü our ray, our arrow.*
> *A rare ear, our aery Yahweh.*
> (Murray 2014, 118)

In fact, even though a casual reader might not recognise it as such or make out only a few of the words, this is perfectly good English, and it could be paraphrased (if paraphrase were not a heresy) roughly like this: *Ah, there's a commotion in the nest / here you are;*[59] *time to fly, isn't it? Over our original area (yes, at our time of day before your meaningless noise begins) we fly around, this way and that way, sensing the aura of our model of the world* (an 'orrery' being "a mechanical model, usually clockwork, devised to represent the motions of the earth and moon [. . .] around the sun", according to the OED) – or 'aura-ing our aura' (cf. Malay 2018, 163) – *our strange 'ü' (sound), our (sonic) ray, our arrow*. The genius of Murray's verses is that, if read quickly, they are perfectly incomprehensible, even to ears that are well-attuned to the English language. They are an accommodation, in human language, of the utterly strange, non-human communication of bats. For the Catholic poet Murray, the "arrow" points straight to God, "our aery Yahweh", whose "rare ear" is attuned not only to humans but also to the non-human animals (Leighton 2017, 162). The poem's last stanza approximates bat-sound in human language, asking its readers or listeners to pay extra attention to the sonic qualities of language, beyond conventional meaning and beyond its merely communicative function. Its final stanza transcends a representational use of language and opens a rift between written and spoken language: while the sound (meaningless noises, at least for most listeners on a first hearing) imitates what bats' echoic voices might sound like if we could hear them, the written

---

59 In some recordings, Murray is said to have pronounced "eyrie-ire" as "here you are" (Malay 2018, 163).

words are all more or less ordinary English words that one would find in any dictionary, and they are combined into a grammatically correct sentence. The contradictory sonic and graphemic actualisations of these verses accentuate the alienness of bats to humans, albeit a form of strangeness that is presented as part of God's plan for creation ("our aery Yahwe"). Only God's perfect hearing is "rare" enough to understand human and non-human creatures alike.

Beyond a theological reading, writing here serves above all as a technology for recording sounds – sounds that may appear meaningless at first but that can be unscrambled with some effort as meaningful human speech. Thus "Bats' Ultrasound" makes a poetic comment on the distance between words and meaning, on the always already mediated and mediating function of language, and on the human use of language as a technology of making sense and finding one's way in the world. Where bats have ultrasound, humans have language. It also engages with a long tradition of representing sounds visually, typographically. Almost inevitably, our discussion of sound has led us to vision. In the next chapter, we will turn to the relationship between literature and seeing to develop this further.

10 Vision: Text and Image

The connection between literature and visuality is a very old one. Traditionally, it has often been described as a similarity between words and images: *ut pictura poesis* – poetry is "like a picture" or "like a painting", according to the Roman poet Horace (65–8 BCE) in his Epistle to the Pisos (*Ars poetica*), l. 361. The earlier Greek poet Simonides of Ceos (c. 556–468 BCE) is quoted by Plutarch as saying that 'painting is silent poetry, and poetry is a speaking picture'. In the early modern period, these words were frequently quoted in the *paragone* or competition between different art forms (Hagstrum 1958), but now more often to emphasise their differences. For Shaftesbury (1671–1713) as well as Lessing (1729–1781), the differences between literature and the visual arts outweighed anything they had in common. In his treatise on painting and poetry, *Laocoön* (1766), Lessing asserts the main difference as one of temporality: whereas painting or sculpture is essentially static, depicting a single moment, literature is dynamic because it tells stories that develop over time.

This difference is crucial for understanding how literature differs from the visual arts. Its visuality is never direct but always mediated, an experience that takes time. In narratology, there is a distinction between 'telling' and 'showing', but even what is meant by 'showing' in a narrative is different from how images show something. We may visualise characters, scenes, and events when we read a novel or a story, but this is still a very different experience from seeing an actual picture or watching a film – it is much more "imperfect", "partial", and "hazy", closer, perhaps, to daydreaming (Mendelsund 2014, 403) than actually seeing something real. There are different ways of seeing that need to be explored further.

Ways of Seeing

The sense of sight has long been associated with ideas of truth and knowledge. In classical Greek, the expression 'I know' (οἶδα) literally means 'I have seen', relating to a Proto-Indo-European root '*weyd', 'to see'. Othello, in Shakespeare's tragedy, demands "the ocular proof" (3.3.365) of Desdemona's infidelity, to see and thus to know the truth with his own eyes. In the nineteenth century, the art theorist, painter, writer, and social critic John Ruskin (1819–1900) wanted, above all else, to teach people to "see things as they are", "simply endeavouring to enable the student to see natural objects clearly and truly" (2004 [1858], 95). In the modern world, however, the connections between seeing and knowing have come under intense pressure and have in many cases been entirely severed. As the writer and art critic John Berger (1926–2017) explains in *Ways of Seeing* (1972):

> It is seeing which establishes our place in the surrounding world; we explain that world with words, but words can never undo the fact that we are surrounded by it. The relation between what we see and what we know is never settled. Each evening we *see* the sun set. We *know* that the earth is turning away from it. Yet the knowledge, the explanation, never quite fits the sight. (Berger 2008, 7)

All seeing, then, is first *relational*. Berger's book (and the TV series it was based on) alerted a large audience to the intricacies of visual representation that intervene between our eyes and brains and the realities in which we live. Images (or other visual media) and literary texts do not simply compete, nor can either of them claim a higher or more accurate 'way of seeing' than the other, since words and images are both embedded in social, political, and economic conditions of representation. This chapter will trace their relationship from Romanticism to modernism, in brief case studies on William Blake, Henry James, Ezra Pound, and T. S. Eliot.

Literary forms that combine visual and textual elements have been around for a long time. Medieval manuscripts were often illuminated with colourful visual elements or pictorial illustrations. After the arrival of print, such elements would still sometimes be added by hand after printing. A fairly cheap way of adding printed illustrations was the woodcut, an image carved into a block of wood and then printed off. In the early modern period, ballads printed on 'broadsides' (single sheets of paper printed on one side only) typically included woodcut illustrations (see ch. 3). Another popular form in early modern print culture was the emblem book, which combined woodcut images (*picturae*) with a title and a text, usually in verse (the *subscriptio*), often combining allegory with a moral message about virtues and vices, illustrated with reference to mythological or historical characters. The text frequently moves towards a proverbial conclusion; for example, the fall of Icarus, who flew too close to the sun, is presented as a warning against hubris, or the fate of Damocles as an encouragement to the poor to accept their fate rather than envy their rulers. Geoffrey Whitney's (c. 1548 – c. 1601) *A Choice of Emblemes* (1586) introduced this European form, best known in Alciati's (1492–1550) *Emblemata* (1531), to Britain. Combining the media of text and image, the emblem book encouraged its readers to see both as interdependent and related, and to create meaning by applying both visual and textual information to their experience of the world. The pictures are not merely illustrations of the text, and the text is not merely an explanation of the picture, but they form a new aesthetic unity, anticipating later forms of text-image combination such as the comic or the graphic novel.

William Blake

A special place in this history belongs to the Romantic poet and engraver William Blake (1757–1827). Blake had complete control over every stage in the writing, printing, and publication of his works. He produced his books not for a mass market but privately, in small numbers, and he worked together with his wife Catherine, selling his books to patrons and connoisseurs of his art. He developed a technique of 'illuminated printing', which combined text and illustrations during the printing process. Like other engravers of his day, Blake used copper plates, but in contrast to his contemporaries he painted and wrote directly on the plates, using an acid-resistant varnish. In the production process, acid was then applied to the plates to etch away the surface and to raise the art, which would then be transferred as a mirror image onto paper. This technique, known as relief printing, allowed Blake to integrate text and images much more seamlessly (fig. 15). Conventionally, illustrations would be inserted later during the process, but Blake created them simultaneously, blending text and image into a unity. Among his earliest books produced in this way is the collection of his lyric poems *Songs of Innocence and of Experience* (1794), which contains many of his best-known poems like "The Lamb", "The Chimney-Sweeper", "The Tyger", and "London". He would sell these books unbound, with the expectation that the buyer would choose his own binding, so that in some extant copies the sequence of poems varies. Yet Blake, among all the Romantic poets, was the one who had most control – total, in fact – of the way in which his poems would appear on the printed page.[60]

Illustrations

New technologies of engraving on copper and later on steel plates made illustrations increasingly easier and cheaper to include in newspapers and printed books. Charles Dickens started out as a provider of text to accompany a series of "cockney sporting plates" by Robert Seymour which became *The Pickwick Papers* (1836–1837). Later, Hablot K. Brown (1815–1882), known as 'Phiz', became Dickens's chief illustrator and produced many memorable images of his eccentric characters. George Cruikshank (1792–1878) illustrated some of Dickens's early

---

[60] Blake's works, including his colour plates, can be read and viewed on http://www.blakearchive.org/. See http://www.blakearchive.org/exhibit/illuminatedprinting for a detailed explanation of Blake's printing technique. Date of access: 13 Dec. 2021.

Fig. 15: William Blake, *Songs of Innocence and Experience* (1794), plate 47. Colour-printed relief etching with watercolour on moderately thick, slightly textured, cream wove paper. Source: Yale Center for British Art, Paul Mellon Collection, B1978.43.1578.

work, most notably *Oliver Twist* (1838). William Thackeray, the author of *Vanity Fair* (1848), a panoramic novel subtitled *Pen and Pencil Sketches of English Society*, worked as his own illustrator. Many of his illustrations interact with the text by adding their own layers of meaning and irony to the story.

For many nineteenth-century novelists, illustration was not seen as detrimental to their novels but as a welcome addition. Other writers were more critical of the spread of images. Regarding popular newspapers such as the *Illustrated London News* (a weekly starting in 1842) as the epitome of stupidity and bad taste, in 1846, the poet laureate William Wordsworth, then in his seventies, wrote a sonnet attacking "Illustrated Books and Newspapers" (even though he was not, in principle, opposed to illustrations accompanying his poems):

> Discourse was deemed Man's noblest attribute,
> And written words the glory of his hand;
> Then followed Printing with enlarged command
> For thought – dominion vast and absolute
> For spreading truth, and making love expand.
> Now prose and verse sunk into disrepute
> Must lacquey a dumb Art that best can suit
> The taste of this once-intellectual Land.
> A backward movement surely have we here,
> From manhood – back to childhood; for the age –
> Back towards caverned life's first rude career.
> Avaunt this vile abuse of pictured page!
> Must eyes be all in all, the tongue and ear
> Nothing? Heaven keep us from a lower stage!
> (Wordsworth 1896, 184–185)

Wordsworth's scathing critique contains all the familiar tropes of cultural pessimism: intellectual decline ("this once-intellectual Land"), regression to an infantile stage of human development ("back to childhood") and to a less civilised phase, a "lower stage" of human history ("caverned life's first rude career"), and so on. Wordsworth compares readers of the "pictured page" to illiterate, image-loving Neanderthals. While his response to new media is familiar, it is informed by specific anxieties about modern visual culture ("a dumb Art"), sensationalist journalism, and class. He used the sonnet, an established poetic form, to demarcate a territory of "intellectual" high culture from cheap popular entertainment. In other words, "he worried that the emerging media ecology would be a hostile environment for his poetry" (Mole 2017, 47). This concern focused on the combination of texts and images in print. Nineteenth-century poets did not object so much to the widespread use of their poems as subjects for paintings. Painters like John Atkinson Grimshaw (1836–1893), William Maw Egley (1826–1916), and John William Waterhouse (1849–1917) painted scenes from Tennyson's ballad

"The Lady of Shalott" (1833/1842), for example. Some Victorian poets, including Dante Gabriel Rossetti (1828–1882) and William Morris (1834–1896), were themselves painters and illustrated their own work, with Morris even becoming his own printer and designing a medievalist visual aesthetic for the presentation of his works (cf. ch. 3 for Morris's edition of Chaucer).

While illustrated fiction was not deemed so problematic in the Victorian age, this changed during the nineteenth century's final quarter when the novel became more respectable as a literary form. In the 1880s, writers like Walter Besant (1836–1901) and Henry James began to speak of the "art of fiction" (Spilka 1973). Illustrations were now often seen as a distraction and a debasement of the art of writing, similar to Wordsworth's fear of "prose and verse" becoming a 'lackey', a lowly servant, within a largely visual culture. For these writers, the visuality of literature was to be a purely imaginative one – a visuality of the mind, not of the eyes. Illustrations were relegated to the cultural margins of popular entertainment, of cartoons and comic strips. Only much later, in the twentieth and early twenty-first century, a new form of serious comics or 'graphic novels' (Baetens and Frey 2015) returned to combine texts and drawings in often sophisticated ways (see below).

Writers who consider their writing a form of art will have difficulties accepting another art form jostling theirs. For example, the French poet Charles Baudelaire (1821–1867), writing about the *salon* of 1859 (a regular art exhibition in Paris) abhorred photography: "If photography is allowed to supplement art in some of its functions, it will soon have supplanted or corrupted it altogether. [. . .] It is time, then, for it to return to its true duty, which is to be the servant of the sciences and arts – but the very humble servant, like printing or shorthand, which have neither created nor supplemented literature" (1981, 154).

Henry James offers the best illustration of this competition between literature and photography. The New York edition of his novels and tales (1907–1909) was expected to feature illustrations on the frontispiece to each volume. This gave James, the foremost psychological novelist and stylist of his time, affectionately and respectfully known as 'the Master', a not inconsiderable amount of anxiety. James's biographer, Leon Edel, tells the story best:

> From the first, Henry James had taken it for granted that each volume of his definitive edition would have a frontispiece. The tradition was well established. A long line of illustrators, not least Cruikshank, had added pictures to prose fiction. James himself had been illustrated by [George] du Maurier as early as *Washington Square* [1880]. In his tale of "The Real Thing" [1892] the narrator is an illustrator preparing a series of drawings for a "definitive edition" designed to be "the tribute of English art" to a representative of letters. James in reality wanted to be spared such a tribute. He had always resented illustration. For one thing, it delayed publication; his prose had to lie about the magazine office waiting for the illustrator to get his drawings done. One [sic] more important grounds, he

felt that pictures – much as he loved them – when combined with text, were an affront to the written word. The English language did not need visual aids. James was "jealous" of illustration. He looked askance at any effort "to graft or 'grow' at whatever point, a picture by another hand on my own picture." (Edel 1972, 333)

In 1905, James had met a young American photographer, Alvin Langdon Coburn (1882–1966), and he warmed to the idea that, instead of having drawings, Coburn could add his photographs to the edition. "His illustrations would be 'optical' symbols. They would be photographs of general scenes, material objects. They would enhance, but in no way intrude with irrelevant images upon James's own literary images. Photographs could have a total 'objectivity', an impersonal quality necessary for illustrating the edition" (Edel 1972, 334). He dispatched Coburn to Paris, to Venice, and accompanied him to London, where the photograph for the *Golden Bowl* frontispiece was taken: the front of an antiquarian shop. For the second volume of *The Golden Bowl*, James chose Coburn's photograph of a hansom cab and Portland Place in a haze (fig. 16).

Fig. 16: Portland Place, London. Photograph by Alvin Langdon Coburn, c. 1905. Source: Granger Historical Picture Archive / Alamy Stock Photo.

In his preface to *The Golden Bowl* for the New York edition, James at first treads carefully around the issue of illustration, but he uses a number of visual metaphors to describe the "desirable vividness" by which his writing is to "display" characters to be 'seen' by the reader (1987, 21): "We see Charlotte also at first, and we see Adam Verver, let alone our seeing Mrs Assingham, and every one and every thing else, but as they are visible in the Prince's interest" (22). The preface returns again and again to this evocation of visuality, of "aspects and visibilities" (35.) "The essence of any representational work", James adds, "is of course to bristle with immediate images" (23). He admits Coburn's photographs not as illustrations in the conventional sense, but as "*mere* optical symbols or echoes, expressions of no particular thing in the text" (24, my emphasis).

James's evocation of the visual sense, of literature's power to stimulate the imagination, may sound like an echo of a famous phrase by Joseph Conrad some years earlier (1897) on the novelist's "task": "My task which I am trying to achieve is, by the power of the written word to make you hear, to make you feel, – it is, before all, to make you *see*" (Conrad 1991, 5, emphasis original). But James had already taken this a step further in 1884 when he declared that his goal in writing was "to guess the unseen from the seen" (James 1986, 172; see also Griem 2008). This "moment of vision" (Conrad 1991, 7), incited by what narratologists would later call 'focalisation', was not to be disturbed by illustrations, because literature was already sufficiently visual.[61] Its images were to be seen in the mind's eye.

Modernist Typography and Visual Thinking

In an even more basic sense, printed literature was designed for the eyes to take in by means of typography. After 1900, writers and artists began to pay more attention to aspects of design and layout. Some set out to found their own small presses, as Nancy Cunard (1896–1965) did with the Hours Press in 1928, which published early work by Samuel Beckett and the legendary *Negro* anthology of Black literature and art (1934). Many modernists made the typography of their texts a part of their artistic intention, at times disrupting the reader's experience in ways that Laurence Sterne would have recognised (see ch. 6), at times choosing new fonts to signal their departure from Victorian and Edwardian fashion. The Italian futurist Filippo Tommaso Marinetti (1876–1944) is an example of this trend, with his poem *Zang Tumb Tuuum* (1912–1914) scattering words and letters across the pages. In his manifesto *Typographic Revolution* (1913), Marinetti calls for a revolution

> against the idiotic and nauseating concepts of the outdated and conventional book, with its handmade paper and seventeenth century ornamentation of garlands and goddesses, huge initials and mythological vegetation [. . .]. The book must be the Futurist expression of our Futurist ideas. [. . .] my revolution is directed against what is known as the

---

[61] On literature and illustration, see also Miller 1992; on Henry James and photography, Burrows 2008.

typographic harmony of the page, which is contrary to the flux and movement of style. Therefore, we will employ three or four different colored inks and twenty different typefaces on the same page if necessary. [. . .] A new concept of the pictorial typographic page. (Marinetti qtd. in Drucker 1994, 114)

Concrete poetry had existed before; a famous earlier example is the poem "Easter Wings" by George Herbert (1593–1633) from *The Temple* (1633), a poem shaped like an angel's outstretched wings. But this arrangement of words into an image was in the service of religious allegory. The new avantgarde movements all over Europe set out to destroy the old and create something new: "make it new", in Ezra Pound's memorable phrase (1935). In France, Guillaume Apollinaire (1880–1918) published his *Calligrammes* in 1918, a collection of poems in free verse, with the words or letters arranged in a pattern to yield an image: vertical lines to indicate rain ("Il pleut") or words arranged in the shape of the Eiffel tower ("Salut monde"), or a tie and a watch ("La cravate et la montre"). In Russia, Ilia Zdanevich (1894–1975) did similar work between 1916 and 1923 (Drucker 168–192), as did the Dadaists in Switzerland and Germany. There were many further experiments within Surrealism and Lettrism in the twentieth century. British writers and artists played a rather less significant role in this field. The only genuine contender is *Blast,* a short-lived magazine edited (and mostly written) by Wyndham Lewis (1882–1957). Only two issues were published, in 1914 and 1915. The magazine was associated with an equally short-lived movement called Vorticism; the War killed many of its key members. As Pound writes in 1914, in an essay titled "Vortex", which was published in the first issue of *Blast* (June 20, 1914):

> The vortex is the point of maximum energy.
> It represents, in mechanics, the greatest efficiency.
> We use the words "greatest efficiency" in the precise sense – as they would be used in a text book of MECHANICS.
> [. . .]
> All experience rushes into this vortex. All the energized past, all the past that is living and worthy to live. [. . .]
> [. . .] All the past that is vital, all the past that is capable of living into the future, is pregnant in the vortex, NOW. (Pound 1980, 151)

This avantgarde had given up the cult of beauty, celebrated by aestheticism and decadence in the 1890s, by the likes of Walter Pater, Oscar Wilde, and Aubrey Beardsley (1872–1898), for a cult of the machine and of technology. Ironically, many of its advocates were literally crushed to death by the new fighting machines of the Great War.

As Joanna Drucker has shown, "[t]he avant-garde poets of the 1910s became the graphic designers, teachers, and systematic theorists of the 1920s and

1930s" (238). If one wonders why the typeface of a Penguin paperback looks so different from anything printed in the nineteenth century, the answer is: because its letters were designed by the typographer Eric Gill (1882–1940). Gill pronounced better design and more easily legible type to be a crucial part of designing better lives. Such ideas of social and political reform were closely associated with modernism. Radical politics on the left and right often came with their own design choices, both desiring to leave established and outmoded forms behind. "The world is not yet clothed in garments which befit it", Gill writes in 1931; "in architecture, furniture, clothes, we are still using and wearing things which have no real relation to the spirit which moves our life. We are wearing and using them simply because we are accustomed to them" (2013, 6). Gill's suggestions for modern typography, inspired by the Arts and Crafts movement, is a plain and efficient form, "designed for modern machine production", which allows for easy reading and is still beautiful to look at without being "fancy" (132). In the 1910s, Gill had assisted in designing the letters for the London Underground. His own creations include the Gill Sans typeface; with its classic line, inspired by Roman models, it embodies his ideals of modern design. This was adopted by Allen Lane for his Penguin paperbacks in 1935.[62]

The modernists' fascination with form and vision, even with the visual shape of letters, also shows in Ezra Pound's interest in Chinese characters. Pound (1885–1972), an American poet who settled in London in 1908 and stayed until 1920, was a key figure of literary modernism. He edited the scholar Ernest Fenollosa's study on *The Chinese Written Character as a Medium for Poetry* in 1918. While Fenollosa's theories about the Chinese language and its writing system never had too many friends among sinologists, his book, via Pound's mediation, had a lasting impact on modern American poetics (Saussy 2008). It, or Pound's reading of it, advocated "ideogrammic" thinking as a model for poetic thinking in images: treating words not as signs for something but as "the picture of a thing; of a thing in a given position or relation, or of a combination of things. It *means* the thing or the action or situation, or quality germane to the several things that it pictures" (Pound 1960 [1934], 21). This matched Pound's longing for concrete rather than abstract expressions – "direct treatment of the 'thing'" (Pound 1968 [1918], 3) or, as the American poet William Carlos Williams (1883–1963) put it in 1927, "no ideas but in things" (1991, 263). For Pound, the power of poetry lay in the energy and luminosity of such a single, powerful image:

---

[62] It is a bitter irony of history that this important sculptor and typographer, who in his work aimed to design better lives, was a monster in private who sexually abused his sisters and daughters (and his dog). This was only revealed in a biography published in 1989 (MacCarthy 1989).

> An 'Image' is that which presents an intellectual and emotional complex in an instant of time. [. . .]
> It is the presentation of such a 'complex' instantaneously which gives that sense of sudden liberation; that sense of freedom from time limits and space limits; that sense of sudden growth, which we experience in the presence of the greatest works of art.
> It is better to present one image in a lifetime than to produce voluminous works.
> (Pound 1968 [1918], 4)[63]

From 1914–1917, Pound was part of a group of seven poets who called themselves 'the Imagists' and who published four annual anthologies and a manifesto: next to Pound, these were fellow Americans H. D. (Hilda Doolittle, 1886–1961), John Gould Fletcher (1886–1950), Amy Lowell (1874–1925), and the British poets Richard Aldington (1892–1962), F. S. Flint (1885–1960), and D. H. Lawrence (who was co-opted by Amy Lowell and never quite convinced he belonged). Of these, only Pound and Lawrence are still well known, though the latter mainly for his novels, in particular the once scandalous *Lady Chatterley's Lover* (1928). Imagism was a reaction against the soft-spoken and late Romantic bloom of 'Georgian' poetry, which dominated the English scene at the time. Against this Victorian survival, the Imagists promoted a distinctly modern style of poem. When D. H. Lawrence wrote a poem beginning "The morning breaks like a pomegranate / In a shining crack of red" (from "Wedding Morn", 1913), or "The sky was apple-green, / The sky was green wine held up in the sun" (from "Green", 1915), he was a galaxy away from the conventional fruit imagery that was a staple of Georgian poetry, as in John Drinkwater's (1882–1937) "Moonlit Apples" from the anthology *Georgian Poetry IV 1918–1919*, which has no other metaphors than the cliché "moonlit apples of dreams" (l. 11). As Pound wrote in 1913: "Don't use such an expression as 'dim lands of *peace*'. It dulls the image. It mixes an abstraction with the concrete. It comes from the writer's not realizing that the natural object is always the *adequate* symbol" (1968, 5).

The kind of poem that Pound wanted to write, and wanted others to write, is best exemplified in the famous "In a Station of the Metro":

> The apparition   of these faces   in the crowd :
> Petals   on a wet, black   bough .

This is the first version – not an extract, but the entire poem – as it appeared in *Poetry* magazine in April 1913 (Pound 1913, 12). Note how individual phrases are emphasised by the spacing, which gives the poem an unusual visual as well as auditory rhythm. It resembles Japanese haiku without exactly replicating the strict syllable count of that form (which usually follows a 5 – 7 – 5 pattern in

---

[63] This part of Pound's 1918 essay "A Retrospect" was first printed as "A Few Don'ts" in 1913.

three phrases). This association with East Asian literature and culture may also impact how readers see the white and black image of faces/petals, possibly associating the ideogram, Chinese calligraphy, or a Hokusai print. Note also that there is no longer a conventional lyric speaker in this poem, and, even more radically, it does not contain a single verb. Instead, there are two more or less well-connected observations, perceptions of a moment, visual impressions rendered in a montage without any analysis, commentary, or reflection. Pound connects the moment when faces become visible in an underground station (most likely the Paris Métro) with flower petals on the wet limb of a tree, a strongly visual image that works like a cinematic montage of two separate shots from a camera. He juxtaposes these two images, which thereby form a visual comparison, a resemblance. Perhaps they merge into a single image in an 'objective' way – at least according to the poetics of 'ideogrammic' thinking that Pound would develop later. It is a poem about vision as well as visuality – breath-taking in its brevity and yet complex not only in its imagery but also its sound pattern. "Crowd" and "bough" form an assonance or near-rhyme. The syllable count is interesting too: 5 – 4 – 3 / 2 – 4 – 1. There are twelve syllables in the first line, seven in the second. Looking at stress patterns, the first line is (close to) a hexameter, line two a pentameter; this alternation is typical of elegiac metre in Greek and Latin, but there is not much metrical regularity here to make this more than a subtle allusion to classical tradition.

Like a photographic snapshot, the imagist image according to Pound "presents an intellectual and emotional complex in an instant of time" (1968, 4). The image is to hit the mind directly and as unmediated as possible. The use of objects as symbols resembles what T. S. Eliot called the "objective correlative" (1921, 92), a phrase that has led to much confusion but is perhaps best understood in this context: "a set of objects, a situation" by which a "*particular* emotion [. . .] is immediately evoked" (ibid.). "In a Station of the Metro": the title still refers to a concrete object, to a situation of being in a particular place. The image is a potential attitude towards the object, capturing a perception of what the object is or appears to be like. There is tension in the uncommon correlation between the object and the image that is being evoked without being explained – a gap that only readers can fill (by thinking about the ways in which faces can be compared to petals, a metro station with a branch of a tree, etc.). As to its emotional resonance, this is largely left open to readers as well. It can range from an appreciation of this scene as an aesthetic object (like a Japanese print) to less pleasant associations with crowds, wetness, and darkness. Above all, it is highly impersonal – an object without a subject.

As a form of cubism by means of language, imagism intends to liberate objects from the tyranny of single-point perspective and to set free the activity of perception. Like the other arts, avantgarde forms of literature in the early twentieth century moved away from representation towards experiments with form and language, trying out multiple perspectives, multiple styles (as in Joyce's *Ulysses* and Eliot's *The Waste Land*, 1922), or even the absence of style altogether, as in Beckett's alleged ideal to 'write without style'.[64]

The Waste Land

Ezra Pound's influence on T. S. Eliot is best seen in *The Waste Land* (1922). A facsimile edition of the manuscript, edited in 1971 by Eliot's second wife Valerie (Eliot 2010), shows how much textual advice Pound gave to Eliot, considerably reducing the poem's length and turning it into a monument of modernism, heavily influenced by Pound's notion of the image and the combination of images rather than the sequential, analytic, or logical combination of objects and abstractions usual in the Western tradition.

Eliot's poetic voice is striking, even strident; his sound is fresh and more colloquial than his contemporaries', sometimes even cynical. There are discontinuities and sudden jumps from one image to another. In one of the early poems that made him famous, "The Love Song of J. Alfred Prufrock" (1915), the distance from conventional poetic imagery is even more pronounced than in what we have seen so far: "Let us go then, you and I, / When the evening is spread out against the sky / Like a patient etherised upon a table" (Eliot 1989, 13, ll. 1–3). The attack is direct, including the reader as an addressee in the "us" and "you" and the injunction "let us go then", the word "then" less a temporal deixis ("then – when") than perhaps an expression of fatigue or disillusionment counteracting the impulse to leave. The evening "spread out against the sky" might lead one to expect a conventional image, possibly a metaphor in the next line, but Eliot goes for a simile, less daring, more traditional, as in the epic simile that was a hallmark of Spenser's *Faerie Queene* (1590/1596); but no, the simile itself is a radical break: "Like a patient etherised upon a table". If anything, this echoes the cynical tone of some of Baudelaire's *Les fleurs du mal* (*The Flowers of Evil*, 1857) with its address to the reader as "my likeness, my brother".[65] Instead of a rural evening sky, we get urban squalor. The fatigue is more radical than just being tired: "etherised" means the patient is down under

---

[64] The phrase has been attributed to Beckett as one of his motivations for writing in French and has since become a commonplace in Beckett studies (Gessner 1957, 32n.; see also Plat 2016).

[65] "– Hypocrite lecteur, – mon semblable, – mon frère" ("Au Lecteur"), as translated by Eli Siegel in 1968. https://fleursdumal.org/poem/099. Date of access: 13 Dec. 2021.

a strong anaesthetic, they are on the operating table soon to undergo an operation – perhaps in a life-and-death situation. Poetry in English would never quite be the same again.

Eliot's long poem *The Waste Land* (1922) manages to uphold this challenge throughout. Images and cultural references are heaped up to create the impression of a cacophony of "different voices" (Eliot 2010, 4), different textual traces superimposed on each other, like a palimpsest of older writings. The chaos of the present is contrasted with the 'better' (but irretrievably lost) order of the mythic or literary past. The opening of *The Waste Land*, "April is the cruellest month", alludes to Chaucer's prologue to *The Canterbury Tales* ("whan that Aprill with his shoures soote"), offering a negation to the hope (fertility, etc.) usually connected with springtime. Eliot added explanatory notes to the poem, tracing allusions, quotations and semi-quotations, echoes and parodies of authors and sources as varied as John Webster (c. 1580–c. 1632), Thomas Kyd (1558–1594), Dante, Paul Verlaine (1844–1896), Baudelaire, the Bible, the legend of the Holy Grail, and James George Frazer's work of cultural anthropology and comparative mythology *The Golden Bough* (1890–1915). He later claimed that these notes were red herrings, "bogus scholarship" meant to mislead critics and to fill space in the otherwise slim book in which it was published, "to provide a few more pages of printed matter" (Eliot 1957, 109). But this claim has since been proven as itself bogus (Kaiser 2007). Like Spenser's annotations to the *Shepherdes Calender*, Eliot's notes serve as a frame that helps to present the poem as an instant classic, a text in need of annotation. Even though Eliot himself later dismissed these 433 lines of verse as "a piece of rhythmical grumbling" (Eliot 2010, 1), it did become a classic and was soon hailed as a literary milestone – the combination of lyricism and cynicism, harshness and spiritual yearning was particularly appealing to the postwar generation.

The Waste Land is pervaded by a sense of loss, desolation, and disorientation; imagery of death is omnipresent: dead trees, dead land, bones of dead men. The death imagery comes close to the "death in life" or "buried life" *topos* of Victorian poetry (cf. Matthew Arnold's poem "The Buried Life"). It is not merely a reference to mass extinction in World War One but also "a lament for the living death that the war symbolically bequeathed to the world in marking the end of a cultural cycle and the shattering of its fundamental values, beliefs and aspirations" (Poplawski 2008, 581–582). It connotes "the spiritual death of western civilisation" through its "imagery of dryness and sterility" (582). The pervasive sense of disorientation, chaos and anarchy is to some extent counteracted by a motif of a search for enlightenment, represented by the allusions to the Holy Grail quest, a search for understanding or (rather) metaphysical, spiritual "Peace which passeth understanding", as Eliot glossed the last three words of the text: the Sanskrit words "Shantih, shantih, shantih", an incantation from the *Upanishads* (ancient Hindu scriptures).

In part three of *The Waste Land*, "The Fire Sermon", the references to London as the main topographical setting of the poem pile up: the Thames, the Cannon Street Hotel, the Metropole, the Strand, Queen Victoria Street, Greenwich, the Isle of Dogs, and other place names are thick on the ground. Different times and places merge: Elizabeth I and the earl of Leicester are rowing on the (modern) Thames, accompanied by quotations from Richard Wagner's *Das Rheingold* (part of his Ring cycle, a nineteenth-century operatic dramatisation of Norse mythology). London is invoked as an "Unreal City" (l. 207). It is paralleled with the mythic land of a king without offspring: the city is a place where people live indifferent lives indifferently. This is contrasted with old stories of romantic or passionate love (Cleopatra, *She Stoops to Conquer*, Dante and Beatrice, Elizabeth and Leicester, the Romance of the Rose). The modern world is 'unreal', as London gives way to other modern cities in the last section, "What the Thunder Said". The modern world for Eliot is the end of culture: a profound antipathy towards the modern condition pervades the poem.

The final stanza takes us back to the shore of the river, with a reference to the mythic Fisher King. "Shall I at least set my lands in order?" (l. 425), the speaker asks, combining sadness with hope for renewal: "These fragments I have shored against my ruins" (l. 430). They are the fragments of which the poem consists (broken-up allusions and echoes of a rich array of mythology and literature), perhaps also referring to the fragmented nature of the modern experience that yearns for a spiritual perspective, supplied here by references to the Hindu wisdom scriptures and their moral teachings: what the thunder said (revealing the voice of the god Prajapati), is "DA DA DA", interpreted as "Datta. Dayadhvam. Damyata" (l. 432), which means (roughly) "self-control, alms-giving, and compassion". As the gods, men, and demons in the Hindu fable must interpret the fragmentary sayings of Prajapati, the reader in *The Waste Land* has to piece together the allusive fragments of the text, from the ruins of civilisation – aided, today, fortunately, by search engines.

All these fragments are difficult to identify since they are placed into a new context. The lack of context directs one's attention to the motivation for this lack, this loss of connectivity. Images appear as fragments, assembled in a collage of different, often contradictory items. There is a clash, an interference of images – broken images that can no longer be decoded. They suggest instead "that reality has emancipated itself from any image" (Iser 1966, 391). If reality can no longer be represented by images, even poetic images in Pound's sense, poetry can only present an endless array of bizarre combinations. In the poem's last line, all activities of interpretation must cease.

One response to this overload of conflicting images is, indeed, blindness. Tiresias, the blind seer, is for Eliot "the most important personage in the poem, uniting all the rest" (Eliot 1989, 82). The flood of images in modernity has led to a "denigration of vision" (Jay 1993; cf. Crary 1992), a denial or suppression of the visual and a privileging of other senses, because this flood can be perceived as threatening the integrity of the subject. Literary forms of visuality intervene in (socially and culturally dominant) regimes of vision and the domains of the visible and the invisible. Literature is already by definition characterised by "optical poverty" (Iser 1978, 138) since its images are for the most part mental rather than real ones and thus far less concrete. Henry James was well aware of this when he bristled against illustration. But it is an even more troublesome step to go from this to the denial of even those images that literature *can* present – as is the case, for example, in Samuel Beckett's late short fiction, most notably in *Imagination Dead Imagine* (1965). Has modern literature gone blind as a medium, has it given up all access to visuality?

Blindness

This is the question that is broached in Henry Green's (Henry Vincent Yorke, 1905–1973) debut novel *Blindness* (1926), published four years after *The Waste Land*. In this novel, John Haye, a young man who aspires to become a writer, loses his eyesight in a railway accident. His hope to develop a more profound insight into life is gradually crushed because of a pervasive social and cultural blindness that goes beyond the physical. This metaphorical blindness of his biases prevents John from really 'seeing' his surroundings, other people around him, and himself. His development is stunted: as a man, he remains under his stepmother's domination; as a writer, he will be unable to free himself from stifling conventions and traditions (Tripp 2014). His imagination is confined to vague memories of things he has seen before his accident, and he can no longer clearly associate words to concepts:

> He felt himself sinking into a pit of darkness. At the top of the pit were figures, like dolls and like his friends, striking attitudes at a sun they had made for themselves, till sinking he lost sight of them, to find himself in the presence of other dolls in the light of a sun that others had made for them. Then it did not work, and he was back in the darkness, on the lawn again. Nothing seemed real.
>
> He said 'tree' out loud and it was a word. He saw branches with vague substance blocked round them, he saw lawn, all green, and he built up a picture of lawn and tree, but there were gaps, and his brain reeled from the effort of filling them. (Green 2008, 394)

"Nothing seemed real": in passages like this, Green's novel can be read as an allegory of (modernist) literature itself, or a modernist attitude to literature that is no longer viewed as an appropriate or as the best possible medium to represent reality. Images have been cut off from objects; people have become indistinguishable from dolls; words and other signs have been cut off from their referents; even the sun – the master signifier – is artificial, leaving behind the real, as inert, dead matter, "vague substance", to make sense of itself. The sun, normally blinding, cannot illuminate anything here. The extract can be read as a critique of traditional Western 'ocularcentrism' (Jay 1993). Its sun is closer to the horribly ugly sun as invoked by the French writer Georges Bataille (1897–1962) in "The Solar Anus" (1927) and "Rotten Sun" (1930; see Jay 1993, 223), or as deconstructed as a central metaphor of Western epistemology by Jacques Derrida (1930–2004) in "White Mythology" (1974). But it is also, intentionally or unintentionally, a statement of a poetics that would be followed by later writers including Beckett – the programme for a radically anti-mimetic literature in which the access to reality has been radically cut off.

The Graphic Novel and Other Forms of Sequential Art

"And he built up a picture [. . .] but there were gaps" (Green 2008, 394). In 1990, the cartoonist Martin Rowson (1959–) published his visual adaptation of Eliot's *The Waste Land* as a graphic novel or, rather, graphic poem. He combined motifs and themes from the poem with an American *film noir* visual style and a plot that resembles the detective novels of Raymond Chandler (1888–1959), with Chandler's detective Philip Marlowe searching for those who killed his partner. In this meta-literary hell of a gloomy and nightmarish 1920s London, "Henry James, Aldous Huxley and Richard Wagner share an ice cream aboard a Thames pleasure steamer" (Rowson 2012, back cover). Because the Eliot estate did not allow Rowson to use extensive quotations from the original poem, the artist had to find ingenious visual solutions. Thus, instead of a verbal reference to the "dried tubers" in l. 7 of *The Waste Land*, Rowson gives us an image of shrivelled *tubas* – a visual-verbal pun (2012, n. p., ch. 1, frame 2) that compensates for the legally imposed textual, rather than visual, poverty of his work (Glaubitz 2013). As in Wolfgang Iser's theory of aesthetic response (1978) and in Scott McCloud's *Understanding Comics* (1994) and his definition of comics as "sequential art" (1994, 9), the gaps – between words, but also between words and images, and in the gutters between panels in a comic strip or a graphic novel – are the spaces where connections are made and meanings are created.

In the later twentieth century, the graphic novel developed into a multimodal art form, combining images and text in ways that William Blake would have recognised but that also added substantial innovations in narrative form (Baetens and Frey 2015). This very diverse field that integrates literary and visual modes of storytelling has emancipated itself from the earlier newspaper comic strip that is part of its origins, or the superhero comics of the mid-twentieth century. Moreover, it is not limited to adaptations of literary texts like Martin Rowson's *The Waste Land* or Catherine Anyango's and David Zane Mairowitz's justly praised adaptation of Joseph Conrad's *Heart of Darkness* (2010). Some of the most original contributions to this form have been written by the English author Alan Moore (1953–), such as the dystopian thriller *V for Vendetta*, illustrated by David Lloyd (1982), and Moore's take on the murders of Jack the Ripper, *From Hell* (1989–1998), with art by Eddie Campbell. But the possibilities of the form are explored and expanded to their utmost in Moore's and Dave Gibbons's *Watchmen* (1986–1987). Set in an alternate reality in the 1980s, *Watchmen*'s gritty revision of the superhero narrative and its complex layers of meaning make it one of the defining literary works of the atomic age and the later Cold War period.

Combinations of text and image persist as appealing art forms in modernity beyond modernism. Some art works present typographic text, as in the LOVE image (1965) by Robert Indiana (1928–2018), in Jenny Holzer's (1950–) 'word art' installations, or in the kind of digital poetry that uses Flash animation to project a sequence of words on a screen, for example by Young-Hae Chang Heavy Industries (*Dakota*, 2001). Other visual artists have turned to the form of the art book or to using old books as a substrate for visual interventions, such as Tom Phillips's (1937–) *A Humument* (1970, 2016).[66] Even though moving images have come to dominate – something we will explore in the next chapter – the single or sequential image or object persists as a (rarely static) mode of expression.

---

66 On book art and the artist's book, see Borsuk 2018, 115–195.

11 Screen: Literature and the Moving Image

Seeing Mrs. Bathurst

In Rudyard Kipling's short story "Mrs. Bathurst" (1904), a group of British naval officers in South Africa begin to talk about a common acquaintance, a very attractive woman named Mrs. Bathurst, who used to keep a little hotel near Auckland, New Zealand. They talk about a fellow officer named Vickery who has developed an obsession for this woman; one member of the group, Pyecroft, recalls how Vickery took him to a circus, where they watched a film made in London in which, suddenly, Vickery recognised Mrs. Bathurst. Vickery demanded Pyecroft to accompany him to the circus on four nights in a row to watch this film. The destructive effect of Mrs. Bathurst on Vickery's mind was such that he apparently became a deserter, left his station, and was only seen again later when his charred remains were found after a forest fire (identified only by his false teeth and a tattoo that was still visible)– together with a second, unidentified body – which may or may not have been that of Mrs. Bathurst.

This rather enigmatic story, which leaves a lot to read between the lines, such as the precise nature of the relationship between Vickery and Mrs. Bathurst, is an early instance of literature responding to the new medium of cinema. It proceeds from a similar narrative setting as several turn-of-the-century novels and stories by Joseph Conrad (e.g., *Heart of Darkness*, 1899; *Lord Jim*, 1900) and Henry James (e.g., *The Turn of the Screw*, 1898): a group of friends telling each other stories, with several speakers filling in details but none of them having sufficient knowledge to tell the entire story. Like Conrad, who desired to make his readers "see" (1991, 5), Pyecroft is trying the same when he talks about Mrs. Bathurst. But one of his interlocutors, Hooper, who will later report on the discovery of Vickery's body, interjects: "I don't *see* her yet somehow" (Kipling 1994b, 587). Only new media technologies provide a different way of acquiring knowledge, as Pyecroft admits: "I used to think seein' and hearin' was the only regulation aids to ascertainin' facts, but as we get older we get more accommodatin'. The cylinders work easier, I suppose . . ." (588). At this point, he asks the others whether they are familiar with "a new turn of a scientific nature called 'Home and Friends for a Tickey'", also known as the "cinematograph" (589). When he tells them about the film showing, Pyecroft emphasises its visual realism: "You 'eard a little dynamo like buzzin', but the pictures were the real thing – alive and movin'" (590). Hooper concurs: "Of course they are taken from the very thing itself – you see" (590), and Pyecroft continues:

Open Access. © 2022 Ingo Berensmeyer, published by De Gruyter. This work is licensed under the Creative Commons Attribution-NonCommercial-NoDerivatives 4.0 International License.
https://doi.org/10.1515/9783110784459-011

> Then the Western Mail came in to Paddin'ton on the big magic lantern sheet. First we saw the platform empty an' the porters standin' by. Then the engine come in, head on, an' the women in the front row jumped: she headed so straight. Then the doors opened and the passengers came out and the porters got the luggage – just like life. Only – only when any one came down too far towards us that was watchin', they walked right out o' the picture, so to speak. (590)

The arrival of a train was indeed one of the earliest motifs of film, and the experience of audiences fearing to be run over by the train on the screen is a commonplace of early reports on cinema. One of these short films that have survived is *The Arrival of a Train at La Ciotat* by the Lumière brothers (1896). Kipling's narrator stresses the film's realism ("just like life") but also the point where watching a film is different from seeing an object in reality: "when any one came down too far towards us [. . .] they walked right out o' the picture". The ghostly appearance of Mrs. Bathurst in this film drives Vickery mad, with the effect that he too, in a manner of speaking, 'walks right out' of his life. He has 'seen' Mrs. Bathurst with a vengeance. How did literature 'see' the cinema?

Early Cinema and Literary Modernism

Cinema and its possibilities held a great fascination for many modernist writers. There were undoubtedly "significant affinities between early cinema and literary modernism" (Trotter 2007, 1). But the moving image had been a staple of the literary imagination even before the arrival of cinema. In the previous chapter, we have seen how earlier writers compared poetry and narrative to static images and statues. In the nineteenth century, George Eliot (1819–1880) compared the historical novelist's craft with that of an illusionist, a 'sorcerer' who "undertakes to reveal [. . .] far-reaching visions of the past" in "a single drop of ink for a mirror" (1985 [1859], 7). In her novel *Middlemarch* (1871–1872), she also referred to the diorama and to the magic lantern and its moving picture sequences as analogues of the human mind: "Our moods are apt to bring with them images which succeed each other like the magic-lantern pictures of a doze" (ch. 20; Eliot 1994, 193–194). "The memory has as many moods as the temper, and shifts its scenery like a diorama" (ch. 53; ibid., 522). The magic lantern was a fashionable parlour toy in the Victorian era. Similarly, in Robert Louis Stevenson's *The Strange Case of Dr. Jekyll and Mr. Hyde* (1886), one character responds to the tale of another as "a scroll of lighted pictures" "before his mind" (1979, 37). Novelists and storytellers were intrigued by the visual imagination and its technological supports well before the invention of the cinematograph.

From its early appearances in circuses, vaudeville theatres, and variety shows towards the end of the nineteenth century, the cinema soon advanced to remodelled or purpose-built 'theatres' or 'picture houses'. In 1909, James Joyce set up Ireland's first cinema, the *Volta Electric Theatre,* in Dublin. But it was not a success, and he gave it up after a few months (Ellmann 1982, 300–303). By then, "motion pictures had clearly become a large industry" (Czitrom 2019, 177). In London, several members of the Bloomsbury Group set up a Film Society in 1925. The less well-known Pool Group founded their own film company in 1927 and made five films (van Schlun 2017, 257). Several (female) modernists edited and contributed to the film magazine *Close Up,* the first British journal of film theory (1927–1933), including H. D., Bryher (Annie Winifred Ellerman, 1894–1983), and Dorothy Richardson (1873–1957) (Shail 2012, 5).

The cinema was also, early on, hungry for literary source material that might be adapted into films, or new stories – soon to be called 'treatments' and 'screenplays' – to be turned into new films, so that the film industry came to provide further professional opportunities for writers. It was cheaper, of course, to film classics that were out of copyright; but a few authors and publishers could make a handsome profit from selling the film rights to their works. For example, many novels by the Victorian bestselling writer Ouida (Maria Louise Ramé, 1839–1908) proved to be highly profitable for the publisher Chatto & Windus in the early twentieth century when some of her novels were adapted into successful films (Lesser 2019, 326–327). In the 1930s, the popular writer Hugh Walpole (1884–1941) sold the film rights to his novel *Vanessa* (1933) to MGM for $ 12,500 (Feather 2006, 165), which roughly amounts to a million dollars in today's money. The film *Vanessa: Her Love Story* was released in 1935. At this time, there were 4,500 cinemas in Britain, and 907 million tickets were sold in 1935 (Perelli 1983, 372, 375). For comparison, there were only 775 in the UK in 2018, with a mere 177 million admissions.[67] In 1944, MGM paid W. Somerset Maugham (1874–1965) $ 250,000 for the film rights to his novel *The Razor's Edge*, money that Maugham used to set up a prize for young writers, which is still awarded annually in his name. Some authors even received money for film options that were never realised (Nash 2016a, 32).

In the early twentieth century, films could dramatically boost book sales – as they can still do today. Ian McEwan's novel *Atonement* (2001), for example, was selling steadily in paperback by 2007, but the movie release catapulted it to the number one spot on the *New York Times* bestseller list (Thompson 2012,

---

[67] According to https://www.statista.com/topics/1854/the-uk-film-industry/. Date of access: 25 February 2020.

281–283). Modernist authors were often fascinated by the aesthetic possibilities of cinema but also wary of its competition against literature (see below for a discussion of Virginia Woolf's essay on cinema), but cinema posed no risk to publishing – on the contrary. It also created new opportunities for writers. In the US, F. Scott Fitzgerald (1896–1940) and William Faulkner (1897–1962) are probably the best-known modernist literary authors who tried their hand at screenwriting; while in Britain, Anthony Powell (1905–2000), Aldous Huxley (1894–1963), and Agatha Christie all at some point wrote for the cinema. Huxley went to Hollywood in 1937 to work mostly on screen adaptations of English literary classics, such as *Pride and Prejudice* and *Jane Eyre*. For Walt Disney, he wrote a screenplay in 1945 titled *Alice and the Mysterious Mr. Carroll* (based on Lewis Carroll's *Alice in Wonderland*, 1865) but this was never produced – with Disney being on record with the comment "It was so literary I could understand only every third word" (Nissley 2014, 384). It took a long time for screenplays to be accepted as literary works in their own right and sometimes published in book form (Korte and Schneider 2000). Some novels were originally commissioned as film scripts or scenarios, such as Graham Greene's (1904–1991) *The Third Man* (1950) or V. S. Naipaul's (1932–2018) *A Flag on the Island* (1967) (Nash 2016a, 32–33).

Attempts to make the cinema more 'literary' and thus more respectable included many early film adaptations of Shakespeare, not only from British and US companies but also, for example, Italian film producers. While the first film of this kind depicted a scene from a stage production of *King John* (UK, 1899), later films used a genuinely cinematic language and camera effects to achieve a sort of visual realism that would not have been possible on stage. The special effects of some of these early films, such as *The Tempest* (UK, 1908), are quite spectacular by any standard (see *Silent Shakespeare*, n. d.).

Cinema began to be a genuine competition for writers from the 1920s onwards, as yet another new form of entertainment ate into the time and money people could spend on leisure; even more severely so after the introduction of sound film in 1927. Many modernist authors were fascinated by the cinema, often in rather ambivalent ways. T. S. Eliot lamented the passing of the music hall and the replacement of its participatory entertainment by what he saw as the "listless apathy" promoted by "the cheap and rapid-breeding cinema" ("Marie Lloyd", 1922, qtd. in Hammond 2016, 32). In an essay of 1926, "The Cinema", Virginia Woolf compares a cinema audience to "savages" delighted at some primitive form of entertainment. "[T]he art of the cinema", she writes, "seems a simple and even a stupid art" (2008a, 172). She repeats several of the by now well-known arguments of a culture-critical nature against new media technologies, deploring the spatial and temporal disconnection of images from their real-life referents. She then picks up the topic of competition between cinema and literature:

> So many arts at first stood ready to offer their help [to the new art of cinema]. For example, there was literature. All the famous novels of the world with their well known characters and their famous scenes only asked to be put on the films. What could be easier, what could be simpler? The cinema fell upon its prey with immense rapacity and to this moment largely subsists upon the body of its unfortunate victim. But the results have been disastrous to both. The alliance is unnatural. Eye and brain are torn asunder ruthlessly as they try vainly to work in couples. The eye says, 'Here is Anna Karenina', and a voluptuous lady in black velvet wearing pearls comes before us. The brain exclaims, 'That is no more Anna Karenina than it is Queen Victoria!' For the brain knows Anna almost entirely by the inside of her mind – her charm, her passion, her despair, whereas all the emphasis is now laid upon her teeth, her pearls and her velvet. (173)

Here, Woolf laments the inevitable focus of film on surfaces, on Anna Karenina's "teeth", "pearls", and "velvet" instead of "the inside of her mind", which is what readers get to see in Tolstoy's novel. She also regards cinema as a predator, a kind of Dracula, a vampire who "subsists upon the body of its unfortunate victim"; indeed, she sees it as a "parasite" (174). The violent metaphors she uses to describe the relationship between cinema and literature are extended to the viewer's experience when Woolf writes that "[e]ye and brain are torn asunder ruthlessly", describing a dissociation of the viewer's sensory perception and cognition. She goes on to ridicule the 'illiteracy' of film, its tin ear for nuances of literature: "A kiss is love. A smashed chair is jealousy. A grin is happiness" (174). What she suggests instead is for film to find its own language, to avoid words altogether and focus on the visual: "the cinema has within its grasp innumerable symbols for emotions that have so far failed to find expression" (174). She imagines a cinema of the future composed of "[s]omething abstract, something moving, something calling only for the very slightest help from words or from music to make itself intelligible" (175). And this new form of cinema could even be superior to literature: "The most fantastic contrasts could be flashed before us with a speed which the writer can only toil after in vain. The past could be unrolled, distances could be annihilated. [. . .] We should have the continuity of human life kept before us [. . .]" (ibid.).

In phrases such as these, it becomes clear that what Woolf is describing here as an ideal for cinema can also be applied back to her own narrative art, moving away from conventional realism and towards a depiction of consciousness, of "emotions mingling together and affecting each other", and of "the continuity of human life" (175) beyond discrete events in a novel. This may remind us of the "myriad impressions" Woolf writes about as an "incessant shower" in her essay "Modern Fiction" (first published in 1919 under the title "Modern Novels"), where she uses a visual, almost cinematic metaphor to describe how we experience our lives: "Life is not a series of gig lamps symmetrically arranged; life is a luminous halo, a semi-transparent envelope surrounding us from the beginning of consciousness to the end" (2008b, 9).[68] Using another modern image, derived from atomic theory, she calls upon writers to "record the atoms as they fall upon the mind in the order in which they fall, let us trace the pattern, however disconnected and incoherent in appearance, which each sight or incident scores upon the consciousness" (9). It was this restless and ever-changing mobility of consciousness that Woolf tried to capture in her novels such as *Mrs Dalloway* (1925), *To the Lighthouse* (1927), and *The Waves* (1931), as well as in shorter pieces such as "Kew Gardens" and "The Mark on the Wall" (1917).

As the writer B. S. Johnson (1933–1973) argued, Joyce's and other modernists' early engagement with cinema made them realise "that film must usurp some of the prerogatives which until then had belonged almost exclusively to the novelist":

> Film could tell a story more directly, in less time and with more concrete detail than a novel; certain aspects of character could be more easily delineated and kept constantly before the audience (for example, physical characteristics like a limp, a scar, particular ugliness or beauty); no novelist's description of a battle squadron at sea in a gale could really hope to compete with that in a well-shot film; and why should anyone who simply wanted to be told a story spend all his spare time for a week or weeks reading a book when he could experience the same thing in a version in some ways superior at his local cinema in only one evening? (Johnson 1977, 151)

For Johnson – an author of experimental novels in the 1960s – the conclusion to be drawn from this media competition was clear: "the only thing the novelist can with any certainty call exclusively his own is the inside of his own skull: and that is what he should be exploring, rather than anachronistically fighting a battle he is bound to lose" (152). Writers should focus not on events but on style: "What happens is nothing like as important as how it is written" (152).

One modern novelist who anticipated this idea is Henry Green, the author of *Blindness* (1926; see ch. 10). Green was addicted to the cinema early on. In his novels, he often aspired to an "intensely visual" quality, but he explicitly disallowed one of these novels (*Party Going*, 1939) to be made into a film, and he grew increasingly hostile to the idea of having his novels filmed or adapted for radio (Treglown 2000, 182). Green's novel *Living* (1929) uses a montage technique (Holmesland 1985, 14) to capture life in and around a factory, combining passages of lyrical narrative description with dialogue in a Birmingham working-class dialect.

---

68 Gig-lamps are the headlights of a horse-drawn carriage.

Its approach to prose signals its experimental character also because any definite or indefinite articles have been eliminated. In their free time, factory workers liked to frequent the cinema, where this novel follows them several times, first in a more conventional narrative fashion (Green 1993, 216–217), the second time (224–225) in a way that imitates the musical ambience of the film theatre:

> They were in cinema. Band played tune tum tum did dee dee. She hugged Dale's arm. She jumped her knees to the time.
> Couple on screen danced in ballroom there. She did not see them. Dee dee did da.
> Tum tum tum tum tum. Dale did not budge. Dee dee de did dee. She hummed now. She rolled his arm between her palms. Da da did dee – did dee dee tum, ta.
> 'I do love this tune' she said.
> 'Ah' he said.
> Did dee dee tum ta. Tune was over. She clapped hands and clapped. Applause was general. But film did not stop oh no heroine's knickers slipped down slinky legs in full floor.
> eeeee Lily Gates screamed.
> OOEEE the audience.
> And band took encore then. Tum tum ti tumpy tum.   (224)

For the novel's heroine, the young Lily Gates, cinema is indeed a 'dream factory' (cf. 311) that makes her dream of a better life. Film here is not a copy of reality but "a metaphorical reflection of the spectators' emotional needs" (Holmesland 1985, 18).

In passages like this one, Green captures the audience's experience of watching a silent film, with a live band playing along, including an attendant who shouts "Order please" (224) when the audience becomes too unruly. It emphasises the importance of music, of rhythm over the visuality of cinema in this passage, and in attempting to imitate the band's music and the audience's vocal responses, gives up meaningful words for the sake of sequences of letters representing non-verbal sound: *Tum tum ti tumpy tum, OOEEE*. Here, a novelist attempts to describe the effect of 'picture-going' in words that leave conventional requirements of grammar and syntax behind in order to capture a new grammar of experience, a new "structure of feeling" (Williams 1977, 132) born out of new media practices. In contrast to Woolf, Green is less interested in the new aesthetics of film than in the audience's responses to it and in the new social space provided by cinema.

Green's narrative technique embraces cinematic montage, the device of juxtaposing shots to tell a story. According to the Russian film director and theorist Sergei Eisenstein (1898–1948), writing in the same year when Green's novel *Living* was published, the relation of two shots is characterised by dynamic conflict and confrontation, out of which a new 'concept' emerges that could not have been contained in either of the two shots on its own (Eisenstein 1977 [1929], 30). "[M]ontage is conflict", Eisenstein declares (38; cf. Holmesland 1985, 28–29). This, not the invention of cinema as such, was a modern idea (Shail 2012, 4), and we have already seen it at work in the collage technique of Eliot's *The Waste Land* and in the "sequential art" of comics (McCloud 1994, 9). Montage generates an insight that can be far more effective than verbal analysis or description. Many modernist novels and poems share the violence of moving rapidly from one image or scene to the next. Green comments on this technique in a letter to his friend Nevill Coghill in the late 1920s, while at work on *Living*: "I think you will like the book I am on now. It's written in a very condensed kind of way in short paragraphs, hardly ever much longer than 1½ to 2 printed pages and often very much shorter. A kind of very disconnected cinema film" (qtd. in Taylor 2008, 253). Green uses cinema in analogy to the "disconnected", broken images of his own writing, not as a "model of mimetic representation" (Holmesland 1985 17). Like a film director using montage, Green wants his prose to pick up "fragments of reality" (21) and give them a new meaning by arranging them in a sequence.

I am a Camera

By contrast, some modernist writers embraced the (supposed) objectivity of the camera as an ideal for their prose, which could aspire to the status of a direct and unfiltered recording of reality. One of the best-known examples that spring to mind is Christopher Isherwood's (1904–1986) "I am a camera". This sentence is spoken by the narrator of Isherwood's largely autobiographical novel *Goodbye to Berlin* (1935), his portrayal of bohemian Berlin in the final years of the Weimar Republic. At the beginning of a section titled "A Berlin Diary (Autumn 1930)", the narrator looks out of his window and observes the street on which he lives: "I am a camera with its shutter open, quite passive, recording, not thinking. Recording the man shaving at the window opposite and the woman in the kimono washing her hair. Some day, all this will have to be developed, carefully printed, fixed" (Isherwood 1999, 243). Already ten years earlier, the New Zealand writer Katherine Mansfield (1888–1923), in conversations published shortly after her early death, compared herself to a camera: "I've been a camera. [. . .] I've been a selective camera, and it has been my attitude that has determined the selection" (Orage 1924, 38).

In such comparisons between authorship and camera work, the camera is more likely to be a photo rather than a film camera, given the insistence on developing, printing, and fixing a recorded image rather than a sequence of movements. This idea of the camera corresponds to an ideal of neutral observation and recording of everyday impressions, as in a diary, but free of thoughts or interpretations, in a style that is associated with the Documentary Film Movement around John Grierson (1898–1972) and with the post-expressionist artistic ideals of the New Objectivity that advocated for a cooler, more matter-of-fact approach to artistic realism. But the words "carefully printed", in the passage from Isherwood, likewise allude to the process of publishing a literary text. In Isherwood's prose, the cinematic influence can also be detected in the way he introduces one of his main characters, Sally Bowles, in "a sequence of cinematic shots" alternating between close-ups and two-shots (Lodge 1992, 69). Such effects, which remediate the experience of cinema in narrative, soon became quite commonplace in fiction.

In poetry, W. H. Auden embraced film in the 1930s – in particular, the British Documentary Movement – in *Night Mail,* a 1936 film about the nightly postal train connecting London and Glasgow. The film, directed by Harry Watt and Basil Wright, with a musical score by Benjamin Britten, ends with a verse commentary by Auden, which celebrates the human connections and communities achieved by the conveyance of letters, news, and gossip. Its closing vision of the sleeping citizens of Edinburgh, Glasgow, and Aberdeen anticipates the dreamlike quality of Dylan Thomas's *Under Milk Wood* by almost twenty years (see ch. 9). Auden's poem, moreover, was written with a stopwatch in hand to time the lines precisely to fit the shots in the finished film (Fuller 1998, 188).

If later writers used montage as a technique of achieving a quasi-cinematic kind of 'photorealism', relying on their readers' familiarity with the conventions of film editing, T. S. Eliot's montage technique in *The Waste Land* still had the opposite aim: even more radically to de-realise and disconnect individual images instead of giving them new meaning by connecting them. "People in themselves want nothing but reality", asserts the heroine of Dorothy Richardson's novel sequence *Pilgrimage,* but she adds the telling question: "Why can't reality exist in the world?" (1979 [1921], 188) Eliot would answer: because "human kind / Cannot bear very much reality" (1989, 189). Many modernists felt with Virginia Woolf that writing should not merely be 'about' life, it should be itself *alive* – giving, that is, a sudden, illuminating shape to the fleeting impressions of the mind. This way pointed inward, into consciousness as an inner space, rather than outward into space, time, and action – elements which were relegated to genre fiction, like mystery novels or science fiction – further deepening the divide between 'highbrow' literature and vernacular or popular forms of writing and other forms of entertainment, including film. This "great divide" (Huyssen 1986) has perhaps never been quite overcome in the past century or so, even though there were several attempts to bridge the gap between 'high' and 'low' culture. We still live with a separation between 'literary' and 'genre' fiction, for instance when Ian McEwan insisted that his novel *Machines Like Me* (2019) was not science fiction, even though it would count as such by any definition – a future scenario of artificial intelligence embedded in an alternative past (Ditum 2019). The need for literary fiction to cordon itself off from popular fiction may have been exacerbated by its competition with so many other modern media, from film to TV and beyond.

Next to this sense of competition and the felt need to distinguish 'valuable' forms of literature from less valuable ones or to keep them free from incursions of other media, there is, in modernity, also a cultural anxiety about visual stimuli circumventing the brain and having a direct (and morally damaging) impact on people, on individuals or entire populations – similar to the anxieties about the nervous system that accompanied the 'railway novels' in the nineteenth century or rock music in the twentieth (see ch. 6 and 9). This impact is illustrated, for instance, in Anthony Burgess's *A Clockwork Orange* (1962), where the juvenile delinquent Alex is subjected to an experimental behaviour modification therapy that involves being forced to watch extremely violent films; this cures him of finding pleasure in violence, but it also robs him of his free will. When director Stanley Kubrick turned this novel into a particularly violent film in 1971, he stoked the fires of moral outrage, leading Burgess to disavow the film. Many novelists before and since have felt that their work was 'betrayed' by filmmakers. They rarely worked with the other medium themselves to explore its opportunities.

One modernist author who worked with film (and later TV) was Samuel Beckett. His *Film* from 1964, starring the American comedian and film director Buster Keaton (1895–1966), is a meditation on the topic of identity and visuality: being seen as a condition of being in the world, following George Berkeley's (1685–1753) dictum *esse est percipi*, 'to be is to be perceived'. Keaton's character in the film is afraid of being seen, but not – as in Orwell's *Nineteen Eighty-Four* – for political reasons. He suffers from what Beckett in his screenplay calls "anguish of perceivedness" (1986, 323). The camera that pursues him is revealed (in the screenplay) not to be an external entity that watches him but his own "self" (323). When at one point the camera faces the man, he "cringes away from perceivedness" (328–329), and then there is a cut, so we see what he sees – but we do not see a camera but a close-up of the man's eye: "Long image of the unblinking gaze" (329). In an interview, Beckett said: "self-perception is the most frightening of all human observations [. . .] when man faces himself, he is looking into the abyss" (Beckett 1969, 210). His *Film*, then, is not about uncovering the mediality of cinema – since, in the fiction, we are made to believe that the technical array of the camera is not there, just as in classical mainstream cinema – but a philosophical take on human self-observation or self-perception. It plays into the "denigration of vision" (Jay 1993) that we already discussed (ch. 10), which is an established pattern in Beckett's work, from the short story "Yellow" (1934) – "What were the eyes anyway? [. . .] They were safer closed" (Beckett 1993, 173) – to *Ill Seen Ill Said* (1981) – "this filthy eye of flesh" (1996, 65) – and the voyeuristic "eye of prey" in *Imagination Dead Imagine* (1995, 185). Yet Beckett was exceptional in writing for *all* available media during his lifetime, from novels to plays, film, radio, and television.

The Rise of Television

After radio and the cinema, television was the next major competitor to the publishing industry. The first experimental TV broadcasts were made in 1929. In 1936, BBC television began its regular service, broadcasting from Alexandra Palace in North London, with an average duration of four hours per day. The TV service was suspended during World War Two but resumed in 1946. By 1947, there were 54,000 licensed viewers in the UK, more than in the US at that time.

Here too, as with cinema and other new media, there was much enthusiasm but also scepticism and worry about the social and cultural changes that television would bring. "Sensation without commitment" was Richard Hoggart's judgement on these new, "shiny" and, in his view, insipid forms of entertainment (1963 [1957], 202–205). A similar argument about television was made by J. B. Priestley's (1894–1984) in his essay "Televiewing" from the same year, 1957. Here, he recounts his own experience in front of a TV set as one of passivity and stupor:

> I have already passed uncounted hours half-hypnotised by the jiggling and noisy images. Sometimes I wonder if I am going out of my mind. We have been told that the worst is over after about four years, but long before that my outlook will have been so completely changed that I shall be a different person. I shall probably be removed to an old man's home. Let us hope these places are equipped with good TV sets. (Priestley 1969, 232)

The TV industry at the time also addressed "the harm that wrong viewing can do", meaning by this, however, not any potentially detrimental effects on society but merely visual problems of the "correct viewing distance" and "reflection" on the screen (Kroll 1957).

George Orwell, who had worked for BBC radio during the Second World War, included a future version of television in his dystopian satire *Nineteen Eighty-Four* (1949), depicting a future Britain as a totalitarian state in which the Party defines what counts as reality, and a downtrodden population is constantly under supervision from their 'telescreens'. Here the TV not only broadcasts official programmes or peddles "jiggling and noisy images" (Priestley 1969, 232), it also monitors its viewers. There is, we learn, a huge communications industry in this future world: "There were the huge printing shops with their sub-editors, their typography experts and their elaborately-equipped studios for the faking of photographs. There was the tele-programmes section with its engineers, its producers and its teams of actors specially chosen for their skill in imitating voices. There were the armies of reference clerks [. . .]" (Orwell 2013, 49). This inflated bureaucracy, an only slightly exaggerated version of the BBC that Orwell knew well, serves to produce what we would now call 'fake news' or 'alternative facts' – it creates the reality that the people of Oceania live in. Orwell had realised the power of the mass media to shape 'what we know about the world' (cf. Luhmann 2000b, 1). In this world, the population is brainwashed by "rubbishy newspapers containing almost nothing except sport, crime and astrology, sensational five-cent novelettes, films oozing with sex, and sentimental songs which were composed entirely by mechanical means" (Orwell 2013, 50). In this world, there are still novels, but they are not written by individual authors anymore but by committees and teams with the help of "novel-writing machines" (149). "Books were just a commodity that had to be produced, like jam or bootlaces" (149–150). Small wonder, then, that the first "decisive act" (9) of disobedience of the hero, Winston Smith, is to buy an old notebook, "a peculiarly beautiful book" with "smooth creamy paper [. . .] of a kind that had not been manufactured for at least forty years past" (8), and to begin writing with "an archaic instrument", a pen "with a real nib" (9).

Orwell's "novel-writing machines" hark back to George Gissing's "Literary Machine" (2016, 96) in the 1890s (see ch. 6), and even further back to Jonathan Swift's satirical imagination of a writing machine in *Gulliver's Travels* (1726), part 3, ch. 5, where professors at the Academy of Lagado have invented an "Engine" that arranges words into random sequences; in this way, they argue, "the most ignorant Person [. . .] may write Books in Philosophy, Poetry, Politicks, Law, Mathematicks and Theology, without the least Assistance from Genius or Study" (Swift 1986, 183). A century later, Thomas Carlyle complained in 1829 "that books are not only printed, but, in a great measure, written and sold, by machinery" (1986, 66). Similar anxieties about literature and automation are also found in much twentieth-century science fiction, from E. M. Forster's "The Machine Stops" (discussed in ch. 8) to Fritz Leiber's (1910–1992) *The Silver Eggheads* (1961), Michael Frayn's (1933–) *The Tin Men* (1965), and Arthur C. Clarke's (1917–2008) "The Steam-Powered Word Processor" (1986) (Kirschenbaum 2016, 38–39).

Nineteen Eighty-Four continues a trend of cultural criticism that can be traced back to Victorian times. As satire, it contains a strong indictment of modernity and of what Adorno and Horkheimer around the same time termed the 'culture industry'. Orwell's critique of popular culture and modern media, and his ambivalent views of the 'proles', the underclass in *Nineteen Eighty-Four*, owes much to middle-class sentiments, the Victorian art critic John Ruskin, the Fabians, and the Arts and Crafts movement of the late nineteenth century. This concealed elitism was recognised and exploited by Apple when this company used a *Nineteen Eighty-Four* scenario for a commercial for the Macintosh in 1984. We see a grey army of workers marching in step, *Metropolis*–style, and gathering in a central hall to watch and listen to a message from Big Brother when a young woman, dressed in a white top and red gym shorts, swings a hammer and destroys the telescreen. As the camera pans across the rows of stunned viewers, a male voiceover reads the words that slowly move from below across the screen: "On January 24th, Apple Computer will introduce Macintosh. And you'll see why 1984 won't be like '1984.'" This was seen at the time as a critique of the predominance of IBM in the world of computers. Like the slogan "Think different", Apple's use of Orwell's novel emphasised individuality and creativity over corporate uniformity – not in order to sell creamy notepaper, obviously, but computers – giving Orwell's novel a decidedly less nostalgic and more techno-optimistic spin.

Despite Orwell's misgivings about television, a TV adaptation of *Nineteen-Eighty Four* massively and immediately boosted the sales of the book in 1954, reportedly selling "1000 hardback and 18,000 paperback copies within five days" (Nash 2016a, 32). The revenge of television on *Nineteen Eighty-Four* was complete when a Dutch producer came up with the idea to use the name *Big Brother* for a reality TV competition show (starting in 1999) featuring people living together in a house isolated from the outside world, under constant surveillance from cameras and microphones. The show became an international franchise spanning the globe from Albania to Zambia.[69]

It was only four years after the publication of *Nineteen Eighty-Four* that TV "became a mass medium" in the UK, when millions watched the BBC broadcast of Elizabeth II's coronation in 1953. Two years later, "numbers of viewers overtook numbers of radio listeners" (Feather 2006, 201). Also in 1955, the BBC got its first commercial competitor, ITV. Programming expanded further with the launch of BBC2 in 1964 and Channel 4 in 1982 (Crisell 2002). With successive technological improvements, from colour TV in the 1960s to flatscreens, cable TV, smart TV, and streaming services today, the number of people who watch TV regularly has increased steadily. Already in the 1980s, 98 % of the UK

---

[69] See https://en.wikipedia.org/wiki/Big_Brother_(franchise). Date of access: 27 February 2020.

population were regular viewers – virtually everybody, that is – while 58 % also "still claimed to read books regularly" (Feather 1988, 219). Now it is not quite clear what 'regularly' means; every day or once a year? A study in 2014 found that the number of people reading (books) daily had decreased to 28 %, while 45 % "said they prefer watching TV [. . .] to reading a novel".[70] A similar study conducted ten years earlier showed that a significantly higher percentage of women than men read for pleasure (40 vs. 25 %) (Feather 2006, 209).

Yet, just like cinema, while certainly eating into the time available for reading, TV also offered new channels of distribution for literature, and yet more opportunities for writers, either as authors of new TV drama, as adaptors of literary classics or their own or their colleagues' work, or as authors of contemporary novels adapted for television, or as authors of TV 'spin-off' books, etc. The latter category "dominate[d] the best-seller lists" in the 1970s (Feather 1988, 222). Companies found that the mutual exchange of "content that could be repurposed" (Thompson 2012, 105) was a win-win situation. Thus, the BBC became its own publisher while also working closely with other publishing houses, and from the 1980s onwards major international conglomerates became interested in exploiting these market synergies to achieve 'vertical integration' as media businesses (Thompson 2012). But even dead writers and their work could profit, if posthumously, from having their novels adapted for television, as happened to Orwell in 1954. In 1967, the BBC adapted John Galsworthy's (1867–1933) *Forsyte Saga* in twenty-six episodes. Galsworthy's Forsyte novels, chronicling several generations of an upper-middle-class family, had been published in the first two decades of the twentieth century (*The Man of Property*, 1906; *In Chancery*, 1920; *To Let*, 1921), and he continued it with a sequel trilogy in the 1930s. He won the Nobel Prize in Literature in 1932. His novels had been frequently adapted for radio and cinema before but the 1967 TV series, repeated in 1968–69, was a breakthrough. "On Sunday nights, when the Saga was on, social life stopped. Dinner parties were scheduled around it, and evening service at some churches was moved to allow churchgoers to watch!"[71] The final episode of the 1969 broadcast was reportedly watched by eighteen million viewers.[72]

Such viewing figures are now unthinkable, given the broad variety of programmes on offer at any time. But there are many other TV series with strong literary connections, and now both literary classics and newly published fiction are frequently adapted for television. To give just one recent example, Sally

---

70 Based on a Booktrust survey of 1,500 adults. See https://www.bbc.com/news/education-26515836. Date of access: 26 February 2020.
71 https://www.bbc.co.uk/programmes/p0167578. Date of access: 26 February 2020.
72 http://www.screenonline.org.uk/tv/id/1071033/index.html. Date of access: 26 February 2020.

Rooney's (1991–) bestselling novel *Normal People*, first published in 2018, was adapted for BBC Three and Hulu in 2020. The novels of Jane Austen and Charles Dickens are a perennial source for successive waves of adaptations, which certainly help keep their works alive in cultural memory. Only two earlier examples of classics reaching a new audience through TV can be mentioned here, both adaptations leading to the revival of a half-forgotten author. One was the 1970 BBC miniseries based on Anthony Trollope's novel *The Way We Live Now* (1875), which led to that novel's inclusion in Penguin's "English Library" and generated steady sales (Lesser 2019, 418).

The other, more spectacular case is the Granada/ITV adaptation of Evelyn Waugh's 1945 novel *Brideshead Revisited* in 1981. Set in the 1920s to 1940s, the eleven-part series turned Waugh's tragicomic novel of class snobbery, Catholicism, and country houses into a prime example of 'heritage TV'. This series is the ancestor of *Downton Abbey* (2010–2015) with its nostalgia for the past as it never really was, often seen as symptomatic of Britain during the Thatcher era rediscovering conservative values. But if that is what it (also) was, there are moments in this adaptation that hint at irreversible social change – none more so than when viewers got to see the two male friends at the heart of the story sunbathing naked on the roof, and the camera lingered over the naked backsides of the actors Anthony Andrews (1948–) and Jeremy Irons (1948–) for at least three seconds. Even though the hedonism of the 1980s would soon be shaken by the AIDS crisis, homosexuality or at least homoeroticism was no longer much of a taboo on TV after this (De Vito and Tropea 2010, 63).[73] The series also had an impact on fashion, starting a vogue for pastel colours, flannel trousers, and a lot else, besides creating a taste for a rose-tinted view of the past, and also quite possibly influencing a slew of novels in the 1980s that explored the British past and the unreliability of memory, such as Kazuo Ishiguro's *The Remains of the Day* (1989), Penelope Lively's (1933–) *Moon Tiger* (1987), and Alan Hollinghurst's (1954–) *The Swimming-Pool Library* (1988) – which, incidentally, includes a rather similar gay sunbathing scene.

Like many other new media, watching films and TV (whether old-style network TV, YouTube, or streaming services) provide plenty of opportunities for distraction that cut into the time people might spend reading. But, as we have seen, at least for some books, cinema and TV can also work wonders and win them an audience of a different order of magnitude. As with previous 'new

---

73 Apparently, the first gay kiss on TV was shown on 6 August 1970 in a BBC broadcast of Christopher Marlowe's *Edward II*, with Ian McKellen as Edward passionately kissing James Laurenson's Gaveston. See https://fakehistoryhunter.wordpress.com/2019/12/21/not-the-first-same-sex-kiss-on-tv/. Date of access: 26 February 2020.

media' like radio and cinema, the impact and influence of television on literature is not always detrimental but often productive, giving rise to new opportunities and constellations. In the next and final chapter, we will have a look at how an even more disruptive new technology and media configuration has transformed the literary world during the past thirty years: the Internet, the World Wide Web, and social media.

12 Web: Literature in the Digital Age

In Russell Hoban's 1987 novel *The Medusa Frequency*, unsuccessful middle-aged novelist Herman Orff is trying to communicate with the mysterious world conjured up by the green letters appearing on the screen of his Apple II computer:

> This screen isn't like a piece of paper; the words come out of a green dancing and the excitation of phosphors. I'm the one who makes the words appear but I don't always know who or what is speaking. [. . .] I'm not the final authority on such things [. . .] at three o'clock in the morning when the words come out of the green dancing and the singing comes from thousands of miles away. (Hoban 2021, 2–3)

In the 1980s, such machines changed the experience of writing dramatically, at least for those authors who were willing to adopt the new technology, by changing the material medium or writing surface from "a piece of paper" to a screen and by switching from actual inscription to the manipulation of virtual and unstable "dancing" letters.

The first working digital computer – "a general-purpose machine for manipulating and storing arbitrarily encoded symbols" (Kirschenbaum 2016, xi) – was built by Konrad Zuse (1910–1995) in his parents' living room in Berlin in 1936, using old 35 mm celluloid film for punched tape to control the computer's operations (Manovich 2001, 25). In the same year, the English mathematician Alan Turing (1912–1954) wrote his paper "On Computable Numbers, with an Application to the Entscheidungsproblem" (1937), which was to provide the theoretical groundwork for a universal computing machine that could perform any calculation that was possible: "a single machine which can be used to compute any computable sequence" (Turing 1937, 241). From the 1940s onwards, computers – so large that they filled entire rooms – were built for "large organizations, aiding administrations, scientific research, and the military" (Heyer and Urquhart 2019, 290). In the late 1960s, IBM marketed its MT/ST (Magnetic Tape Selectric Typewriter) machines to business customers as an alternative to paper-based office work, indeed as a remedy for the 'paperwork explosion', as their dramatic advertising film of 1967 put it (Kirschenbaum 2016, 173).[74] But things began to change with the invention of the microprocessor by Ted Hoff in 1969, which was first produced by Intel in 1971.

The advent of microchip technology made computer circuitry considerably smaller and led to its proliferation also in other areas, including domestic appliances. In the late 1970s and early 1980s, the personal computer made computer

---

[74] See https://www.youtube.com/watch?v=_IZw2CoYztk. Date of access: 19 March 2020.

Open Access. © 2022 Ingo Berensmeyer, published by De Gruyter. This work is licensed under the Creative Commons Attribution-NonCommercial-NoDerivatives 4.0 International License.
https://doi.org/10.1515/9783110784459-012

technology available to virtually everyone, at least in the industrialised parts of the world. "[A]n individual working at home now had access to information-processing capacities that previously had been the sole preserve of large institutions" (Heyer and Urquhart 2019, 290). Since the arrival of the World Wide Web and the smartphone, these developments have been considerably speeded up even further. Now we are used to carrying the world's information in our pocket wherever we go. In this chapter, we will look at the impact of computers, the Internet, and social media on the production, distribution, and reception of literature.

Publishing and the Digital Revolution

How have computers and the networked media environment affected literature? First, they have changed our perception, and the actual material practice, of writing. As Russell Hoban's fictional novelist in *The Medusa Frequency* was well aware, writing on a screen differs radically from writing on paper or other surfaces, even from typing on a typewriter. Older forms of writing either directly or indirectly inscribed symbols on a surface. On a computer screen, by contrast, writing is no longer a form of inscription but a highly abstract form of "algorithmic symbol manipulation" (Kirschenbaum 2016, 82) mediated by digital technology. It may now seem 'natural' but fifty years ago, "pressing a key on a keyboard and watching the corresponding letter, number, or symbol wink into existence on a glowing glass screen must have seemed like something out of a space opera" (93). The arrival of word processing in the 1970s led to new techniques and routines of textual composition, often involving multiple phases of handwriting, typing, and computer software. These did not completely replace older forms of writing but complemented them in complex ways.

These changes in technology not only affected authors, obviously. Increased automation and computerisation also made publishing easier. Among the many advances in printing, one needs to mention phototypesetting and offset printing, from the late 1950s onwards. Since the 1990s, the digital revolution has transformed "the entire book production process, from the creation of the original text to the typesetting, design and printing of the book", further reducing production costs (Thompson 2012, 155). The first British book with computer-aided typesetting was an edition of Dylan Thomas's *Collected Poems* in the Everyman's Library series in 1966, published by J. M. Dent (Feather 2006, 215). In ch. 6, we have looked at the 'paperback revolution' of the twentieth century, in which books became an omnipresent, cheap popular commodity and an important part of popular culture. This is now the point to return to that story and continue it in the light of more recent technological, commercial, and cultural developments.

The first million-selling British paperback was Paul Brickhill's (1916–1991) *The Dam Busters*, in 1956, a non-fiction book about the bombing of German dams (Möhne, Eder, and Sorpe) during World War Two. It was made into a film in 1955, and the film's success also drove sales of the paperback. The overall output of books has grown dramatically since the 1950s. Apparently, publishing did not suffer, as many had feared, under the competition from other media such as cinema or television. On the contrary, commercial publishing became big business. Processes of conglomeration and globalisation have led to new economies of scale in trade publishing, with a few multinational conglomerates now dominating the market (Penguin Random House, Hachette, Simon and Schuster, HarperCollins). These few companies own many smaller imprints who acquire and produce books, but they have the economic power to sell them in large quantities across the globe, aided by large bookselling chains such as Waterstones in the UK (founded in 1982) and, obviously, online sales, most notably via Amazon (founded in 1995) – of which more later. In the shadow of the big companies, some independent smaller publishing firms like Virago and Canongate were launched in the 1970s, and more recent ones like Galley Beggar Press (founded in 2012) have had some major successes with their titles, such as Eimear McBride's (1976–) *A Girl is a Half-formed Thing* (2013) and Lucy Ellmann's (1956–) *Ducks, Newburyport* (2019). In 1995, the Net Book Agreement came to an end in the UK, meaning that booksellers throughout the country were no longer obliged to sell books for the same price. This deregulation of the market proved beneficial for bigger companies, but it did not 'kill the book', as many had feared at the time (Feather 2006, 226–227). In fact, publishing boomed even further in the 1990s, with almost twice as many new titles published in the UK in 1999 than in 1989. The Man Booker Prize, established in 1968, has since developed into one of the most important literary awards short of the Nobel Prize. Its award ceremony is broadcast on live television, significantly boosting book sales and authors' reputations, while also making literary fiction appear "more consumer-oriented" (Richard Todd, qtd. in Nash 2016b, 414).

In the second half of the twentieth and the first two decades of the twenty-first century, there has been a steep rise in the number of new titles published every year in the UK (see tab. 1).[75] Of course, this includes all kinds of books, non-fiction as well as fiction, scholarly as well as trade books. But it does give

---

75 Data from Feather 2006, 208; Thompson 2012, 242; WIPO 2020, 9.

an indication of the size of the publishing industry and the book market, within which literature in the narrower sense has its commercial habitat.

Tab. 1: Number of new book titles published per year in the UK between 1950 and 2018.

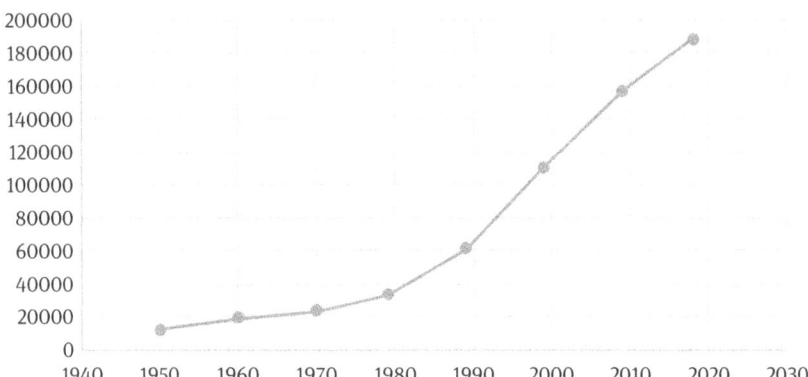

A publishing story that illustrates many of these changes in the early twenty-first century is the worldwide success of J. K. Rowling's (1965–) *Harry Potter* books. What began in the mind of a solitary author in an Edinburgh café in the 1990s has since grown into an entertainment empire with films, websites, dedicated shops selling merchandise, even theme parks. This was not something planned by publishing executives, but a phenomenon that no one could have imagined in 1997. Harry Potter's magic attracted many young readers to the power of literature and the pleasures of reading. It also transformed Bloomsbury, then a small London publishing house that had only been around for ten years, into a global player in an increasingly consolidated market. The books themselves and their publishing story are, to quote Martin Puchner, "an odd mixture of old and new" (2017, 329).

This is epitomised also by the fact that Rowling, in 2007, produced seven handwritten and illustrated copies of *The Tales of Beedle the Bard*, a sequence of Harry Potter-related fairy tales. When one of these manuscript books was put up for auction at Sotheby's for charity, it was bought by Amazon for just under two million pounds – the highest price ever paid for a modern literary manuscript until then – apparently as a 'thank you' after selling more than twelve million copies of the *Harry Potter* books (Cleland 2007). The only comparable English novel to have generated a similar cross-media franchise is J. R. R. Tolkien's *The Lord of the Rings* (1954–1955), a book that was initially expected to make a financial loss (Lesser 2019, 397) but instead sold more than 150 million copies. A trilogy of films (2001–2003) launched this franchise into the new millennium, and (at time of writing) is about to be expanded into an Amazon-produced TV series. The 250 million dollars Amazon reportedly paid for the television rights to *The Lord of the Rings* makes two million pounds for a Rowling manuscript look like peanuts.

Corporate interests and profit margins now dominate the world of publishing, apart from the tiny niche of small presses that are still independent. The vast majority of authors will never come anywhere near such truly staggering figures. Most of them need to subsidise their literary work by other means or other jobs. Income from literature alone is very hard to generate. Marketing budgets in big publishing companies are large but they are concentrated on a few 'big books' each year that promise success.[76] Decisions are increasingly rationalised and data-driven. But such calculations remain – fortunately – "limited by the inherent unpredictability of publishing" (Lesser 2019, 439). No one in the 1950s could have foreseen Tolkien's success, just as nobody in the 1990s could have predicted Rowling's. In the shade provided by these huge successes, many a literary niche thrives in the undergrowth of the vast publishing jungle.

Electronic Literature

But what about more material changes to the ways we can experience text in non-paper-based formats, such as e-books? For writers, the experience already changed significantly when word processing software became widely available on personal computers in the late 1970s. The programme that would come to dominate this market, Microsoft Word, was launched in 1983. Matthew Kirschenbaum's study *Track Changes: A Literary History of Word Processing* (2016) offers a magisterial overview of the impact of this new way of writing on literary authors. Kirschenbaum identifies Len Deighton's (1929–) techno-thriller *Bomber* (1970) as the first novel that was written with the help of word processing, using an IBM MT/ST (Kirschenbaum 2016, 166–183): "For likely the first time in history, a newly composed work of full-length literary fiction existed not just in however many leaves of manuscript or typescript [. . .] but in another format as well, a format composed entirely of codes (actually minute fluctuations across a band of magnetic tape coated in iron oxide)" (182). This ultimately led to a "hidden revolution" in publishing (Thompson 2012, 326) because once texts were produced

---

[76] See Lesser 2019, 437 for a brief outline of the marketing campaign around Zadie Smith's first novel *White Teeth* (2000).

as digital files they could easily be "delivered in whatever form the market demanded", including e-books (ibid.).

For most readers, this change only came much later, from reading texts online in the 1990s to the introduction of the Sony Reader in 2006 and the Amazon Kindle in 2007, made possible by the late 1990s invention of E Ink at MIT, which "uses an electric charge to reconfigure black-and-white microparticles on the screen" (Borsuk 2018, 237) to simulate a printed page (fig. 17). But this also has a literary history. In his comedy science fiction series *The Hitchhiker's Guide to the Galaxy* (on BBC radio in 1978, followed by a 'trilogy' of five books), Douglas Adams (1952–2001) 'invented' the guidebook as a form of electronic book or tablet, displaying text on a screen – effectively breaking with a long tradition of science fiction depicting computers or artificial intelligence as menacing (Kirschenbaum 2016, 112). After all, "it has the words DON'T PANIC inscribed in large friendly letters on its cover" (Adams 1981 [1979], 3). This e-book, looking "rather like a largish electronic calculator", is imagined as having "about a hundred tiny flat press buttons and a screen about four inches square on which any one of a million 'pages' could be summoned at a moment's notice" (27). Its main selling point is, fittingly, *space*: "The reason why it was published in the form of a micro sub meson electronic component is that if it were printed in normal book form, an interstellar hitchhiker would require several inconveniently large buildings to carry it around in" (27).

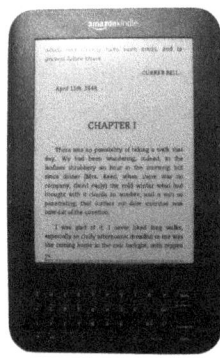

Fig. 17: Amazon Kindle 3rd generation (2010/2011) displaying a page from *Jane Eyre*.
Source: Ingo Berensmeyer.

If we look at literary media history as the history of the "portable supports through which we read" (Borsuk 2018, 202), we see the impact of the digital revolution in the early twenty-first century. This revolution changes the physical form of books but it also, even more radically, transforms texts into data, which can be used by and accessed through many different interfaces: computers, e-readers, tablets, mobile phones. It is not an exaggeration to say that "the digital download [has become] the first serious alternative to the codex in a thousand years" (Lesser 2019, 414). As Lev Manovich explains, "[a]ll existing media are translated into numerical data accessible for the computer" and thus "media become new media" (2001, 25). This translation and transformation also leads to an increasing convergence of media.

Convergence

"Optical fiber networks" and, later, wireless networks lead to a convergence of previously distinct media – "television, radio, telephone, and mail" into "a standardized series of digitized numbers", "a total media link on a digital base" that, as Friedrich Kittler presciently wrote in 1986, "will erase the very concept of medium" (1999, 1–2). In the early 2000s, Henry Jenkins similarly argued that old and new media had increasingly come together. What Kittler did not foresee was the participatory element that the World Wide Web would introduce to the world of publishing, information, and entertainment. Stories are more and more being distributed across different media simultaneously, especially in large media franchises like *Star Wars* and *Marvel*, and this "convergence culture" (Jenkins 2006) is facilitated by the participatory character of web 2.0 technologies and social media, which encourage users to share and generate their own content. Media convergence is thus not merely a technological reality but a new kind of (social as well as individual) experience, a different "structure of feeling" as defined by Raymond Williams: a new "practical consciousness of a present kind, in a living and interrelating continuity" (Williams 1977, 132).

The World Wide Web was created in the early 1990s on top of an existing structure, the Internet, a computer network that originated in the US but was already connecting many countries and institutions in the 1970s and 1980s before Tim Berners-Lee (1955–) and his colleagues at CERN (the European Organization for Nuclear Research) in Switzerland came up with a plan for a more systematic connection. Berners-Lee's foundational idea was to turn the Web into "a pool of human knowledge" (Berners-Lee et al. 1994, 76) that would allow global access to information not only as text but also in the form of images, videos, and other data formats. Beginning in 1989, his team created essential features of the Web, such as HTTP (hypertext transfer protocol), HTML (hypertext markup language) and URLs (universal resource locators). The ubiquity of personal computers and cheaper access to the Internet via privatised phone companies contributed to the quick adoption of the World Wide Web. The first browser to display images together with text, instead of in a separate window, was Mosaic in 1993, soon followed by Netscape Navigator in 1994.

Pioneers of the Web revelled in its possibilities of global connectivity – exemplified by the first webcams that transmitted photos or video from remote places or depicting odd objects. The very first webcam was pointed at the coffee machine in a computer lab at the University of Cambridge from 1991 to 2001. The coming of Web 2.0 around 2000 led to an even wider distribution of user-generated content on the web, with blogs, social networking sites, wikis, video-sharing sites, and other participatory services proliferating – aided by the proliferation of handheld devices such as PDAs (personal digital assistants) and later smartphones.

The omnipresence of networked digital devices has changed how we think about the historical variety of material supports for literature, from medieval manuscripts to printed books and beyond. These devices have mostly remediated the experience of reading physical printed books (Bolter and Grusin 1999), that is they translated this experience into a new medium, while preserving many of the older medium's features. But e-books are for the most part merely digitised books. They have not radically transformed what we read and how; they have not taken advantage of the new possibilities of interaction and connection afforded by new media. The benefits of e-readers such as size and storage capacity need to be offset by their (many) downsides – they are harder to read in the sun or the bath, it's impossible to flip through the pages, there are no page numbers, and so on. Some readers may also dislike being under electronic surveillance while reading. For these reasons and many more, e-books have not, as of now, managed to replace physical books. On the contrary, there seems to be, as with vinyl records in the age of music streaming services, a revival of physical artefacts in the digital era. People still like to read novels, and they still buy physical books. In 2016, e-book sales "dropped in both the United States and the United Kingdom" while "print book sales in the United States actually rose 3.3 percent" (Borsuk 2018, 238). More recent statistics predict a decline of physical book sales in the US until 2025 but a rise in the UK and no significant change in the EU or worldwide.[77] Audiobooks, e-books, and other new formats have expanded our options as readers, but they have not replaced the codex as "an aesthetically pleasing form" and "a social object" (Thompson 2012, 316).

---

[77] "Bücher – Weltweit", *Statista*, Statista GmbH, https://de-statista.com.emedien.ub.uni-muenchen.de/outlook/amo/medien/buecher/weltweit; "Bücher – EU 27", *Statista*, Statista GmbH, https://de-statista.com.emedien.ub.uni-muenchen.de/outlook/amo/medien/buecher/eu-27; "Bücher – Vereinigtes Königreich, USA", *Statista*, Statista GmbH, https//:de-statista-com.emedien.ub.uni-muenchen.de/outlook/amo/medien/buecher/vereinigtes-koenigreich?comparison[]=usa. Date of access: 3 Dec. 2021.

For a while, 'electronic literature' was touted as a new form of literature adequate to the new media of computers and the Internet. Hypertext, a technology invented in 1967, which made it possible to link texts or parts of a text to other texts, was seen to provide entirely new formal possibilities for literature, and to create "a new aesthetic intimately tied to the procedural capabilities of digital media" (Kirschenbaum 2016, 24). These possibilities of nonlinear reading and writing were aided by the Storyspace software developed by Jay David Bolter (1951–) and Michael Joyce (1945–) in the 1980s. Pioneers of electronic literature began to experiment with these possibilities in the 1980s and 1990s, for example by creating 'hypertext fiction', such as Michael Joyce's *afternoon: a story* (1987). These technological innovations remediated older (paper-based) forms of 'interactive fiction', such as the 'Choose Your Own Adventure' type of books, or combinations of stories and games (Montfort 2005, Meifert-Menhard 2013, Rettberg 2019).

Since then, this field has diversified into various directions including cybertext, hypermedia, and digital poetry. Critics have begun to discover the new forms of materiality in new media, electronic literature, artists' books, and the printed book in a digital environment (Hayles 2002, Rettberg 2019). Increasingly in recent years, there has also been some overlap between interactive fiction and video games, or "ergodic literature" (Aarseth 1997; Domsch 2013), with the question arising whether video games should be considered as 'literature' or not. The boundaries are becoming more fluid.

Most writers, however, have been content to adopt the computer as a writing tool for word processing but otherwise continue writing as usual, producing conventional novels, thrillers, or romances. Commercially, hypertext fiction never became a viable product. Other novels used digital production technology to integrate images, specially designed typographies, or even reproductions of handwriting to create 'multimodal' novels or multimedia books (e.g., *S.* by J. J. Abrams and Doug Dorst, 2013). Authors have experimented with e-mail instead of conventional letters for a new kind of epistolary novel, as Matt Beaumont did in his novel *e* (2000) and David Lodge in *Thinks . . .* (2001) or they have integrated a chapter in the style of a PowerPoint presentation into a novel, as Jennifer Egan (1962–) did in *A Visit from the Goon Squad* (2011) (Starre 2015; Löschnigg and Schuh 2018). The digitalised media environment of authorship rarely becomes thematic in literary fiction – one notable exception being Jeanette Winterson's *The PowerBook* (2000). This novel's title alludes to the PowerBook line of Mac laptops (1991–2006) (see fig. 18), and its chapter titles are phrases familiar from working on a computer: "Search", "New Document", "Really Quit?", etc. Winterson's novel explores literary forms of virtual reality – i.e., fiction – in concert with newly available online realities, but it remains tethered to a conventional form: the novel and the printed book. The novel did not appear in blog form but was published by Winterson's regular publisher, Jonathan Cape.

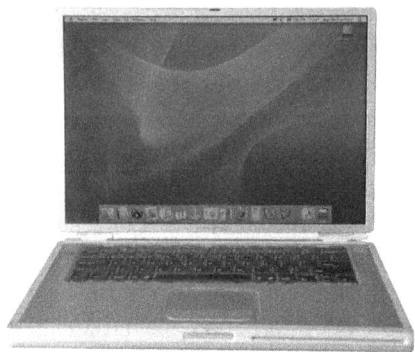

Fig. 18: Apple's PowerBook G4 (2001). Source: Ingo Berensmeyer.

More innovative literary forms of 'overwriting' and 'erasure' have become much easier due to widespread tools of word processing (Kirschenbaum 2016, 188–192, 204–206). The ability to copy-paste and then manipulate large amounts of text has made "secondary authorship" (Cook 2019) and literary mashups at least technically easier: Seth Grahame-Smith's (1976–) *Pride and Prejudice and Zombies* (2009) is the prime example of this form, which splices Jane Austen's classic with a gory new zombie fiction storyline. Patience Agbabi's *Telling Tales* (2014), mentioned in ch. 3, is a modernised 'remix' of Chaucer's *Canterbury Tales* that brings them up to date not only in terms of its language and more diverse cast of characters but also new media and the 'secondary orality' of texting language.

What has changed dramatically, since texts have taken on a digital life, is not literature as such but its sheer availability. Access to a previously unimaginable quantity of texts is now the norm. Project Gutenberg was "the first provider of free electronic books", now hosting over 60,000 titles.[78] Its beginnings go back to 1971, when a student at the University of Illinois typed the Declaration of Independence and uploaded it to a server; six people downloaded the 5K text file (Borsuk 2018, 213–215). The Internet Archive and Open Library also preserve many digitised books. Google Books, launched in 2005, now has a digital archive of more than twenty-five million books, most of them available only in 'snippets' because they are still in copyright.

---

[78] https://www.gutenberg.org/wiki/Gutenberg:About. Date of access: 1 March 2020.

Literature in the Age of Platform Capitalism

New fiction is also produced and published online in many ways, sidestepping traditional forms of print publication, for instance on fan fiction platforms such as Commaful or Archive of Our Own, but also via self-publishing services such as CreateSpace (founded in 2000). Yet the most dominant force in this field in the new millennium is neither a conventional publisher nor a conventional bookseller, but one of the corporate giants of the Internet age: Amazon. Amazon not only sells physical books online and thus poses a threat to high-street bookshops; it is also by far the biggest seller of e-books. Amazon "handled approximately 95 % of UK e-book purchases" in 2015 (Lesser 2019, 452). How does literary fiction work in the "Age of Amazon" (McGurl 2016)? Amazon, now "the world's largest online marketplace" (Wikipedia), has merged selling books with publishing on a global scale. It acquired the self-publishing platform CreateSpace in 2005, the audiobook company Audible in 2008, and the popular reviewing site Goodreads in 2013. Through Kindle Direct Publishing, Amazon encourages authors to become digital entrepreneurs: "The Man of Letters as a Man of E-Commerce" (McGurl 2016, 456), or woman, is firmly oriented towards customer satisfaction because they are being paid not by the number of copies downloaded but by the number of pages read. Yet the income for authors is far lower than in conventional publishing, with 90% of self-published authors making less than £ 7,000 per year and the bottom 20 % making an annual net loss (Lesser 2019, 455, based on data from 2015).

Although it existed long before the Internet, fan fiction has thrived on the possibility of self-publishing at no cost or risk to its authors on platforms where fans can easily communicate with like-minded people. Based on established works of fiction, from Arthur Conan Doyle's Sherlock Holmes stories to *Harry Potter*, yet often with a playful irreverence for those works' pieties, online fan fiction revises plot conventions or character constellations, frequently from the perspective of socially marginalised groups or non-normative sexual orientations (Hellekson and Busse 2014). The first AI-generated *Harry Potter* fan fiction was produced in 2017 by Botnik Studios. Although some critics argue that this day will never come, because computers cannot think in metaphors (Fletcher 2021), it remains to be seen when (rather than whether) Bayesian algorithms based on machine learning processes and/or neural networks will produce poems or novels that are indistinguishable from human efforts. Ian McEwan's 2019 novel *Machines Like Me*, while most likely still written by a single human author named Ian McEwan, already banks on the moment when a humanoid robot is taken for the more cultured and sensitive human being than its owner. The US writer Philip K. Dick (1928–1982) famously asked *Do Androids Dream of Electric Sheep?* in the novel (1968) that was later filmed as *Blade Runner* (1982). The question now is whether they will write and read electric novels.

One answer to this depends on whether AI will develop feelings and the need for communities that characterise human society. Literature has always had a strongly interactive, social component, from oral storytelling to the most literary novel that is discussed in reading groups, reviewed on Goodreads, or recommended by your local bookseller, who hopefully still exists because she attracts a loyal customer base through readings and other events that can only happen locally, and because she provides personal advice. Literature, in this sense, has always been 'social media', long before that term was applied to the new interconnected platforms on and off the Web. Algorithms have merely picked up and intensified (some might say perverted) what was already an established human need for recommendations and conversation, something that literary magazines have also been doing for quite a while. The danger now is that the bubble, however limited in scope, turns into solitary – the window on the world into a windowless monad feeding on nothing but itself.

It is important to state once again that literature (however we wish to define it) was throughout its long history never tied to just a single medium, never only based on paper or the codex, even though these still survive. More immediate modes of performance, or modes that suggest a higher degree of immediacy, have always coexisted with other modes and other technological developments. Poetry now flourishes again in live performances, in poetry slams, or on Instagram, Twitter, TikTok, or Tumblr, often in combination with visuals. For example, the poet Kae (formerly Kate) Tempest (1985–) has published poetry collections in book form as well as performing and recording their poems. Their spoken word performance *Brand New Ancients* won the Ted Hughes Award in 2012. Internationally, so-called Instapoetry became a phenomenon with the Canadian poet Rupi Kaur (1992–) in 2014; her book *milk and honey* sold more than 2.5 million copies, an unheard-of figure for poetry, which rarely sells more than a thousand copies and often much less. At the inauguration of President Biden in 2021, the US National Youth Poet Laureate Amanda Gorman (1998–) stole the show with the graceful recitation of her poem "The Hill We Climb". Gorman, a self-described "wordsmith" and "change-maker",[79] has revived the somewhat dusty tradition of the commissioned poem, and of literature that is committed to an activist cause, in front of a global audience of millions. (The first poet to read an inaugural poem was Robert Frost in 1961, at the inauguration of John F. Kennedy.) Another recent trend is for self-published

---

[79] www.theamandagorman.com, date of access: 20 Feb. 2021.

books, like Kaur's, to be picked up by trade publishers when they are successful. The most notorious success story of this kind is E. L. James's (1963–) *Fifty Shades of Grey* (2011), which began life as online fan fiction and ended up outselling the *Harry Potter* books with its decidedly more adult kind of fantasy.[80]

The present situation has its critics, and rightly so, because the pervasiveness of social media has also led to more efficient forms of spreading hatred and propaganda, and to "new forms of surveillance, by making it easier to identify connections between activists" (Standage 2019, 318), for example. Far from the utopian ideas about global connectivity and a new age of enlightenment, the World Wide Web and social media have become increasingly corporatised, and user-generated data monetised. The world has seen not only the benefits of social media but also its ugly side: "Racism, sexism, bigotry, incivility, and ignorance abound in many online discussion forums. Twitter allows anyone to send threats or abuse directly to other users" (Standage 2019, 319). Tom Standage has pointed out that these forms of interaction take us back to the media configuration of the seventeenth and eighteenth centuries, with online networks as "the new coffeehouses" (322), allowing more direct exchanges than "through the privileged bottleneck of broadcast media" (322). He regards social media not as something new, but a "rebirth".

Likewise, Bronwen Thomas has explored the interconnections between literature and social media as enabling both new ways of "creative expression" and the rediscovery of older works and established authors (Thomas 2020, blurb). Bookstagram, BookTube, and BookTok, i.e., Instagram posts and YouTube and TikTok videos dedicated to books, have become a growing alternative to literary reviews in print media, tailored to younger audiences. This democratisation of literary discussion and criticism, which is also ongoing in reading groups and on web platforms like Goodreads, may scare traditional gatekeepers, but these platforms undoubtedly attract new audiences to literature and the printed book while driving sales primarily in the commercial sectors of young adult and new adult fiction. The literary market, meanwhile, remains as unpredictable as ever ("nobody knows anything").[81] Critically and commercially

---

80 In 2012, the *Daily Telegraph* and other UK papers announced that *Fifty Shades of Grey* had outsold *Harry Potter* (https://www.telegraph.co.uk/culture/books/booknews/9459779/50-Shades-of-Grey-is-best-selling-book-of-all-time.html, date of access: 19 March 2020). By 2015, it had sold a staggering 125 million copies worldwide (according to Wikipedia), making it the best-selling book of the decade in the US (https://www.nbcnews.com/pop-culture/books/fifty-shades-grey-was-best-selling-book-decade-n1105731, date of access: 19 March 2020).
81 Originally coined by the screenwriter William Goldman to describe the film industry, particularly Hollywood, this phrase is often applied to publishing as well; see, e.g., Wagner 2017, 105.

successful novels are now quickly adapted for TV and enjoy a lot of attention on social media as well – consider the example of Sally Rooney's novel *Normal People* (2018, TV miniseries 2020), which has received 53,317 reviews on Goodreads alone (early September 2021). Literature and literary studies are both in the process of changing, and both may profit from new social and technological developments (Hammond 2016, Murray 2020).

As with older 'new media' that I have been discussing in this book, from writing to print, the phonograph, cinema, and television, it is well to remember that new technologies do not radically change everything overnight. Media technologies develop in concert with other historical and social changes. So far, the printed book as a material object has not been replaced, despite some pessimistic predictions of the end of the 'Gutenberg era' (Birkerts 2006, 2015). Many things have changed over the past few decades, but there seems to be no need to fear 'the end of the book' or 'the end of literature'. On the contrary, as Jim Collins has argued, the early twenty-first-century media environment has led to a resurgence of literary reading and to the rise of what he has called "popular literary culture" (2010, 1), further eroding if not completely erasing the long embattled divide between 'elite' and 'popular' expressions of culture (see Birke 2014 for a case study). The "materialities of communication" (Gumbrecht and Pfeiffer 1994), the media environments in which we live, certainly have an impact on our practices of writing and reading literature (and doing literary studies); but these practices are never completely determined by technologies. We now live in a world that is saturated by a multiplicity of media and characterised by the ubiquity of computing devices – in stark contrast to earlier periods of history, in which most people would have had access to only very few media such as pictures or books. In our world, these media do not seem to cancel each other out, even though there are many opportunities for distraction. On the contrary, they constitute a media landscape in which many different media intersect and interact with our senses, cultural techniques, and practices, shaping and reshaping our 'structures of feeling'.

Acknowledgements

This book began life as a lecture series at the University of Munich in the summer of 2020. Because of the pandemic, I had to transfer into the new media setting of online videos, Moodle folders, and Zoom discussions. I would like to thank the students for putting up with my first forays into online teaching. Here was some future media history to be written, certainly, but at the time, it seemed more comforting to remediate older stuff. Some of this material comes from earlier survey courses I had taught at the universities of Siegen and Giessen. I am indebted to my Giessen students and colleagues for untold inspirations; in particular, I would like to thank my former co-workers Martin Spies and Stefanie Rück. Yet in many ways, this book still breathes the 'Siegen spirit' of my student and postgraduate days. Back then, I thought everyone in literary studies was thinking about literature and media together. Now I know how special that constellation of scholars was: a big thank you to Brigitte Pichon, Bernd Schulte, Peter Gendolla, Karl Riha, Volker Roloff, but above all K. Ludwig Pfeiffer, whose formidable knowledge, keen intelligence, and enthusiasm for the humanities are unparalleled.

My text went through several successive drafts as the pandemic dragged on. Through the Cambridge-LMU partnership, I was fortunate to get to know Leo Mellor and David Trotter, who added some much-needed conceptual precision. At LMU, thanks are due in particular to Gero Guttzeit, Georgina Nugent-Folan, Daniel Schneider, Joanna Rostek, Raphaela Loosen, and Patricia Dewhirst. Special thanks to Sonja Trurnit for helping to compile the index and for checking my manuscript for errors. At De Gruyter, I am grateful to Ulrike Krauss and Katja Lehming for shepherding the book through the production process.

Many thanks to my family and friends for keeping me in good spirits; you know who you are. For their helpful comments on individual chapters, I would like to thank Eva von Contzen, Ursula Lenker, and Anne Enderwitz. Ludwig Pfeiffer read an earlier draft of the entire book. For this relief much thanks! All remaining errors, flaws, sins of omission or commission, and other things of darkness I acknowledge mine.

Timeline

Prehistory
BCE
c. 70,000	cognitive revolution
c. 35,000	first graphic symbols

Ancient Empires
c. 3000	cuneiform writing on clay tablets (Mesopotamia)
2900	oldest extant papyrus rolls (Egypt)
2100	Epic of Gilgamesh
1900	earliest surviving literary manuscript (Prisse Papyrus, Egypt)
1600	writing on animal membrane
1300	wax tablet
c. 1000	oldest sources of Hebrew Bible

Classical Antiquity
c. 800	Homeric epic: *Iliad* and *Odyssey*
300	Library of Alexandria
200	punctuation (Rome)
197	Library of Pergamum (Pergamon)
170	perfection of parchment production in Pergamum
39	first public library in Rome

CE
65–100	New Testament
105	paper invented in China
150	codex
220	earliest woodblock printing (China)

Middle Ages
675	word separation (Ireland)
731	Bede, *Historia ecclesiastica gentis anglorum*
c. 1000	*Beowulf* manuscript
1066	Battle of Hastings
1078	first European paper mill (Sativa, Spain)
c. 1200	Laʒamon, *Brut*
1309	first use of paper in England
c. 1390	Chaucer, *The Canterbury Tales* (printed 1476)
1450	printing press, metal type, oil-based ink (Gutenberg, Mainz)
1450–1501	incunable period
1456	Gutenberg Bible

Renaissance/Early Modernity
1476	first printing press in England (William Caxton, Westminster)
1495	papermaking introduced to England (John Tate, Hertfordshire)

Open Access. © 2022 Ingo Berensmeyer, published by De Gruyter. This work is licensed under the Creative Commons Attribution-NonCommercial-NoDerivatives 4.0 International License.
https://doi.org/10.1515/9783110784459-014

c. 1500	Towneley cycle (plays)
1557	first printed anthology of English poems (Tottel, *Songes and Sonettes*)
1561	first English tragedy: *Gorboduc* (Norton and Sackville)
1576	James Burbage builds The Theatre in Shoreditch (first purpose-built playhouse)
1623	First Folio of Shakespeare (Heminges and Condell)

Restoration/18th Century

1697	Dryden's translation of Virgil published by subscription
	Swift writes *The Battle of the Books* and *A Tale of a Tub*
1702	first regular daily newspaper (*The Daily Courant*)
1710	Copyright Act (Statute of Anne)
1725	stereotyping (William Ged)
1741	Richardson, *Pamela*
1755	Johnson, *Dictionary of the English Language*
1759–67	Sterne, *Tristram Shandy*
1774	*Donaldson v. Becket* strikes down perpetual copyright

Romanticism

1788	illuminated printing (Blake)
1798	lithography (Senefelder)
1800	cast iron printing press (Stanhope)
1800	Wordsworth and Coleridge, *Lyrical Ballads*
1807	Fourdrinier machine (paper production on continuous rolls)
1814	first steam press (at *The Times*)
1814	Scott's *Waverley* inaugurates the format of the three-volume novel
1816	photography (Nièpce)

Victorianism

1837	electrical telegraph
1842	Mudie's Select Library (until 1937)
1842	*Illustrated London News* (first illustrated weekly news magazine; until 2003)
1842	Tauchnitz launches *Collection of British Authors*
1843	paper made from wood pulp
1848	first railway station bookshop
1850	Tennyson, *In Memoriam*
1858	first transatlantic telegraph cable
1860	Collins, *The Woman in White*
1876	telephone (Bell, USA)
1877	phonograph (Edison, USA)
1886	Linotype (Mergenthaler)
1886	Berne Convention on Copyright
1889	kinetoscope (Edison, USA)
1890s	photomechanical reproduction of photographs (halftone)
1891	Gissing, *New Grub Street*

1894	three-volume novel format is defunct
1895	cinematograph (Lumière brothers, France); gramophone (Emil Berliner)
1897	Stoker, *Dracula*
1899	Net Book Agreement

Modernism/Early 20th Century

1901	first transatlantic wireless message (Marconi)
1902	Kipling, "Wireless"
1904	Kipling, "Mrs. Bathurst"
1904	The Times Book Club
1907–1909	Henry James, New York Edition
1913	Marinetti, *The Typographic Revolution*
1913	Pound, "In a Station of the Metro"
1914	*BLAST* (Wyndham Lewis)
1919	Woolf, "Modern Novels" (later "Modern Fiction")
1922	BBC radio
1922	Eliot, *The Waste Land*
1922	Joyce, *Ulysses*
1926	Woolf, "The Cinema"
1927	sound film; jukebox
1927	Green, *Living*
1932	audiobooks (USA)
1935	Penguin paperbacks
1936	BBC television
1936	first working digital computer (Zuse)
1936	Turing, "On Computable Numbers"
1938	Welles, *The War of the Worlds* (radio play)
1949	Orwell, *Nineteen Eighty-Four*

Postmodernism/Late 20th Century

1951	inkjet printer (Siemens)
1954	Thomas, *Under Milk Wood* (radio play)
1955	Universal Copyright Convention
1956	first British paperback to sell a million copies (Brickhill, *The Dam Busters*)
1957	Hoggart, *The Uses of Literacy*
1959	Xerox 914 commercial photocopier
1960	*R v Penguin Books* (*Lady Chatterley* trial)
1962	Burgess, *A Clockwork Orange*
1964	Beckett, *Film*
1966	first British book with computer-aided typesetting
1967	Hypertext (Nelson and van Dam); ISBN introduced
1967	*Forsyte Saga* (BBC); IBM MT/ST
1969	Booker Prize (for best English-language novel published in UK)
1970	first novel written with a word processor (Deighton, *Bomber*)
1971	Project Gutenberg (Hart)
1972	Dynabook (Kay)

1973	British Library (world's largest library)
1981	*Brideshead Revisited* (ITV)
1982	first Waterstone's bookshop in London (since 2012: Waterstones)
1983	Microsoft Word
1984	Apple Macintosh
1985	CD-ROM
1989	World Wide Web (Berners-Lee); Ishiguro, *The Remains of the Day*
1991	first webcam (Trojan Room coffee pot, Cambridge)
1992	Sony Data Discman
1993	Mosaic web browser
1994	PlayStation; Netscape Navigator
1995	end of Net Book Agreement
1995	Amazon ('world's largest bookstore')
1995	Audible (audiobooks)
1996	Internet Archive (Kahle)
1997	E-Paper / E-Ink (Jacobson)
1997	Netflix; Rowling, *Harry Potter and the Philosopher's Stone*
1998	Google
1999	*Big Brother* TV show; *The Matrix* (film)

Twenty-First Century/Contemporary

2001	Wikipedia; Creative Commons
2004	Facebook
2005	Google Books
2005	Amazon acquires Create Space (self-publishing service)
2008	Amazon acquires Audible
2006	Sony Reader
2007	Apple iPhone
2007	Amazon Kindle
2007	BBC iPlayer
2007	Rowling, *The Tales of Beedle the Bard*
2008	Pottermore website
2010	Apple iPad
2013	merger of Penguin and Random House
2014	Booker Prize extended to any English-language novel
2017	AI-generated *Harry Potter* fan fiction
2021	Ishiguro, *Klara and the Sun*

List of Illustrations and Table

Fig. 1	Reconstruction of an Anglo-Saxon village hall. West Stow, Suffolk, 2018 Source: Ingo Berensmeyer —— **32**	
Fig. 2	First page of *Beowulf* manuscript (Cotton Vitellius A. XV, f. 132) Source: British Library, Wikimedia Commons —— **39**	
Figs. 3 and 4	A page from Caxton's edition of *The Canterbury Tales* (1483), woodcut and letterpress, and a page from the Kelmscott Chaucer (1896), letterpress Source: Paul Mellon Collection, Yale Center for British Art —— **56**	
Fig. 5	Interior of the Swan playhouse. Copy by Aernout van Buchel of a sketch by Johannes de Witt (1596); from Arnoldus Buchelius, *Adversaria*, fol. 132r Source: Utrecht University Library Special Collections Ms. 842, Wikimedia Commons —— **70**	
Fig. 6	Mr Garrick in Hamlet. Mezzotint by James MacArdell after a painting by Benjamin Wilson, 1754 Source: Metropolitan Museum of Art, Wikimedia Commons —— **80**	
Fig. 7	The Brain-sucker, or the Miseries of Authorship (1787), etching attrib. to Thomas Rowlandson Source: Royal Collection, London —— **96**	
Fig. 8	A Country Churchyard. Verse from Gray's Elegy, 1790. Aquatint on paper by Marie C. Prestel after Thomas Gainsborough. Source: Paul Mellon Collection, Yale Center for British Art Source: Paul Mellon Collection, Yale Center for British Art —— **100**	
Fig. 9	James Grant, *Bothwell* (London: Routledge, n.d. [c. 1884]), priced at 2s and part of Routledge's Railway Library Source: Ingo Berensmeyer —— **114**	
Fig. 10	Mudie's Select Library sticker, n. d Source: Ingo Berensmeyer —— **116**	
Fig. 11	First page of *All the Year Round,* June 16, 1860, with an instalment of Wilkie Collins's *The Woman in White* Source: Ingo Berensmeyer —— **119**	
Fig. 12	The first Penguin paperback, 1935. Cover and page spread Source: Ingo Berensmeyer —— **125**	
Fig. 13	The Eastern Telegraph Company network in 1901 Source: Alamy Stock Photo —— **155**	
Fig. 14	An early 'audiobook': Caedmon TC 2005, vinyl LP and sleeve, 1956 Source: Ingo Berensmeyer —— **163**	
Fig. 15	William Blake, *Songs of Innocence and Experience* (1794), plate 47. Colour-printed relief etching with watercolour on moderately thick, slightly textured, cream wove paper Source: Yale Center for British Art, Paul Mellon Collection, B1978.43.1578 —— **182**	

ᔒ Open Access. © 2022 Ingo Berensmeyer, published by De Gruyter. This work is licensed under the Creative Commons Attribution-NonCommercial-NoDerivatives 4.0 International License.
https://doi.org/10.1515/9783110784459-015

Fig. 16	Portland Place, London. Photograph by Alvin Langdon Coburn, c. 1905 Source: Granger Historical Picture Archive / Alamy Stock Photo —— **185**
Fig. 17	Amazon Kindle 3rd generation (2010/2011) displaying a page from *Jane Eyre* Source: Ingo Berensmeyer —— **218**
Fig. 18	Apple's PowerBook G4 (2001) Source: Ingo Berensmeyer —— **222**
Tab. 1	Number of new book titles published per year in the UK between 1950 and 2018 —— **216**

References

Aarseth, Espen. 1997. *Cybertext: Perspectives on Ergodic Literature*. Baltimore: Johns Hopkins University Press.
Abrams, M. H. 1984. *The Correspondent Breeze: Essays on English Romanticism*. New York: Norton.
Abravanel, Genevieve. 2012. "English by Example. F. R. Leavis and the Americanization of Modern England". *Americanizing Britain. The Rise of Modernism in the Age of the Entertainment Empire*. Oxford: Oxford University Press. 110–130.
Ackerman, Robert W. 1957. "'Pared out of Paper': *Gawain* 802 and *Purity* 1408". *Journal of English and Germanic Philology* 56.3: 410–417.
Adams, Douglas. 1981. *The Hitchhiker's Guide to the Galaxy*. New York: Pocket.
Adams, Thomas R., and Nicolas Barker. 2006. "A New Model for the Study of the Book". *The Book History Reader*. Ed. David Finkelstein and Alistair McCleery. London/New York: Routledge. 47–65.
"Adventures of a Quire of Paper". 1779. *The London Magazine, Or Gentlemans Monthly Intelligencer* 48 (Aug.): 355–358; (Sept.): 395–398; (Oct.): 448–52.
Agbabi, Patience. 2014. *Telling Tales*. Edinburgh: Canongate.
Alcuin. 1895. "Alcuini epistola 124". *Epistolae Karolini aevi II*. Ed. Ernst Dümmler. (Monumenta Germaniae Historica) Berlin: Weidmann. 181–184. https://periodika.digitale-sammlungen.de/wsa. Date of access: 2 March 2020.
Alexander, Gavin. 2004. "Introduction". *Sidney's 'The Defence of Poesy' and Selected Renaissance Literary Criticism*. Ed. Gavin Alexander. Harmondsworth: Penguin. xvii–lxxix.
Alfano, Veronica. 2017. *The Lyric in Victorian Memory. Poetic Remembering and Forgetting from Tennyson to Housman*. Basingstoke: Palgrave Macmillan.
Anderson, Benedict. 2006 *Imagined Communities. Reflections on the Origin and Spread of Nationalism*. 1983. Rev. ed. London/New York: Verso.
Andrews, Malcolm. 2006. *Charles Dickens and His Performing Selves. Dickens and the Public Readings*. Oxford: Oxford University Press.
Aristotle. 2013. *Poetics*. Trans. Anthony Kenny. Oxford: Oxford University Press.
Arnold, Matthew. 1965. *The Poems of Matthew Arnold*. Ed. Kenneth Allott. London: Longmans.
Ashcroft, Bill, Griffiths, Gareth, and Helen Tiffin. 2007. "Orality". *Post-Colonial Studies. The Key Concepts*. 2nd ed. London and New York: Routledge. 151–153.
Ashe, Laura, ed. 2015. *Early Fiction in England. From Geoffrey of Monmouth to Chaucer*. London: Penguin.
Astington, John. 2001. "Playhouses, Players, and Playgoers in Shakespeare's Time". *The Cambridge Companion to Shakespeare*. Ed. Margreta de Grazia and Stanley Wells. Cambridge: Cambridge University Press. 99–113.
Auden, W. H. 2005. "In Memory of W. B. Yeats". 1939. *W. H. Auden. Poems Selected by John Fuller*. London: Faber and Faber.
Austin, J. L. 1975. *How to Do Things with Words*. 2nd ed. Ed. J. O. Urmson and Marina Sbisà. Cambridge, MA: Harvard University Press.
Bachman, Maria K. 2006. "Scandalous Sensations: *The Woman in White* on the Victorian Stage". *The Victorian Newsletter*. Spring. 1–9.
Baetens, Jan, and Hugo Frey. 2015. *The Graphic Novel: An Introduction*. Cambridge: Cambridge University Press.

Bakhtin, Mikhail. 1981. *The Dialogic Imagination. Four Essays*. Ed. Michael Holquist. Trans. Caryl Emerson and Michael Holquist. Austin: University of Texas Press.
Ballard, J. G. 1963. "The Sound-Sweep". *The Four-Dimensional Nightmare*. London: Gollancz. 41–79.
Ballaster, Ros. 1992. *Seductive Forms. Women's Amatory Fiction from 1684 to 1740*. Oxford: Clarendon Press.
Balzac, Honoré de. 2004. *Lost Illusions*. 1837–1843. Trans. Herbert J. Hunt. 1971. London: Penguin.
Bassett, Troy J. 2010. "Living on the Margin: George Bentley and the Economics of the Three-Volume Novel, 1865–70". *Book History* 13: 58–79.
Bate, Jonathan. 2008. *Soul of the Age. The Life, Mind and World of William Shakespeare*. London: Penguin.
Baudelaire, Charles. 1981. *Art in Paris 1845–1862: Salons and Other Exhibitions. Reviewed by Charles Baudelaire*. Trans. and ed. Jonathan Mayne. Ithaca: Cornell University Press.
Beckett, Samuel. 1969. "Samuel Beckett talks about Beckett". *Vogue*. December. 210.
Beckett, Samuel. 1986. *The Complete Dramatic Works*. London and Boston: Faber and Faber.
Beckett, Samuel. 1993. *More Pricks than Kicks*. Paris, London, New York: Calder.
Beckett, Samuel. 1995. *The Complete Short Prose, 1929–1989*. Ed. S. E. Gontarski. New York: Grove.
Beckett, Samuel. 1996. *Nohow On. Company, Ill Seen Ill Said, Worstward Ho*. New York: Grove.
Beckwith, Sarah. 2009. "Drama". *The Cambridge Companion to Medieval English Literature 1100–1500*. Ed. Larry Scanlon. Cambridge: Cambridge University Press, 2009. 83–94.
Bede. 2008. *The Ecclesiastical History of the English People. The Greater Chronicle. Bede's Letter to Egbert*. Ed. Judith McClure and Roger Collins. Oxford: Oxford University Press.
Bell, David N. 2006. "The Libraries of Religious Houses in the Late Middle Ages". *The Cambridge History of Libraries in Britain and Ireland*. Vol. 1: *To 1640*. Ed. Elisabeth Leedham-Green and Teresa Webber. Cambridge: Cambridge University Press. 126–151.
Benjamin, Walter. 2008. "The Work of Art in the Age of its Technological Reproducibility". Second Version. *The Work of Art in the Age of its Technological Reproducibility, and Other Writings on Media*. Ed. Michael W. Jennings et al. Trans. Edmund Jephcott et al. Cambridge, MA/London: Belknap Press of Harvard UP. 19–55.
Berensmeyer, Ingo. 2009. "Eighteenth-Century English Poetry and the Novel: Decline vs. Rise or 'Novelization'?" *Germanisch-Romanische Monatsschrift* 59.2: 239–255.
Berensmeyer, Ingo. 2012. "From Media Anthropology to Media Ecology." *Travelling Concepts for the Study of Culture*. Ed. Birgit Neumann and Ansgar Nünning. Berlin and Boston: De Gruyter. 321–335.
Berensmeyer, Ingo. 2013. "Stage(d) Life: Shakespeare and the Ecology of Media". *New Theories, Models and Methods in Literary and Cultural Studies*. Ed. Greta Olson and Ansgar Nünning. Trier: WVT. 81–97.
Berensmeyer, Ingo. 2014. "Grub Street Revisited: Late Eighteenth-Century Authorship Satire and the Media Culture of Print". *Anglistentag 2013 Konstanz Proceedings*. Ed. Silvia Mergenthal and Reingard M. Nischik. Trier: WVT. 127–136.
Berensmeyer, Ingo. 2016. "'The *musique concrète* of civilization': Responding to Technological and Cultural Change in Postwar British Literature". *REAL: Yearbook of Research in English and American Literature* 32. 169–186.
Berensmeyer, Ingo. 2017. "Komik im britischen Rundfunk". *Komik. Ein interdisziplinäres Handbuch*. Ed. Uwe Wirth. Stuttgart: Metzler. 395–397.

Berensmeyer, Ingo, ed. 2019. *Handbook of English Renaissance Literature*. Berlin and Boston: De Gruyter.
Berensmeyer, Ingo. 2020. "Female Authorship in Modern Fiction: Stevie Smith's *Novel on Yellow Paper* (1936) and the History of Fictional Women Writers". *Authorship* 9.1: 1–14. www.authorship.ugent.be.
Berensmeyer, Ingo, Guttzeit, Gero, and Alise Jameson. 2015. "'The Brain-Sucker: Or, the Distress of Authorship': A Late Eighteenth-Century Satire of Grub Street". *Authorship* 4.1. www.authorship.ugent.be.
Berger, Harry Jr. 1965. "The Renaissance Imagination: Second World and Green World." *Centennial Review of Arts and Sciences* 9: 36–78.
Berger, John. 2008. *Ways of Seeing*. 1972. London: Penguin.
Berners-Lee, Tim et al. 1994. "The World-Wide Web". *Communications of the ACM* 37.8: 76–82.
Bethke, Katrin. 2021. "Love's Accountants: Double-Entry Bookkeeping and the Sonnet Form in Early Modern England". *Forms at Work. New Formalist Approaches in the Study of Literature, Culture, and Media*. Ed. Elizabeth Kovach, Imke Polland, and Ansgar Nünning. Trier: WVT. 25–40.
Birke, Dorothee. 2014. "Challenging the Divide? Stephen King and the Problem of 'Popular Culture'". *The Journal of Popular Culture* 47.3: 520–536.
Birkerts, Sven. 2006. *The Gutenberg Elegies. The Fate of Reading in an Electronic Age*. New York: Farrar, Straus and Giroux.
Birkerts, Sven. 2015. *Changing the Subject. Art and Attention in the Internet Age*. Minneapolis: Graywolf Press.
Blagden, Cyprian. 1960. *The Stationers' Company. A History, 1403–1959*. London: Allen and Unwin.
Bland, Mark. 1998. "The Appearance of the Text in Early Modern England". *Text* 11: 91–154.
Blayney, Peter W. M. 1997. "The Publication of Playbooks". *A New History of Early English Drama*. Ed. J. D. Cox and D. S. Kastan. New York: Columbia University Press. 383–422.
Blayney, Peter W. M. 2013. *The Stationers' Company and the Printers of London, 1501–1557*. Cambridge: Cambridge University Press.
Böker, Uwe. 1987. "'The Distressed Writer': Sozialhistorische Bedingungen eines berufsspezifischen Stereotyps in der Literatur und Kritik des frühen 18. Jahrhunderts". *Erstarrtes Denken. Studien zu Klischee, Stereotyp und Vorurteil in englischsprachiger Literatur*. Ed. Günther Blaicher. Tübingen: Narr. 140–153.
Bolter, Jay David, and Richard Grusin. 1999. *Remediation: Understanding New Media*. Cambridge, MA: MIT Press.
Borsuk, Amaranth. 2018. *The Book*. Cambridge, MA and London: MIT Press.
Boswell, James. 1992. *The Life of Samuel Johnson*. 1791. London: Everyman's Library.
Brandstetter, Gabriele. 2015. *Poetics of Dance. Body, Image, and Space in the Historical Avant-Gardes*. Oxford: Oxford University Press.
Briggs, Asa. 1961. *The History of Broadcasting in the United Kingdom*. Vol. 1. *The Birth of Broadcasting*. London: Oxford University Press.
Briggs, Asa. 1965. *The History of Broadcasting in the United Kingdom*. Vol. 2. *The Golden Age of Wireless*. London: Oxford University Press.
Briggs, Asa. 1979. *The History of Broadcasting in the United Kingdom*. Vol. 4. *Sound and Vision*. London: Oxford University Press.
Brook, Peter. 1996. *The Empty Space*. 1968. New York: Touchstone.
Brown, Erica, and Mary Grover, eds. 2012. *Middlebrow Literary Cultures. The Battle of the Brows, 1920–1960*. Basingstoke: Palgrave Macmillan.

Browning, Robert. 2014. "Mr. Sludge, 'the Medium'". *The Poems of Robert Browning*. Ed. John Woolford, Daniel Karlin and Joseph Phelan. Vol. 4: 1862–1871. London and New York: Routledge. 200–279.

Bruton, Elizabeth. 2019. "Technologies of Romance: Valentine from a Telegraph Clerk ♂ to a Telegraph Clerk ♀: The Material Culture and Standards of Early Electrical Telegraphy". *Science Museum Group Journal* 12: n. p. http://journal.sciencemuseum.org.uk/browse/issue-12/valentine-from-a-telegraph-clerk/. Date of access: 9 Mar. 2022.

Bullough, Donald A. 1993. "What has Ingeld to Do with Lindisfarne?" *Anglo-Saxon England* 22: 93–125.

Burgess, Anthony. 2012. *A Clockwork Orange. The Restored Edition*. Ed. Andrew Biswell. New York and London: Norton.

Burke, Kenneth. 1961. "Literature as Equipment for Living". *The Philosophy of Literary Form. Studies in Symbolic Action*. 1941. New York: Vintage. 253–262.

Burrows, Stuart. 2008. *A Familiar Strangeness: American Fiction and the Language of Photography, 1839–1945*. Athens, GA and London: University of Georgia Press.

Butterfield, Ardis. 2009. "England and France". *A Companion to Medieval English Literature and Culture, c. 1350-c. 1500*. Ed. Peter Brown. Malden, MA and Oxford: Blackwell. 199–214.

Callens, Johan. 2009. "The Wooster Group's *Hamlet*, According to the True, Original Copies". *Theatre Journal* 61: 539–561.

Campbell, Lewis, and William Garnett. 1882. *The Life of James Clerk Maxwell with a Selection from his Correspondence and Occasional Writings* [. . .]. London: Macmillan.

Carlyle, Thomas. 1986. "Signs of the Times". 1829. *Selected Writings*. Ed. Alan Shelston. Harmondsworth: Penguin. 61–85.

Carrière, Jean-Claude, and Umberto Eco. 2012. *This is Not the End of the Book. A Conversation Curated by Jean-Philippe de Tonnac*. 2009. Trans. Polly McLean. New York: Vintage.

Cave, Terence. 2016. *Thinking with Literature*. Oxford: Oxford University Press.

Cerquiglini, Bernard. 1989. *Éloge de la variante*. Paris: Seuil.

Chambers, Matthew. 2020. *London and the Modernist Bookshop*. Cambridge: Cambridge University Press.

Chaucer, Geoffrey. 1987. *The Riverside Chaucer*. 3rd ed. Gen. ed. Larry D. Benson. Oxford: Oxford University Press.

Christ, Carol T. 1975. *The Finer Optic: The Aesthetic of Particularity in Victorian Poetry*. New Haven, CT and London: Yale University Press.

Christie, Agatha. 2011. *4:50 from Paddington*. 1957. New York: Harper.

Clarke, Danielle, ed. 2000. *Isabella Whitney, Mary Sidney and Aemilia Lanyer: Renaissance Women Poets*. London: Penguin.

Classen, Constance. 2012. *The Deepest Sense. A Cultural History of Touch*. Urbana, IL: University of Illinois Press.

Clegg, Cyndia S. 2001. *Press Censorship in Jacobean England*. Cambridge: Cambridge University Press.

Cleland, Gary. 2007. "Amazon admits to record Harry Potter bid". *The Daily Telegraph*, 14 Dec. 2007. https://www.telegraph.co.uk/news/uknews/3669918/Amazon-admits-to-record-Harry-Potter-bid.html. Date of access: 3 March 2020.

Coldiron, A. E. B. 2015. *Printers without Borders. Translation and Textuality in the Renaissance*. Cambridge: Cambridge University Press.

Coleman, Joyce. 2010. "Where Chaucer Got His Pulpit: Audience and Intervisuality in the *Troilus and Criseyde* Frontispiece". *Studies in the Age of Chaucer* 32. 103–128.

Collins, Jim. 2010. *Bring on the Books for Everybody. How Literary Culture Became Popular Culture*. Durham, NC: Duke University Press.
Conrad, Joseph. 1991. *Typhoon and Other Stories*. New York: Knopf.
Conrad, Joseph, and Ford Madox Ford. 1999. *The Inheritors. An Extravagant Story*. 1901. Liverpool: Liverpool University Press.
Cook, Daniel. 2019. "Copyright and Literary Property. The Invention of Secondary Authorship". *The Cambridge Handbook of Literary Authorship*. Ed. Ingo Berensmeyer, Gert Buelens, and Marysa Demoor. Cambridge: Cambridge University Press. 384–399.
Cooper, Helen. 2014. *Shakespeare and the Medieval World*. 2010. London: Bloomsbury.
Coppola, Manuela. 2016. "A Tale of Two Wives: The Transnational Poetry of Patience Agbabi and Jean 'Binta' Breeze". *Journal of Postcolonial Writing* 52.3: 305–318.
Corns, Thomas N. 2007. *A History of Seventeenth-Century Literature*. Malden and Oxford: Blackwell.
Crary, Jonathan. 1992. *Techniques of the Observer: On Vision and Modernity in the Nineteenth Century*. Cambridge, MA: MIT Press.
Crisell, Andrew. 2002. *An Introductory History of British Broadcasting*. 2nd ed. London and New York: Routledge.
Culler, Jonathan. 1977. "Apostrophe". *Diacritics* 7.4: 59–69.
Czitrom, Daniel. 2019. "Early Motion Pictures". *Communication in History. Stone Age Symbols to Social Media*. Ed. Paul Heyer and Peter Urquhart. London and New York: Routledge. 175–183.
Dalley, Stephanie, ed. and trans. 2008. *Myths from Mesopotamia. Creation, the Flood, Gilgamesh, and Others*. Rev. ed. Oxford: Oxford University Press.
Daly, Nicholas. 1999. "Railway Novels: Sensation Fiction and the Modernization of the Senses". *ELH* 66.2: 461–487.
Darnton, Robert. 1982. "What is the History of Books?" *Daedalus* 111.3: 65–83.
Davenport-Hines, Richard. 2009. "Smith, William Henry (1825–1891), Newsagent and Politician". *Oxford Dictionary of National Biography*. Date of access: 25 Feb. 2020.
Defoe, Daniel. 1704. *An Essay on the Regulation of the Press*. London: n. p.
Derrida, Jacques. 1992. "Ulysses Gramophone. Hear Say Yes in Joyce". *Acts of Literature*. Ed. Derek Attridge. New York/London: Routledge. 253–309.
De Vito, John, and Frank Tropea. 2010. *Epic Television Miniseries. A Critical History*. Jefferson, NC: McFarland.
de Voogd, Peter J. 2006. "*Tristram Shandy* as Aesthetic Object". *Laurence Sterne's* Tristram Shandy: *A Casebook*. Ed. Thomas Keymer. Oxford: Oxford University Press. 108–119.
Dickens, Charles. 1975. *The Public Readings*. Ed. Philip Collins. Oxford: Clarendon Press.
Ditum, Sarah. 2019. "'It drives writers mad': why are authors still sniffy about sci-fi?" *The Guardian* 18 April. https://www.theguardian.com/books/2019/apr/18/it-drives-writers-mad-why-are-authors-still-sniffy-about-sci-fi. Date of access: 27 Feb. 2020.
Domsch, Sebastian. 2013. *Storyplaying. Agency and Narrative in Video Games*. Berlin and Boston: De Gruyter.
Downie, J. A. 2014. "Paying for Poetry at the Turn of the Eighteenth Century, with Particular Reference to Dryden, Pope, and Defoe". *Digital Defoe: Studies in Defoe and His Contemporaries* 6.1: 1–18.
Drucker, Joanna. 1994. *The Visible Word. Experimental Typography and Modern Art, 1909–1923*. Chicago and London: University of Chicago Press.
Dussinger, John A. 2012. "Richardson, Samuel (bap. 1689, d. 1761), Printer and Author". *Oxford Dictionary of National Biography*. Date of access: 1 July 2020.

Edel, Leon. 1972. *Henry James. The Master. 1901–1916*. Philadelphia and New York: Lippincott.
Ehland, Christoph, and Cornelia Wächter, eds. 2016. *Middlebrow and Gender, 1890–1945*. Leiden and Boston: Brill Rodopi.
Eisenstein, Sergei. 1977. "The Cinematographic Principle and the Ideogram". 1929. *Film Form. Essays in Film Theory*. Ed. and trans. Jay Leyda. New York and London: Harvest. 28–44.
Eliot, George. 1985. *Adam Bede*. 1859. Ed. Stephen Gill. Harmondsworth: Penguin.
Eliot, George. 1994. *Middlemarch*. Ed. Rosemary Ashton. Harmondsworth: Penguin.
Eliot, T. S. 1921. *The Sacred Wood. Essays on Poetry and Criticism*. New York: Knopf.
Eliot, T. S. 1957. "The Frontiers of Criticism". *On Poetry and Poets*. London: Faber and Faber. 103–121.
Eliot, T. S. 1989. *Collected Poems 1909–1962*. London: Faber and Faber.
Eliot, T. S. 2010. *The Waste Land: A Facsimile and Transcript of the Original Drafts Including the Annotations of Ezra Pound*. Ed. Valerie Eliot. 1971. Rev. ed. London: Faber and Faber.
Ellmann, Richard. 1982. *James Joyce*. Oxford: Oxford University Press.
Enderwitz, Anne. 2015. *Modernist Melancholia. Freud, Conrad and Ford*. Houndmills: Palgrave Macmillan.
Engelsing, Rolf. 1974. *Der Bürger als Leser: Lesergeschichte in Deutschland 1500–1800*. Stuttgart: Metzler.
Ensslin, Astrid. 2014. *Literary Gaming*. Cambridge, MA and London: MIT Press.
Epstein, Josh. 2019. "'We Are a Musical Nation': *Under Milk Wood* and the BBC Third Programme". *Modern Drama* 62.3: 249–271.
Eyles, Leonora. 1952. *Sex for the Engaged*. London: Robert Hale.
Ezell, Margaret J. M. 2019. "Renaissance Englishwomen as Writers, Readers, and Patrons". *Handbook of English Renaissance Literature*. Ed. Ingo Berensmeyer. Berlin and Boston: De Gruyter. 182–202.
Fairer, David, and Christine Gerrard, eds. 2015. *Eighteenth-Century Poetry: An Annotated Anthology*. 3rd ed. Malden, MA and Oxford: Wiley Blackwell.
Farmer, Alan B., and Zachary Lesser. 2005. "The Popularity of Playbooks Revisited". *Shakespeare Quarterly* 56.1: 1–32.
Feather, John. 1988. *A History of British Publishing*. London and New York: Routledge.
Feather, John. 2006. *A History of British Publishing*. 2nd ed. London and New York: Routledge.
Ferber, Michael. 2012. *The Cambridge Introduction to British Romantic Poetry*. Cambridge: Cambridge University Press.
Fergus, Jan. 2006. *Provincial Readers in Eighteenth-Century England*. Oxford: Oxford University Press.
Fielding, Heather. 2015. "Kipling's Wireless Impressionism: Telecommunication and Narration in Early Modernism". *MFS: Modern Fiction Studies* 61.1: 24–46.
Fielding, Henry. 1985. *Joseph Andrews*. Ed. R. F. Brissenden. Harmondsworth: Penguin.
Fielding, Henry. 2004. *An Apology for the Life of Mrs. Shamela Andrews*. Ed. Catherine Ingrassia. Peterborough, Ontario: Broadview Press.
Fielding, Henry. 2005. *The History of Tom Jones, A Foundling*. Ed. Thomas Keymer and Alice Wakely. London: Penguin.
Finkelstein, David. 1993. "'The Secret': British Publishers and Mudie's Struggle for Survival 1861–64." *Publishing History* 33: 5–35.
Finlayson, John. 1980/81. "Definitions of Middle English Romance". *Chaucer Review* 15.1-2:44–62, 168–81.

Fletcher, Angus. 2021. "Why Computers Will Never Write Good Novels". *Nautilus* 95 (10 Feb.). https://nautil.us/issue/95/escape/why-computers-will-never-write-good-novels. Date of access: 20 Feb. 2021.

Ford, Ford Madox. 2012. *Parade's End*. London: Penguin.

Forster. E. M. 2001. "The Machine Stops". 1909. *Selected Stories*. Ed. David Leavitt and Mark Mitchell. London: Penguin. 91–123.

Frank, Joseph. 1961. *The Beginnings of the English Newspaper 1620–1660*. Cambridge, MA: Harvard University Press.

Fulk, R. D., Bjork, Robert E., and John D. Niles, eds. 2008. *Klaeber's Beowulf and the Fight at Finnsburg*. 4th ed. Toronto, Buffalo, and London: University of Toronto Press.

Fuller, John. 1998. *W. H. Auden: A Commentary*. Princeton and Oxford: Princeton University Press.

Fuller, Matthew. 2005. *Media Ecologies. Materialist Energies in Art and Technoculture*. Cambridge, MA and London: MIT Press.

Fumerton, Patricia. 1991. *Cultural Aesthetics. Renaissance Literature and the Practice of Social Ornament*. Chicago, IL and London: University of Chicago Press.

Furniss, Tom, and Michael Bath. 2007. *Reading Poetry: An Introduction*. 2nd ed. Harlow: Pearson.

Gabel, Tobias. 2022. *The Miltonic Sensorium. Sensory Discourse and Literary Epistemology in the Writings of John Milton*. Heidelberg: Universitätsverlag Winter.

Gameson, Richard. 1992. "The Cost of the Codex Amiatinus". *Notes and Queries* 237: 2–9.

Gameson, Richard. 2012. "Anglo-Saxon Scribes and Scriptoria." *The Cambridge History of the Book in Britain. Vol. 1. c. 400–1100*. Ed. Richard Gameson. Cambridge: Cambridge University Press.

Gessner, Niklaus. 1957. *Die Unzulänglichkeit der Sprache. Eine Untersuchung über Formzerfall und Beziehungslosigkeit bei Samuel Beckett*. Zürich: Juris.

Gibson, James J. 1973. "The Theory of Affordances". *Perceiving, Acting, and Knowing. Toward an Ecological Psychology*. Ed. Robert Shaw and John Bransford. Hillsdale, NJ: Lawrence Erlbaum Associates. 67–82.

Gill, Eric. 2013. *An Essay on Typography*. 1931. London: Penguin.

Gillespie, Alexandra. 2006. *Print Culture and the Medieval Author. Chaucer, Lydgate, and Their Books 1473–1557*. Oxford: Oxford University Press.

Gissing, George. 2016. *New Grub Street*. 1891. Ed. Katherine Mullin. Oxford: Oxford University Press.

Gitelman, Lisa. 2006. *Always Already New: Media, History and the Data of Culture*. Cambridge, MA: MIT Press.

Gitelman, Lisa. 2014. *Paper Knowledge. Toward a Media History of Documents*. Durham, NC and London: Duke University Press.

Gitelman, Lisa. 2019. "Inscribing Sound". *Communication in History. Stone Age Symbols to Social Media*. Ed. Paul Heyer and Peter Urquhart. London/New York: Routledge. 163–167.

Glaubitz, Nicola. 2013. "Vernacular Modernism: Martin Rowson's *The Waste Land*". *Anglistentag 2012 – Proceedings*. Ed. Katrin Röder, Ilse Wischer. Trier: WVT. 245–252.

Green, Henry. 1993. *Loving. Living. Party Going*. New York: Penguin.

Green, Henry. 2008. *Nothing, Doting, Blindness*. London: Vintage.

Greenblatt, Stephen, gen. ed. 1997. *The Norton Shakespeare*. New York: Norton.

Greenspan, Ezra, and Jonathan Rose. 1998. "An Introduction to *Book History*". *Book History* 1.1: ix–xi.

Grenby, M. O., ed. 2013. *Little Goody Two-Shoes and Other Stories: Originally Published by John Newbery*. Basingstoke: Palgrave Macmillan.
Griem, Julika. 2008. "Visuality and its Discontents. On Some Uses of Invisibility in Edgar Allan Poe, George Eliot, and Henry James". *Victorian Visual Culture*. Ed. Renate Brosch. Heidelberg: Winter. 245–265.
Griest, Guinevere L. 1970. *Mudie's Circulating Library and the Victorian Novel*. Bloomington: Indiana University Press.
Griffiths, Eric. 1993. "Tennyson's Breath". *Critical Essays on Alfred Lord Tennyson*. Ed. Herbert F. Tucker. New York: G. K. Hall. 28–47.
Griffiths, Eric. 2018. *The Printed Voice of Victorian Poetry*. 2nd ed. Oxford: Oxford University Press.
Grimes, Hilary. 2011. *The Late Victorian Gothic. Mental Science, the Uncanny, and Scenes of Writing*. Farnham and Burlington: Ashgate.
Gumbrecht, Hans Ulrich. 2008. "Shall We Continue to Write Histories of Literature?" *New Literary History* 39.3. 519–532.
Gumbrecht, Hans Ulrich, and K. Ludwig Pfeiffer, eds. 1994. *Materialities of Communication*. Trans. William Whobrey. Stanford: Stanford University Press.
Gunn, Thom. 1957. *The Sense of Movement*. London: Faber and Faber.
Gurr, Andrew. 1997. "The Shakespearean Stage". *The Norton Shakespeare*. Gen. ed. Stephen Greenblatt. New York: Norton. 3281–3301.
Guttzeit, Gero. 2017. *The Figures of Edgar Allan Poe. Authorship, Antebellum Literature, and Transatlantic Rhetoric*. Berlin and Boston: De Gruyter.
Hagstrum, Jean. 1958. *The Sister Arts. The Tradition of Literary Pictorialism and English Poetry from Dryden to Gray*. Chicago: University of Chicago Press.
Hammond, Adam. 2016. *Literature in the Digital Age. An Introduction*. New York: Cambridge University Press.
Hammond, Brean. 1997. *Professional Imaginative Writing in England, 1670–1740: 'Hackney for Bread'*. Oxford: Clarendon Press.
Hammond, Brean, and Shaun Regan. 2006. *Making the Novel. Fiction and Society in Britain, 1660–1789*. Houndmills: Palgrave Macmillan.
Happé, Peter. 1972. "Introduction". *Tudor Interludes*. Ed. Peter Happé. Harmondsworth: Penguin. 7–34.
Harari, Yuval Noah. 2015. *Sapiens. A Brief History of Humankind*. New York: Vintage.
Hayles, N. Katherine. 2002. *Writing Machines*. Cambridge, MA and London: MIT Press.
Haynes, Christine. 2005. "Reassessing 'Genius' in Studies of Authorship: The State of the Discipline". *Book History* 8: 287–320.
Heal, Felicity. 2014. *The Power of Gifts. Gift-Exchange in Early Modern England*. Oxford: Oxford University Press.
Heaney, Seamus. 2019. *Beowulf: A Verse Translation*. 2002. Ed. Daniel Donoghue. New York: Norton.
Heider, Fritz. 1926. "Ding und Medium." *Symposion* 1.2: 109–157.
Hellekson, Karen, and Kristina Busse, eds. 2014. *The Fan Fiction Studies Reader*. Iowa City, IA: University of Iowa Press.
Heyer, Paul, and Peter Urquart, eds. 2019. *Communication in History. Stone Age Symbols to Social Media*. London and New York: Routledge.

Hines, John. 1990. "The Runic Inscriptions of Early Anglo-Saxon England". *Britain 400–600: Language and History*. Ed. Alfred Bammesberger and Alfred Wollmann. Heidelberg: Winter. 437–455.
Hoban, Russell. 2021. *The Medusa Frequency*. 1987. London: Penguin.
Hoggart, Richard. 1963. *The Uses of Literacy: Aspects of Working Class Life with Special Reference to Publications and Entertainments*. 1957. Harmondsworth: Penguin.
Hollander, John. 1961. *The Untuning of the Sky. Ideas of Music in English Poetry 1500–1700*. Princeton, NJ: Princeton University Press.
Holmesland, Oddvar. 1985. *A Critical Introduction to Henry Green's Novels: The Living Vision*. London: Macmillan.
Houston, Natalie M. 2016. "Reading the Visual Page in the Digital Archive". *Research Methods for Reading Digital Data in the Digital Humanities*. Ed. Gabriele Griffin and Matt Hayler. Edinburgh: Edinburgh University Press. 36–50.
Howe, Nicholas. 2002. "The Cultural Construction of Reading in Anglo-Saxon England." *Old English Literature: Critical Essays*. Ed. R. M. Liuzza. New Haven, CT and London: Yale University Press. 1–22.
Hühn, Peter. 1995. *Geschichte der englischen Lyrik. Band I: Vom 16. Jahrhundert bis zur Romantik*. Tübingen and Basel: Francke.
Humble, Nicola. 2001. *The Feminine Middlebrow Novel, 1920s to 1950s. Class, Domesticity, and Bohemianism*. Oxford: Oxford University Press.
Hunter, G. K. 1997. *English Drama 1586–1642. The Age of Shakespeare*. Oxford: Clarendon Press.
Huyssen, Andreas. 1986. *After the Great Divide. Modernism, Mass Culture, Postmodernism*. Bloomington and Indianapolis, IN: Indiana University Press.
Ingrassia, Catherine. 2004. "Introduction". Eliza Haywood, *Anti-Pamela; or, Feign'd Innocence Detected*; Henry Fielding, *An Apology for the Life of Mrs. Shamela Andrews*. Ed. Catherine Ingrassia. Peterborough, Ontario: Broadview Press. 7–43.
Innis, Harold. 2007. *Empire and Communications*. 1950. Toronto: Dundurn Press.
Iser, Wolfgang. 1966. "Image und Montage. Zur Bildkonzeption in der imagistischen Lyrik und in T. S. Eliots *Waste Land*". *Immanente Ästhetik, ästhetische Reflexion. Lyrik als Paradigma der Moderne*. Ed. Wolfgang Iser. Munich: Fink. 361–393.
Iser, Wolfgang. 1978. *The Act of Reading. A Theory of Aesthetic Response*. 1976. London: Routledge and Kegan Paul.
Isherwood, Christopher. 1999. *The Berlin Novels*. London: Vintage.
Jack, George. 1994. "Introduction". *Beowulf. A Student Edition*. Oxford: Clarendon Press. 1–26.
Jahraus, Oliver. 2003. *Literatur als Medium. Sinnkonstitution und Subjekterfahrung zwischen Bewußtsein und Kommunikation*. Weilerswist: Velbrück.
James, Henry. 1986. "The Art of Fiction". 1884. *The Art of Criticism: Henry James on the Theory and the Practice of Fiction*. Ed. William Veeder and Susan M. Griffin. Chicago, IL and London: University of Chicago Press. 165–183.
James, Henry. 1987. *The Golden Bowl*. 1904. London: Penguin.
Jay, Martin. 1993. *Downcast Eyes. The Denigration of Vision in Twentieth-Century French Thought*. Berkeley, Los Angeles, and London: University of California Press.
Jenkins, Henry. 2006. *Convergence Culture. Where Old and New Media Collide*. New York and London: New York University Press.

Johnson, B. S. 1977. "Introduction to *Aren't You Rather Young to be Writing Your Memoirs?*" 1973. *The Novel Today: Contemporary Writers on Modern Fiction*. Ed. Malcolm Bradbury. Manchester: Manchester University Press. 151–168.

Johnson, Samuel. 1755. *A Dictionary of the English Language*. 2 vols. London: Strahan.

Johnson, Samuel. 2014. From *The Adventurer* no. 115, Tuesday, December 11, 1753 [The Age of Authors]. *The Age of Authors. An Anthology of Eighteenth-Century Print Culture*. Ed. Paul Keen. Peterborough, Ontario: Broadview Press. 209–212.

Johnson, Samuel. 2016. *The Life of Mr Richard Savage*. Ed. Nicholas Seager and Lance Wilcox. Peterborough, Ontario: Broadview Press.

Johnson, Samuel. 2020. *Samuel Johnson*. Ed. David Womersley. 2018. Oxford: Oxford University Press.

Jones, Susan. 2013. *Literature, Modernism, and Dance*. Oxford: Oxford University Press.

Kaiser, Jo Ellen Green. 2007. "Disciplining *The Waste Land*, or How to Lead Critics into Temptation". *T. S. Eliot's* The Waste Land. Ed. Harold Bloom. New York: Chelsea House. 235–252.

Keats, John. 1988. *The Complete Poems*. Ed. John Barnard. 3rd ed. London: Penguin.

Keen, Suzanne. 2015. *Narrative Form. Revised and Expanded Second Edition*. Houndmills: Palgrave Macmillan.

Kern, Stephen. 2019. "Wireless World". *Communication in History. Stone Age Symbols to Social Media*. Ed. Paul Heyer and Peter Urquhart. London/New York: Routledge. 145–148.

Kesson, Andy, and Emma Smith, eds. 2013. *The Elizabethan Top Ten. Defining Print Popularity in Early Modern England*. New York and London: Routledge.

Keymer, Thomas, and Peter Sabor, eds. 2001. *The Pamela Controversy: Criticisms and Adaptations of Samuel Richardson's* Pamela, *1740–1750*. 6 vols. London: Pickering and Chatto.

Keymer, Thomas, and Peter Sabor. 2005. *Pamela in the Marketplace. Literary Controversy and Print Culture in Eighteenth-Century Britain and Ireland*. Cambridge: Cambridge University Press.

Kiernan, Kevin, ed. 2015. *Electronic Beowulf 4.0*. https://ebeowulf.uky.edu/ Date of access: 6 August 2020.

Kipling, Rudyard. 1965. *Rudyard Kipling to Rider Haggard. The Record of a Friendship*. Ed. Morton Cohen. London: Hutchinson.

Kipling, Rudyard. 1994a. "'Wireless'". 1902. *Collected Stories*. New York: Knopf. 553–573.

Kipling, Rudyard. 1994b. "Mrs. Bathurst". 1904. *Collected Stories*. New York: Knopf. 577–597.

Kipling, Rudyard. 1994c. "With the Night Mail. A Story of 2000 A.D." 1905. *Collected Stories*. New York: Knopf. 649–676.

Kipling, Rudyard. 2015. *Stories and Poems*. Ed. Daniel Karlin. Oxford: Oxford University Press.

Kirk, Elizabeth D., and Judith H. Anderson, eds. 1990. *Piers Plowman: An Alliterative Verse Translation by E. Talbot Donaldson*. New York: Norton.

Kirschenbaum, Matthew G. 2016. *Track Changes. A Literary History of Word Processing*. Cambridge, MA: The Belknap Press of Harvard University Press.

Kittler, Friedrich A. 1997. "Dracula's Legacy". 1982. Trans. William Stephen Davis. *Literature, Media, Information Systems: Essays*. Ed. John Johnston. Amsterdam: OPA. 50–84.

Kittler, Friedrich A. 1999. *Gramophone Film Typewriter*. Trans Geoffrey Winthrop-Young and Michael Wutz. Stanford: Stanford University Press.

Klinck, Anne L. 1992. *The Old English Elegies. A Critical Edition and Genre Study*. Montreal: McGill-Queen's University Press.

Korte, Barbara, and Ralf Schneider. 2000. "The Published Screenplay – A New *Literary* Genre?" *AAA – Arbeiten aus Anglistik und Amerikanistik* 25.1: 89–105.
Kroll, Natasha. "Designing a Room for Television". *Radio Times*. 8 March 1957. 57.
Kurlansky, Mark. 2016. *Paper: Paging through History*. New York: Norton.
Lakoff, George, and Mark Johnson. 1980. *Metaphors We Live By*. Chicago, IL: University of Chicago Press.
Lamarque, Peter. 2009. *The Philosophy of Literature*. Malden, MA and Oxford: Blackwell.
Langland, William. 2006. *Piers Plowman*. Ed. Elizabeth Robertson and Stephen H. A. Shepherd. New York and London: Norton.
Lapidge, Michael. 2019. "*Beowulf* and Perception". 2001. *Beowulf: A Verse Translation*. Trans. Seamus Heaney. Ed. Daniel Donoghue. New York: Norton. 242–268.
Latham, Sean. 2019. "Industrialized Print: Modernism and Authorship". *The Cambridge Handbook of Literary Authorship*. Ed. Ingo Berensmeyer, Gert Buelens, and Marysa Demoor. Cambridge: Cambridge University Press. 165–182.
Leavis, F. R. 1930. *Mass Civilisation and Minority Culture*. Cambridge: The Minority Press.
Leavis, F. R. 1962. *Two Cultures? The Significance of C. P. Snow*. London: Chatto & Windus.
Leavis, Q. D. 1979. *Fiction and the Reading Public*. 1932. Harmondsworth: Penguin.
Le Goff, Jacques. 1980. *Time, Work, and Culture in the Middle Ages*. Trans. Arthur Goldhammer. Chicago, IL and London: University of Chicago Press.
Lehmann, Hans-Thies. 2006. *Postdramatic Theatre*. Trans. Karen Jürs-Munby. London: Routledge.
Leighton, Angela. 2017. "Incarnations in the Ear: On Poetry and Presence". *Poetic Revelations. Word Made Flesh Made Word*. Ed. Mark S. Burrows, Jean Ward, and Małgorzata Grzegorzewska. London and New York: Routledge. 149–163.
Lerer, Seth. 1991. *Literacy and Power in Anglo-Saxon Literature*. Lincoln, NE: University of Nebraska Press.
Leroi-Gourhan, André. 1993. *Gesture and Speech*. 1964. Trans. Anna Bostock Berger. Cambridge, MA and London: MIT Press.
Lesser, Zachary, ed. 2019. *The Book in Britain. A Historical Introduction*. Hoboken, NJ and Chichester: Wiley Blackwell.
Levin, Harry. 1952. *The Overreacher. A Study of Christopher Marlowe*. Cambridge, MA and London: Harvard University Press.
Levine, Caroline. 2015. *Forms: Whole, Rhythm, Hierarchy, Network*. Princeton: Princeton University Press.
Lichtenberg, Georg Christoph. 1994. *Schriften und Briefe*. 4 vols. Ed. Wolfgang Promies. Frankfurt am Main: Zweitausendeins.
Lodge, David. 1992. *The Art of Fiction. Illustrated from Classic and Modern Texts*. Harmondsworth: Penguin.
Löschnigg, Maria, and Rebekka Schuh, eds. 2018. *The Epistolary Renaissance. A Critical Approach to Contemporary Letter Narratives in Anglophone Fiction*. Berlin and Boston: De Gruyter.
Love, Harold. 1993. *Scribal Publication in Seventeenth-Century England*. Oxford: Clarendon Press.
Love, Harold. 2001. "Roger L'Estrange's Criticism of Dryden's Elocution". *Notes and Queries* 48.4: 398–400.
Love, Harold. 2003. "Vocal Register in Behn's *Love-Letters Between a Nobleman and His Sister*". *ELN: English Language Notes* 41.1: 44–53

Luckhurst, Roger. 2002. *The Invention of Telepathy. 1870–1901*. Oxford: Oxford University Press.
Luhmann, Niklas. 1987. *Archimedes und wir. Interviews*. Ed. Dirk Baecker and Georg Stanitzek. Berlin: Merve.
Luhmann, Niklas. 2000a. *Art as a Social System*. Trans. Eva M. Knodt. Stanford, CA: Stanford University Press.
Luhmann, Niklas. 2000b. *The Reality of the Mass Media*. Trans. Kathleen Cross. Stanford, CA: Stanford University Press.
Lukács, Georg. 2000. "From *The Theory of the Novel*". *Theory of the Novel: A Historical Approach*. Ed. Michael McKeon. Baltimore, MD and London: Johns Hopkins University Press. 185–264.
Lupton, Christina. 2012. *Knowing Books. The Consciousness of Mediation in Eighteenth-Century Britain*. Philadelphia, PA: University of Pennsylvania Press.
Lycett, Andrew. 1999. *Rudyard Kipling*. London: Weidenfeld and Nicolson.
MacCarthy, Fiona. 1989. *Eric Gill*. London: Faber and Faber.
Macdonald, Kate, ed. 2011. *The Masculine Middlebrow, 1880–1950: What Mr. Miniver Read*. Basingstoke: Palgrave Macmillan.
Machen, Arthur. 2019. *The Great God Pan and Other Horror Stories*. Ed. Aaron Worth. Oxford: Oxford University Press.
Malay, Michael. 2018. *The Figure of the Animal in Modern and Contemporary Poetry*. Basingstoke: Palgrave Macmillan.
Manovich, Lev. 2001. *The Language of New Media*. Cambridge, MA and London: MIT Press.
Marczek-Fuchs, Maria. 2015. *Dance and British Literature: An Intermedial Encounter (Theory – Typology – Case Studies)*. Leiden and Boston: Brill Rodopi.
Marino, James J. 2013. *Owning William Shakespeare. The King's Men and their Intellectual Property*. Philadelphia, PA: University of Pennsylvania Press.
Marlowe, Christopher. 1999. *The Complete Plays*. Ed. Mark Thornton Burnett. London: Dent; Vermont: Tuttle.
Marotti, Arthur F. 1990. "Shakespeare's Sonnets as Literary Property". *Soliciting Interpretation. Literary Theory and Seventeenth-Century English Poetry*. Ed. Elizabeth D. Harvey and Katherine Eisaman Maus. Chicago and London: University of Chicago Press. 143–173.
Marotti, Arthur F. 1995. *Manuscript, Print, and the English Renaissance Lyric*. Ithaca, NY and London: Cornell University Press.
Martin, Robert Bernard. 1980. *Tennyson. The Unquiet Heart*. Oxford: Oxford University Press.
Marvin, Carolyn. 1988. *When Old Technologies Were New: Thinking about Electric Communication in the Late Nineteenth Century*. New York and Oxford: Oxford University Press.
May, Steven. 1980. "Tudor Aristocrats and the Mythical 'Stigma of Print'". *Renaissance Papers* 10: 11–18.
McCabe, Richard A. 2010. "Authorial Self-Presentation". *The Oxford Handbook of Edmund Spenser*. Oxford: Oxford University Press. 462–484.
McCloud, Scott. 1994. *Understanding Comics. The Invisible Art*. New York: William Morrow.
McDonald, Peter D. 1997. *British Literary Culture and Publishing Practice, 1880–1914*. Cambridge; Cambridge University Press.
McGill, Meredith L. 2016. "Literary History, Book History, and Media Studies". *Turns of Event: American Literary Studies in Motion*. Ed. Hester Blum. Philadelphia: University of Pennsylvania Press. 23–39.

McGurl, Mark. 2016. "Everything and Less: Fiction in the Age of Amazon". *Modern Language Quarterly* 77.3: 447–471.
McKenzie, D. F. 1999. "The Book as an Expressive Form". *Bibliography and the Sociology of Texts*. Cambridge: Cambridge University Press. 9–29.
McLuhan, Marshall. 1962. *The Gutenberg Galaxy*. Toronto: University of Toronto Press.
McLuhan, Marshall. 1994. *Understanding Media. The Extensions of Man*. (1964) Cambridge, MA and London: MIT Press.
McPherson, David. 1974. "Ben Jonson's Library and Marginalia: An Annotated Catalogue". *Studies in Philology* 71.5: 1, 3–106.
Meifert-Menhard, Felicitas. 2013. *Playing the Text, Performing the Future. Future Narratives in Print and Digiture*. Berlin and Boston: De Gruyter.
Mendelsund, Peter. 2014. *What We See When We Read. A Phenomenology with Illustrations*. New York: Vintage.
Menke, Richard. 2019. *Literature, Print Culture, and Media Technologies, 1880–1900. Many Inventions*. Cambridge: Cambridge University Press.
Mienert, Melanie, Keiderling, Thomas, Welz, Stephan, and Dietmar Böhnke. 2017. *Baron der englischen Bücher. Der Leipziger Verlag Bernhard Tauchnitz 1837–1973*. Beucha/Markkleeberg: Sax-Verlag.
Mill, John Stuart. 1859. "Thoughts on Poetry and its Varieties". (1833) *Discussions Political, Philosophical, and Historical*. 2 vols. London: John W. Parker and Son. Vol. 1. 63–94.
Miller, Ashley. 2018. *Poetry, Media, and the Material Body. Autopoetics in Nineteenth-Century Britain*. Cambridge: Cambridge University Press.
Miller, J. Hillis. 1992. *Illustration*. Cambridge, MA: Harvard University Press; London: Reaktion.
Miller, J. Hillis. 2009. *The Medium is the Maker. Browning, Freud, Derrida and the New Telepathic Ecotechnologies*. Brighton and Portland: Sussex Academic Press.
Miller, Mark. 2009. "Subjectivity and Ideology in the *Canterbury Tales*". *A Companion to Medieval English Literature and Culture*, Ed. Peter Brown. Malden, MA and Oxford: Blackwell. 554–568.
Milton, John. 1953. *Complete Prose Works of John Milton*. Vol. 2. 1643–1648. Ed. Don M. Wolfe. New Haven, CT: Yale University Press.
Milton, John. 1998. *Paradise Lost*. Ed. Alastair Fowler. 2nd ed. London: Longman.
Misson, [François-Maximilien]. 1719. *M. Misson's Memoirs and Observations in his Travels over England. With Some Account of Scotland and Ireland [. . .]*. Translated by Mr. Ozell. London: Printed for D. Browne [. . .].
Moeller, Hans-Georg. 2006. *Luhmann Explained. From Souls to Systems*. Chicago and La Salle, IL: Open Court.
Mole, Tom. 2017. *What the Victorians Made of Romanticism. Material Artifacts, Cultural Practices, and Reception History*. Princeton: Princeton University Press.
Montfort, Nick. 2005. *Twisty Little Passages. An Approach to Interactive Fiction*. Cambridge, MA and London: MIT Press.
Moretti, Franco. 2000. *The Way of the World. The* Bildungsroman *in European Culture*. Trans. Albert Sbragia. 1987. London and New York: Verso.
Moretti, Franco. 2013. *Distant Reading*. London and New York: Verso.
Morton, Timothy. 2007. *Ecology without Nature: Rethinking Environmental Aesthetics*. Cambridge, MA: Harvard University Press.
Moshenska, Joe. 2014. *Feeling Pleasures. The Sense of Touch in Renaissance England*. Oxford: Oxford University Press.

Mosse, Ramona. 2014. "Hamlet als Metakommentar des Theaters". *Hamlet-Handbuch. Stoffe, Aneignungen, Deutungen*. Ed. Peter W. Marx. Stuttgart and Weimar: Metzler. 107–114.

Mulholland, James. 2008. "Gray's Ambition: Printed Voices and Performing Bards in the Later Poetry". *English Literary History* 75.1: 109–134.

Mullaney, Steven. 1988. *The Place of the Stage. License, Play and Power in Renaissance England*. Chicago and London: University of Chicago Press.

Mullaney, Steven. 2005. "Shakespeare and the Liberties". *Encyclopaedia Britannica*. https://www.britannica.com/topic/Shakespeare-and-the-Liberties-1086252. Date of access: 30 June 2020.

Murdoch, Iris. 2004. *The Bell*. 1958. London: Vintage.

Murphy, Peter. 2019. *The Long Public Life of a Short Private Poem. Reading and Remembering Thomas Wyatt*. Stanford, CA: Stanford University Press.

Murray, Les. 2014. *New Selected Poems*. New York: Farrar, Straus and Giroux.

Murray, Simone. 2020. *Introduction to Contemporary Print Culture: Books as Media*. London and New York: Routledge.

Myers, F. W. H. 1967. "Tennyson as Prophet". 1889. *Tennyson: The Critical Heritage*. Ed. John D. Jump. London: Routledge. 395–413.

Myers, Robin, ed. 2001. *The Stationers' Company: A History of the Later Years, 1800–2000*. London: Worshipful Company of Stationers and Newspaper Makers.

Nagel, Thomas. 1979. *Mortal Questions*. Cambridge: Cambridge University Press.

Nash, Andrew. 2016a. "The Material History of the Novel I: 1940–1973". *British and Irish Fiction Since 1940*. Ed. Peter Boxall and Bryan Cheyette. The Oxford History of the Novel in English, vol. 7. Oxford: Oxford University Press. 21–36.

Nash, Andrew. 2016b. "The Material History of the Novel II: 1973–Present". *British and Irish Fiction Since 1940*. Ed. Peter Boxall and Bryan Cheyette. The Oxford History of the Novel in English, vol. 7. Oxford: Oxford University Press. 401–416.

Niles, John D. 2016. *Old English Literature: A Guide to Criticism with Selected Readings*. Malden, MA and Oxford: Wiley-Blackwell.

Nissley, Tom. 2014. *A Reader's Book of Days. True Tales from the Lives and Works of Writers for Every Day of the Year*. New York and London: Norton.

Norrick-Rühl, Corinna. 2019. *Book Clubs and Book Commerce*. Cambridge: Cambridge University Press.

North, Richard. 2006. *The Origins of Beowulf. From Vergil to Wiglaf*. Oxford: Oxford University Press.

Nünning, Ansgar. 1992. "Mimesis und Poiesis im englischen Roman des 18. Jahrhunderts: Überlegungen zum Zusammenhang zwischen narrativer Form und Wirklichkeitserfahrung". *Neue Lesarten, Neue Wirklichkeiten. Zur Wiederentdeckung des 18. Jahrhunderts durch die Anglistik*. Ed. Gerd Stratmann and Manfred Buschmeier. Trier: WVT. 46–69.

Ong, Walter J. 2002. *Orality and Literacy. The Technologizing of the Word*. 1982. 2nd ed. New York and London: Routledge.

Orage, A. R. 1924. "Talks with Katherine Mansfield". *Century Magazine*, November. 36–40.

Orchard, Andy. 2003. *A Critical Companion to* Beowulf. Cambridge: D. S. Brewer.

Ortolano, Guy. 2009. *The Two Cultures Controversy. Science, Literature and Cultural Politics in Postwar Britain*. Cambridge: Cambridge University Press.

Orwell, George. 2012. *Essays*. Ed. John Carey and Peter Davison. New York: Knopf.

Orwell, George. 2013. *Nineteen Eighty-Four. The Annotated Edition*. 1949. Ed. D. J. Taylor. London: Penguin.
Osborn, Marijane. 2019. "The Great Feud: Scriptural History and Strife in *Beowulf*". 1978. *Beowulf: A Verse Translation*. Trans. Seamus Heaney. Ed. Daniel Donoghue. New York: Norton. 139–153.
Oswald, John. 1787. "The Brain-Sucker, or the Distress of Authorship". *The British Mercury* 1–2:14–27, 43–48.
Owen, Alex. 1989. *The Darkened Room. Women, Power, and Spiritualism in Late Nineteenth Century England*. London: Virago.
Parker, Patricia. 1985. "Introduction". *Lyric Poetry: Beyond New Criticism*. Ed. Chaviva Hošek and Patricia Parker. Ithaca, NY and London: Cornell University Press. 11–28.
Parnell, Tim. 2003. "Explanatory Notes". Laurence Sterne, *A Sentimental Journey and Other Writings*. Ed. Ian Jack and Tim Parnell. Oxford: Oxford University Press. 223–262.
Parsons, Talcott. 1977. "Social Structure and the Symbolic Media of Interchange". 1975. *Social Systems and the Evolution of Action Theory*. New York: Free Press. 204–228.
Pearsall, Derek. 1997. "Courtesy and Chivalry in *Sir Gawain and the Green Knight*: the Order of Shame and the Invention of Embarrassment". *A Companion to the* Gawain-*Poet*. Ed. Derek Brewer and Jonathan Gibson. Cambridge: D. S. Brewer. 351–362.
Pearsall, Derek, ed. 1999. *Chaucer to Spenser. An Anthology*. Malden, MA and Oxford: Blackwell.
Perelli, Patricia. 1983. "Statistical Survey of the British Film Industry". *British Cinema History*. Ed. James Curran and Vincent Porter. London: Weidenfeld and Nicolson. 372–382.
Pfeiffer, K. Ludwig. 2002. *The Protoliterary. Steps Toward an Anthropology of Culture*. Stanford, CA: Stanford University Press.
Picker, John M. 2001. "The Victorian Aura of the Recorded Voice". *New Literary History* 32.3: 769–786.
Plat, Julien. 2016. "Fiction(s) de genèse, l'exemple de *Molloy* de Samuel Beckett". 2012. *La Réserve*, 9 Jan. http://ouvroir-litt-arts.univ-grenoble-alpes.fr/revues/reserve/313-fiction-s-de-genese-l-exemple-de-molloy-de-samuel-beckett. Date of access: 13 Dec. 2021.
Plumb, J. H. 1982. "The Commercialization of Leisure in Eighteenth-Century England". *The Birth of a Consumer Society: The Commercialization of Eighteenth-Century England*. Ed. Neil McKendrick, John Brewer, and J. H. Plumb. Bloomington, IN: Indiana University Press. 265–286.
Pope, Alexander. 2006. *The Major Works*. Ed. Pat Rogers. Oxford: Oxford University Press.
Poplawski, Paul, ed. 2008. *English Literature in Context*. Cambridge: Cambridge University Press.
Postman, Neil. 1974. *Media Ecology: Communication as Context*. New York: Speech Communication Association.
Pound, Ezra. 1913. "In a Station of the Metro". *Poetry* 2.1 (April): 12.
Pound, Ezra. 1935. *Make It New*. New Haven, CT: Yale University Press.
Pound, Ezra. 1960. *ABC of Reading*. 1934. New York: New Directions.
Pound, Ezra. 1968. "A Retrospect". 1918. *Literary Essays of Ezra Pound*. Ed. T. S. Eliot. New York: New Directions. 3–14.
Pound, Ezra. 1980. *Ezra Pound and the Visual Arts*. Ed. Harriet Zinnes. New York: New Directions.
Pound, Ezra. 2010. *New Selected Poems and Translations*. Ed. Richard Sieburth. New York: New Directions.

Priestley, J. B. 1969. "Televiewing". 1957. *Essays of Five Decades*. London: Heinemann. 232–236.
Puchner, Martin. 2017. *The Written World. How Literature Shaped History*. London: Granta.
Rainey, Lawrence. 2009. "Pretty Typewriters, Melodramatic Modernity: Edna, Belle, Estelle". *Modernism/modernity* 16.1: 105–122.
Raven, James. 2018. *What is the History of the Book?* Cambridge and Medford, MA: Polity Press.
Reinfandt, Christoph. 2009. "Literatur als Medium". *Grenzen der Literatur. Zu Begriff und Phänomen des Literarischen*. Ed. Simone Winko, Fotis Jannidis, and Gerhard Lauer. Berlin and New York: de Gruyter. 161–187.
Rettberg, Scott. 2019. *Electronic Literature*. Cambridge and Medford, MA: Polity Press.
Rhys, Ernest. 1932. "Introduction". *The Reader's Guide to Everyman's Library. Being a Catalogue of the First 888 Volumes*. By R. Farquarson Sharp. London and Toronto: J. M. Dent & Sons; New York: E. P. Dutton. ix–lxiv.
Richardson, Dorothy. 1979. *Pilgrimage*. Vol. 3. *Deadlock* [1921]. *Revolving Lights* [1923]. *The Trap* [1925]. London: Virago.
Richardson, Samuel. 1964. *Selected Letters of Samuel Richardson*. Ed. John Carroll. Oxford: Clarendon Press.
Ricoeur, Paul. 1984. *Time and Narrative. Volume I*. Trans. Kathleen McLaughlin and David Pellauer. Chicago, IL and London: University of Chicago Press.
Rippl, Gabriele, ed. 2015. *Handbook of Intermediality. Literature – Image – Sound – Music*. Berlin and Boston: De Gruyter.
Rives, Rochelle. 2012. *Modernist Impersonalities. Affect, Authority, and the Subject*. Basingstoke: Palgrave Macmillan.
Roberts, Ivy. 2017. "'Edison's Telephonoscope': The Visual Telephone and the Satire of Electric Light Mania". *Early Popular Visual Culture* 15.1: 1–25.
Roberts, Lewis. 2006. "Trafficking in Literary Authority: Mudie's Select Library and the Commodification of the Victorian Novel". *Victorian Literature and Culture* 34.1: 1–25.
Ronell, Avital. 1989. *The Telephone Book. Technology, Schizophrenia, Electric Speech*. Lincoln, NE and London: University of Nebraska Press.
Rowson, Martin. 2012. *The Waste Land*. 1990. London, New York, and Calcutta: Seagull Books.
Rubery, Matthew. 2016. *The Untold Story of the Talking Book*. Cambridge, MA and London: Harvard University Press.
Rubery, Matthew, ed. 2011. *Audiobooks, Literature, and Sound Studies*. London and New York: Routledge.
Rushdie, Salman. 2010. *Imaginary Homelands. Essay and Criticism 1981–1991*. 1991. New York: Vintage.
Ruskin, John. 2004. "Cambridge School of Art: Inaugural Address". 1858. *Selected Writings*. Ed. Dinah Birch. Oxford: Oxford University Press. 93–104.
Saenger, Paul. 1997. *Space Between Words. The Origins of Silent Reading*. Stanford: Stanford University Press.
Sale, William D. 1950. *Samuel Richardson: Master Printer*. Ithaca, NY and London: Cornell University Press.
Salmon, Richard. 2013. *The Formation of the Victorian Literary Profession*. Cambridge: Cambridge University Press.
Salzman, Paul, ed. 1998. *An Anthology of Elizabethan Prose Fiction*. (1987) Oxford: Oxford University Press.

Sanders, Andrew. 2004. *The Short Oxford History of English Literature*. 3rd ed. Oxford: Oxford University Press.
Sargant, William. 1957. *Battle for the Mind. A Physiology of Conversion and Brain-Washing*. Melbourne/London/Toronto: Heinemann.
Saunders, J. W. 1951. "The Stigma of Print: A Note on the Social Bases of Tudor Poetry". *Essays in Criticism* 1: 139–164.
Saussy, Haun. 2008. "Fenollosa Compounded: A Discrimination". *The Chinese Written Character as a Medium for Poetry*. By Ernest Fenollosa and Ezra Pound. A Critical Edition. Ed. Haun Saussy, Jonathan Stalling, and Lucas Klein. New York: Fordham University Press. 1–40.
Schaeffer, John D., and David Gorman. 2009. "Ong and Derrida on Presence: A Case Study in the Conflict of Traditions". *Academic Writing, Philosophy and Genre*. Ed. Michael A. Peters. Malden, MA and Oxford: Wiley-Blackwell. 38–54.
Schellenberg, Betty A. 2019. "The Eighteenth Century: Print, Professionalization, and Defining the Author". *The Cambridge Handbook of Literary Authorship*. Ed. Ingo Berensmeyer, Gert Buelens, and Marysa Demoor. Cambridge: Cambridge University Press. 133–146.
Schwanitz, Dietrich. 1990. *Systemtheorie und Literatur: Ein neues Paradigma*. Opladen: Westdeutscher Verlag.
Scott, Allison V. 2006. *Selfish Gifts. The Politics of Exchange and English Courtly Literature, 1580–1628*. Madison and Teaneck, NJ: Fairleigh Dickinson University Press.
Scott-Warren, Jason. 2005. *Early Modern English Literature*. Cambridge / Malden, MA: Polity.
Scragg, Donald. 2012. "Old English Homiliaries and Poetic Manuscripts". *The Cambridge History of the Book in Britain. Vol. 1: c. 400–1100*. Ed. Richard Gameson. Cambridge: Cambridge University Press. 553–562.
Sellars, Simon. 2009. "Stereoscopic Urbanism: J. G. Ballard and the Built Environment". *Architectural Design* 79.5: 88–81.
Sennett, Richard. 2002. *The Fall of Public Man*. 1977. London: Penguin.
Shail, Andrew. 2012. *The Cinema and the Origins of Literary Modernism*. New York and London: Routledge.
Shakespeare, William. 1997. *The Norton Shakespeare*. Gen. ed. Stephen Greenblatt. New York: Norton.
Sharp, Michele Turner. 2002. "Elegy unto Epitaph: Print Culture and Commemorative Practice in Gray's "Elegy Written in a Country Churchyard'". *Papers on Language and Literature* 38.1: 3–28,
Shelley, Percy Bysshe. 2006a. "A Defence of Poetry" [Extracts]. (1821). *Romanticism: An Anthology*. Ed. Duncan Wu. 3rd ed. Malden, MA and Oxford: Blackwell. 1184–1199.
Shelley, Percy Bysshe. 2006b. "Ode to the West Wind". (1820). *Romanticism: An Anthology*. Ed. Duncan Wu. 3rd ed. Malden, MA and Oxford: Blackwell. 1175–1177.
Shillingsburg, Peter. 2010. "Three- or Triple-Decker". *The Oxford Companion to the Book*. Ed. Michael F. Suarez and H. F. Woudhuysen. Vol. 2. Oxford: Oxford University Press.
Sidney, Sir Philip. 2002. *The Major Works*. Ed. Katherine Duncan-Jones. Oxford: Oxford University Press.
Siemens, Ray et al. 2014. *A Social Edition of the Devonshire Manuscript (BL Add 17,492)*. https://en.wikibooks.org/wiki/The_Devonshire_Manuscript. Date of access: 16 February 2017.
Silent Shakespeare. N. d. DVD. 88 mins. London: BFI.

Simons, Olaf. 2009. *Statistic of Titles in the English Short Title Catalogue Categorised as 'Fiction', 1600–1799*. https://commons.wikimedia.org/wiki/File:1600-1799-estc-fiction.png. Date of access: 18 Aug. 2021.

Simons, Olaf. 2010. *London's Book Market 1700*. https://commons.wikimedia.org/wiki/File:1700_London%27s_Book_Market_according_to_Term_Catalogues.png. Date of access: 18 Aug. 2021.

Sinfield, Alan. 1986. *Alfred Tennyson*. Oxford: Blackwell.

Siskin, Clifford. 1998. *The Work of Writing: Literature and Social Change in Britain, 1700–1830*. Baltimore, MD: Johns Hopkins University Press.

Skinner, John. 2001. *An Introduction to Eighteenth-Century Fiction. Raising the Novel*. Houndmills and New York: Palgrave.

Smith, Barbara Herrnstein. 1978. *On the Margins of Discourse*. Chicago, IL: University of Chicago Press.

Solopova, Elizabeth, and Stuart D. Lee. 2007. *Key Concepts in Medieval Literature*. Houndmills: Palgrave Macmillan.

Spearing, A. C. 2015. *Medieval Autographies. The 'I' of the Text*. Notre Dame, IN: University of Notre Dame Press.

Spilka, Mark. 1973. "Henry James and Walter Besant: The 'Art of Fiction' Controversy". *Novel: A Forum on Fiction* 6.2: 101–119.

Standage, Tom. 2019. "Social Media Retweets History". *Communication in History. Stone Age Symbols to Social Media*. Ed. Paul Heyer and Peter Urquhart. London/New York: Routledge. 317–322.

Starre, Alexander. 2015. *Metamedia. American Book Fictions and Literary Print Culture after Digitization*. Iowa City: University of Iowa Press.

Stein, Jordan Alexander. 2020. *When Novels Were Books*. Cambridge, MA and London: Harvard University Press.

Stern, Tiffany. 2009. *Documents of Performance in Early Modern England*. Cambridge: Cambridge University Press.

Sterne, Jonathan. 2019. "The Making of the Phonograph". *Communication in History. Stone Age Symbols to Social Media*. Ed. Paul Heyer and Peter Urquhart. London and New York: Routledge. 169–173.

Sterne, Laurence. 1985. *The Life and Opinions of Tristram Shandy Gentleman*. Ed. Graham Petrie. Harmondsworth: Penguin.

Sterne, Laurence. 1986. *A Sentimental Journey through France and Italy*. Ed. Graham Petrie. Harmondsworth: Penguin.

Sterry, Emma. 2017. *The Single Woman, Modernity, and Literary Culture. Women's Fiction from the 1920s to the 1940s*. Basingstoke: Palgrave Macmillan.

Stevenson, Robert Louis. 1979. *The Strange Case of Dr Jekyll and Mr Hyde and Other Stories*. Ed. Jenni Calder. Harmondsworth: Penguin.

Stirling, Christopher, and John M. Kitross. "The Golden Age of Programming". *Communication in History. Stone Age Symbols to Social Media*. Ed. Paul Heyer and Peter Urquhart. London and New York: Routledge. 211–217.

Stock, Brian. 1983. *The Implications of Literacy. Written Language and Models of Interpretation in the Eleventh and Twelfth Centuries*. Princeton, NJ: Princeton University Press.

Suerbaum, Almut, and Manuele Gragnolati. 2010. "Medieval Culture 'betwixt and between': An Introduction". *Aspects of the Performative in Medieval Culture*. Ed. Manuele Gragnolati and Almut Suerbaum. Berlin and New York: De Gruyter. 1–13.

Sutherland, John. 2006. *Victorian Fiction: Writers, Publishers, Readers*. 2nd ed. Houndmills: Palgrave Macmillan.
Swift, Jonathan. 1986. *Gulliver's Travels*. Ed. Paul Turner. Oxford: Oxford University Press.
Swift, Jonathan. 2008. *A Tale of a Tub and Other Writings*. Ed. Angus Ross and David Woolley. 1986. Oxford: Oxford University Press.
Symes, Colin. 2005. "From *Tomorrow's Eve* to *High Fidelity*: Novel Responses to the Gramophone in Twentieth Century Literature". *Popular Music* 24.2: 193–206.
Tally, Robert T. 2014. *Poe and the Subversion of American Literature: Satire, Fantasy, Critique*. New York: Bloomsbury Academic.
Taylor, D. J. 2008. *Bright Young People. The Rise and Fall of a Generation 1918–1940*. 2007. London: Vintage.
Taylor, Gary et al. 2017. *The New Oxford Shakespeare: Critical Reference Edition*. Vol. 2. Oxford: Oxford University Press.
Tease, Amy Woodbury. 2016. "Call and Answer: Muriel Spark and Media Culture". *MFS: Modern Fiction Studies* 62.1: 70–91.
Tennyson, Alfred. 2014. *Tennyson. A Selected Edition*. Ed. Christopher Ricks. Rev. ed. London and New York: Routledge.
Tennyson, Hallam. 1897. *Alfred Lord Tennyson. A Memoir by his Son*. 2 vols. London: Macmillan.
Thomas, Bronwen. 2020. *Literature and Social Media*. New York and London: Routledge.
Thomas, Dylan. 1988. *Under Milk Wood. A Play for Voices*. 1954. London: Dent.
Thompson, John B. 2012. *Merchants of Culture. The Publishing Business in the Twenty-First Century*. 2nd ed. New York: Plume.
Thorn, Michael. 1992. *Tennyson*. London: Abacus.
Tolkien, J. R. R. 1936. *Beowulf: The Monsters and the Critics*. London: Humphrey Milford.
Tolkien, J. R. R. 1975. *Sir Gawain and the Green Knight. Pearl* and *Sir Orfeo*. Ed. Christopher Tolkien. London: George Allen & Unwin.
Travis, Alan. 2000. *Bound and Gagged. A Secret History of Obscenity in Britain*. London: Profile.
Treglown, Jeremy. 2000. *Romancing. The Life and Work of Henry Green*. London: Faber and Faber.
Treharne, Elaine, and Claude Willan. 2020. *Text Technologies. A History*. Stanford, CA: Stanford University Press.
Treharne, Elaine, ed. 2010. *Old and Middle English c. 890–1450. An Anthology*. 3rd ed. Malden, MA and Oxford: Wiley-Blackwell.
Tripp, Ronja. 2014 "Visualisierung und Narrativierung in Erzähltexten der Moderne (H. Green: *Blindness*)". *Handbuch Literatur & Visuelle Kultur*. Ed. Claudia Benthien, Brigitte Weingart. Berlin and New York: De Gruyter. 462–477.
Trollope, Anthony. 1995. "The Telegraph Girl". 1877. *Later Short Stories*. Ed. John Sutherland. Oxford: Oxford University Press. 354–385.
Trotter, David. 2007. *Cinema and Modernism*. Malden, MA and Oxford: Blackwell.
Trotter, David. 2013. *Literature in the First Media Age. Britain Between the Wars*. Cambridge, MA and London: Harvard University Press.
Trotter, David. 2017. "Literature Between Media". *The Cambridge History of Modernism*. Ed. Vincent Sherry. Cambridge: Cambridge University Press. 386–403.
Trotter, David. 2020. *The Literature of Connection. Signal, Medium, Interface, 1850–1950*. Oxford: Oxford University Press.

Tuppen, Sandra. "John Milton's Publishing Contract for *Paradise Lost*". 27 April 2017. https://blogs.bl.uk/english-and-drama/2017/04/john-miltons-publishing-contract-for-paradise-lost.html. Date of access: 13 Feb. 2020.
Turing, Alan. 1937. "On Computable Numbers, with an Application to the Entscheidungsproblem". *Proceedings of the London Mathematical Society*, 2nd series, 42.1: 230–265. https://www.cs.virginia.edu/~robins/Turing_Paper_1936.pdf. Date of access: 9 Mar. 2022.
Turner, Marion. 2019. *Chaucer: A European Life*. Princeton: Princeton University Press, 2019.
Turner, Mark. 1998. *The Literary Mind. The Origins of Thought and Language*. 1996. Oxford: Oxford University Press.
Twycross, Meg. 2008. "The Theatricality of Medieval English Plays". *The Cambridge Companion to Medieval English Theatre*. Ed. Richard Beadle and Alan J. Fletcher. Cambridge: Cambridge University Press. 26–74.
van der Weel, Adriaan. 2004. "*Scripta manent*: The Anxiety of Immortality". *Living in Posterity. Essays in Honour of Bart Westerweel*. Ed. Jan Frans van Dijkhuizen et al. Hilversum: Uitgeverij Verloren. 321–332.
van Schlun, Betsy 2017. *The Pool Group and the Quest for Anthropological Universality. The Humane Images of Modernism*. Berlin and Boston: De Gruyter.
Vernon, John. 1979. *Poetry and the Body*. Urbana, Chicago, IL and London: University of Illinois Press.
von Contzen, Eva. 2018. "Narrative and Experience in Medieval Literature. Author, Narrator, and Character Revisited". *Narratologie und mittelalterliches Erzählen. Autor, Erzähler, Perspektive, Zeit und Raum*. Ed. Eva von Contzen and Florian Kragl. Berlin and Boston: De Gruyter. 61–80.
Wagner, Erica. 2017. "Literary Reviews: Past, Present, Future". *The Literary Market in the UK*. Ed. Amrei Katharina Nensel and Christoph Reinfandt. Tübingen: Eberhard Karls Universität Tübingen. 101–108.
Walker, Greg. 1998. *The Politics of Performance in Early Renaissance Drama*. Cambridge: Cambridge University Press.
Walker, Greg, ed. 2000. *Medieval Drama: An Anthology*. Oxford: Blackwell.
Waltz, Gwendolyn. 2006. "Filmed Scenery on the Live Stage". *Theatre Journal* 58.4: 547–573.
Warkentin, Germaine. 1980. "Sidney's *Certain Sonnets*: Speculations on the Evolution of the Text." *The Library* 6th ser. 2: 430–444.
Warner, William. 1998. *Licensing Entertainment. The Elevation of Novel Reading in Britain, 1684–1750*. Berkeley, Los Angeles, CA and London: University of California Press.
Watt, Diane. 2009. "John Gower". *The Cambridge Companion to Medieval English Literature 1100–1500*. Ed. Larry Scanlon. Cambridge: Cambridge University Press. 153–164.
Watt, Ian. 1957. *The Rise of the Novel. Studies in Defoe, Richardson and Fielding*. Berkeley and Los Angeles, CA: University of California Press.
Watt, Tessa. 1994. *Cheap Print and Popular Piety, 1550–1640*. Cambridge: Cambridge University Press.
Waugh, Evelyn. 2003. *Vile Bodies*. (1930) London: Penguin.
Waxenberger, Gaby. 2017. "The Development of the Old English Rune Row". *From Hieroglyphs to Netspeak: On the Relation of Script and Sound*. Ed. Gaby Waxenberger, Hans Sauer, and Kerstin Kazzazi. Wiesbaden: Reichert. 209–247.
Weimann, Robert. 2000. *Author's Pen and Actor's Voice*. Cambridge: Cambridge University Press.

Weinbrot, Howard D. 1978. "Gray's *Elegy*: A Poem of Moral Choice and Resolution". *Studies in English Literature* 18.3: 537–551.
Wellbery, David E. 1996. *The Specular Moment. Goethe's Early Lyric and the Beginnings of Romanticism*. Stanford, CA: Stanford University Press.
Wellek, René, and Austin Warren. 1956. *Theory of Literature*. 1949. 3rd ed. New York: Harvest.
Wershler-Henry, Darren. 2005. *The Iron Whim: A Fragmented History of Typewriting*. Ithaca and New York, NY: Cornell University Press.
Wexler, Joyce Piell. 1997. *Who Paid for Modernism? Art, Money, and the Fiction of Conrad, Joyce, and Lawrence*. Fayetteville, AR: University of Arkansas Press.
Williams, Paul. 2020. *Dreaming the Graphic Novel: The Novelization of Comics*. New Brunswick: Rutgers University Press.
Williams, Raymond. 1977. *Marxism and Literature*. Oxford: Oxford University Press.
Williams, Raymond. 1983. *Keywords. A Vocabulary of Culture and Society*. 1976. New York: Oxford University Press.
Williams, William Carlos. 1991. "Paterson". (1927) *The Collected Poems of William Carlos Williams*. Ed. A. Walton Litz and Christopher MacGowan. Vol. 1. 1909–1939. New York: New Directions. 263–266.
Wilson, Charles. 1985. *First with the News. The History of W. H. Smith 1792–1972*. London: Jonathan Cape.
WIPO. 2020. *The Global Publishing Industry in 2018*. Geneva: World Intellectual Property Organization. https://www.wipo.int/edocs/pubdocs/en/wipo_pub_1064_2019.pdf. Date of access: 14 Dec. 2021.
Wolf, Werner. 1999. *The Musicalization of Fiction. A Study in the Theory and History of Intermediality*. Amsterdam and Atlanta, GA: Rodopi.
Woodmansee, Martha. 1984. "The Genius and the Copyright: Economic and Legal Conditions of the Emergence of the 'Author'". *Eighteenth-Century Studies* 17.4. 425–448.
Woolf, Virginia. 2006. *To the Lighthouse*. Ed. David Bradshaw. Oxford: Oxford University Press.
Woolf, Virginia. 2008a. "The Cinema". (1926). *Selected Essays*. Ed. David Bradshaw. Oxford: Oxford University Press. 172–176.
Woolf, Virginia. 2008b. "Modern Fiction". (1919). *Selected Essays*. Ed. David Bradshaw. Oxford: Oxford University Press. 6–12.
Wordsworth, William. 1896. *The Poetical Works of William Wordsworth*. Ed. William Knight. Vol. 8. London: Macmillan.
Worthen, B. W. 2008. "*Hamlet* at Ground Zero. The Wooster Group and the Archive of Performance". *Shakespeare Quarterly* 59.3: 303–322.
Woudhuysen, H. R. 1996. *Sir Philip Sidney and the Circulation of Manuscripts 1558–1640*. Oxford: Clarendon Press.
Wu, Duncan, ed. 2006. *Romanticism: An Anthology*. 3rd ed. Malden, MA and Oxford: Blackwell.
Young, Edward. *Conjectures on Original Composition. In a Letter to the Author of Sir Charles Grandison. The Complete* Works, *Poetry and Prose*. Ed. James Nichols. London: Tegg, 1854. Rpt. Hildesheim: Olms, 1968. Vol. 2. 547–586.
Zumthor, Paul. 1972. *Essai de poétique médiévale*. Paris: Seuil.
Zumthor, Paul. 1990. *Oral Poetry: An Introduction*. 1983. Trans. Katherine Murphy-Judy. Minneapolis, MN: University of Minnesota Press.

Index

Abel 41
Aberdeen 205
Abraham 64
Abrams, J. J. 221
– S. 221
Abrams, M. H. 133
Abstraction 21–22, 73, 189, 191
actor 14–15, 65, 67–69, 71–72, 75–82, 91, 128–129, 168, 208, 211
Adams, Douglas 218
– *The Hitchhiker's Guide to the Galaxy* 218
adaptation 14, 17, 22, 55, 81, 168, 195–196, 200, 209, 211
– co-adaptation 5
Addison, Joseph 93–94
Admiral's Men 71
Adorno, Theodor 123, 209
adventure 37, 47–48, 86
– *The Adventurer* 89
– "Adventures of a Quire of Paper" 105
– *The Adventures of Master F. J.* (Gascoigne) 58
– *The Adventures of Rivella* (Manley) 110
– Choose Your Own Adventure 221
advertising, *see also* commercial 5–6, 92, 105, 116, 167, 213
Ælfric 45
Aeneid (Virgil) 29, 37
Aesop 90
aestheticism 122 187
aesthetics 3, 15, 21, 124, 175, 203
Æthelwold 63
– *Regularis Concordia* 63
affirmation 124, 170
affordance 8, 14, 25, 59, 144
Africa 172, 197
Agbabi, Patience 51, 55, 222
– *Telling Tales* 51, 55, 222
age 16, 77, 85, 87, 95, 107–108, 113, 128, 137, 159, 162, 183, 220, 223, 225
– 'Age of Amazon' 223
– age of authors 88–89
– "The Age of Paper" (song) 103
– age of print 149

– age of representation 16, 144
– age of the novel 101
– atomic age 196
– digital age 213–226
– 'Golden Age' of detective fiction 172
– jet age 170
– Middle Ages 3, 12, 27–28, 30, 42–44, 63–64, 149, 229
– Victorian age 184
agent 1, 87, 157
– literary agent 15, 114
agriculture 22
AI (artificial intelligence) 223–224, 232
AIDS 211
Aix 162
– "How they brought the good news from Ghent to Aix" (Browning) 162
Albatross Books 125
Alciati 180
– *Emblemata* 180
Alcuin 40–41, 45
Aldington, Richard 189
Aldde, Elizabeth 58
Alexander the Great 24, 50
Alexandra Palace 207
Alfred the Great 31–32, 34
algorithm 214, 223–224
All Alive and Merry 108
Allde, Elizabeth 58
Allde, Margaret 58
allegory 66, 180, 187, 195
alliteration 33, 35, 38, 46–47
allusion, *see also* intertextuality 6, 40, 48, 100, 171, 190, 192–193, 205, 221
Almereyda, Michael 81–82
– *Hamlet* (film) 81–82
amateur 87, 95, 157
Amazon 215–218, 223, 232
Ambrose (bishop of Milan) 34
America 3, 118, 122, 142–143, 148, 162, 167, 172, 185, 188–189, 195, 206
amphitheatre 63
anarchy 192
Andreas (poem) 36
Andrews, Anthony 211

Ә Open Access. © 2022 Ingo Berensmeyer, published by De Gruyter. [CC BY-NC-ND] This work is licensed under the Creative Commons Attribution-NonCommercial-NoDerivatives 4.0 International License.
https://doi.org/10.1515/9783110784459-017

angel 64–65, 171, 187
Angles 30, 44
Anglo-Christian 41
Anglo-French 44
Anglo-Irish 87, 111
Anglo-Norman 44
Anglo-Saxon 30, 32–33
animal 21–22, 25–26, 29, 131–132, 175–176, 229
animism 132
annotation 192
anthology 58, 92, 131, 186, 189, 230
anthropology 15, 21, 192
anthropomorphism 132–133, 175
antiquity 24, 69, 229
anxiety 159, 184, 206
Anyango, Catherine 196
– *Heart of Darkness* (graphic novel) 196
aphorism 57
Apollinaire, Guillaume 187
– *Calligrammes* 187
apostrophe 131–132, 138
Apple 209, 213, 222, 231–232
The Archers (BBC drama) 168
archive
– Archive of Our Own 223
– digital archive 222
– Internet Archive 104, 222, 232
aristocracy 47, 53, 58, 67, 109
Aristotle 10–11, 63, 73, 77
– *Poetics* 10, 63, 73
Armitage, Simon 47
– *Sir Gawain and the Green Knight* (transl.) 47
Arnold, Matthew 134, 192
– "The Buried Life" 134, 192
art 6, 11–12, 22, 56, 93, 124, 170, 179–181, 183–184, 186, 189, 191, 196, 200–201
– art book 196
– art for art's sake 122–123
– art history 11
– art of fiction 184
– art of writing 184
– book arts 15
– liberal arts 2
– mimetic art 63
– multimodal art 196

– narrative art 201
– sequential art 195–196, 204
– verbal art 12, 22
– visual arts 179
– word art 196
artificial intelligence, *see* AI
artist 120, 137, 186–187, 195–196, 221
– artist novel 164
Arts and Crafts 124, 188, 209
Arundel, Thomas 50
assonance 190
astrology 208
Auckland 155, 197
Auden, W. H. 134, 205
– *Night Mail* 205
Audible 223, 232
audience 1, 23, 34–36, 38–41, 44, 47–48, 51, 55, 58–59, 61–82, 85–86, 101, 110, 117, 120, 127, 129–131, 140, 142, 156, 167, 172, 180, 198, 200, 202–203, 211, 224–225
audio 164, 168
audiobook 1–2, 127, 159, 162–163, 220, 223, 231–232
audio-visual 13
auditor, *see also* listener 130–131
Augustine of Canterbury 30
Augustine of Hippo 30, 34
– *Confessions* 34
aurality 38, 75, 101, 170
Austen, Jane 12, 117, 211, 222
Austin, J. L. 6
Australia 154, 175
authenticity 55, 79, 106, 109, 130, 150
author, *see also* writer 1, 3, 24, 27–28, 40, 44, 46, 48–51, 53–55, 61, 65, 67, 85–92, 95–98, 106, 108, 111, 113–114, 116–118, 123, 127, 129, 136, 146, 149, 153, 156, 160, 162, 164–165, 183, 192, 196, 199–200, 202, 206, 210–211, 213–217, 221, 223, 225
– *The Case of Authors* (Ralph) 95
authority 33, 54, 67, 69, 78, 85, 125, 141, 159, 213
authorship 4, 15, 57, 86–87, 97, 103, 116, 136, 159, 162, 204, 221
– "The Brain-Sucker Or, the Distress of Authorship" 97

- secondary authorship 222
autobiography 49, 204
autonomy 6, 97, 136
Ayenbite of Inwit 27
Azarias (poem) 36

Bach, Johann Sebastian 173
Bacon, Francis 5
Baker, Nicholson 166
- *Vox* 166
Bakhtin, Mikhail 127
Baldwin, William 50
- *The Mirror for Magistrates* 50
Bale, John 67
- *The Impostures of Thomas à Beckett* 67
- *The King's Two Marriages* 67
ballad 61, 180, 183
Ballard, J. G. 174–175
- *Crash* 174
- "The Sound-Sweep" 174–175
Balzac, Honoré de 112
- *Lost Illusions* 112
Band Waggon (British sitcom) 167
bard 127–128
- *The Tales of Beedle the Bard* (Rowling) 216, 232
Barker, Nicola 175
- *H(a)ppy* 175
Bartlett, Mike 78
- *King Charles III* 78
Bataille, Georges 195
- "Rotten Sun" 195
- "The Solar Anus" 195
Bate, Jonathan 75
battle 37, 89–90, 202
- battlefield 90
- battle-king 46
- Battle of Hastings 229
- *The Battle of the Books* (Swift) 89–90
- battle of the brows 123
- battle-scene 46
Baudelaire, Charles 184, 191–192
- *Les fleurs du mal* 191
Baudry (reprint publisher) 118
BBC 166–170, 207–211, 218, 231–232
Beardsley, Aubrey 187
Beaumont, Francis 76

- *The Knight of the Burning Pestle* 76
Beaumont, Matt 221
- *e* 221
beauty 25, 34, 74, 137, 150, 165, 170–171, 175, 187, 202
Becket, Thomas 92
Beckett, Samuel 168, 186, 191, 194–195, 206–207, 231
- *All That Fall* 168
- *Cascando* 168
- *Embers* 168
- *Film* 206–207, 231
- *From an Abandoned Work* 168
- *Ill Seen Ill Said* 207
- *Imagination Dead Imagine* 194, 207
- *Krapp's Last Tape* 168
- *The Old Tune* 168
- *Rough for Radio* 168
- *Words and Music* 168
- "Yellow" 207
Bede 30–31, 33–34, 229
- *The Ecclesiastical History of the English People* 30–31, 33–34, 229
Beethoven, Ludwig van 173
- Ninth Symphony 173
Behn, Aphra 106–107, 110
- *Oroonoko* 106
Bell (inn) 69
Bell, Alexander Graham 161, 230
Bel Savage (inn) 69
Benjamin, Walter 3
- "The Work of Art" 3
Bentley, George 116–117
- *Standard Novels* (reprint series) 116–117
Bentley, Richard 89–90
Bent's Monthly Literary Advertiser 104
Beowulf 12, 27, 29, 35–42, 46, 229
Beowulf (character) 38–40
Berger, Harry 11, 22
Berger, John 180
- *Ways of Seeing* 180
Bergvall, Caroline 55
- *Alisoun Sings* 55
Berkeley, George 206
Berlin 204, 213
- *Goodbye to Berlin* (Isherwood) 204
Berliner, Emil 161, 231

Berne Convention 230
Berners-Lee, Tim 219, 232
Besant, Walter 184
bestseller 21, 58–59, 62, 94, 113, 124, 199
Betjeman, John 122
Bevis of Hampton 44
Bible, *see also* Scripture 12, 23, 25–26, 34, 36, 37, 49, 61, 64, 68, 85, 91, 140, 192, 229
Big Brother 209
Big Brother (TV series) 209, 232
bildungsroman, *see also* novel 107
binding 45, 60, 110, 113, 117, 181
biography 88, 97–98, 188
biology 21
Birch, Thomas 95
Birkerts, Sven 5
Birmingham 202
– Birmingham Repertory Theatre 79
black letter 61
Blackwood (publishers) 118
– *Blackwood's Magazine* 118
Blade Runner (film) 224
Blair, Robert 98
Blake, William 131–132, 135, 180–182, 196
– "The Chimney Sweeper" 181
– "The Lamb" 181
– "London" 181
– *Songs of Innocence and of Experience* 181–182
– "The Tyger" 181
blending 14, 37, 41, 181
blindness 166, 194, 202
blog 220, 222
Bloom, Allan 5
Bloomsbury (place) 123, 199
Bloomsbury (publisher) 216
bob and wheel 47
Boccaccio 51
– *Il Decamerone* 51
– *Il Filostrato* 51
Bodleian 34
Bodley Head 123
body 14, 16, 27, 36, 38, 54, 64, 90, 110, 129, 137–139, 159–160, 170, 197, 201
Boethius, Anicius Manlius Severinus 28
Boeve de Haumtone 44

Bolter, Jay David 221
Bombay 154–155
bone 21, 36, 192
book, *see also* audiobook, chapbook, codex, paperback 1, 4–5, 10, 12, 15, 17, 25–27, 31, 37, 43–44, 46, 49, 51, 54–63, 85–94, 103–108, 110–118, 120–126, 151, 156, 159, 168, 172, 180–181, 186, 188, 192, 196, 200, 202, 204, 208–211, 214–226, 231
– advice book 27, 172
– art book 112, 196
– artist's book 196, 221
– *The Battle of the Books* (Swift) 89–90, 230
– book club 124
– book format 1, 60, 63, 126, 220
– book history, *see also* history of the book 2–4, 15, 78, 115
– book market 59, 85–86, 88, 104–105, 216
– Book of Common Prayer 61
– book of Genesis 40
– *Book of Kells* 43
– *The Book of Margery Kempe* 49
– Book of the Machine (Forster) 159
– Book of the Month Club 124
– book piracy 92, 118
– book prices 92, 118
– book review 168
– bookscape 130
– book series 113
– Book Society 124
– bookstall 113, 115
– book-table 124
– book trade 57–58, 60, 68, 85, 95, 104–106
– children's book 110
– commonplace book 63
– conduct book 108
– e-book 2, 4–5, 126, 217–220, 223
– electronic book 218, 222
– emblem book 180
– Exeter Book 28, 42–43
– Google Books 222, 232
– gospel-book 29
– guidebook 218
– "Illustrated Books and Newspapers" (Wordsworth) 183

– manuscript book 43, 216
– multimedia book 221
– newsbook 93
– notebook 24–25, 208
– part book 94
– phonographic book 162
– physical book 5, 13, 25, 220, 223
– play-book 68
– *The PowerBook* (Winterson) 221
– printed book 1, 4, 43, 57, 60, 63, 110, 181, 214, 220–222, 225–226
– rule book 63
– textbook 24, 187
– trade book 215
– TV 'spin-off' book 210
– Vercelli book 37
bookbinder 15, 60
Booker Prize 215, 231–232
bookkeeping 60
bookseller *or* bookselling 15, 56, 59–60, 92, 95, 97, 104, 199, 215, 223–224
– *The Bookseller* (periodical) 104
bookshop 104, 114–115, 123, 223, 230–231
– "Bookshop Memories" (Orwell) 122
Bookstagram 225
BookTok 225
BookTube 225
Boots Booklovers' Library 122
boredom 11, 77
Boswell, James 88
– *Life of Johnson* 88
Botnik Studios 223
Bowles, Sally (character) 205
boys' companies 71
Braddon, Mary 113
– *Lady Audley's Secret* 113
brain 21–22, 87, 139, 141, 150, 156, 180, 194, 201, 206
– "The Brain-Sucker" 96–97
– brainwashing 123, 208
Branagh, Kenneth 81–82
– *Hamlet* (film) 82
– *Henry V* (film) 81
– *Much Ado About Nothing* (film) 81
Brawne, Fanny 158
Brayne, John 69
breath 127–144, 190

Brecht, Bertolt 82
Breeze, Jean 'Binta' 55
– "The Wife of Bath in Brixton Market" 55
Brickhill, Paul 215, 231
– *The Dam Busters* 215, 231
Brideshead Revisited 211, 232
Bridge Theatre 82
Bright Young People 166
Britain *or* British 12, 30–31, 44, 46, 56, 88, 91–92, 112–113, 115, 117–118, 124–125, 148, 152, 154, 156, 166–169, 170, 172–174, 180, 187, 189, 197, 199–200, 207, 211, 214–215, 230–231
Britain, Thomas of 44
– *Tristan* 44
Britannia 156
British Broadcasting Company *or* Corporation *see* BBC
British Documentary Movement 205
British Empire 12, 118, 153, 164
British Isles 30, 67, 92, 148
British Library 27, 34, 37, 39, 86, 232
The British Magazine 105
British Museum 121
Britons 30
Brittany 30
Britten, Benjamin 205
– *Night Mail* 205
broadcast *or* broadcasting 6–7, 9, 80–81, 156–157, 160, 166–169, 207, 209–211, 215, 225
broadside 61, 180
Broadway 78, 81
Brontë, Charlotte 118
– *Jane Eyre* 118
Broome, Joan 58
Brown, Hablot K. 181
Browning, Robert 138, 141–144, 147, 158, 162
– "Mr. Sludge, 'the Medium'" 141–144, 147, 158
brows, battle of the 123–124
browser 219, 232
Bruges 56–57
Bryher (Annie Winifred Ellerman) 199
Bull (inn) 69
Burbage, James 69, 72, 230

Burbage, Richard 72, 76
Burgess, Anthony 173–174, 206, 231
– *A Clockwork Orange* 173–174, 206, 231
Burke, Kenneth 11
Burns, Robert 132
Burton, Richard 81–82, 169
Burton, Robert 5
Byron, George Gordon, Lord 78, 87, 135
– *Manfred* 78

cable 148–149, 153–154, 156, 209, 230
cacophony 175, 192
cadence 174
Cædmon 29, 33–36
Caedmon records 162–163
Caesar (Gaius Julius Caesar) 72, 76
Cain 40–41
calligraphy 190
Calvinism 61
Cambridge 34, 74, 90, 140, 220, 232
camera 80, 190, 200, 204–206, 209, 211
Campbell, Eddie 196
– *From Hell* 196
canon (literature) 55, 85
canon (music) 45
Canongate 215
canon law 73
Canterbury 27, 30, 50–52, 54
The Canterbury Tales (Chaucer) 51–56, 61, 85, 192, 222, 229
Cape, Jonathan 222
capital 13, 61, 151
capitalism 6, 72, 97, 172, 223
Carlyle, Thomas 118, 208
Carter, Lincoln J. 81
– *Chattanooga* 81
cartoon 162, 184, 195
Cary, Elizabeth 78
– *The Tragedy of Mariam* 78
Cassiodorus 25, 161
The Castle of Perseverance (play) 66
cast 55, 79, 222
casting 79
– colour-blind casting 79
– colour-conscious casting 79
Castorp, Hans (character) 161

catalogue 27, 54, 104, 115
– term catalogue 104
Catawba 142
catharsis 11
Catholicism 30, 67, 176, 211
Cave, Terence 11
Caxton, William 50, 55–57, 61, 85, 229
CBS 168
CD-ROM 232
censorship, *see also* licensing 15, 90–91, 115–116
Cerquiglini, Bernard 28
Chamberlain's Men, *see* Lord Chamberlain's Men
Chambers, Robert 141
– *Vestiges of the Natural History of Creation* 141
Chambers's Encyclopaedia 104
Chandler, Raymond 195
Chandos, *see* Wallace
change 1, 3–4, 7, 11, 16, 51, 68, 79, 88, 118, 153, 214, 216–218, 220, 222, 224, 226
– cultural change 5, 63, 172, 207
– literary change 3, 170
– media change 3, 5
– social change 63, 104, 134, 152, 207, 211, 226
– technological change 4, 149, 152, 170, 174, 214
channel 152, 154, 158, 168, 210
Channel 4 (TV) 209
chaos 192
chapbook 60, 63
Chapman & Hall 117
character 3, 14, 39–41, 48, 50–53, 55, 64, 66, 72–73, 76–79, 106, 108, 115, 121, 127–128, 136–138, 164, 166, 169–171, 179, 181, 185, 188, 198, 201–202, 205–206, 222–223
charta 25
Chatto & Windus 199
Chaucer, Geoffrey 28, 48, 50–57, 60, 78, 85, 184, 192, 222, 229
– *The Canterbury Tales* 51–56, 61, 85, 192, 222, 229
– *The Parson's Tale* 48

- *Troilus and Criseyde* 28, 50–52, 60
- *The Workes of Geffray Chaucer* (ed. Thynne) 85
- *The Works of Geoffrey Chaucer* (ed. Morris) 55–56, 184

Chekhov, Anton 168
Chester 64
- Chester cycle 64–65
Chesterfield (Philip Stanhope, 4th Earl of) 88
children 35, 110
- "Among School Children" (Yeats) 173
- Children of the Chapel 71
- Children of the Queen's Revels 72
- Children of Paul's 71
- Children's Hour 167
chivalry 46–48, 53, 73
Christ, *see also* Jesus 37, 40, 54, 63–65
Christ I–III (poems) 36
Christ and Satan (poem) 36
Christianity 24, 26, 30–31, 33–34, 36–37, 40–41, 49, 53, 63, 65–66, 105, 138, 142, 167
Christie, Agatha 171–172, 200
- *4:50 from Paddington* 171
Christmas 48
church 32–33, 49, 54, 63–64, 67, 87, 157, 210
Church Fathers 37, 67
Cibber, Colley 128
cinema, *see also* montage 4, 14, 79–81, 197–207, 210–212, 215, 226, 231
cinematograph 197–198, 231
circulation 59, 77, 104, 117
circus 197, 199
Civil War, English 90, 93
civilisation 23–24, 60, 123, 130, 155, 160, 164, 174, 192–193
Clare, John 131–132, 135
Clarissa (character) 109
Clarissa (novel) 109
Clarke, Arthur C. 208
- "The Steam-Powered Word Processor" 208
class 60, 79, 92, 95, 110, 115, 117–118, 120, 122–123, 135, 152, 172–173, 183, 202, 209–211
classic 13, 105, 117, 124–126, 192, 199–200, 210–211, 222

clay 15, 23–24, 127, 229
Cleanness (poem) 48
Clegg, Cyndia 90
Cleopatra 193
close-up 205–206
Close Up (magazine) 199
Coburn, Alvin Langdon 185–186
code 47, 61, 73, 75, 134, 147, 152, 217
- Morse code 148
codex, *see also* book 1, 5, 25–26, 37, 43, 219–220, 224, 229
- Codex Amiatinus 26, 32
- Nowell codex 36–37
coffeehouse 93–94, 225
Coghill, Nevill 204
cognition 11, 14, 201
Coleridge, Samuel Taylor 133, 135–136, 230
- "The Eolian Harp" 133
collage 193, 204
Collins, Jim 226
Collins, Wilkie 113, 117–118
- *The Moonstone* 120
- *The Woman in White* 113, 119–120, 164, 230
Collins Illustrated Pocket Classics 125
Cologne 56
colony 154
colour 69, 79, 117, 125, 150, 169, 180–182, 209, 211
- colour-blind casting 79
- colour-conscious casting 79
Comédie Française 79
comedy 48, 53–54, 65–66, 69, 72–73, 75, 77, 107, 169, 218
- *A Comedy of Danger* (Hughes) 167
- *Divine Comedy* (Dante) 147
comic 117, 180, 184, 195–196, 204
Commaful 223
commemoration 101, 138
commerce 5–6, 54, 58–59, 62–63, 78, 85–86, 97, 104, 110, 115–116, 123–124, 126, 132, 139, 142, 156, 162, 164, 209, 215–216, 221, 225
commercial, *see also* advertising 209
commission 87, 95, 200, 224
commodity 3, 60, 85, 112–113, 121, 126, 154, 208, 214

commonplace 57, 63, 123, 191, 198, 205
communication 1–3, 6–10, 13, 15–16, 33–34, 42, 57, 61, 77, 93–94, 101, 103, 111, 139, 141, 147, 149, 151–154, 156–157, 159, 161, 164–165, 171, 176, 208
– communication studies 8
– communications circuit 15
– literary communication 153
– mass communication 2
– materiality of communication 12, 138, 226
– print communication 94
– spiritual communication 142
– telecommunication 147
– telephonic communication 166
community 16, 23, 26, 31, 33–34, 39, 42, 53, 65, 101, 111, 123, 127, 131, 169–173, 205, 224
– imagined community 170
– reading community 58
– textual community 33
comparison 23, 130, 155, 190, 199, 204
competition 1, 4, 72, 124, 167, 179, 184, 200–202, 206, 209, 215
compilation 37, 95
complexity 53, 66, 107, 144
computer 4, 209, 213–214, 217–221, 223, 231
Condell, Henry 85, 230
configuration 1, 8, 11, 14, 63
– media configuration 1, 3, 8, 15–17, 120, 130, 212, 225
conflict 40, 54, 72–73, 89, 108, 110, 112, 194, 203–204
Congreve, William 106
connection, *see also* contact 1, 8–9, 13–16, 22, 28, 34, 37, 47, 92, 103, 129, 134, 136, 144–145, 151–154, 156–157, 159, 162–163, 165–166, 170, 173, 179, 195, 205, 210, 219–220, 225
– "Only connect" (Forster) 155
connectivity 8–9, 13, 16, 144, 148, 151, 159, 165–166, 193, 220, 225
Conrad, Joseph 165, 186, 196–197
– *Heart of Darkness* 196–197
– *The Inheritors* 165
– *Lord Jim* 197
consumer 106, 215

consumption 4, 74, 101, 106, 113, 121, 158
contact, *see also* connection 7, 54, 79, 131, 139, 143, 147, 149–151, 156
– contact zone 76
content 1–2, 7, 11, 22, 34, 39, 61, 95, 132, 149, 167–168, 210, 219–220
context 3–4, 12, 37–38, 42, 47, 58, 67, 71, 101, 114, 130, 139, 150, 152, 154–156, 159, 164, 190, 193
contract 48, 86, 113
convergence 219–221
conversation 93, 161, 166, 204, 224
conversion 3, 30, 64
Cooke and Wheatstone telegraph 148
copy 21, 24, 26–28, 43, 50, 55, 57, 60–61, 63, 70, 86, 91, 93–95, 99, 104, 107, 112, 115, 125, 150, 167, 181, 203, 209, 216, 223–225, 231
– copy-paste 222
– master copy 67
copyright 15, 57, 86, 88, 91–92, 95, 118, 125, 136, 199, 222, 230–231
– Berne Convention on Copyright 230
– Copyright Act 91, 230
– Universal Copyright Convention 231
coranto 93
Cornhill Magazine 118
Corns, Thomas 76
Cornwall 30
corruption 54, 91, 164, 184
cosmology 65
costume 79
coterie 58–59
Cotton, Sir Robert 27
– Cotton Caligula (manuscript) 46
– Cotton Nero (manuscript) 46
– Cotton Vitellius (manuscript) 37, 39
couplet 44
court, *see also* Inns, love 38, 44, 46–48, 51–52, 58, 67–68, 72
– tennis court 69
courtier 47, 68–69
Cowper, William 132
CreateSpace 223
creation 11, 28, 33, 37, 54, 64, 77, 92, 101, 124, 136, 141, 151, 177, 188, 214
Creative Commons 232

creativity 121, 129, 136, 160, 164, 209, 225
creator 27, 35, 137
credit 60
crime 66, 106, 123, 208
criminal 69, 74, 106
crisis 11, 174, 211
critic 38, 41, 78, 88, 90, 122–124, 129, 137, 179–180, 192, 209, 221, 223, 225
Critical Review 94, 105
criticism 53–54, 77, 128, 144, 158, 167, 183
– cultural criticism 200, 208
– literary criticism 15, 94, 225
– New Criticism 14
critique 40, 91, 128, 147, 183, 195, 209
Cromwell, Thomas 67
Cronin, A. J. 124
– *The Citadel* 124
cross 37, 65
– Ruthwell Cross 37
Cross Keys (inn) 69
crowd 89, 135, 189–190
– crowdfunding 87
crucifixion 37, 64–65
Cruikshank, George 181, 184
cubism 190
cult 151, 187
cultural studies 2, 172
culture, *see also* change, decline, pessimism, value 5, 11–12, 24, 30, 33, 37, 44–45, 63, 73, 94, 101, 109, 122–124, 136, 164, 174, 183, 190, 192–193, 205, 226
– convergence culture 219
– culture industry 71, 123, 209
– culture war 172
– literary culture 57, 226
– mass culture 172
– media culture 130
– oral culture 12, 33, 35
– pop culture *or* popular culture 172–173, 209, 214, 226
– print culture 16, 85–101, 103, 112–116, 121, 180
– 'two cultures' debate 123–124
– visual culture 183–184
Cumberbatch, Benedict 81
Cumbria 130

Cunard, Nancy 186
cuneiform 23, 229
Curll, Edmund 91
– *Venus in the Cloister* 91
curtain 69, 71
Curtain (theatre) 69
cybernetics 165, 172
cybertext 221
Cynewulf 29

Dada 187
Daily Courant 93, 230
Daily Graphic 162
Daily Telegraph 225
Damocles 180
dance 14, 72, 75, 172–173, 203
Daniel (poem) 36
Daniell, John 148–149
Danish, *see* Denmark
Dante Alighieri 147, 192–193
– *The Divine Comedy* 147
Darnton, Robert 15
Darwin, Charles 115, 141
– *The Origin of Species* 115
data 2, 215, 217–219, 223, 225, 231
– database 135
– Data Discman 231
decadence 187
deception 49, 166
decline 81, 135, 220
– cultural decline 4, 16, 122–123, 170, 172–173
– intellectual decline 183
– religious decline 30
Defoe, Daniel 91, 94, 106
– *Robinson Crusoe* 91, 106
– *The Review* 94
– *The Shortest Way with the Dissenters* 91
degeneration 164–165, 173
Deighton, Len 217, 231
– *Bomber* 217, 231
Dell, Ethel M. 123
Deloney, Thomas 58
– *Jack of Newbury* 58
democracy *or* democratisation 6, 225
Denmark *or* Danish 30, 38
Dent, J. M. 124–125, 214

Derrida, Jacques 195
– "White Mythology" 195
description 4–5, 8, 11, 13, 15–16, 22–23, 26, 28–29, 36, 48, 70, 80, 87, 90, 129, 171, 175, 201–204
design 40, 61, 75, 79, 112, 114, 124–126, 155, 184, 186–188, 214, 221
desire 53, 57, 105–106, 108, 115, 142–143, 165, 169
determinism 6–7, 9, 17, 158, 226
device 35, 61, 111, 147, 181, 203, 220, 226
– plot device 171
devotion 26, 54
De Witt, Johannes 70
de Worde, Wynkyn 57
dialect 30, 46, 202
dialogue 54, 64, 166, 168, 202
diary 164, 204–205
Dick, Philip K. 223
– *Do Androids Dream of Electric Sheep?* 223
Dickens, Charles 97, 117–118, 120, 127, 181, 211
– *All the Year Round* 117, 119–120
– *Dombey and Son* 117
– *Household Words* 117
– *Oliver Twist* 183
– *The Pickwick Papers* 117, 181
digital, *see also* archive, environment, media, poetry, revolution, technology, text 4, 81, 126, 213–226, 231
– *Digital Donne* 59
– digitalisation 2, 221
– digitisation 220, 222
diorama 198
director 79, 81, 166, 203–204, 206
disbelief, suspension of 71
disconnection 16, 163, 165–166, 200, 202, 204–205
discourse 25, 32, 38, 77, 111, 158, 162, 170–171, 173, 183
– genius discourse 136
discovery 16, 138, 140, 197
disease 28, 97, 137
disguise 66, 69, 71
Disney, Walt 200
disorder 63, 97
disorientation 192

display type 61
dissent 61, 124
– *The Shortest Way with the Dissenters* 91
dissociation 159, 165–166, 201
distance 8–11, 16, 21–22, 101, 127, 130, 135, 147, 149–150, 154, 156, 158, 160, 165, 170, 177, 191, 201, 207
distinction 1, 7–8, 10, 13, 22, 34, 40, 53, 76–77, 179
distribution 6, 9, 13, 15–16, 67, 93, 101, 104, 110, 113, 122, 156, 170, 210, 214, 219–220
diversity 55, 58, 63, 67, 72, 79, 101, 222
divinity, *see also* theology 104, 151
document 15, 58, 68, 164, 172
Donaldson, Alexander 92
Donaldson v. Becket 230
Donne, John 59, 128, 149, 151
– *Digital Donne* 59
– "Hail Bishop Valentine" 149
Doolittle, Hilda, *see* H. D.
doppelganger 41
Dorst, Doug 221
– *S.* 221
double 41
– double-entry 60
– doubling 9
Doyle, Arthur Conan 161, 163, 169, 223
– "The Japanned Box" 161, 163, 169
– Sherlock Holmes stories 223
Downes, Geoff 4
Downton Abbey 211
Dracula (Stoker) 163–164, 231
Dracula (character) 164–165, 201
Drake, Francis 156
drama, *see also* play 1, 53, 63–82, 85–86, 107, 128, 135, 168
– closet drama 78
– dramatisation 162, 168, 193
– metadrama 75–77
– proto-drama 63
– radio drama 168–170
– religious drama 64
– secular drama 64
– TV drama 210
– verse drama 78
drawing 21, 70, 156, 162, 184–185

dream 33, 49, 120, 135, 137, 139, 142, 169, 189, 203, 205
– daydreaming 179
– dream factory, see also Hollywood 203
– *The Dream of the Rood* 36–37
– *A Midsummer Night's Dream* 77, 82, 86
Drinkwater, John 189
– "Moonlit Apples" 189
Drucker, Joanna 187
Drury Lane (theatre) 79
Dryden, John 86–87, 90, 97, 128, 230
– *Amphitryon* 128
– translation of Virgil 86, 90, 230
Dublin 43, 199
Duffy, Carol Ann 149
– "Valentine" 149
Du Maurier, George 162, 184
Dutch 209
dystopia 168, 196, 207

earth 35–36, 64, 133, 176, 180
– middle-earth 30, 35
e-book, see also e-reader 2, 4–5, 126, 217–218, 220, 223
echo 53, 107, 130, 157, 165, 176, 186, 191–193
Eco, Umberto 4, 17
ecology, see media
economics 2, 6, 15, 23, 56, 60, 85
economy 87, 123, 215
– affective economy 60
– gift economy 86
ecstasy 170–171
Edel, Leon 184–185
Eder 215
Edgar (character) 150
Edinburgh 92, 205, 216
Edison, Thomas 121, 161–162, 230
edition 29, 37, 55–56, 61–62, 78, 85, 92, 95, 98–99, 108, 111–112, 114, 117, 126, 141, 151, 184, 214
– Aldine editions 61
– edition binding 110
– facsimile edition 191
– limited edition 123
– New York edition (James) 184–185, 231

– paper-covered edition 124
– reprint edition 116
education 32, 45, 74, 89, 93, 124, 167
– self-education 107
– Universal Education Act 152
Edwardian 155, 161, 186
Egan, Jennifer 221
– *A Visit from the Goon Squad* 221
Egley, William Maw 183
Egypt 141, 229
Einstürzende Neubauten (band) 175
Eisenstein, Sergei 203–204
ekphrasis 13
Elder, see Smith, Elder
electricity 4, 148
electromagnetism 156, 158–159
electron 148
electronics 174
elegy 101, 139, 147
– *Elegy Written in a Country Church-Yard* (Gray) 98–101
Elene (poem) 36
Eliot, George 118, 120, 157, 198
– "The Lifted Veil" 157
– *Middlemarch*
Eliot, T. S. 51, 78, 123, 127, 137, 143, 180, 190–195, 200, 204–205, 231
– *The Cocktail Party* 78
– "The Love Song of J. Alfred Prufrock" 191
– *Murder in the Cathedral* 78
– *The Waste Land* 51, 127, 143, 191–195, 204–205, 231
Eliot, Valerie 191
Elizabeth I, Queen of England and Ireland 73, 193
Elizabeth II, Queen of the United Kingdom 209
Elizabethan era or period 1, 58, 61, 70–71, 77, 85
Ellmann, Lucy 215
– *Ducks, Newburyport* 215
elocution 128
eloquence 128, 130
e-mail 221
emblem 52, 112, 171, 174, 180
– *A Choice of Emblemes* (Whitney) 180

– *Emblemata* (Alciati) 180
emotion 11, 49, 77–79, 109–110, 134, 149–150, 162, 169, 189–190, 201, 203
empire 113, 216, 239
– British Empire 12, 118, 153–155, 164
– Roman Empire 30, 63
England *or* English 3, 5, 10, 12, 15, 27, 30–38, 42–50, 52, 55–61, 63–64, 66–67, 73–74, 80–81, 86, 88–94, 97, 109, 114, 117–118, 120, 122, 126, 128–129, 131, 155, 170, 176–177, 183–185, 189, 192, 196, 200, 213, 216, 229–232
– Anglo-Saxon England 33
– Elizabethan England 77, 85
– *English Illustrated Magazine* 155
– English Library (Penguin book series) 211
– Englishness 61
– Hiberno-English 38
– medieval England 30, 33, 63
– Middle English 27, 43–45, 50, 55
– 'Mother England' 156
– Northern England 30, 64, 130
– Old English 23, 27–38, 43–46, 105, 162
– *A Song of the English* (Kipling) 154–155
– standard English 167
engraving 21, 24, 112, 117, 181
Enkidu 23
enlightenment 192, 225
entertainment 4, 9–10, 40, 67–68, 73, 75, 85, 106, 113, 160, 167, 172, 183–184, 200, 205, 207, 216, 219
environment 29, 45, 151, 183
– cognitive environment 11
– digital environment 221
– media environment 214, 221, 226
– natural environment 154
– sensory environment 1
– sonic environment 170
– textual environment 131
epilogue 76, 86
epistemology 111, 156, 195
e-reader, *see also* e-book 126, 218, 220
eroticism 59, 91, 151
– homoeroticism 211
error 55, 150

essay 3, 87–89, 94, 104–105, 107, 122, 136, 175, 187, 189, 200–201, 207
etymology 34
Europe 4, 12, 25–26, 60, 67, 69, 91, 94, 118, 135–136, 164–165, 172, 180, 187, 229
Eve 151
– *Tomorrow's Eve* (Villiers de l'Isle-Adam) 161
The Eve of St. Agnes (Keats) 158–159
Everyman (character) 66
Everyman's Library 124, 214
evolution 5, 11, 21, 141
– co-evolution 5
Exeter Book 28, 42–43
exile 31, 41
Exodus (poem) 36
expectation 87, 95, 116, 181
experience 9–10, 16, 49, 53–54, 77, 79–80, 82, 105–108, 127, 135–138, 140, 159, 163, 168, 171, 173–175, 179–180, 187, 189, 193, 198, 201, 203, 205, 207, 213, 217, 219
– aesthetic experience 15, 77
– mystical experience 49, 140
– reading experience 134, 186, 220
– *Songs of Innocence and Experience* (Blake) 181–182
– subjective experience 10, 13
– tactile experience 150
– visual experience 112
experientiality 15
expressivism 136
Eyles, Leonora 172–173

Fabian Society 209
fable 193
– beast fable 52
fabliau 52
Facebook 232
facsimile 99, 191
faith 64, 141, 151
Falstaff (character) 73
fame 13, 39, 46, 55, 74, 88, 95–96, 98, 113
family 9, 22, 44, 50, 58, 65, 92, 106, 109, 121, 142, 167, 169, 210
– *The Family Herald* 117

fantasy 77, 123, 139–140, 157, 162, 170, 225
Faraday, Michael 149
farce 69
fascination 143, 159–160, 171, 188, 198
fashion 21, 59, 61, 66, 74, 93, 100, 103, 107, 113, 122, 129, 186, 198, 211
fate 30, 37, 40, 98, 113, 180
- *The Fates of the Apostles* (poem) 36
Faulkner, William 200
fear 4, 31, 51, 113, 132, 135, 141, 160, 164, 171, 174, 184, 198, 215, 226
femininity 124, 153
feminism 78
Fenollosa, Ernest 188
- *The Chinese Written Character a a Medium for Poetry* 188
Ferrar, Nicholas 58
feudalism 165
fiction, *see also* art, non-fiction 9–11, 22, 44, 49, 51, 53–54, 69, 76, 94, 104–105, 117–118, 123, 128, 143, 156, 164, 174, 184, 205–206, 210, 215, 221, 223
- amatory fiction 107, 110
- detective fiction 172
- erotic fiction 91
- fan fiction 223, 225, 232
- *Fiction and the Reading Public* (Leavis) 123
- genre fiction 123, 205–206
- gothic fiction 156
- horror fiction 156
- hypertext fiction 221
- illustrated fiction 184
- interactive fiction 221
- literary fiction 123, 205–206, 215, 217, 221, 223
- middlebrow fiction 123
- "Modern Fiction" (Woolf) 201, 231
- modernist fiction 112
- narrative fiction 124, 128
- new adult fiction 225
- phonographic fiction 169
- popular fiction 58, 116–117, 206
- postmodernist fiction 112
- romance fiction 110
- science fiction 107, 123, 154, 159–160, 168, 174, 205–206, 208, 218
- sentimental fiction 151

- serial fiction 116–120
- short fiction 120, 194
- young adult fiction 225
- zombie fiction 222
fictionality 3, 11, 15, 25
field 10, 13, 15, 69, 86, 90, 123, 187, 196, 221, 223
Fielding, Henry 92, 95, 107, 109, 111
- *Amelia* 92
- *Joseph Andrews* 107
- *Shamela* 109
- *Tom Jones* 92
figure 31, 50–51, 54, 66, 74, 99, 132, 137, 188, 194
film 4, 14, 21–22, 47, 71, 74, 80–82, 170, 173, 179, 197–208, 211, 213, 215–216, 224, 232
- Documentary Film Movement 205
- *Film* (Beckett) 206, 231
- film company 199
- film editing 205
- film industry 199, 225
- film magazine 199
- *film noir* 195
- Film Society 199
- film theatre 203
- film theory 199
- silent film 203
- sound film 200, 231
- theatrofilm 81
Finch, Ann 98
- "A Nocturnal Rêverie" 98
fitt 47
Fitzgerald, F. Scott 200
Flash 196
flaxseed 105
Fletcher, John Gould 189
Flint, F. S. 189
foliation 43
folio 26, 43, 60, 68, 85, 87–88
- First Folio (Shakespeare) 61, 68, 85, 230
font 186
Ford, Ford Madox 165
- *The Inheritors* 165
- *Some Do Not. . .* 165
form 1–2, 4–8, 11, 13–14, 16, 21–23, 29, 34–35, 43–45, 49–50, 53–54, 57–58,

60–65, 68, 73, 75–77, 79, 81, 85, 94, 96–97, 99, 101, 103, 108, 110–112, 124, 127, 138–140, 143, 149, 161, 168, 171, 175, 180, 184, 188–189, 191, 196, 200, 205–207, 214, 218–223, 224–225
– epistolary form 109
– formal patterning 15
– form of speech 127, 129–130, 132, 134, 138, 167
– letter form 31
– literary form 3, 8, 13, 32, 103–104, 106–107, 168, 180, 184, 194
– lyric form 101
– material form 1–2, 6–7, 12, 15–16
– narrative form 196
– serial form 94, 117–118
– sonnet form 149, 183
– symbolic form 22
format, *see also* folio, quarto
– codex format 5
– one-volume format 122
– serial format 118
– shilling shocker format 117
– triple-decker format 115, 230
formula 35
Forster, E. M. 155, 159, 165, 208
– *Howards End* 155
– "The Machine Stops" 159, 165, 208
Fourdrinier machine 103, 230
fragment 33, 49, 54, 193, 204
– Worcester Fragments 45
frame 10, 77, 80, 128, 155, 192, 195
– freeze-frame 80
– time frame 153
framework 73, 75
France *or* French 21, 26, 44–46, 48, 50, 60, 73, 75, 86, 91, 112, 122, 128, 142, 151, 163, 184, 187, 191, 195, 231
Frayn, Michael 208
– *The Tin Men* 208
Frazer, James George 192
– *The Golden Bough* 192
freedom, *see also* liberty 11, 21, 91, 134, 152, 164, 189
Freud, Sigmund 137

friend *or* friendship 23, 52, 58, 88, 96–97, 101, 108–109, 113, 118, 138, 142, 147, 156–157, 188, 194, 197, 204, 211
Frisians 30
frontispiece 51, 184–185
Frost, Robert 224
Fry, Christopher 78
– *The Lady's Not for Burning* 78
future 78, 99, 152, 165, 187
futurist 186

Gaddis, William 166
– *J R* 166
Galignani (publisher) 118
Galley Beggar Press 215
Galsworthy, John 210
– *The Forsyte Saga* 210
game, *see also* playing 9–10, 14, 48, 53, 168, 221
– parlour game 162
– video game 4, 14, 221
Garrick, David 79–80
Gascoigne, George 58
– *The Adventures of Master F. J.* 58
Gaveston (character) 211
Gawain (character) 47–49
Ged, William 230
gender 2, 44, 71, 79, 148
Genesis 23, 40
Genesis A (poem) 36
Genesis B (poem) 36
genius 50, 97, 120, 136, 176, 208
genre, *see also* fiction, subgenre 1, 3, 44, 48–50, 52, 54, 63–64, 75, 85–86, 97–98, 103, 105–107, 128, 149, 151, 156, 164
gentleman 89, 95, 97, 111
The Gentleman's Magazine 104
gentry 55, 66, 85
Georgian Poetry (anthology) 189
German *or* Germany 14, 25, 30–31, 112, 118, 126, 175, 187, 215
Germanic 30–31, 33, 37, 40
Ghent 162

– "How they brought the good news from Ghent to Aix" (Browning) 162
ghost 82, 133, 138, 140, 159, 163–164, 198
– ghost story 158
– ghost-writer 88
Gibbons, Dave 196
– *Watchmen* 196
Gibson, James J. 8
gift 33, 86
Gilgamesh 23–24, 48, 147, 229
Gill, Eric 172, 188
Gill Sans (typeface) 188
Gissing, George 120–122, 208, 230
– *New Grub Street* 120–122, 230
– *The Unclassed* 120
Glasgow 205
global *or* globe 12, 15, 21, 81, 118, 127, 154, 156, 209, 215–216, 219–220, 223–225
globalisation 154, 172, 215
Globe Theatre 72, 76–77
gloss 26, 32, 50, 192
Gloucester (character) 150
god *or* God 23–24, 33–35, 37, 40–41, 46, 49, 52, 65–67, 99, 131, 141, 156, 176–177, 193
goddess 186
Golden Hind (ship) 156
Goldman, William 225
Goldsmith, Oliver 95
– *She Stoops to Conquer* 193
Gollancz 125
Goodreads 223–226
Google 232
– Google Books 222, 232
Gorman, Amanda 224
– "The Hill We Climb" 224
government 38, 67, 93, 152, 156
Gower, John 49–50, 52
– *Confessio Amantis* 50
grace 31, 33, 66
Grahame-Smith, Seth 222
– *Pride and Prejudice and Zombies* 222
grammar 22, 26, 32, 203
gramophone 161, 231
Granada 211
graphic novel 14, 180, 184, 195–196
graphism 21

graveyard 98–99, 101, 130
Gray, Thomas 98–101, 122, 130
– *Elegy Written in a Country Church-Yard* 98–101, 130
Greece *or* Greek 24–25, 60, 73, 126, 131, 133, 143, 165, 168, 179, 190
Green, Henry 194–195, 202–204, 231
– *Blindness* 194, 202
– *Living* 202–204, 231
– *Party Going* 202
Greene, Graham 200
– *The Third Man* 200
Greene, Robert 58
– *Pandosto* 58
The Green Knight (film)
Greenwich 193
Grendel (character) 38, 40–41
Grierson, John 205
Griffiths, Ralph 105
Grimshaw, John Atkinson 183
Grove, William 148–149
Grub Street 95–97, 120
The Guardian 94
Gui de Warewic 44
guild 53, 57, 64–65
Gumbrecht, Hans Ulrich 1, 12
Gunn, Thom 173
Gutenberg, Johannes 4, 26, 229
– Gutenberg Bible 229
– Gutenberg era 226
– *Gutenberg Galaxy* (McLuhan) 6
– Project Gutenberg 222, 231
Guthlac (poem) 36
Guy of Warwick 44
Guyau, Jean-Marie 163

habit, *see also* reading 15, 58, 104–106, 128, 172
Hachette 215
hack 95, 97, 120
Haggard, H. Rider 159
haiku 189
halftone 230
hall 31–33, 40–41, 64, 66, 69, 77, 129, 209
– music hall 200
– Stationer's Hall 57
Hall, Abraham (character) 151–152

Hall, Radclyffe 91
- *The Well of Loneliness* 91
Hall, Steven 175
- *The Raw Shark Texts* 175
Hallam, Arthur Henry 138–139, 147
Hamlet 76–77, 80–82, 107, 111
Hamlet (character) 73, 76
hand 5, 21–23, 26–27, 41, 58, 105, 109, 111–112, 128, 142, 151, 153–154, 165, 180, 183, 185, 203
- handbill 103
- handheld devices 220
- handwriting, see also manuscript 43, 68, 101, 214, 216, 221
- second-hand books 114
- shorthand 184
- Tremulous Hand 45
Harari, Yuval Noah 21
- *Sapiens* 21
hardback 125, 209
Harker, Mina (character) 164
harmony 66, 105, 151, 174, 187
HarperCollins 215
Harry Potter, see also Pottermore, Rowling 216, 223, 225, 232
Hart, Michael S. 231
Hawthorne, Nathaniel 143
Hayles, N. Katherine 8
Haywood, Eliza 108–110
- *Anti-Pamela* 109
H. D. (Hilda Doolittle) 199
Heaney, Seamus 38
hearing 128, 132, 152, 165, 174, 176–177
heart 34, 131, 135, 138–139, 141, 148–150, 163, 171, 211
- *Heart of Darkness* (Conrad) 196–197
heaven 33, 35, 40–41, 64–65, 74, 135, 151, 171, 174, 183
Heider, Fritz 13
hell 37, 41, 65, 195
- *The Descent into Hell* (poem) 36
- *From Hell* (graphic novel) 196
Hemans, Felicia 135
Heminges, John 85, 230
Hengist 30
Henrietta Maria, Queen of England, Scotland and Ireland 91

Henry IV, King of England 50
Henry IV (play) 73
Henry VIII, King of England 67
Heorot 40–41
Herbert, George 187
- "Easter Wings" 187
- *The Temple* 187
Hercules 22
heresy 176
- Pelagian heresy 31
heritage 123, 211
hero 33, 37–41, 47, 49, 90, 161, 208
- heroic epic 164
- heroism 40, 46
- mock-heroic 90
- superhero 196
heroine 36, 108–110, 203, 205
Hertz, Heinrich 156
- Hertzian waves 157–158
heteroglossia 127
heterosexuality 149
hifi 173
Higginson, Thomas Wentworth 129
highbrow 123–124, 205
Hill, Aaron 110
Hinduism 193
historicism 79
history 1–5, 7–8, 10, 12, 15, 17, 21, 30, 44, 57–58, 64–65, 77, 82, 94, 96, 103, 105–106, 109, 126–127, 168, 183, 188, 217, 226
- art history 1
- big history 21
- cultural history 15
- *Ecclesiastical History* (Bede) 33–34
- *Historia regum Britanniae* 44
- history of literature *or* literary history 1, 3, 5, 8, 12, 16–17, 49, 218, 224
- history of media *or* media history 3–5, 7, 13, 15, 17, 42, 184, 218
- history of print media 2
- history of publishing 15
- history of the book, see also book history 3, 15, 92
- history play 75, 78
- prehistory 229
- theatre history 82

Index — 273

– *Vestiges of the Natural History of Creation* 141
Hoban, Russell 213
– *The Medusa Frequency* 213
Hoccleve, Thomas 27, 50
– *The Regiment of Princes* 27, 50
Hoff, Ted 213
Hoggart, Richard 172–173, 175, 207, 231
– *The Uses of Literacy* 172, 175, 231
Hokusai 190
Hollinghurst, Alan 211
– *The Swimming-Pool Library* 211
Hollywood 200, 225
Holmes, Sherlock (character) 223
Holofernes 36
Holy Church 49
Holy Grail 92, 192
Holy Spirit 65
Holywell Street 115
Holzer, Jenny 196
Homer 24, 55, 90, 143, 147, 229
– *The Iliad* 24, 29, 37, 86–87, 90, 229
– *The Odyssey* 24, 37, 126, 229
homoeroticism 211
homosexuality 211
honour 39–40, 47, 73–74
Horace (Quintus Horatius Flaccus) 73, 179
– *Ars poetica* 73, 179
Horkheimer, Max 123, 209
Horn, Trevor 4
horror 74, 156, 160, 163
Horsa 30
Hours Press 186
House of Lords 92
Housman, A. E. 132
Howard, Henry, earl of Surrey 60
Howards End (Forster) 155
Howe, Nicholas 33
Hrothgar (character) 38, 40
HTML 219
HTTP 219
Hughes, Richard 167
– *A Comedy of Danger* 167
Hughes, Ted 224
– Ted Hughes Award 224
Hühn, Peter 10
Hulme, T. E. 137

Hulu 211
human *or* humanity *or* humankind 3, 7, 11, 14, 16, 21–24, 29, 40–41, 44, 51, 65–66, 73, 77, 108, 111, 126–127, 131–133, 138, 140, 149, 151, 153–154, 159–165, 168, 171, 174–177, 183, 198, 201, 205–206, 219, 223–224
– humanoid robot 160, 223
– inhuman 160
– non-human 29, 40, 176–177
– post-human 175
– superhuman 171, 175
humanist 75
humanities 2
humour 39, 53, 169
Hutton, Matthew 67
Huxley, Aldous 195, 200
– *Alice and the Mysterious Mr. Carroll* 200
– *Jane Eyre* (screenplay) 200
– *Pride and Prejudice* (screenplay) 200
hybrid 81
Hytner, Nicholas 82

IBM 209, 213, 217, 231
Ibsen, Henrik 168
Icarus 180
icon 12
ideal *or* idealism 46, 54, 97, 120, 137, 140, 143, 151, 170, 188, 191, 201, 204, 205
– ideal type 16
identification 15, 22, 36, 43, 66, 143, 197, 225
– nonidentificatory acting 82
identity 11, 28, 55, 87, 206
– gender identity 71
– social identity 69, 71
ideogram 188, 190
ideology 53
ignorance 66, 112, 208, 225
Iliad 24, 29, 37, 86–87, 90, 229
illiteracy 34, 49, 61, 99–100, 183, 201
illusion 71, 138
– *Lost Illusions* (Balzac) 112
illusionist 198
illustration 33, 53, 61, 65, 70, 73, 88, 93, 112–113, 117, 125, 180–181, 183–186, 194, 196, 206, 216

– Collins Illustrated Pocket Classics 125
– *English Illustrated Magazine* 155
– "Illustrated Books and Newspapers" (Wordsworth) 183
– *Illustrated London News* 183, 230
image 5, 13, 21, 22, 47, 97, 112, 132, 134, 137, 142, 179–183, 185–196, 198, 200, 202, 204–208, 219, 221
– literary image 185
– mirror image 181
– moving image 196–198
– recorded image 204
– static image 198
– text-image combination 180–183, 196, 221
– visual image 13, 190
imagery 29, 148, 189–192
imaginary 11, 14, 97, 99, 128, 157, 171
imagination 10, 22, 127, 186, 194, 208
– *Imagination Dead Imagine* (Beckett) 194, 207
– imaginative literature *or* writing
– imagined community 9, 170
– literary imagination 158, 161, 198
– visual imagination 198
imagism *or* Imagists 189–190
imitation 3, 10, 13, 38, 58, 61, 87, 90, 94, 131, 175–176, 203, 208
immediacy 16, 75, 78, 82, 85, 108, 127, 130, 134, 138, 170, 186, 190, 224
immortality 23, 96, 164
imperialism 155–156
impersonality 136–137, 143, 185, 190
impression 9, 14, 76, 133–134, 192, 201, 205
– visual impression 165, 190
impressionism 159
imprint 77, 215
inauthenticity 54
incunabula 43, 56, 229
Indiana, Robert 196
individual *or* individuality 15, 23, 40, 52–53, 57, 74–75, 79, 87, 89, 98, 106, 111, 127, 134–136, 138, 140, 151, 162, 169, 206, 208–209, 214, 219
information 2, 6–10, 16, 25, 27, 60, 71, 93–94, 106, 154, 167, 180, 214, 219
– information-processing 214
– Ministry of Information 168

infrastructure 1, 113, 153
ink 24–25, 111, 187, 198, 229
– E-Ink 218, 232
– inkjet printer 231
Inner Temple 73
innovation 17, 69, 75, 90, 112, 125, 171, 196, 221–222
Inns of Court 69
inscription 31, 58, 99–100, 127, 213–214, 218
inspiration 51, 97, 108, 125, 129, 136, 139, 150, 156–158, 160, 162, 164, 168, 188
Instagram 224–225
Instapoetry 224
institution 3–4, 6–7, 12, 54, 63, 120, 122, 124, 140, 153, 166, 214, 219
intellect 90, 110, 120
intention 15, 73, 168, 195
interaction 3, 8, 16, 54, 58, 94, 166, 172, 183, 220, 225–226
interactivity 8–9, 16, 221, 224
interiority, *see also* inwardness 77
interlude 66–67, 73
intermediality 13–14
internationality 108, 110, 118, 156, 209–210, 224
Internet 4–5, 9, 212, 214, 219, 221, 223
– Internet Archive 104, 222, 232
interpretation 16, 33–34, 36, 40, 47, 124, 142, 170, 193, 205
intertextuality 100
interwar period 123, 166
intimacy 22, 101, 111, 139, 149, 166, 172
inwardness, *see also* interiority 40, 150, 205
iPad (Apple) 232
iPhone (Apple) 232
iPlayer (BBC) 232
Iraq 23
Ireland *or* Irish 25, 30, 38, 148, 199, 229
– Anglo-Irish 87, 111
Irons, Jeremy 211
irony 22, 51, 98–99, 113, 150, 152, 159, 170, 183, 187–188
Isaac 65
Iser, Wolfgang 195
Iseut 44
Isherwood, Christopher 204–205

– *Goodbye to Berlin* 204
Ishiguro, Kazuo 160, 211, 232
– *Klara and the Sun* 160, 232
– *Never Let Me Go* 160
– *The Remains of the Day* 211, 232
Isle of Dogs 193
Italy *or* Italian 50, 60, 73, 151, 162, 186, 200
ITV 209, 211, 231

Jacobean period 71, 90
Jacobson, Joseph 232
James I, King of England and Ireland 72
James V, King of Scotland 67
Dr. James's Fever Powder 110
James, E. L. 225
– *Fifty Shades of Grey* 225
James, Henry 153, 160, 164, 180, 184–186, 194–195, 197, 231
– *The Golden Bowl* 185
– "In the Cage" 153
– "The Real Thing" 184
– *The Turn of the Screw* 197
– *Washington Square* 184
Japan 189–190
"The Japanned Box" (Doyle) 161, 163, 169
jazz 172
Jenkins, Henry 219
Jesus 65
jet 171–172
– jet age 170
– jet airliner 174
– jet plane 170–172
– jet turbine 174
Johnson, B. S. 202
Johnson, Samuel 88–89, 94, 96–99, 109, 230
– *Dictionary of the English Language* 88, 96, 230
– *The Idler* 94
– *Irene* 88
– *Life of Johnson* (Boswell) 88
– *Life of Savage* 97–98
– *Lives of the Poets* 88
– *The Rambler* 94–95
– *Rasselas* 88
joke 22–23, 52, 105, 107, 151

Jonson, Ben 66, 68, 73
– *The Devil is an Ass* 66
– *Workes* 68
journal 94, 104–105, 107–108, 117–118, 120, 168, 199
– *The London Journal* 117
– penny journal 117–118
journalist *or* journalism 2, 15, 107, 113, 183
journey 24, 49, 52, 66, 88, 113, 122, 125, 127, 147
– *Sentimental Journey* (Sterne) 151
Joyce, James 143, 161, 191, 199, 202, 231
– *Ulysses* 143, 161, 191, 231
Joyce, Michael 221
– *afternoon: a story* 221
judgement 51–52, 207
– Last Judgement 64
– *The Last Judgement* (play) 65
Judith (poem) 36
Judith 36
jukebox 172, 231
Julian of Norwich 49
Juliana (poem) 36
justice 49, 107
Jutes 30

Kahle, Brewster 232
Karenina, Anna (character) 201
Kaur, Rupi 224–225
– *milk and honey* 224
Kay, Alan C. 231
Keaton, Buster 206
Keats, John 87, 131–132, 135–138, 142–143, 147, 158–159
– *Endymion* 137
– *The Eve of St. Agnes* 158–159
– "Lamia" 142
– "On First Looking into Chapman's Homer" 147
– "Sleep and Poetry" 132
Kempe, Margery 49
– *The Book of Margery Kempe* 49
Kennedy, John F. 224
kenning 36
Kindle, *see also* Amazon 218, 232
– Kindle Direct Publishing 223

kinetoscope 230
king *or* kingship, *see also* monarch, monarchy 23–24, 30–32, 36, 38–41, 44, 46, 50, 67, 77–78, 193
– Fisher King 193
– *King Charles III* (play) 78
– *King John* (film) 200
– *King Lear* 79, 150
– King's Men 72, 85
kingdom 35, 87
– *Kingdom's Intelligencer* 93
– United Kingdom 103, 220
kinship 31
Kipling, Rudyard 121–122, 153–159, 161, 165, 197–198, 231
– "The Deep-Sea Cables" 153
– "En-dor" 158
– *The Light that Failed* 121
– "The Mark of the Beast" 157
– "Mrs. Bathurst" 197–198, 231
– *The Naulahka* 121
– "The Sending of Dana Da" 158
– *The Seven Seas* 153
– *A Song of the English* 154–155
– "The Three-Decker" 122
– "Wireless" 157–158, 165, 231
– "With the Night Mail" 154
Kipling, Trix 158
Kirkman, Francis 104
Kirschenbaum, Matthew 217
Kittler, Friedrich 164, 171, 219
knight 46–48, 52
– Green Knight (character) 47
– *The Green Knight* (film) 47
– *The Knight of the Burning Pestle* (play) 76
– Knights of the Round Table 46
– Knight's Tale (Chaucer) 53
– *Sir Gawain and the Green Knight* 46–48
knowledge 3, 9–10, 21, 23, 40, 46, 48, 89, 159, 179, 180, 197, 219
Kubrick, Stanley 21, 173, 206
– *2001: A Space Odyssey* 21
– *A Clockwork Orange* (film) 173, 206
Kyd, Thomas 192

labour 26, 95, 97, 121
– division of labour 2

Lake District 130
Lamarque, Peter 136
landscape 47–48, 98, 152, 226
Lane, Allen 125, 188
Langland, William 49
– *Piers Plowman* 49
language 6, 11–14, 21–22, 30–31, 33–35, 43–44, 59, 66, 73, 118, 129, 131–132, 141, 143, 148, 176–177, 185, 190–191, 222
– Chinese language 188
– cinematic language 200–201
– hypertext markup language 219
– literary language 171
– media language 61
– poetic language 149, 169, 175
– scientific language 149
– spoken language 176
– texting language 55, 222
Lanyer, Aemilia 58
Latimer, John 106
Latin 24–26, 31–34, 41, 44–46, 50, 59, 64–66, 69–70, 73, 90, 126, 129, 133, 190
Laurenson, James 211
law 41, 52, 57, 91–92, 118, 208
– canon law 73
– copyright law 91–92, 118
– laws of nature 148
– lawsuit 92
– libel laws 91
– sumptuary laws 69
Lawrence, D. H. 91, 189
– "Green" 189
– *Lady Chatterley's Lover* 91, 189
– "Wedding Morn" 189
lawyer 69
Laȝamon 46
– *Brut* 46
layout 112, 126, 186
Lean, David 170
– *The Sound Barrier* 170
learning 12, 31, 75, 89–90, 96, 106
– "An Act for the Encouragement of Learning" 91–92
– machine learning 223
Leavis, F. R. 123–124, 137, 172

Leavis, Q. D. 122–124
- *Fiction and the Reading Public* 123
LeCompte, Elizabeth 81
Lee, Vernon 137
Left Book Club 124
Le Goff, Jacques 154
Leiber, Fritz 208
- *The Silver Eggheads* 208
Leicester, Robert Dudley, Earl of 193
- Earl of Leicester's Men 71
Leigh's New Picture of London 114
leisure 89, 106, 114, 153, 200
Lennox, Charlotte 95
Leroi-Gourhan, André 21–22
- *Gesture and Speech* 21
Lessing, Gotthold Ephraim 179
- *Lacoön* 179
L'Estrange, Roger 128
letter 23, 25–26, 31–32, 40, 43, 57, 63, 80–81, 88, 96–97, 107–110, 136, 139, 149, 159, 184, 186–188, 203–205, 213–214, 218, 221
- black letter 61
- familiar letter 108
- fictional letter 108
- letter form 31
- letterpress 56
- *Letters Written to and for Particular Friends* (Richardson) 108
- man of letters 88, 128, 223
- novel in letters 108
Lettrism 187
Levine, Caroline 8
Lewis, Wyndham 187, 231
- *Blast* 187, 231
liberties 69
librarian 24
library 15, 25–26, 85, 115–116, 121, 124, 126
- Argosy & Sundial Libraries 122
- Bodleian Library 34
- Boots Booklovers' Library 122
- British Library 27, 34, 37, 39, 86, 232
- circulating library 93, 104, 106, 115–116, 120, 122
- English Library (Penguin series) 211
- Everyman's Library (book series) 124, 214
- Foyle's Libraries 122
- Library of Alexandria 229
- library of Pergamum 24, 229
- Mudie's Select Library 115–116, 122, 230
- mushroom library 122
- Open Library 222
- public library 116, 229
- *Railway Library* (book series) 113–114, 116
- royal library 89
- St James's Library 89
- Sir Robert Cotton's library 27
- *The Swimming-Pool Library* (novel) 211
- *Traveller's Library* (book series) 113
- twopenny library 122
- William Andrews Clark Memorial Library 99
licence *or* licensing 57, 72, 90–91, 157, 207
- artistic license 70
- Licensing Act 90
Lichtenberg, Georg Christoph 80–81
life 9, 11, 27, 29, 36, 39, 45, 47, 49–52, 54, 60, 66, 73, 75, 77, 79, 88, 90, 92, 97–98, 106–107, 109, 121–122, 129, 139–141, 149, 158, 160, 163, 165, 175, 183, 188, 193–194, 198, 201–203, 205, 225
- afterlife 143
- authors' lives 136
- "The Buried Life" (Arnold) 134, 192
- civic life 63
- court life
- cultureless life 123
- death in life 192
- everyday life 49, 108
- inner life 108, 169
- life-and-death situation 192
- *The Life and Opinions of Tristram Shandy* 111
- life force 139
- lifeless life 163
- lifelike acting 75
- *Life of Johnson* (Boswell) 88
- *Life of Savage* (Johnson) 97
- *Life on the Mississippi* (Twain) 164
- life-story 38
- life-writing 49
- literary life 48, 87, 97
- lives of the poets 98

– *Lives of the Poets* (Johnson) 88
– low life 69
– religious life 32
– saint's life 32, 49, 52, 64
– social life 210
– urban life 174
Lindsay, David 67
– *Ane Satyre of the Thrie Estaitis* 67
linen 103, 105, 139
linguistics 6, 55
Lintot, Bernard 86
lion 22
– LION (database) 135
– Red Lion (inn) 69
listener, *see also* auditor 12, 15, 41, 53, 130–131, 167–170, 173, 176
– *The Listener* 168
– radio listeners 209
literacy *or* literate 12, 15, 23, 33–35, 38, 42, 60, 63, 75, 94–95, 100, 152
– *The Uses of Literacy* (Hoggart) 172, 175, 231
literary studies 2–3, 8, 226
literature *passim*
– anti-mimetic literature 195
– Black literature 186
– children's literature 110
– electronic literature 217, 221
– English literature 3, 12, 15, 30, 34, 37, 49, 117, 126
– ergodic literature 221
– European literature 12
– imaginative literature 12
– Middle English literature 43–45
– national literature 12
– Old English literature 29–31
lithography 112, 230
– chromolithography 113
liturgy 31, 63
Lively, Penelope 211
– *Moon Tiger* 211
liveness 1, 4, 16, 35, 75, 80–82, 85, 167, 172, 203, 215, 224
Lloyd, David 196
– *V for Vendetta* 196
Lloyd, Marie 200
Lloyd's Penny Weekly Miscellany 117
locus 76

Lodge, David 166, 221
– *Thinks. . .* 221
London 27–28, 48, 51, 55, 57, 66, 69, 72, 74, 78, 82, 90, 92–93, 96–97, 101, 104, 114, 120–121, 123, 128, 152, 154, 162, 166, 185, 193, 195, 197, 199, 205, 207, 216, 231
– *Illustrated London News* 183, 230
– "London" (Blake) 181
– *Leigh's New Picture of London* 114
– London and North Western Railway 113
– *London Gazette* 93
– *The London Journal* 117
– *London Magazine* 105
– London Underground 188
Longfellow, Henry Wadsworth 143
Longman 113
Lord Chamberlain's Men 71–72
Lord Strange's Men 71
love 3, 51–53, 99, 106, 108, 118, 121, 132, 148, 150–153, 156, 169, 183, 193, 201
– courtly love 149
– LOVE image (Indiana) 196
– love lyric 58, 149
– "The Love Song of J. Alfred Prufrock" 191
– *Love's Victory* (Wroth) 78
– *Shakespeare in Love* (film) 74
– *Vanessa: Her Love Story* (film) 199
Love, Harold 128
Lovelace (character) 109
lowbrow 124
Lowell, Amy 189
Luhmann, Niklas 3, 8–11, 13, 76
Lumière brothers 198, 231
– *The Arrival of a Train at La Ciotat* (film) 198
Lydgate, John 50
– *The Fall of Princes* 50
Lyell, Charles 141
– *Principles of Geology* 141

Machen, Arthur 156–157, 160
– "The Great God Pan" 156–157
machine 22, 112, 132, 158–161, 164–165, 172, 187–188, 208, 213
– coffee machine 220
– computing machine
– Edison machine 162

- Fourdrinier machine 103, 230
- literary machine 121, 208
- machine learning 223
- *Machines Like Me* 160, 206, 223
- "The Machine Stops" (Forster) 159–160, 165, 208
- novel-writing machines 208
- *The Time Machine* (Wells) 165
- writing machine 208

Macintosh (Apple) 209, 232
Mackenzie, Henry 107
- *The Man of Feeling* 107

MacNeice, Louis 168
magazine 103–105, 117, 120, 122–123, 153, 162, 184, 187, 189, 199, 224, 230
- *Blackwood's Magazine* 118
- *The British Magazine* 105
- *Cornhill Magazine* 118
- *English Illustrated Magazine* 155
- *The Gentleman's Magazine* 104
- *London Magazine* 105

magic 28, 42, 216
- *The Magic Mountain* (Mann) 161
magic lantern 198
Mainz 229
Mairowitz, David Zane 196
- *Heart of Darkness* (graphic novel) 196
Malory, Thomas 55, 57
- *Le Morte Darthur* 55
man 27, 29, 40, 52–53, 58, 64, 71–72, 74, 88–89, 96, 110, 117, 120, 122, 128, 131, 133, 135–136, 139, 143, 147, 153–154, 157–158, 164, 175, 192–194, 204, 206, 210
- dawn of man 21
- extensions of man 7, 22
- *The Invisible Man* (Wells) 160
- jingle-man 129
- ladies' man 48
- Man Booker Prize 215
- man-eating 41
- *The Man of Feeling* (Mackenzie) 107
- Man of Law (Chaucer) 52
- man of letters 88, 128, 223
- *The Man of Property* (Galsworthy) 210
- *The Third Man* (Greene) 200
- *The Tin Men* (Frayn) 208

- wild man 23
Manchester 134
manifesto 186, 189
manipulation 51, 81–82, 213–214, 222
Mankind (play) 66
Mankind (character) 66
Manley, Delarivier 110
- *The Adventures of Rivella* 110
Mann, Thomas 161
- *The Magic Mountain* 161
Manovich, Lev 219
Mansfield, Katherine 204
manuscript, *see also* handwriting 1, 25–29, 32, 34, 37, 42–47, 50–51, 54–61, 63, 65, 67, 90, 101, 109, 114, 130, 149, 180, 191, 216–217, 220, 229
- *Beowulf* manuscript 27, 29, 36–37, 39, 42, 229
- Devonshire manuscript 58
- Eton College manuscript 99
- Findern manuscript 58
- illuminated manuscript 43
- Junius manuscript 36
- manuscript circulation 59
Marconi, Guglielmo 156–157, 230
Marie de France 44
Marinetti, Filippo Tommaso 186–187, 231
- *Typographic Revolution* 186–187, 231
- *Zang Tumb Tuuum* 186
market or marketplace, *see also* supermarket 5, 68, 85, 93, 95, 97, 104, 106, 113–118, 120–121, 123–124, 129–130, 210, 215–218, 223, 225
- book market 59, 85–88, 104–105, 216
- global market
- literary market *or* marketplace
- mass market 113, 124, 126, 181
- print market 58, 94
marketing 61, 161, 213, 217
Marlowe, Christopher 66, 73–75, 211
- *Dido Queen of Carthage* 74
- *Doctor Faustus* 66, 74
- *Edward II* 74, 211
- *The Jew of Malta* 74
- *The Massacre at Paris* 74
- *Tamburlaine* 74–75
Marlowe, Philip (character) 195

marriage 45, 108, 153, 172
- companionate marriage 151
- *The King's Two Marriages* (play) 67
Marsh, Richard 157
- *The Beetle* 157
Marvel 219
materialism 142–143
materiality 2, 10, 12, 138, 221, 226
mathematics 208, 213
The Matrix (film) 232
matter 138, 157, 195
- matter of Britain 56
- printed matter 89, 192
- reading matter 113, 115, 126
- subject matter 45, 86
Maugham, W. Somerset 199
- *The Razor's Edge* 199
Maxwell, James Clerk 148–149, 151, 156
- "Valentine from a Telegraph Clerk ♂ to a Telegraph Clerk ♀ " 148–149
McBride, Eimear 215
- *A Girl is a Half-formed Thing* 215
McCarthy, Tom 175
- *C* 175
McCloud, Scott 195
- *Understanding Comics* 195
McEwan, Ian 160, 199, 206, 223
- *Atonement* 199
- *Machines Like Me* 160, 206, 223
McGill, Meredith 2
McKellen, Ian 211
McLuhan, Marshall 2–3, 6–7, 22
meaning 7, 13, 15–16, 22, 34–35, 58, 66, 76, 107, 141, 144, 154, 170, 173, 176–177, 180, 183, 195–196, 203–205
mechanisation 56, 112, 164
media, *see also* change, culture, history, medium, technology 1–17, 22, 42, 55, 58, 61, 63, 67, 78, 90, 100–101, 107, 120, 130, 144, 149, 155, 157, 159, 161, 164, 166, 175, 180, 203, 206–207, 209–210, 212, 214–215, 219, 225–226
- acoustic media 168
- broadcast media 225
- connective media 8
- cross-media franchise 216
- digital media 12, 16, 221
- ecologies of media *or* media ecology 14, 183
- electronic media 5
- hypermedia 221
- mass media *or* medium 6, 8–9, 13, 61, 208–209
- media event 108
- media shift 3, 16
- media studies 2–3, 6, 8
- multimedia 13, 45, 101, 221
- new media 2, 4, 16, 63, 80, 144, 173, 183, 207, 211–212, 219–222, 226
- performance-based media 16
- print media 2, 94, 225
- representational media *or* media of representation 8, 16
- social media 212, 214, 219, 224–226
- technical media 7
- technological media 164
- visual media 180
mediality 206
mediation, *see also* premediation, remediation 80, 111, 126, 127, 130, 144, 147, 149, 170, 177, 179, 188, 214
- print mediation 2
- technological mediation 165
mediator 134
medieval, *see also* Middle Ages 27–28, 30–33, 38, 43–68, 73, 79, 149, 180, 220
medievalism 79, 184
medium 2–8, 12–17, 22, 58, 60, 75, 77, 94, 100, 105, 108, 110, 126, 130, 137, 138–144, 153–154, 158, 162, 165–166, 168, 170, 174, 188, 194–195, 197, 206, 213, 219, 220, 224
- "Mr Sludge, 'the Medium'" (Browning) 141–144, 147
Medwall, Henry 67
- *Fulgens and Lucres* 67
melancholy 99–100
melody 45, 51, 129, 131, 133, 141, 174
membrane 24–25, 43, 229
memoir 107
memory 21, 24, 48, 100–101, 131, 140, 158, 162–163, 169, 194, 198, 211
- "Bookshop Memories" (Orwell) 122
- cultural memory 100, 211

– *In Memoriam* (Tennyson) 138–140, 147, 230
Menologium (poem) 36
merchandise 108, 216
merchant 50, 52, 56, 154
– *The Merchant of Venice* (Shakespeare) 73
Mercy (character) 66
Mesopotamia 23–24
message 2, 6–7, 15, 42, 48, 121, 142, 147–148, 151–152, 156, 158, 161, 180, 209, 230
metaphor 5, 11, 13–14, 22, 29, 36, 89, 122, 127, 134, 138, 148, 154, 157–158, 165, 175, 189, 191, 194–195, 201–203, 223
– conceptual metaphor 150
– cognitive metaphor theory 14
– visual metaphor 185, 202
metaphysics, *see also* poetry 192
Methuen 123
metonymy 22–23, 36
Metropole 193
metropolis 93, 123, 130
Metropolis (film) 209
MGM 199
microchip 213
microphone 209
microprocessor 213
Microsoft Word 217, 232
Middle Ages, *see also* medieval 3, 12, 27–28, 30, 42–44, 63–64, 149, 229
middlebrow 120, 123–124
Mill, John Stuart 130
Miller's Tale (Chaucer) 52–54
Milton, John 86, 89–90, 99, 101, 151, 171
– *Areopagitica* 89–90
– "Lycidas" 101
– *Paradise Lost* 86, 151
Milvain, Jasper (character) 120
mimesis 10–11, 21, 63, 76–77, 195, 204
mind 10–11, 14, 110–111, 131, 134, 136–137, 147, 159, 184, 186, 190, 197–198, 201–202, 205, 207, 216
miracle 64, 170
mirror 41, 143, 176, 181, 198
– mirror for magistrates *or* princes 50
miscellany 58–59, 63
– *Lloyd's Penny Weekly Miscellany* 117

– *Reynold's Miscellany* 117
Mischief (character) 66
missionary 30
misunderstanding 166
Mitchell, David 160
– *Cloud Atlas* 160
mobile phone 218
mobility 28, 64, 69, 135, 174, 202
model 10, 17, 32, 52, 71, 73, 75, 86–87, 90, 107, 137, 148, 164, 176, 188, 204
– business model 104, 125
– role model 39
– subscription model 86
modernisation 121, 153, 222
modernism 112, 123–124, 127, 143, 159, 164–165, 180, 186–188, 191, 195–196, 198–206, 230–231
modernity 6, 8, 10–13, 56, 60, 78, 101, 126, 129, 155, 164, 171, 194, 196, 206, 209, 229
Möhne 215
monarch *or* monarchy 1, 43
monastery 26–27, 32–33, 40
money 3, 49, 59, 86–87, 92, 94–95, 114–117, 120–121, 153, 158, 199–200
monk 26, 32–34, 40–41, 43, 45, 52, 64
Monkwearmouth-Jarrow 32
Monmouth, Geoffrey of 44
– *Historia regum Britanniae* 44
monologue 55, 169
– dramatic monologue 138, 141, 143
monopoly 56, 152
monster 23, 37–38, 40–41, 154, 163, 188
montage 190, 202–205
Monthly Review 94, 105
mood 39, 198
moon 82, 176
– "Moonlit Apples" (Drinkwater) 189
– *The Moonstone* (Collins) 120
– *Moon Tiger* (Lively) 211
Moore, Alan 196
– *From Hell* 196
– *V for Vendetta* 196
– *Watchmen* 196
Moore, George 116, 122
– *Esther Waters* 116
morality play 64, 66

Moretti, Franco 5
Morris, William 55–56, 184
– *The Works of Geoffrey Chaucer* (edition) 56
Morse, Samuel 148
Morse code 148
mortality 24, 98, 137–138, 163
Le Morte Darthur (Malory) 55
Mosaic 219, 232
Moses 65
Mozart, Wolfgang Amadeus 173
MT/ST 213, 217, 231
Mudie, Charles Edward 115
– Mudie's Select Library 115–116, 122, 230
multilingualism 44–45, 55
multiplicity 2, 13, 15, 31, 69, 87, 226
multitude 89, 120
Murdoch, Iris 170, 174–175
– *The Bell* 170, 174–175
Murray, John 113
Murray, Les 175–176
– "'Bats' Ultrasound" 175–176
Muse 150
music 13–14, 45, 71–72, 80, 82, 103, 128–129, 131, 152, 159, 161, 167–168, 171–175, 200–201, 203, 205–206, 220
– rock music, *see also* rock'n' roll 173, 206
– *Words and Music* (Beckett) 168
mystery *or* mystery play 64, 67, 120, 136, 147, 154, 157, 159, 205, 213
mysticism 49, 140
myth *or* mythology 59, 137, 180, 186, 192–193
– Norse mythology 40, 193
– "White Mythology" (Derrida) 195

Nagel, Thomas 175
Naipaul, V. S. 200
– *A Flag on the Island* 200
narration 48, 111
narrative, *see also* fiction, poem, voice 3, 17, 33, 38, 98, 136, 143, 166, 168, 171, 179, 196–198, 201–203, 205
– Arthurian narrative 55
– epic narrative 24
– eye-witness narrative 106
– fictional narrative 11
– it-narrative 105

– multimodal forms of narrative 14
– superhero narrative 196
– survivor narrative 106
narratology 179, 186
narrator 50–53, 55, 97, 112, 128, 151–152, 157–159, 164–166, 169, 174, 184, 198, 204
Nashe, Thomas 58
– *The Unfortunate Traveller* 58
nation *or* nationality 38, 56–57, 61, 110, 122, 166–167, 172
– multinational conglomerates 215
– National Health Service 124
– nationalism 12, 60
– National Telegraph Department 152
– National Theatre 81
– National Youth Poet Laureate (US) 224
naturalism 122
nature 3, 48–49, 51, 98, 111, 135, 140–141, 150–151, 153, 160, 175
– force of nature 133
– human nature 77, 111, 165
– laws of nature 148
negation 192
negative capability 136, 143
negative space 134, 155
Negro (anthology) 186
Nelson, Ted 231
neoclassicism 98, 137, 143
Neoplatonism 156
Net Book Agreement 114, 215, 231–232
Netflix 232
Netherlands 156
Netscape Navigator 219, 232
network 8, 31, 58, 155, 167, 211, 214, 219–220, 223, 225
Newbery, John 110
– *Goody Two-Shoes* 110
– *A Little Pretty Pocket-Book* 110
New Criticism 14
Newfoundland 148
Newgate novel 107
New Grub Street (Gissing) 120–122, 230
New Guise (character) 66
New Objectivity 205
New Oxford Shakespeare 78
news 6, 93, 120, 162, 166–168, 205, 230
– fake news 208

– *Illustrated London News* 183, 230
newsagent 113, 122
newsbook 93
newspaper 5–6, 9, 90, 93–94, 103, 105, 108, 112–113, 167, 181, 183, 196, 208, 230
– "Illustrated Books and Newspapers" (Wordsworth) 183
New Testament 32, 36, 64, 229
New York 78, 162, 169, 184–185
New York Times 199
New Zealand 154, 197, 204
Nièpce, Nicéphore 230
Nietzsche, Friedrich 164
Night Mail (film) 205
Noah 53, 64
Nobel Prize 210, 215
nobility *or* nobleman 71, 85
noise 10, 53, 161, 170–171, 174–176
non-fiction 115, 215
norm 37, 44, 57, 61, 63, 79, 222–223
Normal People 211, 226
Norman, *see also* Anglo-Norman 43
Norns 40
Northampton 93
The Norton Shakespeare 14
Norton, Thomas 73, 230
– *Gorboduc* 73, 230
nostalgia 5, 56, 122, 130, 132, 170, 209, 211
Nought (character) 66
Nova Scotia 156
novel 4, 9, 14, 88, 91–92, 94, 98, 103–113, 115–118, 120–124, 126–128, 130, 143, 151, 153, 155, 160–162, 164–166, 168, 170–171, 173–174, 179, 183–184, 189, 194–195, 197–203, 206–211, 213, 216–217, 220–224, 226, 231–232
– artist novel 164
– autobiographical novel 204
– Bentley's *Standard Novels* 116
– bildungsroman 107
– detective novel 107, 120, 171, 195
– dystopian novel 168
– epistolary novel 108, 221
– experimental novel 202
– Gothic novel 107
– graphic novel 14, 180, 184, 195–196
– historical novel 107, 115, 198
– horror novel 163
– illustrated novel
– modernist novel 143, 204
– "Modern Novels" (Woolf) 201, 231
– multimodal novel 221
– mystery novel 205
– Newgate novel 107
– *Novel on Yellow Paper* (Smith) 164
– novel sequence 205
– novel-writing machines 208
– one-volume novel 113
– paper-covered novels 122
– psychological novel 108
– railway novel 113, 173, 206
– realist novel 98, 123, 143
– reprints of older novels 116
– rise of the novel 105
– romance novel 123
– science fiction novel 107, 168
– sensation novel 107, 113, 115, 120, 164
– sentimental novel 107
– serialised novel 118, 120
– silver-fork novel 107
– society novel 166
– telephone novel 166
– three-volume novel 115, 230–231
novelette 208
novelisation 14
novelist 92, 111, 117–118, 122, 127, 152, 183–184, 186, 198, 202–203, 206, 213–214
novella 153
novelty 63, 105, 107
Nowadays (character) 66
N-town cycle 65
numeracy 152
nun 26, 32
– Nun's Priest (Chaucer) 52
– *Venus in the Cloister or the Nun in her Smock* 91

object 1, 3, 8, 10–12, 14, 17, 21–22, 29, 35, 76, 173, 105, 131–132, 143, 147–148, 185, 190–191, 195–196, 198, 220, 226
– aesthetic object 190
– book as object 4
– cultural object 94

- inanimate object 131
- natural object 179, 189
- object as symbol 190
- social object 220

objectivity 159, 185, 190, 204
- New Objectivity 205
- objective correlative 190

obscenity 52, 66, 91
- Obscene Publications Act 91

observation or observer 9–11, 147, 170, 172, 190, 204, 206
- self-observation 206
- second-order observation 10–11

ocularcentrism 195
ocular proof 179
ode 131, 133
"Ode to the West Wind" (Shelley) 133–134
Odyssey 24, 37, 126, 229
- 2001: A Space Odyssey (film) 21
Oedipus 37
Ohm (unit) 148
Ohm, Georg 149
Old Testament 32, 36–37, 64
Olivier, Laurence 81
- Hamlet (film) 81
onomatopoeia 175
Open Library 222
opera 75, 129, 193
- opera singer 174
- soap opera 168
- space opera 214

optimism 4, 66, 140, 155, 160, 172–173, 209
orality 33–34, 55, 100, 134
- fictional orality 33
- secondary orality 100, 222

order 11, 34, 54, 153, 165, 192–193, 202–203
- cosmic order 53
- social order 63

originality 27, 29, 38, 61, 87, 95, 121, 136, 150
orrery 176
Orrmulum 27
orthodoxy 30, 33
Orwell, George 122, 168, 206–210, 231
- "Bookshop Memories" 122–123
- Keep the Aspidistra Flying 122
- Nineteen Eighty-Four 168, 206–209, 231

Othello (character) 79, 179
Ouida (Maria Louise Ramé) 199
The Owl and the Nightingale 44
Oxford 34, 90
- Oxford Gazette 93
- Oxford's Men 71
- Oxford Shakespeare 78
- Oxford University Press 125

pagan or paganism 30, 34, 37, 40–41
page 1, 5, 29, 34, 39, 46, 53, 56, 75, 78, 88, 93, 98, 100, 111–112, 118–119, 125, 127, 134, 186–187, 192, 218, 220, 223
- black page 111
- blank or empty page 46, 57, 111
- marbled pages 112
- page number or pagination 43, 220
- pictured page 183
- printed page 1, 111, 127, 134, 181, 204, 218
- title page 60–61

pageant 64
painter 179, 183–184
painting 22, 80, 171, 179, 183
palimpsest 77, 192
Pamela (character) 108–109
pamphlet 91, 93, 95, 98
panpsychism 132
paper, see also newspaper 5, 12, 25, 48, 68, 89, 93, 103, 105, 111–113, 117, 125–128, 134, 144, 180–181, 208, 213–214, 217, 221, 224–225, 229
- "Adventures of a Quire of Paper" 105
- "The Age of Paper" (song) 103
- E-Paper 232
- handmade paper 186
- machine-made paper 103
- notepaper 209
- Novel on Yellow Paper (Smith) 164
- paperback 117–118, 124–127, 188, 199, 209, 214–215, 231
- paper-covered editions or novels 122, 124
- papermaking 103, 112–113, 229–230
- paper mill 229
- paper rationing 125
- paperwork 213
- paper worlds 153
- The Pickwick Papers (Dickens) 117, 181

– touchpaper 150
papyrus 24–25, 229
– Prisse Papyrus 229
paradox 89, 101, 136, 140, 150, 159, 169, 171
paragone 179
parallelism 35
paratext 61
parchment 24–26, 28–29, 42, 229
Paris 44, 89, 93, 118, 184–185
– *The Massacre at Paris* (Marlowe) 74
– Paris Métro 190
Parliament 50
– *Parliamentary Intelligencer* 93
Parnell, Thomas 98
Parnell, Tim 151
parody 45, 51, 53, 66, 108–109, 111, 192
– self-parody 52
parson 52, 54
– Parson's Tale (Chaucer) 48
– Parson Williams (character) 109
– Parson Yorick (character) 111
Parsons, Talcott 3
past 139, 143, 147, 157, 159, 165, 169, 187, 192, 198, 201, 206, 211
pastoral 105
Pater, Walter 122, 187
– *Marius the Epicurean* 122
patron *or* patronage 6, 44, 58–59, 67, 71, 79, 85–90, 181
PDA 220
PDF 15
Pearl (poem) 47
pen, *see also* quill 12, 42, 55, 59, 95, 105, 111, 121, 128, 132, 135, 142, 149, 183, 208
Penguin 91, 125–126, 188, 211, 231–232
Penguin Random House 215, 232
penny blood *or* dreadful 117
pentangle 47
Pentecost (play) 65
perception 3, 10, 29, 111, 190–191, 201, 214
– self-perception 206
– sensory perception 165
performance 14, 16, 35, 45, 63–72, 75–81, 85, 127, 129, 144, 224
– dramatic performance 63
– live performance 80–81, 167, 224

– medieval performance
– musical performance 45
– theatrical performance 16, 68, 75, 81
performativity 4, 6, 10, 33, 42, 77–78, 101, 128, 144
period 1, 3, 9, 17, 34, 45, 226
– Cold War period 196
– early modern period 11, 31, 43, 45–46, 57, 59, 63, 78, 150, 179–180
– Elizabethan period 61
– incunable period 229
– interwar period 123
– Jacobean period 90
– modernist period 123
– Old English period 43
– Romantic period 130
– Victorian period 79
periodical 93–94, 104–105, 112, 117–118, 155–156
– essay periodical 94, 107
– periodical press 116
periodisation 1, 16
person 10, 22, 58, 75, 87, 91, 129, 131–132, 136, 139, 159, 165, 170, 207–208
– first person 29, 105, 173, 176
– second person 176
– third person 131
persona 51, 94, 96
personification 66, 90, 132
perspective, *see also* point of view 1, 9–10, 14, 48–49, 51, 130, 135, 223
– evolutionary perspective 21
– media-historical perspective
– multiple perspectives 94, 191
– single-point perspective 190
– spiritual perspective 193
Perspice Christicola 45
pessimism 39, 226
– pessimism, cultural 5, 183
Peterloo Massacre 134
Petrarch 60, 149
– *S'amor non è* 60
Pfeiffer, K. Ludwig 12
Pharaoh 65
Philides 26
Phillips, Tom 112, 196
– *A Humument* 112, 196

philologist 90
philosopher 30, 128, 163, 175
- *Harry Potter and the Philosopher's Stone* 232
philosophy 107, 132, 208
- cold philosophy 142
phonograph *or* phonography 161–165, 169, 226, 230
photograph *or* photographer *or* photography 184, 185–186, 190, 208, 230
piano 167
Picts 30
picture, *see also* illustration, image, painting 70, 105, 156, 158, 179–180, 183–185, 188, 194–195, 197–198, 226
- Best Picture Oscar 81
- *Leigh's New Picture of London* 114
- motion picture, *see also* film 199
- moving picture 198
- picture-going 203
- picture house, *see also* cinema 199
- *The Picture of Dorian Gray* (Wilde) 122
piety 29, 46, 65, 138
pilgrim *or* pilgrimage 51–52, 54
- *Pilgrimage* (Richardson) 205
Pindar 131
piracy 57, 91–92, 118
Piscator, Erwin 81
platea 76
Platter, Thomas 72
play, *see also* drama 50, 55, 58, 61–79, 81–82, 85–86, 90–91, 108, 128, 167–170, 207, 229
- avantgarde play 168
- history play 75, 78
- moral *or* morality play 64, 66
- mystery play 64, 67
- playbill 75
- play-book *or* text 68, 85
- play cycle 64–65
- playlet 64
- radio play 1, 166–170, 231
- screenplay 199–200, 206
playhouse, *see also* theatre 63, 69–72, 76, 86, 230
- indoor playhouse 77, 80

playing, *see also* game 4, 9, 11, 71–72, 76, 79, 153, 157, 159, 203
PlayStation 232
playwright 59–60, 68, 71, 73–75
pleasure 54, 89, 96, 106, 110, 161, 195, 206, 210, 216
plot 48, 53, 109, 115, 118, 171, 195, 223
plurality 69, 94
Plutarch 179
podcast 1–2
Poe, Edgar Allan 129
- "Loss of Breath" 129
poem 2, 10, 23, 28–31, 33–42, 44–51, 55, 58–61, 63, 74, 88, 92, 96, 98–101, 122, 127–129, 131, 133–134, 136–144, 148–149, 153–159, 162, 173, 175–176, 181, 183, 186–187, 189–195, 204–205, 223–224, 229
- *Collected Poems* (Thomas) 214
- comic epic-poem in prose 107
- commissioned poem 224
- dramatic poem 78
- epic poem 12, 24, 37, 86, 136, 147
- graphic poem 195
- inaugural poem 224
- long poem 49, 61, 137–138, 192
- lyric poem 45, 58, 128, 138
- mock-epic poem 95
- narrative poem 28, 46, 50, 59
- *Poems, Chiefly Lyrical* (Tennyson) 155
poet 4, 28–29, 31, 33–35, 38–40, 44, 47–52, 55, 59–60, 85–87, 92, 97–99, 101, 103, 127–132, 136–138, 140, 143, 147, 158, 162, 168, 175–176, 179, 181, 183–184, 188–189, 224
- avant-garde poet 187
- *Beowulf*-poet 41
- *Lives of the Poets* (Johnson) 88
- national poet 56
- poet laureate 99, 138, 183, 224
- poet-narrator 50
- Poets' Corner 51
- poet-speaker 133
- print-fixated poet 59
- women poets 58
poetics 15, 33, 188, 190, 195
- *Poetics* (Aristotle) 10, 63, 73

poetry 4, 10, 29, 31–38, 43, 55, 58, 78, 92, 97–101, 104, 107, 123, 126–144, 147, 149, 157–159, 162, 175, 179, 183, 188, 192–193, 198, 205, 208, 224
– avantgarde poetry 123
– *The Chinese Written Character as a Medium for Poetry* (Fenollosa) 188
– concrete poetry 187
– *Defence of Poesie* (Sidney) 73
– *Defence of Poetry* (Shelley) 130, 133
– digital poetry 196, 221
– dramatic poetry 74
– Georgian poetry 189
– *Georgian Poetry* (anthology) 189
– heroic poetry 136
– Instapoetry 224
– love poetry 150, 156
– lyric poetry 10, 129, 169
– metaphysical poetry 151
– modernist poetry 127
– oral poetry 16, 31
– *Poetry* magazine 189
– poetry collection 58, 224
– poetry reading 4
– poetry slam 4, 224
– secular poetry 43
– "Sleep and Poetry" (Keats) 132
point of view 40–41, 49
polemic 67, 97, 123
– antitheatrical polemic 68
politician 113, 167
politics 2, 7, 63, 188
Polonius (character) 76, 107
polysemy 150
polyvocity 127
Pool Group 199
Pope, Alexander 86–87, 89, 95, 97
– *The Dunciad* 95
– *Epistle to Dr Arbuthnot* 95
– *The Iliad* (transl.) 86–87
popularity 27, 40, 44, 50, 58, 61–62, 64, 68, 72, 75, 78, 86, 98, 103–105, 114–117, 122–124, 126, 149, 168, 173, 180, 183–184, 199, 205–206, 209, 214, 223, 226
pornography 91
post 94, 149, 154, 205
– postcard 161
– Post Office 152, 166
postcolonial studies 2
postdramatic theatre 82
poster 103, 107
post-expressionism 205
post-human 175
postimperial 170
Postman, Neil 5
post-medieval 149
postmodernism 1, 112, 174, 231
post-punk 175
posture 169, 173
postwar 168, 170–171, 174–175, 192
Pottermore 232
Pound, Ezra 45, 180, 187–191, 193, 231
– "Ancient Music" 45
– "In a Station of the Metro" 189–190, 231
– "Vortex" 187
poverty 106, 194–195
Powell, Anthony 200
power 3, 11, 23, 28–29, 43–44, 69, 74, 89, 105, 120, 130–133, 136, 144
– economic power 215
– PowerBook (Apple) 221–222
– *The PowerBook* (Winterson) 221
– power of literacy 42
– power of literature 186, 216
– power of mass media 208
– power of poetry 132, 188
– power of speech *or* words 66
– power of the written word *or* of writing 42, 159, 186
– PowerPoint 221
– powers of story-telling 142
– purchasing power 86
– "The Steam-Powered Word Processor" (Clarke) 208
practice 6–8, 12, 31, 57, 79, 87, 90, 92, 103, 106, 142–143, 147, 214, 226
– audio-visual practice 13
– cultural practice 33, 127
– devotional practice 26
– media practice 8, 42, 203
– primary practice 6
– scribal practice 28
– stage practices 82

– textual practice 63
pragmatics 6
Prajapati 193
prayer 46, 122
– Book of Common Prayer 61
precept 73, 75
preface 61, 85, 88, 107, 130, 185–186
prefiguration 11, 36, 99–100
prejudice
– antitheatrical prejudice 67
– class prejudice 123
– *Pride and Prejudice* (Austen) 200
– *Pride and Prejudice and Zombies* (Grahame-Smith) 222
premediation 82
presence 81–82, 120, 132–133, 136, 153, 162–163, 189, 194
present, the 3, 6, 16, 79, 89, 157, 165, 169, 192, 225
presentation 1, 3, 46, 50, 63, 65, 184, 189, 221
– self-presentation 54
Presley, Elvis 173
press 6, 59, 89, 91, 112, 186, 217
– Galley Beggar Press 215
– Hogarth Press 123
– Hours Press 186
– Kelmscott Press 56
– Oxford University Press 125
– periodical press 116
– popular press 173
– press regulation 90
– printing press 56–57, 59, 90, 95, 101, 229
– Stanhope press 112, 230
– steam press 112, 230
priest 32, 46, 88
– Nun's Priest (Chaucer) 52
Priestley, J. B. 207
– "Televiewing" 207–208
Prince Henry's Men 72
print *or* printing, see also press 1–7, 12, 15–16, 26, 28–29, 37, 43, 50, 55–61, 63, 67–68, 73, 75, 78, 85–87, 89–91, 93–95, 98–101, 103–106, 110–113, 117, 120–121, 125, 127, 130–131, 134, 149, 180–181, 183–184, 186, 188–190, 192, 204–205, 208, 214, 218, 220–223, 225–226, 229
– illuminated printing 181, 230
– modern printing
– offset printing 214
– print-run 101, 104, 125
– relief printing 181
– reprint 88, 92, 94–95, 104, 106, 114, 116, 118, 124–125, 151–153, 184
– stigma of print 59
– woodblock printing 26, 229
printer 15, 55–61, 68, 85–86, 92, 96, 104, 107, 110, 112
– inkjet printer 231
– printer-publisher 55
production 6, 13, 15–16, 27, 64, 77, 79, 81–82, 90, 92, 96–97, 101, 103, 105, 116, 121, 128, 168–169, 181, 188, 200, 214, 221
– book production 56, 112, 214
– film production 81
– overproduction 121
– paper production 103, 105, 230
– parchment production 229
– text production 15, 96
profession *or* professionalism 12, 27, 57, 63, 69, 71, 87–89, 95, 97, 103, 114, 116, 120–121, 140, 152, 158, 199
– *The Case of Authors by Profession* (Ralph) 95
programming 167–168, 209
Project Gutenberg 222, 231
proles 209
prologue 27, 46, 51, 54–55, 86, 192
pronunciation 167
prop 71, 79
propaganda 225
property 6, 8, 57, 92, 108
– *The Man of Property* (Galsworthy) 210
prophecy 133–134, 140
proscenium 69
prose 29, 32, 37, 52, 55, 58, 95, 97, 129, 134–135, 158, 183–184, 203–205
– comic epic-poem in prose 107
prostitution 120, 152
protagonist 49, 66, 74, 118, 165, 169

protest 56
Protestantism 67–68, 167
Prynne, William 68, 85, 91
– *Histrio-mastix* 68
Psalms (poem) 36
psychoanalysis 158
psychology 8, 51, 76, 108–109, 184
publication *or* publishing 5, 57, 59, 88, 90–93, 103–104, 155, 181, 184, 209
– manuscript publication 59
– Obscene Publications Act 91
– periodical publication 104–105
– print publication 86, 134, 223
– serial publication 94
public domain 92, 162
publicity 59
public speaking *or* speech 22, 140
public sphere 89, 93–94, 130
publisher, *see also* publishing 15, 56–60, 86–87, 89, 91–92, 95–97, 104, 106, 110, 113–114, 116–118, 120–121, 123, 125, 164, 199, 210, 222–223
– hardback publisher 125
– independent publisher 215, 217
– paperback publisher 125
– printer-publisher 55
– *The Publisher's Circular* 104
– trade publisher 225
publishing 4, 6, 15, 58, 61–62, 87, 90, 92, 97, 112–113, 118, 123, 126, 130, 167, 200, 205, 207, 214–217, 219, 223, 225
– Kindle Direct Publishing 223
– publishing firm *or* house 114, 118, 123, 210, 215–216
– self-publishing 223, 232
– trade publishing 215
pulp 103, 112–113, 230
pumice 25
pun 148, 151, 195
Punch 113, 162
punctuation 25, 229
Puritanism 61, 68, 70
purity 6, 54
Pynson, Richard 61

quarto 60, 63, 68, 85
queen 73, 91, 140, 201
– Children of the Queen's Revels 72
– *Dido Queen of Carthage* (Marlowe) 74
– *The Faerie Queene* (Spenser) 61, 191
quill, *see also* pen 28, 149
quotation 14, 144, 157, 192–193, 195

race *or* racism 30, 172–173, 225
radicalism 49, 68, 135, 153, 175, 188, 191, 195, 205, 220, 226
radio, *see also* broadcast, wireless 4, 7, 80, 127, 156–159, 161, 165–170, 202, 207, 209–210, 212, 218–219, 231
– London Radio Repertory Players 167
– Radio 4 168
– radio drama *or* play 1, 166–170, 231
– radio signal
– radio sitcom 167
– radio waves 156, 158–159
– *Rough for Radio* (Beckett) 168
railway, *see also* train 7, 113, 125, 194, 230
– *The Great Western Railway* (Turner) 171
– *Railway Library* (book series) 113–114, 116
– railway literature *or* novel 113, 173, 206
Ralph, James 95
– *The Case of Authors by Profession* 95
Ramé, Maria Louise ('Ouida') 199
rape 28, 109, 159
rationalism 11
reader 7, 9, 11–12, 14–15, 37, 40, 42, 44–45, 47–49, 53–54, 57, 59, 67, 85, 93–94, 99, 104–108, 110–111, 113, 115, 117–118, 120–122, 124, 127, 130–131, 134, 140, 151, 153, 172, 175–176, 180, 183, 185–186, 190–191, 193, 197, 201, 205, 216, 218, 220
– e-reader 126, 218, 220
– publisher's reader 114
– reader response 15
– readership 55, 58–59, 67, 101, 113, 117
– Sony Reader 218, 232
– woman reader 58
– working-class reader 118
reading 4, 14, 24, 27, 32–34, 42, 51, 78, 85, 93–94, 97, 99, 105–106, 110, 113, 115, 120, 126–129, 132–134, 140–141, 147, 161–162, 170, 177, 188, 202, 210–211, 216, 218, 220, 224, 226

290 — Index

- close reading 14
- easy reading 188
- extensive reading 106
- *Fiction and the Reading Public* (Leavis) 123
- light reading 105
- nonlinear reading 221
- novel-reading 110, 122, 210
- poetry reading 4
- public reading 127, 169
- reading aloud 127–128
- reading community 58
- *Reading for the Rail* (book series) 113
- reading group 224–225
- reading habit 15, 58, 106, 172
- Reading Room 121
- reading tour 127
- rereading 139
- silent reading 34, 42, 45, 127, 130

realism 48, 53, 64, 66, 79, 97–98, 106, 108, 116, 120, 144, 157, 167–168, 198, 201
- artistic realism 205
- formal realism 106
- photorealism 79, 205
- visual realism 197, 200

reality 9–13, 16, 21–22, 54, 73, 76–78, 97, 151, 157, 170, 180, 184, 193, 195, 198, 203–205, 207–208, 219, 221
- alternate reality 196
- fictional reality 10–11
- reality TV 209
- second reality 9–11, 22, 76
- virtual reality 221

Reardon, Edwin (character) 120
rebirth, *see also* renaissance 225
reception 6, 13, 16, 96, 128, 214
recitation 2, 23, 31, 33, 51, 128–129, 162, 165, 224
recitative 129
reconstruction 32, 37, 58, 71, 79
record 27, 32, 57, 72, 161, 163
- Caedmon records 162
- gramophone record 161
- long-playing record *or* LP 162
- record-keeper 164
- vinyl record 162, 220

recording, *see also* tape recorder 4, 23, 25, 30, 33–34, 46, 49, 80–81, 100, 161–163, 172, 176, 202, 204–205, 224
- sound recording 160–163, 168–169, 174, 177
- video recording 81

Red Lion (inn) 69
reference 10–12, 24, 35, 40, 48, 63, 65, 76–77, 113, 141, 148–150, 154, 156, 161, 171–172, 180, 190, 192–193, 195, 198
- frame of reference 77
- metareference 82
- reference clerk 208

referent 195, 201
reflection 10–11, 13, 22, 40, 51, 63, 65–66, 75, 86, 98–101, 111–112, 121, 171–172, 190, 203, 207
- metareflection 77
- self-reflection 98–99, 174

reform 49, 67–68, 134, 188
Reformation 27, 30, 60, 67
regiment 168
- *Regiment of Princes* (Hoccleve) 27, 50

Reith, Sir John 166–167
religion 11, 30, 32, 34, 43, 45–47, 49, 54–55, 61, 63–64, 67–68, 73, 75, 85, 95, 105, 110, 140, 167, 170, 187
remediation 81, 127, 134, 205, 220–221
remembering *or* remembrance 47, 76, 82, 99–101, 166
Remington 164
renaissance *or* Renaissance, *see also* rebirth 1, 55, 58, 66, 229
repetition 29, 33, 35, 79, 129, 152, 210
representation 8–10, 13, 16, 21–22, 29, 52, 77–79, 82, 85, 106, 114, 122, 127–129, 143–144, 161, 163, 171, 176–177, 180, 185, 191, 193, 195, 203
- mimetic representation 77, 204
- misrepresentation 112
- symbolic representation 79
- visual representation 180

reprint, *see* print
reproduction 82, 162, 221
- mechanical reproduction 3, 162–163
- photomechanical reproduction 112, 230

reputation 48, 89, 95, 107, 215

Restoration 71, 230
resurrection 65
revenge 38, 40, 209
review *or* reviewer 15, 105, 167–168, 223–226
– *Critical Review* 94, 105
– *Monthly Review* 94, 105
– *The Review* 94
revolution 4, 57, 164, 186, 217–218
– cognitive revolution 21, 229
– communications revolution 151
– digital revolution 4, 214–215, 218
– paperback revolution 214
– *The Typographic Revolution* (Marinetti) 186, 213
reward 52, 59, 85, 109–110
– *Pamela, or Virtue Rewarded* (Richardson) 108–109
rhetoric 60, 75, 128–129, 130, 138
rhyme 73, 103, 161, 190
rhythm 21, 55, 75, 138, 141, 172, 174, 192, 203
– auditory rhythm 189
– bodily *or* body rhythm 126–127, 138
Ricardian 49
Richard II, King of England 47, 50
Richard III, King of England 77
Richards, Grant 123, 125
– World's Classics (book series) 125
Richardson, Dorothy 199, 205
– *Pilgrimage* 205
Richardson, Samuel 107–111, 230
– *The Apprentice's Vade Mecum* 108
– *Clarissa* 109
– *Letters Written to and for Particular Friends* 108
– *Pamela in her Exalted Condition* 108
– *Pamela, or Virtue Rewarded* 108–110, 230
– *Sir Charles Grandison* 109
Ricks, Christopher 141
Ricoeur, Paul 11
riddle 23, 28–29, 36, 42–43, 105
Rieu, E. V. 126
– *The Odyssey* (transl.) 126
right *or* rights, *see also* copyright 57, 91–92, 172, 199, 217

ritual 23, 53, 63–64, 73, 75, 170
robot 160, 233
rock'n'roll, *see also* music 172–173
role 6, 34, 41, 50, 64, 68, 73, 77, 79, 81, 99, 104, 118, 126, 129, 138, 168, 187
– role model 39
Roman 25–26, 30, 32, 61, 63, 73, 86, 161, 179, 188
romance 44, 46–48, 51–53, 61, 86, 105, 110, 123, 131, 160, 221
– Romance of the Rose 193
Romanticism 78, 97, 100, 126, 129–130, 132, 135–138, 140, 143, 180–181, 189, 230
Rome 25, 30, 46, 60, 79, 229
Ronell, Avital 166
– *The Telephone Book* 166
Rooney, Sally 210–211, 226
– *Normal People* 211, 226
Rosalind (character) 71
Rousseau, Jean-Jacques 135
– *Reveries of the Solitary Walker* 135
Routledge, George 113
Routledge (firm) 114, 116–117
– *Railway Library* 113, 114
Rowling, J. K. 216–217, 232
– *Harry Potter*, see also Pottermore 216, 223, 225, 232
– *The Tales of Beedle the Bard* 216
Rowson, Martin 195–196
– *The Waste Land* 195–196
royalties 86
ruler 27, 38, 50, 180
Rushdie, Salman 12
Ruskin, John 179, 209
Ruthwell Cross 37

Sackville, Thomas 73, 230
– *Gorboduc* 73, 230
saint, *see also* life 32, 49, 52, 64, 141
Sais 141
salon 184
Sanskrit 193
satire 87, 89–91, 96–97, 107, 129, 208
– dystopian satire 207
– social satire 174
– verse satire 97

Sativa 229
Savage, Richard 97–98
Saxons 30, 44
Scandinavia 12, 37, 41, 44
scene 22, 36, 48–49, 51, 53, 64, 75–76, 82, 98, 121, 150, 166, 179, 183, 185, 189–190, 200–201, 204, 211
scenery 71, 81, 198
scepticism 134, 144, 155, 170, 207
science 122, 124, 149, 160, 184
– science fiction 107, 123, 154, 159–160, 168, 174, 205–206, 208, 218
– social science 2, 8
Scotland or Scottish 30, 67, 88, 92
Scott, Walter 115, 230
– *Waverley* 115, 230
screen 10, 15, 17, 24, 79, 81–82, 85, 196, 198, 200, 203, 207, 209, 213–214, 218
– aesthetic screen 76
– computer screen 4, 213–214
– flatscreen 209
– telescreen 207, 209
– TV screen 82
screenplay 199–200, 206
screenwriter or screenwriting 200, 225
scribe 23, 26–28, 34, 36–37, 43, 49, 55, 57–58, 63
script 64, 75–76
– film script 200
– runic script 31, 37
scriptorium 26
Scripture, see also Bible 31, 40, 193
scroll 24–25, 198
sculptor or sculpture 100, 179, 188
sea 36, 153–155, 169, 202
– *The Seven Seas* (Kipling) 153
Secunda Pastorum 65
seeing, see also sight 14, 150, 165, 177, 179–180, 185, 194, 197–198
– *Ways of Seeing* (Berger) 180
self or selfhood 60, 135–136, 150–151, 159, 169, 206
– self-censorship 116
– self-consciousness 105, 153, 171
– self-conceit 142
– self-control 141, 193
– self-critique 144

– self-deprecation 51
– self-education 107
– self-experience 135
– self-expression 60, 86, 135–136
– self-fashioning 107
– self-improvement 124
– self-observation 206
– self-parody 52
– self-perception 206
– self-presentation 54
– self-protection 108
– self-publishing 223–224, 232
– self-reflection 98–99, 174
– self-reflexiveness or self-reflexivity 15, 42
– self-sacrifice 40
– self-scrutiny 98
– self-understanding 171
Self, Will 175
– *My Idea of Fun* 175
semantics 22, 132, 134
Seneca, Lucius Annaeus (the Younger) 73
Senefelder, Alois 112, 230
Sennett, Richard 78
sensation, *see also* novel 64, 109, 121, 170, 173–174, 207
sensationalism 98, 110, 183, 208
sense 1, 11, 16, 34, 36, 135, 147, 150–152, 170, 177, 179, 189, 192, 195
– nonsense 174
– sense organ 175
– the senses 2, 7, 9, 17, 150, 165, 194, 226
– visual sense 186
sensibility 99, 131, 151
sensorium 151
sensory 1–2, 16, 126, 151, 165, 201
sentence 13, 37, 91, 151, 166, 177, 204
sepulchre 63
sermon 40, 52, 54, 88, 105, 193
settler 30
sex 54, 150, 170, 188, 208, 211
– sexual imagery 29
– sexual orientation
sexism 225
sexuality 63, 223
– heterosexuality 149
– homosexuality 211

Seymour, Robert 181
Shaftesbury (Anthony Ashley Cooper 3rd Earl of) 179
Shakespeare, William 12, 14, 50, 55, 58–61, 71–79, 81–82, 85–86, 111, 150, 168, 179, 200
– *As You Like It* 71
– First Folio 61, 68, 85, 230
– *Hamlet* 76–77, 80–82, 107, 111
– *Henry IV* 73
– *Henry V* 14, 81
– *Julius Caesar* 72, 76, 79, 82
– *King John* 200
– *King Lear* 79, 150
– *Macbeth* 75, 79
– *M[aste]r William Shakespeare's Comedies, Histories and Tragedies* 68, 85
– *The Merchant of Venice* 73
– *A Midsummer Night's Dream* 77, 82, 86
– New Oxford Shakespeare 78
– Norton Shakespeare 14
– *Othello* 179
– Oxford Shakespeare 78
– *Pericles* 50
– *Romeo and Juliet* 71
– *Shakespeare in Love* (film) 74
– *Silent Shakespeare* 200
– sonnets 60, 150
– *The Tempest* 81, 86, 200
– *Two Gentlemen of Verona* 150
– *Venus and Adonis* 58–59
sheet 25, 43, 60–61, 93, 95, 103, 112, 180, 198
– balance sheet 60
shellac 162
Shelley, Mary 160
– *Frankenstein* 160
Shelley, Percy Bysshe 78, 87, 130–131, 133–135, 137
– *A Defence of Poetry* 130
– "Ode to the West Wind"
– *Prometheus Unbound* 78
She Stoops to Conquer (Goldsmith) 193
ship 35–36, 122, 156
Shoreditch 69, 230
short story 120, 151, 153, 159, 163, 168, 197, 207

Sidney, Sir Philip 60, 73, 149–150
– *Astrophil and Stella* 60, 150
– *Defence of Poesie* 73
Siegel, Eli 191
sight, *see also* seeing 7, 22, 48, 98, 150, 179–180, 194, 202
sign 15, 21–22, 78–79, 85, 132, 157, 162, 188, 195
– sign system 6–7, 12, 78
signal 6, 8, 61, 87, 111, 158–159, 172, 186, 203
– nonverbal signal 152
– radio signal 156–157
– telegraphic signal 154
– ultrasound signal 175–176
– US Army Signal Corps 151
signature 43, 74, 109
signifier 195
silence 26, 33–34, 42, 45, 79, 81, 127, 130, 139–140, 170–171, 174, 179, 203
simile 22, 191
Simmons, Samuel 86
Simon and Schuster 215
Simonides of Ceos 179
simulation 77, 218
simultaneity 159, 181, 219
sin 54, 140
sincerity 108, 130
singularity 129, 137
Sir Charles Grandison (Richardson) 109
Sir Gawain and the Green Knight 46–48
Sir Thopas (Chaucer) 52
sitcom 167
Six-Five Special (TV show) 173
Skelton, John 67
– *Magnyfycence* 67
skin 25–26, 29, 139
– book-skin 46
– calfskin 26
– sheepskin 24, 27
slave *or* slavery 95, 97, 151
smartphone 214, 220
Smee, Alfred 149
Smith, Charlotte 131–132
Smith, Elder (publishers) 118
Smith, Stevie 164
– *Novel on Yellow Paper* 164

Smith, W. H. (firm) 116, 121–122
Smith, William Henry 113, 116
Smith, Winston (character) 208
Smith, Zadie 55, 78, 217
– *White Teeth* 217
– *The Wife of Willesden* 55, 78
Smollett, Tobias 95, 105
– *Launcelot Greaves* 105
soap opera 168
socialism 140
social media 212, 214, 219, 224–226
social sciences 2, 8
society 3, 6, 8, 9–10, 21, 31, 34, 40–41, 49, 63, 67, 108, 111, 160, 183, 207
– Book Society 124
– consumer society 106
– Film Society 199
– human society 41, 224
– modern society
– society novel 166
– warrior society 39
– wireless societies 156
sociology 3, 8
soliloquy 73, 130
song 4, 23, 33, 40, 45, 60, 75, 103, 130, 150, 169, 172, 208
– birdsong 130
– "The Love Song of J. Alfred Prufrock" (Eliot) 191
– *Songes and Sonettes* 58–59, 230
– *A Song of the English* (Kipling) 154–155
– *Songs of Innocence and Experience* (Blake) 181–182
sonnet 60, 149–150, 183
– Petrarchan sonnet 60, 149
Sony 218, 232
– Sony Data Discman 232
– Sony Reader 218, 232
Sorpe 215
soul 90, 132, 135, 138–141, 147–148, 151, 159, 161, 164
sound 7–8, 10, 13, 15, 22, 31, 90, 129–131, 152, 159–162, 168–170, 174–177, 191
– bat-sound 176
– human sound 176
– natural sound 132, 175
– non-verbal sound 203

– recorded sound 80, 162, 177
– sound barrier 171
– *The Sound Barrier* (film) 170
– sound effect 80, 167–168
– sounder 147
– sound film 81, 200, 231
– sound pattern 190
– soundscape 174–175
– "The Sound-Sweep" (Ballard) 171, 174–175
– ultrasound 175–177
– vocal sound 161
South Africa 197
Southampton 44
Southampton, Henry Wriothesley 3rd earl of 59
Southey, Robert 131
Southwark 52
space 1, 7, 23, 43, 71, 76–77, 99, 124, 134, 143, 147, 153–154, 157, 165, 175, 189, 192, 195, 205, 218
– *2001: A Space Odyssey* (film) 21
– CreateSpace 223, 232
– cultural space 124
– inner space 205
– negative space 134, 155
– performance space 71
– private space 166
– public space 63, 69
– social space 77, 203
– space opera 214
– spaceship 21, 174
– space travel 21
– stage space 64, 82
– Storyspace 221
– theatrical space 82
– white space 134
Spain 25, 50, 86, 229
Spark, Muriel 128, 164, 166
– *The Comforters* 164
– *The Girls of Slender Means* 128
– *Memento Mori* 166
speaker 10, 29, 42, 44, 46, 98–99, 127, 132–135, 140, 142–143, 162, 173, 176, 193, 197
– lyric speaker 10, 190
spectacle 67, 78–79, 170

– *De spectaculis* (Tertullian) 67
spectator 203
– *The Spectator* 94
speech 7, 22, 29, 34, 42, 57, 73–75, 78, 100, 127–128, 130, 134, 138, 143, 162–163, 167, 173
– direct speech 99, 138
– *Gesture and Speech* (Leroi-Gourhan) 21
– human speech 175, 177
– imaginary speech 128
– interior speech 100, 129–130
– lyric speech 10
– poetic speech 132, 141, 143
– public speech 140
– speech act theory 6
Spenser, Edmund 55, 59, 61, 191–192
– *The Faerie Queene* 61, 191
– *The Shepherdes Calender* 192
spirit 36, 89–90, 98, 121, 131, 133, 140, 156–157, 188
– Holy Spirit 65
spiritualism 139–141, 143, 147, 158
spirituality 26, 49, 51, 139, 142–143, 151, 192–193
stage 1, 3, 11, 14–15, 22, 63–64, 66, 68, 70–71, 75–82, 168–169, 181, 183, 200
– public stage 63
– stage design 79
– stage performance 81
– stage seat 79
– stage space 64, 82
– staging 53, 76, 101, 173
Standage, Tom 225
Stanhope press 112, 230
stanza 47, 99, 148–149, 173, 176, 193
star 47, 74, 206
– radio star 4
– *Star Wars* 219
starvation 97, 142
state 34, 89, 140, 207
Stationers' Company 57
Stationers' Hall 57
Stationers' Register 57
Statius 37
– *Thebaid* 37
statue 128, 141, 198
Statute of Anne 91, 230

Steele, Richard 94
Stella 150
– *Astrophil and Stella* 60, 150
stereotype 124
stereotyping 113, 230
Sterne, Laurence 111–112, 151, 186, 230
– *Sentimental Journey* 151
– *Tristram Shandy* 111, 230
Stevenson, Robert Louis 117, 198
– *The Strange Case of Dr. Jekyll and Mr. Hyde* 117, 198
stimulation 77, 161, 171, 186
Stockhausen, Karlheinz 174
Stoker, Bram 163–165, 231
– *Dracula* 163–165, 231
stone 21, 24, 31, 99–100, 120
– *Harry Potter and the Philosopher's Stone* 232
– *The Moonstone* (Collins) 120
– touchstone 150
story, *see also* narrative, short story 4, 11, 17, 23–24, 33, 36–39, 46–48, 50–54, 64–66, 74, 77, 87, 97–98, 104–106, 108–110, 120, 149, 151–154, 156–161, 163–165, 174–175, 179, 183–184, 193, 197, 199, 202–203, 211, 215, 219, 221, 223
– *afternoon: a story* (Joyce) 221
– ghost story 158
– love story 151
– publishing story 216
– storytelling 23, 52, 142, 202–203
– success story 225
– *Vanessa: Her Love Story* (film) 199
Strand 115, 193
strategy 29, 61, 130
streaming 5, 209, 211, 220
stream of consciousness 143
structure 10, 16, 23, 35, 47, 55, 95, 134, 219
– five-act structure 73
– grammatical structure 35
– infrastructure 1, 113, 153
– structure of feeling 203, 219, 226
style 7, 21, 88, 108, 126, 129, 173–174, 187, 189, 191, 202, 205, 209, 211, 221
– formulaic style 35
– high style 53

- low style 53
- new style (calendar) 91
- style of performance 64, 68
- visual style 195
- writing style 23, 32, 191
subgenre 66
subject 60, 76, 91, 98, 100, 152, 159, 165, 183, 190, 194
- subject position 53
subjectivity 13, 135
sublime 98, 171
- egotistical sublime 136
- technological sublime 171
subplot 66
subscriptio 180
subscription 86–87, 115, 230
substance 5–6, 112, 194–195
"Sumer is icumen in" (song) 45
sun 9, 29, 98, 153–154, 157, 176, 180, 189, 194–195, 220
- *Klara and the Sun* (Ishiguro) 160, 232
- "Rotten Sun" (Bataille) 195
superhero 196
supermarket 125
supernatural 40, 47, 142, 163
surface 154, 160, 174, 181, 201
- writing surface 24–25, 213–214
surrealism 170, 174, 187
survival 4–5, 23, 25, 27–29, 32–34, 36–37, 40, 42–44, 50, 54–55, 63–68, 70, 89, 108, 120–121, 134, 159, 162, 171, 189, 198, 224, 229
survivor 106
suspense 118
Sutherland, John 117
Swan (playhouse) 70
Sweden 38
Swift, Jonathan 87, 89–90, 96–97, 208, 230
- *The Battle of the Books* 89
- *Gulliver's Travels* 208, 230
- *A Tale of a Tub* 87, 96, 230
symbiosis 164
symbol 3, 15, 21–22, 31, 47, 77–79, 121, 171, 174, 185–186, 189–190, 192, 201, 213–214, 229
sympathy 41, 66, 77, 151
syntax 203

system 10, 21, 54, 59, 86, 94, 104, 115–116, 152, 157, 187, 219
- acoustic system 152
- case and gender system 44
- control system 165
- guild system 64
- hifi stereo system 173
- motor system 22
- nervous system 113, 206
- patronage system 6
- railway system 113
- sign system *or* system of signs 6–7, 12, 78–79
- systems theory 10–11, 13
- technical system 7
- writing system 22, 188

Tabard (inn) 52
tablet 15, 23, 25, 161, 218, 229
tape
- *Krapp's Last Tape* (Beckett) 168
- magnetic tape 22, 213, 217
- punched tape 213
- tape recorder 169
- videotape 82
taste 7, 86, 93, 123–124, 183, 211
Tate, John 229
The Tatler 94
Tauchnitz, Christian Bernhard 118, 124, 230
- *Collection of British Authors* 118, 230
tax 66, 113
Taymor, Julie 81
- *The Tempest* (film) 81
technics 22
technique 35, 48, 75, 106, 109, 112–113, 139, 143, 203, 205, 214
- collage technique 204
- cultural technique 226
- dramatic technique 75
- montage technique 202, 205
- poetic technique 45, 132
- printing technique 56, 181
technocracy 7
techno-determinism 6–7
technology 1–4, 7, 12, 15–17, 21–22, 26, 80–81, 112–113, 127, 144, 147, 149, 151–165, 170–172, 174–175, 177, 181,

187, 198, 209, 212–213, 215, 219, 221, 224, 226
- audio technology 168
- communication technology 153, 159, 161, 164
- computer technology 213–214
- digital technology 16, 214, 221
- media technology 164, 197, 200, 226
- microchip technology 213
- radio technology 156, 158
- text technology 2, 15, 25
- video technology 82
- wireless technology 159
techno-optimism 209
techno-thriller 217
telecommunications 147
telegram 148–149, 152, 161
telegraph *or* telegraphy 7, 147–149, 152–154, 156–157, 160–161, 164–165, 230
- Eastern Telegraph Company 155
- National Telegraph Department 152
- Telegraph Bill 152
- "The Telegraph Girl" (Trollope) 151–153, 156
- wireless telegraphy 156
telekinesis 147
tele-media 8
teleology 17
telepathy 147, 159
telephone 7, 159, 161, 165–166, 219, 230
- *The Telephone Book* (Ronell) 166
- telephone novel 166
tele-programme 208
telescreen 207, 209
television *or* TV 4, 7, 9, 14, 80, 168, 173, 175, 206–207, 209–212, 215, 217, 219, 226, 231–232
- cable TV 209
- colour TV 209
- heritage TV 211
- live television 215
- network TV 211
- reality TV 209
- smart TV 209
- streaming television 5
- TV broadcast 207

- TV drama 210
- TV series 180, 210, 217, 226
- TV set *or* screen 82, 207
- TV spin-off book 210
The Tempest (film) 81, 200
Tempest, Kae 224
- *Brand New Ancients* 224
Temple, Sir William 89–90
temporality, *see also* time 154, 163, 179, 191, 200
Tennyson, Alfred, Lord 128, 138–141, 143–144, 147, 153–155, 157, 161–162, 183, 230
- "The Charge of the Light Brigade" 162
- *In Memoriam A. H. H.* 138–140, 147, 230
- "The Kraken" 153–155
- "Maud" 162
- *Poems, Chiefly Lyrical* 155
tension 54, 60, 73, 75, 101, 127, 149, 190
terror 38, 74
Tertullian 67
- *De spectaculis* 67
text 1–5, 10–11, 14–15, 23–29, 31–38, 40–41, 43–47, 49–50, 53–58, 60–61, 63–64, 75, 87, 89–90, 92, 95–97, 99–101, 106, 109–112, 114, 117, 126–127, 131, 135, 151, 156, 162, 165, 169, 171, 175, 179–181, 183–186, 191–193, 195–196, 205, 214, 217–219, 221–222
- cybertext 221
- digital text 4, 15
- fictional text 94, 104
- hypertext 219, 221, 231
- immaterial text 57
- literary text 11, 14, 31, 171, 175, 180, 196, 205
- material text 15, 31, 105
- paratext 61
- play-text 68, 85
- printed text 28, 61, 67–68, 103, 105, 134
- *The Raw Shark Texts* (Hall) 175
- text block 134
- textbook 24, 187
- texting 55, 222
- text technology 2, 15, 25
- textual community 33

- textual composition 10, 214
- textuality 101
- textual practice 63
- textual transmission 28, 101
- textual variant 43
- typographic text 196
- written text 16, 33, 40, 54, 136
textile 56, 103
texture 139, 170
Thackeray, William 118, 183
- *Vanity Fair* 183
Thames 72, 193, 195
Thatcher, Margaret 211
theatre 63, 69, 71–73, 75, 77–82, 85–86, 92, 199
- amphitheatre 63
- Birmingham Repertory Theatre 79
- Bridge Theatre 82
- commercial theatre 63
- Curtain 69
- film theatre 203
- Globe Theatre 72
- hybrid theatre 81
- metatheatre 75–76, 82
- National Theatre 81
- postdramatic theatre 82
- Swan 70
- Theatre 69, 72, 230
- theatre history 82
- theatricality 53, 77
- theatrofilm 81
- vaudeville theatre 199
- Volta Electrical Theatre 199
Thebaid (Statius) 37
Thebes 37
theology, *see also* divinity 30, 33, 37, 44, 65, 104, 177, 208, 213
theory 1, 13–14, 63, 73, 85, 136, 141, 187–188, 195
- art theory 179
- atomic theory 202
- cognitive metaphor theory 14
- evolution theory
- film theory 199, 203
- oral-formulaic theory 36
- speech act theory 6
- systems theory 10–11, 13

- theory of evolution 141
- *Theory of Literature* (Wellek/Warren) 13
- theory of the novel 107, 127
thinking 204
- ideogrammic thinking 188, 190
- visual thinking 186
Thomas, Bronwen 225
Thomas, Dylan 162, 169–170, 205, 214, 231
- *Collected Poems* 214
- *Under Milk Wood* 169–170, 205, 231
Thomas of Britain 44
- *Tristan* 44
Thomson, James 92
- *The Seasons* 92
thought 121, 129–130, 132–135, 137–138, 156–157, 169, 183, 205
- subconscious thought 158–159
- verbalised thought 129
thriller 221
- airport thriller 113
- dystopian thriller 196
- techno-thriller 217
Thynne, William 85
- *The Workes of Geffray Chaucer* 85
Tietjens, Christopher (character) 165
TikTok 224–225
time, *see also* temporality 3, 7–10, 17, 23, 25, 27, 73, 81, 94, 100, 132, 147, 153–154, 165, 179, 189, 193, 200, 202–203, 205, 210–211
- broadcasting time 167
- deep time 154
- merchant's time 154
- *New York Times* 199
- spare time 202
- timelessness 14, 153, 155
- *The Time Machine* (Wells) 165
- *The Times* 112
- Times Book Club 124, 231
Tiresias 194
tiring house 71
title 28–29, 50, 57–58, 67–68, 104–105, 109, 116–118, 125, 144, 154, 157, 169, 180, 187, 190, 200–201, 204, 215–216, 221–222
- subtitle 109, 183
- title page 60–61

- title role 81
- working title 127
token 41, 47
Tolkien, J. R. R. 29, 47, 216–217
- *The Hobbit* 2
- *The Lord of the Rings* 24, 216–217
- *Sir Gawain and the Green Knight* (transl.) 47
Tolstoy, Lev 201
tone 39, 69, 128–129, 191
Tonson, Jacob 86–87
Tooke, Benjamin 96
tool 17, 21–22, 42, 221–222
Tory 87
totalisation 21
totalitarianism 207
totality 107
Tottel, Richard 58–59, 230
- *Songes and Sonettes* 58–59, 230
touch 7, 139, 142, 147, 150–151, 157, 159–160, 170, 173
- touchpaper 150
- touchstone 150
- touchwood 150
Towneley cycle 65, 230
tradition 3, 23, 33, 36, 46, 59, 67, 70, 72–73, 93, 100–101, 104, 128–129, 131, 149, 156, 162, 171, 175, 177, 179, 184, 191, 194–195, 218, 223–225
- classical tradition 190
- dramatic tradition 82
- literary tradition 44, 48
- oral tradition 37, 100
- poetic tradition 45
- Western tradition 191
tragedy 68, 72–73, 75, 85, 179, 230
- classical tragedy 88, 168
- neo-Senecan tragedy 73
- *The Tragedy of Mariam* (Cary) 78
tragicomedy 75, 211
train, *see also* railway 113, 171, 175, 198, 205
- *The Arrival of a Train at La Ciotat* (film) 198
training 11, 74, 138
transience 1, 16, 45, 98, 163
transcription 37, 45, 58, 63, 166
transformation 5, 10, 14, 75, 77, 108, 138, 149, 154, 159–160, 212, 214, 216, 218–220

translation 10, 27–28, 31–32, 34, 38, 43–44, 47, 55, 60, 73, 81, 86, 90–91, 95, 101, 108, 126, 128, 130–131, 134, 149, 176, 191, 219–220, 230
transmigration 90
transmission 7, 9, 54, 147–148, 156, 158, 160–161, 220
- radio transmission 127, 158, 167
- telephone transmission 161
- textual transmission *or* transmission of text 15, 28, 57, 101
- transmission of voice 101, 161
transmitter 156
transnationalism 12
travel 49–50, 55–56, 69, 72, 107, 118, 135, 154
- *Gulliver's Travels* (Swift) 208
- rail traveller 113
- space travel 21
- *Traveller's Library* (book series) 113
- travel literature *or* writing 106
- *The Unfortunate Traveller* (Nashe) 58
treatise 179
- *Tretise of Miraclis Pleyinge* 67
Treharne, Elaine 31
Tremulous Hand 45
trial 92, 105, 108
- *Lady Chatterley* trial 231
Trinity 31
Trinity College 43
Tristan 44
Tristan (Thomas of Britain) 44
Trojan Room 221, 232
Trojan War 51
Trollope, Anthony 117, 151–153, 156, 211
- "The Telegraph Girl" 151–153, 156
- *The Way We Live Now* 211
trope 97, 101, 183
Trotter, David 8, 9, 13, 16, 151, 166
Troy 143
trust 118, 138, 140, 142, 150
truth 33, 46, 49, 61, 122, 141–143, 150, 179, 183
Tschichold, Jan 126
Tudor 1, 58, 60
Tumblr 224
Turing, Alan 213, 231

- "On Computable Numbers" 213, 231
Turner, J. M. W. 171
- *Rain, Steam and Speed* 171
Turner, Mark 11
TV, see television
Twain, Mark 164
- *Life on the Mississippi* 164
Twitter 224–225
Tynan, Kenneth 169
type 2, 15–17, 26, 36, 53, 61, 66, 74, 103, 114, 122, 160, 164, 169, 188, 221–222
- display type 61
- ideal type 16
- italic type 61
- Linotype 230
- metal type 229
- movable type 26
- Roman type 61
- stereotype 124
- typeface 61, 111, 187–188
- typesetting 214, 231
- typescript 164, 217
- typewriter 164–165, 213–214
typography 111–112, 125–126, 151, 155, 177, 186–188, 196, 208, 221
- *The Typographic Revolution* (Marinetti) 186, 231
typology 41
tyranny 190
tyrant 50, 74

uncanny 41, 156–157, 159, 163
uncertainty 4, 99, 101, 136, 151
unconscious 36, 130, 137, 171
understanding 1–2, 8, 10, 16, 38, 86, 159, 175, 177, 179, 192, 200
- misunderstanding 166
- self-understanding 171
- *Understanding Comics* (McCloud) 195
- *Understanding Media* (McLuhan) 6
uniformity 110, 209
union 64, 154
uniqueness 43, 112, 136, 174
United Kingdom 103, 220
United States 220
unities of place, time, and action 73
unity 13, 69, 138, 153–154, 180–181

universality 24, 87, 89, 137–138, 140, 159, 213
- *The Universal Chronicle* 94
- Universal Education Act 152
- universal resource locator 219
universe 9, 64, 133, 151
university 69, 71, 74
- Oxford University Press 125
- University of Cambridge 220
- University of Illinois 222
- university wits 74
univocality 30
unreliability 211
Upanishads 193
urbanisation 22
URL 219
Uruk 23–24
use 6, 8, 16–17, 21–22, 24–25, 31–32, 35, 43, 54, 61, 77–78, 81, 105, 108, 141, 143, 150, 161–162, 169, 171, 174–175, 183, 190, 209, 229
- language use 22, 176–177
- tool use 21
- usefulness 3, 5, 8–9, 11, 13, 29, 41, 43, 74, 152, 156
- user 57, 219–220, 225
- *The Uses of Literacy* (Hoggart) 172, 175, 231
utopia 159, 225
utterance 23, 128, 133, 165

valentine 148–149, 151, 156
Valentine's Day 149
Valéry, Paul 137
value 39–40, 46, 59, 63, 65, 72, 106, 129, 134, 140, 175, 192
- Christian values 167
- cognitive value 11
- conservative values 211
- cultural value 172
- truth value 61
vampire 163, 201
van Buchel, Aernout 70
van Dam, Andries 231
variant 27, 43, 135
variation 35, 44, 68, 164
variety 3, 12, 51, 53, 85, 116, 142, 210, 220
- variety show 199

vaudeville 199
vellum 26
vengeance 40, 82, 198
Venice 185
– *The Merchant of Venice* (Shakespeare) 73
ventriloquist 138
Venus and Adonis (Shakespeare) 58–59
Venus in the Cloister 91
verisimilitude 106
Verlaine, Paul 192
vernacular 31, 33, 55, 65, 205
Verne, Jules 161
– *The Castle of the Carpathians* 161
verse 34–35, 37–38, 44, 64, 75, 78, 97, 128–129, 133, 138, 142, 149, 158, 176–177, 180, 183–184, 192, 205
– alliterative verse 38, 47
– blank verse 73–75, 78
– free verse 187
– recorded verse 161
– verse chronicle 46
– verse drama 78
– verse miscellany 58
– verse riddle 42
– verse romance 44, 52
– verse satire 97
vice 52, 66, 180
Victoria, Queen of the Kingdom of Great Britain and Ireland 140, 201
– Queen Victoria Street 193
Victorian period 56, 79, 113, 115, 117, 120–122, 127, 137–139, 142–144, 147, 152, 156–157, 161, 184, 186, 189, 192, 198–199, 208–209, 230
victory 41, 74
– *Love's Victory* (Wroth) 78
video 4, 81–82, 219–220, 225
– video conferencing 159
– video game 4, 14, 221
– video-sharing site 220
– videotape 82
viewer 15, 80–81, 167, 201, 207–211
Viking 27, 32
Villiers de l'Isle-Adam, Auguste 161
– *Tomorrow's Eve* 161
vinyl 162

violence 29, 40, 66, 74, 78, 110, 173, 201, 204, 206
Virago 215
Virgil (Publius Vergilius Maro) 37, 61, 86, 90, 230
– *The Aeneid* 29, 37
virtuality 14, 81, 213, 221
virtue 29, 47, 52, 66, 108, 110–111, 143, 180
– *Pamela, or Virtue Rewarded* (Richardson) 108–109
vision 49, 74, 101, 109, 121, 131–132, 153–154, 170, 173, 177, 179, 188, 190, 194, 198, 205
– denigration of vision 194, 207
– double vision 40
– moment of vision 186
visuality 14, 150, 179, 184–185, 190, 194, 203, 206
voice 2, 4–5, 7, 12, 21, 23, 34, 50, 80, 90, 94, 101, 127–129, 131–134, 136–143, 157, 162–166, 168–169, 173, 175–176, 192–193, 208
– human voice 126–127, 161–163, 165, 168, 175
– impersonal voice 137
– lyric voice 129–130, 137
– narrative voice 105
– poetic voice 134, 140, 191
– recorded voice 161–163, 168–169
Volta, Alessandro 149
Volta Electric Theatre 199
volume 24, 26, 37, 87, 94, 106, 111, 114–115, 118, 120, 184–185
– one-volume novel 113, 122
– single-volume reprint 116
– three-volume novel 115, 230–231
vortex 187
– "Vortex" (Pound) 187
Vorticism 187
Vortigern 30

Wagner, Richard 193, 195
– *Das Rheingold* 193
Wakefield 64–65
– Wakefield Master 65–66
– *Wakefield Second Shepherds' Play* 65–66
Waldef 44

Wales *or* Welsh 30, 114, 156, 167, 169–170
Wallace, Chandos Leigh Hunt 139
Walpole, Hugh 199
– *Vanessa* 199
war 40
– Civil War 90, 93
– Cold War 196
– culture war 172
– Great War 187
– nuclear war 171
– price war 114
– *Star Wars* 219
– Trojan War 51
– war in heaven 171
– *The War of the Worlds* (Wells/Welles) 168, 231
– Wars of the Roses 77
– World War One 156, 187, 192
– World War Two 124–126, 128, 207, 215
Warren, Austin 13
warrior 24, 36–37, 39, 90
Warton, Thomas 132
Warwick 106
Waterhouse, John William 183
Waterstones 215, 232
Watt, Harry 205
– *Night Mail* 205
Watt, Ian 105–106
– *The Rise of the Novel* 105
Waugh, Evelyn 166, 211
– *A Handful of Dust* 166
– *Brideshead Revisited* 211
– *Vile Bodies* 166
wave 133, 159, 211
– Hertzian wave 157–158
– radio wave 156, 158–159, 165
– *The Waves* (Woolf) 202
Waverley (Scott) 115, 230
wax 22, 161
– wax cylinder 162
– wax tablet 25, 161, 229
– waxworks 108
wealth 106, 126
webcam 220, 232
Weber, Max 16
Weber, Wilhelm 148–149

Webster, John 192
Weimann, Robert 76
Weimar Republic 204
Wellek, René 1, 13
Welles, Orson 81, 168, 231
– *The War of the Worlds* 168, 231
Wells, H. G. 160, 165, 168
– *The Invisible Man* 160
– *The Island of Doctor Moreau* 160
– *The Time Machine* 165
– *The War of the Worlds* 168
Welsh, *see* Wales
West End 78, 114–115
West Indies 172
Westminster 55, 57, 229
– Westminster Abbey 50
Whig 87
Whitechapel 69
Whitehall 73
Whitney, Geoffrey 180
– *A Choice of Emblemes* 180
Whitney, Isabella 58
Wikipedia 4, 154, 209, 223, 225, 232
Wilde, Oscar 122, 164, 187
– *The Importance of Being Earnest* 122
– *The Picture of Dorian Gray* 122
Wilder, Thornton 169
– *Our Town* 169
wilderness 48, 132
Wilkins, George 50
– *Pericles* 50
Williams, Raymond 5–7, 12, 219
Williams, William Carlos 188
Winterson, Jeanette 160, 221–222
– *Frankisstein* 160
– *The PowerBook* 221–222
wireless, *see also* broadcast, radio 156, 159–160, 165, 167, 219, 231
– "Wireless" (Kipling) 157, 165, 231
wisdom 23–24, 29, 40, 138, 140, 193
woman 36, 44, 47, 52–54, 58, 64, 71–72, 91, 109–110, 116, 152–153, 156–158, 162, 164–165, 167, 197–198, 204, 209–210, 223
– *The Woman in White* (Collins) 113, 119–120, 164–165, 230

- woman poet 58
- woman writer 49, 78
wood 25, 36, 43, 45, 70–71, 99, 112, 180
- touchwood 150
- *Under Milk Wood* (Thomas) 169–170, 205, 231
- woodblock printing 26, 229
- woodcut 56, 61, 93, 112, 180
- wood pulp 103, 230
Woolf, Leonard 123
Woolf, Virginia 123, 165, 200–203, 205
- "The Cinema" 200–201, 231
- "Kew Gardens" 202
- "The Mark on the Wall" 202
- "Modern Fiction" *or* "Modern Novels" 201, 231
- *Mrs Dalloway* 202
- *To the Lighthouse* 165, 202
- *The Waves* 202
Woolley, Bruce 4
Wooster Group 81–82
Worcester Fragments 45
Worcester's Men 71
word 1, 5, 10, 12–14, 22–28, 31–32, 34–36, 38, 40, 42, 45–46, 59, 64, 66, 68, 73, 75, 82, 88, 104, 109, 112, 127, 129, 133–135, 137–140, 147–153, 157, 160–161, 164–165, 176–177, 179–180, 186–188, 191, 193–196, 200–201, 203, 205, 208–209, 213, 218
- headword 58
- *Household Words* (Dickens) 117
- *How to Do Things with Words* (Austin) 6
- keyword 7, 66, 106
- loan word 44
- Microsoft Word 217, 232
- power of words 66
- printed word 94
- spoken word 75, 224
- word art 196
- wordplay 170
- word processing 15, 214, 217, 221–222, 231
- *Words and Music* (Beckett) 168
- word separation 229
- word spacing 134
- written word 7, 31, 33, 42, 176–177, 183, 185–186

Wordsworth, William 130, 132, 135–136, 183–184, 230
- "Illustrated Books and Newspapers" 183
- *Lyrical Ballads* 130, 230
- *The Prelude* 136
work 3, 9–10, 13, 26–28, 34–36, 38, 44, 49–51, 54–55, 57–60, 68–69, 85–88, 91, 95, 97, 106–107, 109, 112, 115, 117, 120, 122, 124, 136, 152, 162, 164–165, 168–169, 174–175, 181, 183–190, 192, 194–195, 199–200, 204, 206–207, 210–211, 214, 217, 221, 223, 225
- camera work 204
- collected works 85
- *From an Abandoned Work* (Beckett) 168
- literary work *or* work of literature 11–12, 29, 67, 162, 168, 196, 200, 217
- manual work 23
- office work 164, 213
- paperwork 213
- reference work 24
- waxworks 108
- *Workes* (Jonson) 68
- *The Workes of Geffray Chaucer* (Thynne) 85
- worker 203, 209
- work of art 11, 189, 196
- "The Work of Art in the Age of its Technological Reproducibility" (Benjamin) 3
- work of fiction 164, 223
- working class 115, 117–118, 122, 172, 202
- work of writing 95
- *The Works of Geoffrey Chaucer* (Morris) 56
world, *see also* war 5–6, 9–11, 13, 22–23, 35–36, 53–54, 58–59, 65, 74, 76, 78, 81, 97, 103–129, 138, 141–143, 147, 151, 153, 154, 156–157, 159, 166, 168, 171–172, 174–177, 179–180, 188, 192, 201, 205–206, 208–209, 213–214, 216, 220, 223–226, 231–232
- alien *or* other world 153, 157
- alternative world 13
- classical world 63
- fallen world 54
- fictional world 76
- future world 159, 208
- inner world 143

- invisible world 156
- literary world 85, 114, 212
- Mediterranean world 25
- modern world 107, 143, 193
- outside world 209
- pagan world 40
- paper world 103–126, 153
- real world 21–22, 49, 144, 156
- second world 10–11, 22
- spirit or spiritual world 140, 156–157
- symbolic world 22
- underworld 23, 147
- worldliness 132
- worldmaking 11
- world of language 22
- World's Classics (book series) 125
- worldview 30, 37, 53
World Wide Web 212, 214, 219, 225, 232
Wright, Basil 205
- *Night Mail* 205
writer, see also author, hack, typewriter 4–5, 11, 14, 27, 32, 42, 46, 49–50, 55, 57–59, 67, 71, 74, 86–90, 95–97, 105, 111, 113, 116–118, 120–121, 123, 127, 143, 164, 168, 172, 174, 179–180, 183–184, 186–187, 189, 194–195, 198–202, 204–205, 210, 217, 221, 223
- bestselling writer 199
- gentleman-writer 95
- ghost-writer 88
- jobbing writer 95
- modernist writer 198, 204
- popular writer 199
- professional writer 120–121
- screenwriter 225
- woman writer 49
- writer-king 24
writing, see also machine 3, 6–8, 12, 21–32, 34, 37, 42–44, 46, 48–49, 60, 87, 89–90, 94–95, 97, 99–100, 105–111, 116–117, 120–121, 127–129, 136, 141, 147, 149–150, 158–159, 161–162, 164–165, 171–172, 177, 181, 184–186, 191–192, 203–205, 207–208, 213–214, 217, 221, 226, 229
- automatic writing 142, 147, 158

- hack writing 120
- handwriting 43, 68, 101, 214, 216, 221
- imaginative writing 3, 10, 143
- industrialization of writing 164
- life-writing 49
- literary writing 100, 136
- middlebrow writing 120
- overwriting 222
- phonetic writing 22
- rewriting 158
- romance-writing 110
- screenwriting 200
- travel writing 106
- typewriting 164
- work of writing 95
- writing at a distance 147
- writing in code 147
- writing system 188
- writing to the moment 108–109
Wroth, Mary 78
- *Love's Victory* 78
Wyatt, Thomas 58, 60

Xerox 231

Yahwe 176–177
Yearsley, Ann 131
Yeats, W. B. 173
- "Among School Children" 173
York 64–65, 67, 90
- York Cycle 63–65, 67
Yorke, Henry Vincent 194
Yorkshire 66
young adult fiction 225
Young, Edward 98, 136
- *Conjectures on Original Composition* 136
Young-Hae Chang Heavy Industries 196
- *Dakota* 196
YouTube 81, 211

Zauberberg, see Mann
Zdanevich, Ilia 187
Zola, Émile 91, 120, 122
Zumthor, Paul 28
Zuse, Konrad 213, 231

www.ingramcontent.com/pod-product-compliance
Lightning Source LLC
Chambersburg PA
CBHW050515170426
43201CB00013B/1969